Sir Walter Ra

A Biography

W. Stebbing

Alpha Editions

This edition published in 2023

ISBN : 9789357957809

Design and Setting By
Alpha Editions
www.alphaedis.com
Email - info@alphaedis.com

Contents

PREFACE

Students of Ralegh's career cannot complain of a dearth of materials. For thirty-seven years he lived in the full glare of publicity. The social and political literature of more than a generation abounds in allusions to him. He appears and reappears continually in the correspondence of Burleigh, Robert Cecil, Christopher Hatton, Essex, Anthony Bacon, Henry Sidney, Richard Boyle, Ralph Winwood, Dudley Carleton, George Carew, Henry Howard, and King James. His is a very familiar name in the Calendars of Domestic State Papers. It holds its place in the archives of Venice and Simancas. No family muniment room can be explored without traces of him. Successive reports of the Historical Manuscripts Commission testify to the vigilance with which his doings were noted. No personage in two reigns was more a centre for anecdotes and fables. They were eagerly imbibed, treasured, and circulated alike by contemporary, or all but contemporary, statesmen and wits, and by the feeblest scandal-mongers. A list comprising the names of Francis Bacon, Sir John Harington, Sir Robert Naunton, Drummond of Hawthornden, Thomas Fuller, Sir Anthony Welldon, Bishop Goodman, Francis Osborn, Sir Edward Peyton, Sir Henry Wotton, John Aubrey, Sir William Sanderson, David Lloyd, and James Howell, is far from exhausting the number of the very miscellaneous purveyors and chroniclers.

Antiquaries, from the days of John Hooker of Exeter, the continuer of Holinshed, Sir William Pole, Anthony à Wood, and John Prince, to those of Lysons, Polwhele, Isaac D'Israeli, Payne Collier, and Dr. Brushfield, have found boundless hunting-ground in his habits, acts, and motives. Sir John Hawles, Mr. Justice Foster, David Jardine, Lord Campbell, and Spedding have discussed the technical justice of his trials and sentences. No historian, from Camden and de Thou, to Hume, Lingard, Hallam, and Gardiner, has been able to abstain from debating his merits and demerits. From his own age to the present the fascination of his career, and at once the copiousness of information on it, and its mysteries, have attracted a multitude of commentators. His character has been repeatedly analysed by essayists, subtle as Macvey Napier, eloquent as Charles Kingsley. There has been no more favourite theme for biographers. Since the earliest and trivial account compiled by William Winstanley in 1660, followed by the anonymous and tolerably industrious narrative attributed variously to John, Benjamin, and James, Shirley in 1677, and Lewis Theobald's meagre sketch in 1719, a dozen or more lives with larger pretensions to critical research have been printed, by William Oldys in 1736, Thomas Birch in 1751, Arthur Cayley in 1805, Sir Samuel Egerton Brydges in 1813, Mrs. A.T. Thomson in 1830,

Patrick Fraser Tytler in 1833, Robert Southey in 1837, Sir Robert Hermann Schomburgk in 1848, C. Whitehead in 1854, S.G. Drake, of Boston, U.S., in 1862, J.A. St. John in 1868, Edward Edwards in the same year, Mrs. Creighton in 1877, and Edmund Gosse in 1886.

Almost every one of this numerous company, down even to bookmaking Winstanley the barber, has shed light, much or little, upon dark recesses. By four, Oldys, Cayley, Tytler, and Edwards, the whole learning of the subject, so far as it was for their respective periods available, must be admitted to have been most diligently accumulated. Yet it will scarcely be denied that there has always been room for a new presentment of Ralegh's personality. That the want has remained unsatisfied after all the efforts made to supply it is to be imputed less to defects in the writers, than to the intrinsic difficulties of the subject. Ralegh's multifarious activity, with the width of the area in which it operated, is itself a disturbing element. It is confusing for a biographer to be required to keep at once independent and in unison the poet, statesman, courtier, schemer, patriot, soldier, sailor, freebooter, discoverer, colonist, castle-builder, historian, philosopher, chemist, prisoner, and visionary. The variety of Ralegh's powers and tendencies, and of their exercise, is the distinctive note of him, and of the epoch which needed, fashioned, and used him. A whole band of faculties stood ready in him at any moment for action. Several generally were at work simultaneously. For the man to be properly visible, he should be shown flashing from more facets than a brilliant. Few are the pens which can vividly reflect versatility like his. The temptation to diffuseness and irrelevancy is as embarrassing and dangerous. At every turn Ralegh's restless vitality involved him in a web of other men's fortunes, and in national crises. A biographer is constantly being beguiled into describing an era as well as its representative, into writing history instead of a life. Within an author's legitimate province the perplexities are numberless and distracting. Never surely was there a career more beset with insoluble riddles and unmanageable dilemmas. At each step, in the relation of the most ordinary incidents, exactness of dates, or precision of events, appears unattainable. Fiction is ever elbowing fact, so that it might be supposed contemporaries had with one accord been conspiring to disguise the truth from posterity. The uncertainty is deepened tenfold when motives have to be measured and appraised. Ralegh was the best hated personage in the kingdom. On a conscientious biographer is laid the burden of allowing just enough, and not too much, for the gall of private, political, and popular enmity. He is equally bound to remember and account, often on the adverse side, for inherent contradictions in his hero's own moral nature. While he knows it would be absurdly unjust to accept the verdict of Ralegh's jealous and envious world on his intentions, he has to beware of construing malicious persecution as equivalent to proof of angelic innocence.

One main duty of a biographer of Ralegh is to be strenuously on the guard against degenerating into an apologist. But, above all, he ought to be versed in the art of standing aside. While explanations of obscurities must necessarily be offered, readers should be put into a position to judge for themselves of their sufficiency, and to substitute, if they will, others of their own. Commonly they want not so much arguments, however unegotistical and dispassionate, as a narrative. They wish to view and hear Ralegh himself; to attend him on his quick course from one field of fruitful energy to another; to see him as his age saw him, in his exuberant vitality; not among the few greatest, but of all great, Englishmen the most universally capable. They desire facts, stated as such, simply, in chronological sequence, and, when it is at all practicable, in the actor's own words, not artificially carved, coloured, digested, and classified. As for failings and infirmities, they are more equitable and less liable to unreasonable disgusts than a biographer is inclined to fancy. They are content that a great man's faults, real or apparent, should be left to be justified, excused, or at all events harmonized, in the mass of good and ill.

No biographer of Ralegh need for lack of occupation stray from the direct path of telling his readers the plain story of an [Pg xi] eventful life. The rightful demands on his resources are enough to absorb the most plentiful stores of leisure, patience, and self-denial. He should be willing to spend weeks or months on loosing a knot visible to students alone, which others have not noticed, and, if they had, would think might as profitably have been left tied. He should collect, and weigh, and have the courage to refuse to use, piles of matter which do not enlighten. He should be prepared to devote years to the search for a clue to a career with a bewildering capacity for sudden transformation scenes. He should have the courage, when he has lost the trace, to acknowledge that he has wandered. He should feel an interest so supreme in his subject, in its shadows as in its lights, as neither to count the cost of labour in its service, nor to find affection for the man incompatible with the condemnation of his errors. Finally, after having arrived at a clear perception of the true method to be pursued, and ends to be aimed at, he should be able to recognize how very imperfectly he has succeeded in acting up to his theory.

W.S.

LONDON:
September, 1891.

AUTHORITIES

Not a few readers and critics, who have been so kind as to speak otherwise only too favourably of the book, have intimated that its value would be increased by references to the authorities.

In compliance with the suggestion, the author now prints the list—a formidable one. He has drawn it up in a form which, he hopes, may enable students without much difficulty to trace the sources of the statements in the text.

The figures in the parentheses ( ) after the title of each authority are the date of the original edition, where that is not the one cited. The figures which follow give the date of the edition actually referred to. The brackets [ ] after the pages of the *Life* contain the pages, or volumes and pages, of the cited works.

Example—
D'ISRAELI, ISAAC, *Cur. Lit.*
(1791-1834), date of original edition.
ed. B. Disraeli, 1849, date of edition referred to.
79, page of *Life*.
[iii. 140], volume and page of *Cur. Lit.*

A.

ARBER, EDWARD, *English Reprints*: p. 83 [No. 29, xiv. 13-22].

Archaeologia (Transactions of the Society of Antiquaries): pp. 130 [xxii. 175], 299 [xii. 271], 368
[xliv. 394]. See also Collier, Monson.

Ashmolean MSS. (Bodleian Library): pp. 368 [DCCLXXXVI, fol. 101], 386.

Aubrey, John, *Letters by Eminent Persons and Lives of Eminent Men*, 1813: pp. 8, 13, 25, 28, 35, 49,
57, 58, 100, 104, 105, 164, 180, 181, 192, 209, 249, 273, 282, 283, 300 [ii. 416 and 494, and 509-21].

Aulicus Coquinarius (published in *Secret History of James I*, 1811)—'supposed to have been compiled
from Bishop Goodman's materials by William Sanderson': p. 210 [173].

B.

BACON, ANTHONY, Correspondence (*MSS. Tenison*, at Lambeth, and *Lambeth Palace MSS.*): pp. 89 [Cat. 162], 108 [Cat. 166].

BACON, FRANCIS, LORD, *Works, Letters, and Life*, ed. James Spedding, R.E. Ellis, and D.D. Heath, 1858-1874.

— *Apophthegms*: pp. 8 [ii. 163], 89 [ii. 129], 155 [ii. 124], 302 [ii. 168].

— *Life*: pp. 359 [vi. 360-2], 361 [vi. 356, 364-5].

BAYLEY, JOHN, *History and Antiquities of the Tower of London*, 1821: p. 250 [Appendix, vol. ii. ch. x].

BEATSON, ROBERT, *Political Index to the Histories of Great Britain and Ireland* (1786), 3rd ed. 1806: pp. 35 [i. 448], 108 [i. 448].

BEAUMONT, CHRISTOPHER DE HARLAY DE, *Lettres à Henri IV* (transcripts by E. Edwards from MSS. Bibliothèque Nationale, Paris): pp. 182, 195, 201, 227, 237, 239, 240.

Biographia Britannica, 1747-1766 (Art. W. Ralegh): pp. 39, 49.

BIRCH, REV. THOMAS, D.D., *Memoirs of Queen Elizabeth*, 1754: pp. 89 [i. 79], 147 [ii. 418].

— *Life of Sir Walter Ralegh* (Oxford ed. of Ralegh's Works): pp. 89 [i. 593], 300 [i. 613].

BLACKSTONE, MR. JUSTICE SIR WILLIAM, *Commentaries on the Laws of England* (1765-1769). Revised by Serjeant Henry John Stephen, 3rd ed. 1853: p. 285 [ii. 475].

BOLINGBROKE, HENRY ST. JOHN, VISCOUNT ('*The Craftsman*, by Caleb D'Anvers, Esq.' 1731-1737. Nos. 160, 163, 164, 175, 274): p. 269.

BRAY. See Manning.

BRAYLEY, EDWARD WEDLAKE, and JOHN BRITTON, *History of Surrey*, 1850: p. 380 [ii. 93-4].

BRUCE, REV. JOHN, *Correspondence of King James VI of Scotland with Sir R. Cecil and others in England* (Camden Society), 1861: pp. 58 [67], 148 [Appendix 82-3, 90], 172 [15], 173 [67], 175 [43], 176 [18-9], 177 [ibid.], 254 [140-60, 219].

BRUSHFIELD, THOMAS NADAULD, M.D., *Raleghana (Burial-place of Walter and Katherine Ralegh)*, 1896: p. 5
(Devon Assoc. Trans. xxviii. 291-4).

—— *(Birthplace of Sir Walter Ralegh)*, 1889: pp. 6, 101 (Devon Assoc. Trans. xxi. 319-21).

—— *(Children of)*, 1896: p. 197 (Devon Assoc. Trans. xxviii. 310-12).

— *London and Suburban Residences of Sir Walter Ralegh:* pp. 103-5 *(Western Antiquary*, iv. 82-7, 109-12).

— *Bibliography of Sir Walter Ralegh* (reprinted from *Western Antiquary*), 1886: pp. 265-76.

— *(Tobacco and Potatoes)*: p. 49 (Devon Assoc. Trans. xxx. 158-97). *Builder, The*, Sept. 17, 1864: p. 105.

BULLEN, A.H. *(Poetical Rhapsody*, ed. Francis Davison, 1602), 1890: pp. 78 [i. 116, and Introd. 83, 84], 79 [i. 28,
and Introd. 86].

— *(England's Helicon*, 1600), 1887: p. 80 [Introd. 22, 23].

BURGHLEY, WILLIAM CECIL, LORD, *State Papers at Hatfield House*, Vol. ii, 1571-1596, ed. Rev. Wm. Murdin:
pp. 93 [ii. 657], 95 [ii. 658], 102 [ii. 675], 152 [ii. 811].

C.

Calendar, Carew MSS. 1515-1624, Lambeth Palace Library, ed. Rev. John S. Brewer and William Bullen, 1868:
pp. 38, 49, 71, 91, 126, 148, 149, 156, 158, 162, 169, 330.

— *State Papers*, Domestic Series, Elizabeth and James I, 1585-1618: pp. 34, 35, 36, 37, 43, 45, 51, 54, 55, 58, 59,
64, 69, 82, 84, 87, 89, 96, 98, 101, 102, 117, 125, 134, 135, 142, 146, 147, 164, 169, 180, 182, 201, 208, 241,
242, 243, 247, 249, 252, 254, 257, 260, 262, 263, 264, 266, 288, 297, 298, 300, 301, 302, 307, 313, 316, 332,
333, 337, 346, 347, 348, 349, 352, 358, 366, 369, 372, 375, 381, 384, 385, 386, 387, 393, 394, 396.

— *Venetian State Papers*, 1581-1591: pp. 50, 64.

CAMDEN, WILLIAM, *Annales, etc. regnante Elizabethâ* (Part I, to 1589, 1615; Part II, 1627), ed. Thomas Hearne,
1717: pp. 9 [i. 198], 66 [ii. 574-5], 89 [iii. 697], 109 [iii. 697], 137 [iii. 741-2].

— *Annales Regni Jacobi I*: p. 275 [9].

— *Epistolae* (containing in appendix the *Annales Jacobi I*), ed. Thomas Smith, 1691: pp. 325 [256], 333 [243].

CAMPBELL, JOHN, LORD, *Lives of the Chief Justices of England*, 1849-1857: p. 209 [i. 210-11].

CAREW, RICHARD, *Survey of Cornwall* (1602), ed. Lord de Dunstanville, 1811: p. 168 [xxv-xxvi].

CARLYLE, THOMAS: p. 279 (see Cromwell).

CARTE, THOMAS, *General History of England*, 1747-1755: p. 205 [iii. 719].

CLARENDON, EDWARD HYDE, FIRST EARL of, *The Difference and Disparity between the Estates and Conditions of George, Duke of Buckingham, and Robert, Earl of Essex*, 'written by the Earl of Clarendon in his younger Dayes' (in *Reliquiae Wottonianae*, 4th ed. 1685, 185-202): p. 145 [190].

COKE, SIR EDWARD, *Third Institute* (1644), 1797: p. 214 [24-5].

COLLIER, JOHN PAYNE (*Notes and Queries*, 3rd Series, vol. v): pp. 244 [7], 246 [7].

— *Archaeologia* (Society of Antiquaries) 1852-1853: pp. 11 [xxxiv. 139], 15 [xxxiv. 139], 21 [xxxiv. 141], 36 [xxxv. 368-71], 42 [xxxiii. 199, and xxxiv. 151], 89 [xxxiv. 160], 90 [xxxiv. 161], 91 [xxxiv. 165], 133 [xxxiv. 168], 164 [xxxiv. 163-4], 165 [xxxv. 214], 244 [xxxv. 217-8], 252 [xxxv. 219-20].

CORNEY, BOLTON, '*Curiosities of Literature*, by I. D'Israeli, Esq., Illustrated by Bolton Corney, Esq.,' 1837: p. 274.

COSTELLO, LOUISA STUART, *Memoirs of Eminent Englishwomen*, 1844: p. 63 [i. 209-10].

Cotton. Library MSS., British Museum: pp. 57 [Galba, C. 9, fol. 157], 132 [Vespas. C. 13, fol. 290], 149 [Julius, F. 6, p. 433], 272 [Julius, C. 3, fol. 311], 316 [Titus, B. 8, fol. 155], 351 [Vitell. C. 17, foll. 439-40], 373 [Titus, C. 6, fol. 93].

Craftsman. See Bolingbroke.

CROMWELL, OLIVER, *Letters and Speeches*, ed. Thomas Carlyle, 1870: p. 279 [ii. 293].

— *Memoirs of the Protector Oliver Cromwell, and of his sons, Richard and Henry*, by Oliver Cromwell, Esq.
(1820), 3rd ed. 1822: p. 279 [i. 369-70].

D.

Declaration of the Demeanour and Carriage of Sir Walter Raleigh, as well in his Voyage, as in and since his
Return, printed by the King's Printers, 1618; reprinted *Harleian Miscellany*, iii, 1809; *Somers Collect,*
ii, 1809: pp. 301 [Harl. iii. 20-3], 389-93 [Harl. iii. 18, *et seq.*].

DEE, DR. JOHN, *Private Diary*, ed. J.O. Halliwell (Camden Society), 1842: p. 104 [54].

DEVEREUX, WALTER B., *Lives and Letters of the Devereux, Earls of Essex*, 1853: pp. 61 [i. 86], 62 [i. 186-8], 130
[i. 376-7], 138 [i. 457].

Devonshire Association for the Advancement of Science, Literature, and Art, Transactions of the (see also
Brushfield): pp. 2 [xv. 163-79], 313 [xv. 459].

D'EWES, SIR SIMONDS, *Journals of all the Parliaments during the Reign of Queen Elizabeth*, ed. Paul Bowes
(1682), 1862: pp. 105 [478, 492], 106 [508-9], 158 [674-6], 159 [629-33].

D'ISRAELI, ISAAC, *Curiosities of Literature* (1791-1834), ed. B. Disraeli, 1849: pp. 79 [iii. 140], 274 [iii. 145-7],
334 [iii. 127], 375 [iii. 141].

— '*Amenities of Literature* (Psychological History of Rawleigh (1840)),' 1841: pp. 59 [iii. 152], 181 [iii. 166-7],
274 [iii. 172-84].

DIXON, WILLIAM HEPWORTH, *Her Majesty's Tower*, 1869-71: pp. 198 [i. 351-4], 266 [i. 369-70].

DREXELIUS, JEREMIAH (*Trismegistus Christianus*), Antwerp, 1643: p. 40 [469].

DRUMMOND, WILLIAM, of Hawthornden, '*Notes of Ben Jonson's Conversations with*—January, 1619'
(Shakespeare Society), ed. David Laing, 1842: pp. 13 [21], 270 [15], 274 [15], 301 [21].

E.

ECHARD, ARCHDEACON LAURENCE, *History of England*, 1711: p. 186 [i. 911].

EDWARDS, EDWARD, *Life of Sir Walter Ralegh*, 1868: p. 26 [i. 54-5].

Egerton Papers—from MSS. belonging to Lord Francis Egerton, ed. J. Payne Collier (for Camden Society),
1840: pp. 36 [94], 183 [377].

ELIOT, SIR JOHN, *Monarchy of Man, MSS. Harleian*, 2228, Brit. Mus. (cf. Forster's *Life of Eliot* [i. 34, 604]):
pp. 375, 397.

EVELYN, JOHN, *Diary and Correspondence*, ed. William Bray (1818-1819), 1872: p. 267 [i. 391].

F.

FEBRE, NICHOLAS LE, *Discours sur le Grand Cordial de Sir Walter Ralegh*, 1664: p. 266.

Flying Chudleigh, Chaplain of the, MSS. Corpus Christi, Oxford: p. 326.

FORSTER, JOHN, *Life of John Eliot*, 1864. See Eliot.

Fortescue Papers; collected by John Packer, Secretary to George Villiers, Duke of Buckingham, ed. S.R.
Gardiner, 1871: pp. 332 [40], 386 [80], 387 [67], 395 [143].

FOSS, EDWARD, *Judges of England*, 1857: pp. 209 [vi. 179], 231 [vi. 159].

FOSTER, MR. JUSTICE SIR MICHAEL, *Trial of the Rebels in 1746, and other Crown Cases* (1st ed. 1762),
new ed. 1809: pp. 214, 222 [234].

FOX (or FOXE), JOHN, *Acts and Monuments* (1554-1562), 1684: p. 5 [iii. 748].

FROUDE, JAMES ANTHONY, *History of England*, 1856-1870: p. 4 [vi. 149].

FULLER, REV. THOMAS, *Church History of Britain*, 1655: p. 7 [170].

— *History of the Worthies of England* (1662), 1811: pp. 24 [i. 287], 166 [ii. 286], 394 [ii. 336].

G.

GAINSFORD, CAPTAIN THOMAS, *Vox Spiritus*, or *Sir Walter Rawleigh's Ghost*, 1620: p. 395 [Fortescue Papers, 143].

GARDINER, SAMUEL RAWSON, *History of England, from the Accession of James I to the Disgrace of Chief Justice Coke*, 1603-1616. 1863: pp. 190 [i. 102], 193 [i. 89], 226 [i. 58-9], 263 [i. 29-32].

— *Prince Charles and the Spanish Marriage, 1617-1623*. 1869: pp. 238 [i. 151], 309 [i. 57-64], 324 [i. 125, 130], 332 [i. 134], 337 [i. 140].

— *The Case against Sir Walter Ralegh (Fortnightly Review*, vol. vii; New Series, vol. i), 1867: pp. 305 [613], 318 [602-14].

GASCOIGNE, GEORGE, *The Glasse of Gouernment* (1576), ed. W.C. Hazlitt (Roxburghe Library), 1870: p. 12 [ii. 178].

GERARD, JOHN, *Herbal, or General History of Plants*, 1597, with dedication to Sir Walter Raleigh: p. 105 [546].

GIBBON, EDWARD, *Life and Works*, ed. John Lord Sheffield (1799), new ed. 1814: pp. 102 [i. 152], 281 [i. 151], 309 [i. 152-3], 398 [i. 153].

Gibson MSS., Lambeth Palace Library: p. 345 [viii. fol. 21].

GIFFORD, WILLIAM, *Ben Jonson's Works, with Memoir by*, 1860: p. 157 [19].

GOODMAN, GODFREY, EX-BISHOP OF GLOUCESTER, *Court of King James the First*, ed. John S. Brewer, 1839: pp. 195 [ii. 93-7], 381 [i. 69].

GORGES, SIR ARTHUR, *A larger Relation of the said Island Voyage* (1607), iv. Purchas, 1938-1969: pp. 136 [iv. 1950], 139 [iv. 1965], 140 [iv. 1938-69].

GOSSE, EDMUND, *Athenaeum*, January 2 and 9, 1886: p. 73.

GUTCH, REV. J., *Collectanea Curiosa*, 1781: pp. 368 [i. 94-5], 367, 372, 373, 374, 376 [ii. 421-4].

H.

HAILES, LORD, *Secret Correspondence of Sir Robert Cecil with James VI*, ed. Lord Hailes, 1766: pp. 171 [116], 174 [9], 175 [29], 176 [68], 180 [231], 182 [107], 254 [140-60, 290].

HAKLUYT, RICHARD, *Voyages, Navigations, Traffics, and Discoveries of the English Nation* (1600). New ed.

1810: pp. 11 [iii. 364], 15 [iii. 186], 44 [iii. 301-6], 45 [iii. 324-40], 47 [iii. 365], 50 [iii. 366], 53 [iii. 364],
67 [ii. 169], 84 [ii. 663-70], 119 [iv. 66].

HALL, BISHOP JOSEPH, *Balm of Gilead* (1660), *Works*, 1837: p. 279 [vii. 171].

HALLAM, HENRY, *Constitutional History of England, Henry VII—George II* (1827), 1850: pp. 183 [i. 354],
199 [i. 353], 204 [i. 354], 225 [i. 353], 285 [i. 277], 293 [i. 352-3], 303 [i. 354].

— *Introduction to the Literature of Europe* (1838-1839), 1847: pp. 79 [ii. 126], 277 [iii. 149].

Hampshire, History of, by Richard Warner, 1795, Woodward, Wilks, and Lockhart (undated) 209 [i. 298-302],
Murray's *Handbook*, 5th ed. 1898: p. 209 [98-9].

HANNAH, ARCHDEACON JOHN, *The Courtly Poets, from Raleigh to Montrose*, 1870: pp. 56 [56],
73 [Introd. xiv-xv], 367 [52-3].

HARINGTON, SIR JOHN (*Nugae Antiquae*, 1804). *A Brief State of the Church of England*: pp. 91 [ii. 127], 101
[ii. 125], 102 [ii. 152], 143 [ii. 129], 164 [ii. 125], 194 [ii. 126], 237 [ii. 99], 273 [ii. 127].

— *Letters*: pp. 90 [i. 348-53], 93 [i. 362], 156 [i. 342], 171 [ibid.], 205 [i. 343], 293 [i. 348-53].

HARIOT (HARRIOT, HERIOTT, or HERIOT), THOMAS, *A Briefe and True Report of the new found Land of*
Virginia, February, 1587; published, London, 1588, and in Latin, by Theodore Bry at Frankfort, 1590;
reprinted from the London edition by Hakluyt (iii. 324-40), 1600; new ed. of Hakluyt, 1810: pp. 45, 49.

Harleian MSS., British Museum: pp. 20 [6993, fol. 5], 21 [1644, fol. 77], 56 [6994, fol. 2], 181 [11402, fol. 88],
210, 218 [xxxix. ff. 277 *et seq.*], [Pg xix] 288 [xxxix. fol. 359], 290 [xxxix. ff. 350-1], 329 [4761, ff. 23-5], 333
[7002, fol. 410].

Harleian Miscellany (from library of Edward, second Earl of Oxford), (1st ed. William Oldys, 1744-1753;
2nd ed. the late William Oldys and Thomas Park, 1808-1813): pp. 381 [iv. 62], 382 [iv. 63], 387 [iii. 63-8].

Hatfield Papers, Hatfield House: pp. 18, 102, 103, 107, 111, 112, 119, 120, 124, 126, 141, 156, 160, 164, 165,

170, 171, 174, 178, 181, 194, 201, 203, 232, 233, 242, 244, 246, 247, 249, 260, 261, 334.

HAWLES, SIR JOHN, *The Magistracy and Government of England Vindicated*, 1689: pp. 186, 224 [35].

HEARNE, THOMAS, *Appendix to Preface to Chronic. Walteri Hemingford, Edw I, II, and III*, 1731: pp. 372, 374 [i. 181].

HENNESSY, SIR JOHN POPE, *Sir Walter Ralegh in Ireland*, 1883: pp. 70 [1-3], 162 [75-9], 272 [142-3].

HEYLIN, REV. PETER, D.D., 'Observation upon some particular persons and passages in a Book intitled *A Compleat History of the Lives and Reigns of Queen Mary and King James*, By a Lover of the Truth, 1656' (ascribed to Carew Ralegh, but queried in British Museum Catalogue as by Peter Heylin): pp. 243, 254, 281.

Historical Account of Sir Walter Raleigh's Voyages and Adventures, 1719: p. 7.

'*Holinshed's Chronicles of England, Scotland, and Ireland* (1st ed. by Raphael Holinshed, 1577; 2nd ed. by Raphael Holinshed, William Harrison, and others, newlie augmented and continued to the yeare 1586 by John Hooker, alias Vowell, Gent.'—the 'supplie' by Hooker, vol. vi, 323-461—1586-1587). Reprint 1807 (to which I refer): pp. 4 [iii. 942], 15 [vi. 107], 16 [vi. 437], 18 [vi. 441-5], 38 [vi. 183], 45 [iv. 598-9].

HOOKER, JOHN, alias VOWELL. See Holinshed. Also, *Epistle Dedicatory*, prefixed to his translation of *The Irish Histories of Giraldus Cambrensis*, and his *Continuation of the Chronicles of Ireland*, in ii. Holinshed, ed. 1587. Reprint 1807, vol. vi, pp. 101-110: pp. 1 [vi. 105-6], 3 [vi. 105], 53 [vi. 107].

HOWELL, THOMAS BAYLY (Cobbett's *Complete Collection of State Trials*, edited by Thomas Bayly Howell, 1809-1815; and by Thomas Jones Howell, 1815-1826): pp. 174 [ii. 48], 228 [ii. 48], 230 [ii. 47-51], 237 [ii. 50], 260 [ii. 950-1].

HOWELL (or HOWEL), JAMES, *Epistolae Ho-Elianae* (1645-1655), 7th ed. 1705: pp. 49 [404], 302 [371], 303 [ibid.], 305 [369], 327 [370].

HUMBOLDT, F.H. ALEXANDER VON, *Personal Narrative of Travels* (1799-1804). Translated by Helen Maria
Williams, 2nd ed. 1827: p. 115 [ii. 439, 446].

HUME, DAVID, *History of England* (1754-1761), new ed. 1848: pp. 120 [iv. 123], 184 [iv. 225], 225 [iv. 226].

HUTCHINS, JOHN, *History and Antiquities of the County of Dorset*, 3rd ed. 1870: pp. 49 [iv. 279], 266 [iv. 276].

HUTCHINSON, MRS. LUCY, *Life of Colonel Hutchinson* (1806), 3rd ed. 1810: pp. 247 [ii. 322], 347 [i. 20], 348
[i. 22, 274].

I.

Irish Correspondence, Eliz. (Record Office): pp. 19 [lxxx. § 82], 20 [lxxxiii. § 16].

IZACKE, RICHARD, *Remarkable Antiquities of the City of Exeter* (1677), enlarged by Samuel Izacke, 1724:
p. 6 [147].

J.

JARDINE, DAVID, *Criminal Trials* (Library of Entertaining Knowledge), 1832: pp. 152 [i. 507], 214 [i. 514-5],
218 [i. 446], 224 [i. 513-4], 303 [i. 518-9].

JONSON, BEN, *Works*, ed. William Gifford (1816), 1860: p. 274 [701].

K.

KING, CAPTAIN SAMUEL, *Narrative of Sir Walter Ralegh's Motives and Opportunities for conveying himself out
of the Kingdom, with the Manner in which he was betrayed*, MS. 1618. (Cited by Oldys in *Life*; and stated
by E. Edwards to be in the British Museum; but not discoverable there by Spedding): pp. 333-342.

KINGSLEY, REV. CHARLES, *Miscellanies*, 1859: pp. 151 [i. 65], 204 [i. 72], 300 [i. 80], 328 [i. 104], 388 [i. 106].

KNIGHT, CHARLES, *London*, 1842: p. 104 [ii. 175-6].

L.

LAING, DAVID (viii. *MSS. Hawthornden*, Antiqu. Society of Scotland; ii, *Drummond Miscel.*): p. 367 [iv. 236-8].

Lansdowne MSS., Brit. Mus.: pp. 1 [clx. fol. 311], 97 [xx. fol. 88], 99 [lxx. fol. 210], 361 [cxlii. ff. 412, &c.].

LAUDONNIÈRE, RENÉ DE, *L'Histoire notable de la Floride*, Paris, 1586. (Only six copies known to be extant): p. 43.

Leicester's Commonwealth. See Parsons.

LINGARD, REV. DR. JOHN, *History of England* (1819-1830), 6th ed. 1855: pp. 192 [vi. 208-9], 227 [viii. 131].

Lismore Papers. Notes and Diaries of Sir Richard Boyle, first Earl of Cork, ed. Dr. Alexander B. Grosart. First
Series, 1886: pp. 95 [v. 242], 103 [i. 289]; Second Series, 1887: pp. 163 [ii. 157], 299 [ii. 81-2], 314 [i. 78,
and ii. 85, 159], 315 [ii. 38-57], 382 [ii. 157-60].

[Pg xxi]

LLOYD, DAVID, *State Worthies*, 1766: pp. 55 [i. 564], 270 [i. 565], 328 [ii. 83-4].

LODGE, EDMUND, *Portraits of Illustrious Personages*, 1824: p. 381 [ii. Portrait 12].

Loseley Manuscripts, Henry VIII—James I, ed. A.J. Kempe, 1835: pp. 295 [377-8], 298 [378-9].

LYSONS, REV. DANIEL, *Environs of London* (1792-96), 2nd ed. 1811: p. 105 [ii. Part II, 481].

M.

MANNING, REV. OWEN, and WILLIAM BRAY, *History and Antiquities of the County of Surrey*, 1814: pp. 49
[ii. 527], 105 [iii. Append. 152], 373 [ii. 527].

MARÊTS, COMTE DES, *Despatches*, MSS. 1616-1617, Bibliothèque Nationale, Paris: pp. 306 [ii. No. 420], 307 [ii.].

MATTHEW, SIR TOBY, *Collection of Letters*, 1660: pp. 189 [181], 199 [285], 219 [285], 229 [279], 237 [285].

Middlesex County Records, ed. John Cordy Jeaffreson, 1886: pp. 13 [i. 110-11], 40 [i. 149].

MONSON, SIR WILLIAM, *Narrative of the Principal Naval Expeditions of English Fleets*, 1588-1603 (*MSS.*
Cotton. Titus, B. viii, ff. 127 et seq. Brit. Mus.). Printed by Sir Henry Ellis in xxxiv. *Archaeologia*, 296-349,
as by an anonymous writer 'closely connected with Sir William Monson, if he was not Sir William
himself'; and as *Sir William Monson's Naval Tracts*, in iii. Churchill's *Collection of Voyages and Travels*,
3rd ed. 1745, pp. 147-508: pp. 71 [iii. 164], 99 [iii. 165], 125 [iii. 167], 127 [iii. 169], 129 [iii. 170], 131
[iii. 172], 136 [iii. 173], 138 [iii. 173, but cf. xxxiv. Archaeol. 324].

MOORE, REV. THOMAS, *History of Devonshire*, 1829: p. 6.

N.

NAPIER, MACVEY, *Lord Bacon and Sir Walter Raleigh*, 1853: pp. 208 [223], 270 [206].

NAUNTON, SIR ROBERT, *Fragmenta Regalia*, or, *Observations on the late Queen Elizabeth, her Times and*
Favourites (1641); reprinted *Harl. Miscel.* ii. 81-108: pp. 16 [ii. 100], 22 [ii. 100], 35 [ii. 101], 109 [ii. 100].

Newes of Sir Walter Rauleigh from the River of Caliana. At the Bell without Newgate, 1618: p. 317.

NICOLAS, SIR NICOLAS HARRIS, *Life and Times of Sir Christopher Hatton*, 1846: pp. 57 [323], 60 [415].

Notes and Queries, Second Series, vol. viii, pp. 64 [107], 247 [107]; Third Series, vol. v, pp. 16 [351], 21 [351];
Fourth Series, vol. v, p. 299 [91], and vol. ix, p. 333 [239]; Fifth Series, vol. viii, p. 5 [515]. See also Collier.

O.

Observation upon a Book, &c. See Heylin.

OLDYS, WILLIAM, *Life of Sir Walter Ralegh* (1735); new ed. prefixed to Oxford edition of Ralegh's *Works*, 1829:
pp. 12 [i. 23], 55 [i. 115], 260 [i. 416], 265 [i. 372, 415, 447], 266 [i. 413, 415], 267 [i. 447], 268 [i. 441-2],
295 [i. 468], 299 [i. 472-3], 301 [i. 479], 375 [i 563].

— Manuscript notes to Gerard Langbaine's *Account of the English Dramatic Poets*, 1691, in Brit. Mus. copy of
Langbaine: p. 301 [ii. 612].

OSBORN, FRANCIS, *Traditional Memoirs on the Reign of King James* (1658).
Reprinted in *Secret History of
James I*, 1811: pp. 180 [379], 230 [384], 258 [413], 280 [387], 296 [382], 368 [382].

OVERBURY, SIR THOMAS, *Trial of Sir Walter Ralegh; MSS. Cotton.* Titus, C. 7,
Brit. Mus.; *MSS. Harleian*,
xxxix; ii. *Somers Collect.*: pp. 219, 221 [ii. 408-20].

Oxford, Register of the University of, ed. Rev. Andrew Clark, 1887-1889: pp. 8
[ii. Part II, 40], 300 [ii. Part II,
297], 381 [ii. Part II. 386].

P.

PARSONS (or PERSONS), REV. ROBERT (alias R. Doleman the Jesuit), *Per D.
Andraeam Philopatrum ad idem
(i.e. *Elizabethae Reginae Edictum*, Nov. 29, 1592) *Responsio*, Lyons, 1592: p.
106.

— *Leicester's Commonwealth*, 'by Robert Parsons, Jesuite, London, 1641'
(according to Lowndes, and the
Dictionary of National Biography, falsely attributed to him. Reprinted IV.
Harleian Miscellany, 576-583.
Originally printed abroad as early as 1584): p. 33.

Physicians, Roll of Royal College of, ed. William Munk, M.D.; 2nd ed. 1878: p.
328 [i. 166].

PINKERTON, JOHN, *Letters of Literature, by Robert Heron*, 1785: p. 283 [213-16].

POLE, SIR WILLIAM, 'Collections towards a Description of the County of Devon
(made by or before 1635).
Now first printed by Sir J.W. de la Pole,' 1791: pp. 1 [119], 101 [162-3].

POLWHELE, REV. RICHARD, *History of Devonshire*, 1797: pp. 1 [i. 267], 2 [ii. 219], 101 [ii. 219].

POPE, ALEXANDER, *Works*, ed. William Roscoe, 1824: pp. 164 [viii. 411-18], 278 [vi. 273].

PRESTON, THOMAS, *Yeomen of the Guard*, 1485-1885. 1886: pp. 35 [11], 108 [11].

PRINCE, REV. JOHN, *The Worthies of Devon* (1710), 2nd ed. 1810: p. 2.

Privy Council, 'Acts of the Privy Council of England; New Series (vols. i-xvi), 1542-1580,' ed. John Roche
Dasent, 1890-1897: pp. 13 [xi. 384, 388-9, 421], 15 [xi. 143].

Privy Council Register, Elizabeth—James I: pp. 51 [ii. 57], 331 [iii. 175], 332 [iii. 233]. 335 [iii. 474-5]. 351
[iii. 510-12].

PURCHAS, REV. SAMUEL, *Purchas his Pilgrimes* (or *Purchas his Pilgrimage*), 1613-1625: pp. 136, 138, 139,
140, 291 [iv. 1938-1969, and 1267].

PUTTENHAM, GEORGE, *The Arte of English Poesie* (1589). Reprinted 1811: p. 77 [ii. 236].

R.

RALEGH, SIR WALTER, *The Works of Sir Walter Ralegh, Kt., now first collected, with the Lives by Oldys and*
Birch. Oxford University Press, 1829.

— *Apology for his Voyage to Guiana*, first printed 1650, and generally annexed to his *Select Essays*, also
published in 1650. Reprinted with the same essays, 1667. In the Oxford ed. of *Works*, viii. 479-506:
pp. 320, 321, 324. 336.

— *Discourse of War in General*: p. 11 [viii. 279].

— *Discourse touching a War with Spain*: p. 17 [viii. 304-5].

— *Instructions to his Son, and to Posterity*: pp. 167 [viii. 563], 187 [viii. 558].

— *Letters*: pp. 20, 42, 56, 87, 88, 92-3, 95, 103, 106, 107, 151-2, 183, 233, 237-8, 257, 262, 293, 317, 324,
329, 349-50 [viii. 627-66].

— *Match between the Lady Elizabeth and the Prince of Piedmont*: p. 256 [viii. 224-36].

— *Marriage between Prince Henry and a Daughter of Savoy*: p. 256 [viii. 237-52].

— *Maxims of State*: p. 286 [viii. 2].

— *Orders to Commanders*: p. 313 [viii. 682-8].

— *Poems*: pp. 12, 56, 72-81, 102, 103, 258 [viii. 697-736].

— *Prerogative of Parliaments*: pp. 148 [viii. 199], 159 [viii. 187], 178 [viii. 178], 259 [viii. 179], 285 [viii. 154], 286 [viii. 213].

— *Relation of Cadiz Action*: pp. 127 [viii. 668], 131 [viii. 674].

— *Report of the Truth of the Fight about the Isle of Azores* (not in *Works*), 1591. See Hakluyt.

— *History of the World*: pp. 10 [vi. 211], 35 [vii. 789], 50 [iv. 684], 52 [v. 318], 65 [vi. 101-2], 66 [vi. 81-2], 85
[vi. 113-4], 134 [vii. 789-90], 137 [vi. 103-5], 162 [ii. 151-2], 167 [vi. 458-63], 204 [v. 210], 208
[ii. Preface, 2], 270 [vi. 83], 396 [vii. 900].

— *Lives*, by Oldys and Birch. See Oldys and Birch.

— CAREW, *Observation upon Sanderson's History*. See Heylin.

Record Office MSS.: pp. 343 [Dom. Cor. James I, xcviii. § 79], 357 [Dom. Cor. James I, xcix. § 74], 373
[Dom. Cor. James I, Nov. 7, 1618], 383 [Dom. Cor. James I, Oct. 5, 1619], 385 [Dom. Cor. James I,
ciii. §§ 76 and 21].

Remains of Sir Walter Raleigh, 1651 and 1656-1657. Lowndes dates 1660. (The contents of this
publication—treatises and letters— are incorporated in the Oxford 1829 edition of the *Works*):
pp. 257, 294, 317.

ROS, LIEUT.-GEN. LORD DE, *Memorials of the Tower of London* (1866), new ed. 1867: pp. 248 [183, 193],
250 [168].

ROSSETTI, DANTE GABRIEL (in *Sonnets of Three Centuries*, ed. T.H. Caine, 1883): p. 265 [170].

RUSHWORTH, JOHN, *Historical Collections of Private Passages of State* (1659-1701). Abridged and improved,
1703: pp. 186 [i. 9], 386 [i. 9].

S.

ST. JOHN, JAMES AUGUSTUS, *Life of Sir Walter Raleigh*, 1868: p. 360 [ii. 339].

SANDERSON, SIR WILLIAM, *A Compleat History of the Lives and Reigns of Queen Mary and King James*, 1656.
'Answer to a scurrilous pamphlet entitled *Observations upon a Complete*

History,' &c., 1656: pp. 210
[284], 297 [459-60].

SCHOMBURGK, SIR ROBERT H., *Discovery of the Empire of Guiana in the year 1595, by Sir Walter Ralegh*, ed.
Sir R.H. Schomburgk (Hakluyt Society), 1848: pp. 110 [25-6], 113 [41], 119 [62], 121 [56-64], 307 [173],
321 [211].

SHIRLEY (JOHN, or BENJAMIN, or JAMES), *Life of the Valiant and Learned Sir Walter Ralegh, Kt.*, 1677: pp. 258
[179], 273.

SIDNEY, HON. ALGERNON, *Discourses Concerning Government* (1698), 1750: pp. 274 [ii. 274], 285 [ibid.].

SMITH, CHARLES, M.D., *County and City of Cork*, 1774: pp. 38 [i. 52-6], 49 [i. 120].

SOMERS, *Collection of Tracts from public and private Libraries, particularly that of Lord Somers*, 2nd ed.
Walter Scott, 1809: pp. 219 [ii. 408-20], 376 [ii. 439-42], 382 [ii. 452-6], 387 [ii. 445-51], 389 [ii. 422-37].

SOUTHEY, ROBERT, *The British Admirals* (Lardner's *Cabinet Cyclopaedia*), 1837: pp. 11 [iv. 210], 55 [iv. 242],
113 [iv. 310].

SPEDDING, JAMES. See Francis Bacon.

SPENCE, REV. JOSEPH, D.D., *Observations, Anecdotes, and Characters of Books and Men*, ed. S.W. Singer (1820),
2nd ed. 1858: p. 278 [235].

SPENSER, EDMUND, *A View of the State of Ireland, in Ancient Irish Histories*, Dublin (1633, ed. Sir James
Ware), 1809: p. 17 [i. 168-9].

STAUNDFORD (STAUNFORD, or STANFORD), MR. JUSTICE SIR WILLIAM, *Les Plees del Coron*, London (1557);
1560: p. 214. See Jardine.

STEELE, SIR RICHARD, *The Englishman*, 1714: p. 269 [Aug. 11, 1611].

STEWART, DUGALD, *Collected Works*, ed. Sir William Hamilton, 1854-1860. *A Dissertation*, Part First:
p. 398 [i. 78].

— *Elements of the Philosophy of the Human Mind*: p. 398 [iii. 376].

STOW, JOHN, *A Survey of London and Westminster* (1598), 6th ed. 1754-1755: P. 371 [ii. 634].

— *Annales, or a Generall Chronicle of England* (1580), continued by Edmond Howes (1615), 1631: p. 146 [788].

STRYPE, REV. JOHN, *Annals of the Reformation—Reign of Elizabeth—with Appendix of original State Papers* (1709-31), new ed. 1824: pp. 55 [iv. 28-41], 97 [iv. 178], 98 [iv. 177], 99 [iv. 181].

STUKELY (or STUCLEY), SIR LEWIS, *Apology* (*MSS. Ashmolean*, Bodleian Library, Oxford; copy in Stukely's own hand), Aug. 10, 1618: p. 386. [Printed in Ralegh's *Works*, viii. 783-5.]

— *Humble Petition and Information of Sir Lewis Stukely*, &c., Nov. 26, 1618; *Somers Collection*, 445-451; *Harleian Miscellany*, 63-68; *Fortescue Papers*, 67: p. 387.

SULLY, MAXIMILIEN DE BETHUNE, DUC DE, *Mémoires* (1634), nouvelle edition, Londres, 1768: pp. 156 [iv. 37], 184 [iv. 340], 254 [iv. 295].

SYDNEY, SIR HENRY, '*Letters and Memorials of State (Queen Mary—Oliver)*, written and collected by Sir Henry Sydney,' ed. from originals at Penshurst, Arthur Collins, 1746: pp. 121 [i. 377], 132 [ii. 24], 133 [ii. 42, 55], 144 [ii. 82, 90], 146 [ii. 96, 117-18], 148 [ii. 178, 139], 151 [ii. 168-9], 160 [ii. 210].

T.

Tanner MSS. (Archbishop Sancroft's, at Bodleian): pp. 271 [xxv. No. 10, fol. 12], 304 [lxxiii. § 160], 368 [ccxcix. fol. 87].

Tenison MSS., Lambeth Palace Library Catalogue: p. 69 [i. 160].

THORESBY, RALPH, *Ducatus Leodensis*, or *The Topography of Leeds* (Musaeum Thoresbyanum), 1715: p. 49 [485].

TIMBS, JOHN, *Curiosities of London*, 1855: p. 248 [796].

TOWNSHEND, HEYWOOD, *Four Last Parliaments of Queen Elizabeth*, 1680: p. 159 [232, 235].

Tubus Historicus, or *Historical Perspective* (described by the publisher, T. Harper, as 'Model to the Heroic
Work, *The History of the World*, by Sir Walter Raleigh'), 1631: p. 282.

TYTLER, PATRICK FRASER, *Life of Sir Walter Raleigh*, 1833: p. 198 [438].

U.

UDAL, REV. JOHN, *Demonstration of the Truth of that Discipline which Christ hath prescribed in his Worde
for the Gouernment of his Church*, 1588: p. 55.

V.

VERE, MARSHAL SIR FRANCIS, *The Commentaries of Sir Francis Vere, written by Himself*. Published from his
manuscript by Dr. William Dillingham, 1657. Reprinted, VII. English Garner, ed. Edward Arber,
1883, pp. 57-184: pp. 134 [vii. 94], 138 [vii. 99].

W.

WALTON, IZAAK, *The Complete Angler* (1653), ed. Sir Harris Nicolas, 1875: pp. 78 [78].

WELLDON, SIR ANTHONY, *Court and Character of King James the First* (1651), reprinted in *Secret History of
the Court of James I*, 1811: pp. 217 [346], 255 [350-1].

Wharton MSS. (Bodleian, Oxford): pp. 221 [vol. lxxx], 230 [lxxx. ff. 440, &c.].

WHEATLEY, H.B., *London Past and Present* (based on Peter Cunningham's *Handbook of London*), 1891:
pp. 104 [i. 540-2], 248 [iii. 76], 371 [ii. 88-9].

WHITE, WALTER, *A Londoner's Walk to the Land's End*, 1855: p. 7 [98-100].

WINSTANLEY, WILLIAM, *English Worthies*, 1660: p. 282 [256-7].

WINWOOD, SIR RALPH, *Memorials of Affairs of State in the Reigns of Queen Elizabeth and King James I*
(Collection of Papers belonging to him), ed. Edmund Sawyer, 1725: pp. 156 [i. 215, 231], 205 [ii. 8],
237 [ii. 11].

WOTTON, SIR HENRY, *Of Robert Devereux, Earl of Essex, and George Villiers, Duke of Buckingham, Some Observations by way of Parallel,* 1641 (in *Reliquiae Wottonianae,* 4th ed. 1685): pp. 23 [162], 40 [175], 56 [162], 139 [180], 145 [190].

WOOD, ANTHONY À, *Athenae Oxonienses,* to which are added *The Fasti* (1691-1692), ed. Rev. Philip Bliss, 1815: pp. 8 [ii. 235], 12 [ibid.], 54 [ii. 299-303], 89 [ii. 237], 270 [ii. 242], 273 [iii. 18], 274 [ii. 626], 300 [iii. 169], 301 [ii. 612], 382 [ii. 244-5].

CORRIGENDA

P.5, l. 12, *for* 'him. It has not been' *read* 'his career. Until lately it had not even.'

P.5, ll. 22-26, *for* 'In fact no trace ... face of Ralegh's words' *read* 'But a few years ago an entry was
discovered in the Registers of St. Mary Major, Exeter, of the burial in that church on February 23,
1581, of "Mr. Walter Rawlye, gentelman." Katherine Ralegh, as appears from her will, found in 1895,
died in 1594.'

P.89, l. 10, *omit* 'published in 1615.'

P.90, l. 2 from bottom, *omit* 'in 1615 by Ralegh and his wife.'

P.102, l. 28, *for* 'absence of the detail of private life' *read* 'barrenness in Oldys's biography of the detail
of private life.'

P.209, l. 7, *for* 'Wolvesey Castle, the old episcopal palace, now a ruin' *read* 'the great Hall of the Castle.'

P.233, l. 20, *for* 'Send me my life' *read* 'Lend me my life.'

P.248, l. 4, *omit* 'and there remained all the years of his imprisonment.'

P.248, l. 8, *for* 'died on Tower Hill' *read* 'was buried in St. Peter's Chapel in the Tower.'

P.256, l. 14, *for* 'the Duke' *read* 'the Dukes.'

P.258, l. 8 from bottom, 'Historical scavengers, Aubrey and Osborn,' *omit* 'Aubrey and Osborn.'

P.269, l. 11, *for* 'against the phrase' *read* 'against misuse of the phrase.'

P.285, l. 12, *for* 'a statement in the Dialogue' *read* 'a statement in the Preface to the History.'

P.317, l. 2, *for* 'November 17' *read* 'November 14, 1617.'

P.324, l. 10 from bottom, *for* '"I know"—or, according to the Apology, "I know not"' *read* '"I know," according to the Apology—or, according to another account, "I know not."'

P.335, ll. 11-14, *omit* sentence 'Mr. ... mob,' which, entirely in error, attributes to Dr. Gardiner the opinion of another writer.

P.373, l. 9 from bottom, *for* 'God hold me and' *read* 'God hold me in.'

P.398, l. 22, *omit* 'and a fund of materials not yet properly manufactured.'

CHAPTER I.

The Raleghs were an old Devonshire family, once wealthy and distinguished. At one period five knightly branches of the house flourished simultaneously in the county. In the reign of Henry III a Ralegh had been Justiciary. There were genealogists who, though others doubted, traced the stock to the Plantagenets through an intermarriage with the Clares. The Clare arms have been found quartered with those of Ralegh on a Ralegh pew in East Budleigh church. The family had held Smallridge, near Axminster, from before the Conquest. Since the reign of Edward III it had been seated on the edge of Dartmoor, at Fardell. There it built a picturesque mansion and chapel. The Raleghs of Fardell were, writes Polwhele, 'esteemed ancient gentlemen.' But the rapacious lawyers of Henry VII had discovered some occasion against Wimund Ralegh, the head of the family in their day. They thought him worth the levy of a heavy fine for misprision of treason; and he had to sell Smallridge.

Ralegh's Parents.

Wimund married into the Grenville family; and in 1497 his son and heir, Walter, was born. Before the boy attained majority the father died. As Dr. Brushfield, a Devon antiquarian, to whose diligence and enthusiasm all students of the life of Walter Ralegh are indebted, has shown, Walter Ralegh of Fardell, on the termination of his minority, in 1518, was possessed, in addition to Fardell, of the manors of Colaton Ralegh, Wythecombe Ralegh, and Bollams. He may be presumed to have succeeded to encumbrances likewise. Part of Colaton was sold by him; and he did not occupy Fardell. As he is known to have owned a bark in the reign of Mary, it has been supposed that he took to commerce. Whether for the sake of contiguity to Exeter, then the centre of a large maritime trade, or for economy, he fixed his residence in East Budleigh parish, on a farm, which was his for the residue of an eighty years' term. His choice may have been partly determined by his marriage to Joan, daughter to John Drake of Exmouth. The Exmouth Drakes were connected with East Budleigh; and Joan's nephew, Robert Drake, bequeathed charitable funds in 1628 for the benefit of East Budleigh parish in which he lived. The dates of Joan's marriage and death are uncertain. It is only known that the two events occurred between 1518 and 1534. Her tomb is in East Budleigh church, with an inscription asking prayers for her soul. She left two sons, George and John. Secondly, Walter married a lady of the family of Darell or

Dorrell, though some genealogists describe her as Isabel, daughter of de Ponte, a Genoese merchant settled in London. She left a daughter, Mary, who married Hugh Snedale. On her death, some time before 1549, Walter married thirdly Katherine, daughter of Sir Philip Champernoun. She was widow of Otho Gilbert, of Compton and Greenway Castles, to whom she had borne the three Gilbert brothers, John, Humphrey, and Adrian. By her marriage to Walter Ralegh of Fardell she had three more children, Carew, and Walter, 'Sir Walter Ralegh,' with a daughter, Margaret, described sometimes as older, and sometimes as younger than Walter.

At the time of Ralegh's birth the family had lost its pristine splendour. But there has been a tendency to exaggeration of the extent of the decadence, by way of foil to the merit which retrieved the ruin. John Hooker, a contemporary Devonshire antiquary, uncle to the author of *The Laws of Ecclesiastical Polity*, described the family as 'consopited,' and as having 'become buried in oblivion, as though it had never been.' Yet Walter Ralegh of Fardell was still a land-owner of importance. His third marriage indicates that he had not fallen out of the society of his class. Not even personally can he and his wife Katherine be set down as altogether : *Their Character.* : obscure. Holinshed names one of them, and Foxe names both. Walter seems to have had much of his great son's restlessness and independence of character, if without the genius and the gift of mounting. After his first wife's death he energetically adopted reformed doctrines. In 1549 during the rising in the West his religious zeal endangered his life.

The story is thus told in Holinshed's *Chronicles*. 'It happened that a certain gentleman named Walter Ralegh, as he was upon a side holy day riding from his house to Exeter, overtook an old woman going to the parish church of Saint Mary Clift, who had a pair of beads in her hands, and asked her what she did with those beads. And entering into further speech with her concerning religion which was reformed, and as then by order of law to be put in execution, he did persuade with her that she should, as a good Christian woman and an obedient subject, yield thereunto; saying further that there was a punishment by law appointed against her, and all such as would not obey and follow the same, and which would be put in execution upon them. This woman nothing liking, nor well digesting this matter, went forth to the parish church, where all the parishioners were then at the service; and being impatient, and in an agony with the speeches before passed between her and the gentleman, beginneth to upbraid in the open church very hard and unseemly speeches concerning religion, saying that she was threatened by the gentleman, that, except she would leave her beads, and give over holy bread and holy water, the gentlemen would burn them out of their houses and spoil them, with many other speeches very false and untrue, and whereof no talk at all had passed between the gentleman and her. Notwithstanding, she had not so soon spoken but that she was believed, and in all haste like a sort of wasps they fling out of the church, and get them to the town which is not far from thence, and there began to intrench and fortify the town, sending abroad into the country round about the news aforesaid, and of their doings in hand, flocking, and procuring as many as they could to come and to join with them. But before they came into the town they overtook the gentleman Master Ralegh aforesaid, and were in such a choler, and so fell in rages with him, that, if he had not shifted - *In Peril of Death.* - himself into the chapel there, and had been rescued by certain mariners of Exmouth which came with him, he had been in great danger of his life, and like to have been murdered. And albeit he escaped for this time, yet it was not long before he fell into their hands, and by them was imprisoned and kept in prison in the tower and church of Saint Sidwell, without the east gate of the city of Exeter, during the whole time of the commotion, being many times threatened to be executed to death.' He was not released till the battle of Clyst, called by Holinshed, Clift, Heath, won on August 4, 1549, by Lords Grey and Bedford near the scene of his misadventure, followed by a second victory on the next day, forced the Catholic insurgents to raise the siege of Exeter, which they had been blockading since July 2.

He was no fair weather theologian. His Protestantism out-lived King Edward. He sympathized with the demonstration in 1553 against the Spanish marriage. On the failure of the Devonshire movement his cousin, Sir Peter Carew, the ringleader at Exeter, is stated in official depositions to have effected his escape abroad through Walter Ralegh, whom he 'persuaded to convey him in his bark' to France from Weymouth. The wording implies active and conscious intervention. The strange thing is that he should not have been punished for complicity. Later in the reign of Mary his wife exposed herself to similar peril, and similarly escaped. Foxe in his *Acts and Monuments* relates that Agnes Prest, before she was brought to the stake in 1557 at Southernhay, had been comforted in Exeter gaol by the visits of 'the wife of Walter Ralegh, a woman of noble wit, and of good and goodly opinion.'

Unless that Walter was churchwarden of East Budleigh in 1561, and that a conveyance by him of the Sidmouth Manor fish tithes proves him to have been - *Death and Burial.* - alive in April, 1578, nothing more is known of him. It has not been ascertained when he and Katherine died, though they are believed to have been dead in 1584. The interest in the East Budleigh farm had by that time run out; and it is surmised they had removed into Exeter, if they had not previously possessed a residence there, perhaps by the Palace Gate. On the authority of a request by their son in 1603 to be buried, if not at Sherborne, beside them in 'Exeter Church,' it has been concluded that they were interred in the Cathedral. A monument erected to Katherine's son by her first marriage, Sir John Gilbert, was long accepted as theirs. In fact no trace of their burial in any Exeter church has been found. The present inclination of local archæologists seems to be to assume that they were not buried at Exeter at all. It is hard to assent in the face of Ralegh's words. At all events, nothing else of any kind is remembered of the pair; or could reasonably be expected to have been remembered. History has told much more of them than of most country gentlemen and their wives.

CHAPTER II.

Walter, the second son by the third marriage of Walter Ralegh of Fardell and Hayes, was born in the reign of Edward VI, it has been supposed, in 1552. The exact date is not beyond doubt; for the registration of baptisms at East Budleigh was not begun till two or three years later. If the inscription on the National Portrait Gallery picture, '1588, aetatis suae 34,' and that on Zucchero's in the Dublin Gallery, 'aet. 44, 1598,' be correct, his birth must have been not in 1552, but about 1554. A similar, or nearly similar, inference may be drawn from the statement, on a miniature of him at Belvoir Castle, of his age as sixty-five in 1618. One *Ralegh's Birthplace.* local writer, R. Izacke, has claimed the honour of his birthplace for a house in Exeter, adjoining the Palace-gate. Probably the rumour points, as I have intimated, to its occupation at some time or other by his parents. Another author asserts that he was born at Fardell. His own testimony, 'being born in that house,' is decisive in favour of his father's Budleigh home, a lonely, one-storied, thatched, late Tudor farmhouse, not a manor-house, of moderate size, with gabled wings, and a projecting central porch. Tradition has marked out the particular room in which he was born, as on the upper floor at the west end, facing southwards. The house, which is a mile west of East Budleigh church, and six from Exmouth, with the exception of some change at the end of the east wing, probably retains its original character. It was restored in 1627 by 'R.D.' For a century past it has been denominated Hayes Barton, or simply Hayes. Previously it had been called, after successive landlords, Poerhayes or Power's Hayes, and Dukes-hayes. The hollow in which it lies, among low hills, is on the verge of a tract of moorland; and Hayes Wood rises close at hand. Through the oak wood to Budleigh Salterton Bay is two miles and a half.

In this quiet spot Ralegh spent his boyhood, in circumstances not very unlike those of more eminent county families with which his was connected. During the earlier half of the sixteenth century the majority of the gentry were continually growing poorer, and a minority were growing richer. The Raleghs, it is plain, had not met with the good fortune of the Russells, and others of their rural peers. They were declining, if hardly in the degree represented subsequently. But an ampler share of prosperity could not have made much difference in young Walter's prospects or training. Three brothers were all before him in the succession to the patrimony. His birthright could not have comprised more than the cadet's prescriptive portion of necessity and brains. It is unfair to the natural curiosity of posterity that his extraordinary endowments in the second respect are not traceable in anecdotes of his childhood. Naturally a local legend reports him to have loved the society of adventurous mariners. Sir John Millais in his 'Boyhood of Ralegh,' which was painted at Budleigh Salterton, has embodied it. In a narrative printed a century after his death a general assertion of his fondness for books of voyages occurs. Otherwise his boyish *At Oxford.* tastes and habits are wholly unknown. The name of his school has not been preserved. The first accepted fact after his birth is his entrance, as a commoner, into Oriel College, of which, says Anthony à Wood, his cousin, C. Champernoun, was a member. According to a statement by Thomas Fuller, of which there is no corroboration either in the books of Christ Church, or elsewhere, he belonged also to Christ Church, before or after his admission into Oriel. For any details of his academical course, as for the dates of its commencement and close, posterity is indebted to Wood, who remarks that he went up to Oriel 'in 1568, or thereabouts,' and, 'after he had spent about three years in that house, left the University without a degree.' Wood declares that 'his natural parts being strangely advanced by academical learning, under the care of an excellent tutor, he became the ornament of the juniors, and was worthily esteemed a proficient in oratory and philosophy.' It is exceedingly likely, Ralegh being Ralegh. At the same time, particulars would have been welcome.

Lord Bacon has enshrined in his Apophthegms an example of Ralegh's wit at Oxford. A cowardly fellow happened to be a very good archer. Having been grossly abused by another, he bemoaned himself to Ralegh, and asked what he should do to repair the wrong that had been offered him. 'Why, challenge him,' answered Ralegh, 'to a match of shooting.' If the sarcasm is not very keen its preservation in academical memory implies an impression of distinction in its author. Perhaps as much may be said for another anecdote of his University career, for which John Aubrey solemnly vouches, that he borrowed a gown at Oxford of one T. Child, and never restored it. Bacon's anecdote, in any case, being contemporary testimony, answers the useful purpose of confirming the reality of Ralegh's membership of the University, *Chronological difficulties.* which otherwise would have to be believed on the faith simply of vague tradition, and of Wood's hasty assertions. No evidence indeed of Ralegh's connection with Oxford has ever been discovered in the College or University papers and books, beyond the entry, a little below the name of C. Champernoun, of 'W. Rawley,' in the list of members of Oriel, dated 1572. It is printed in Mr.

Andrew Clark's valuable *Oxford Register*. This W. Rawley must have been, like Champernoun, an undergraduate; for the name has not the graduate's prefix of 'M^r' or 'S^r'. The presence of the name in the list, with that of Champernoun, would be known to Wood. He may have built upon it the whole of his account of the periods both of Ralegh's admission into Oriel, and his departure after some three years. It would seem to him reasonable enough that Ralegh should have entered about 1568 at sixteen, and be still in residence three or four years later. Unfortunately an interlude, put apparently by Wood several years later, separates 1568 and 1572 in Ralegh's career. His academical course cannot fill up the gap; and it at once renders the chronology of the *Athenae* impossible, and that of the Oriel list hard to understand. Ralegh is known to have been out of England for part, if not the whole, of 1569, and is believed with good cause to have remained abroad over 1572. There are ways of explaining the consequent discrepancies. The W. Rawley on the Oriel list may have been, and probably was, our Walter Ralegh, retained among the number of undergraduates, though he had ceased to reside. A century later the name of the Duke of Monmouth, who had resided for a few months only, was kept on the Corpus books for many years. Again, to take and revise Wood's reference, Ralegh may well have entered long before he was sixteen. If, having been, in accordance with the common belief, born in 1552, he had, like his son Walter, gone up at fourteen, he would, in 1569, have passed three years at Oxford. But at all events Wood is mistaken in the assertion that he resided there about three years from 1568; for in 1569 he certainly was campaigning in France.

In France.

It happened in this way. His maternal kinsmen, the Champernouns, were connected by marriage with the Huguenot Comte de Montgomerie. One of them, Henry, had obtained the leave of Elizabeth to raise a troop of a hundred mounted gentlemen volunteers for the Protestant side. He collected them chiefly from the West. Ralegh is said to have been among those who accepted his invitation; 'admodum adolescens,' writes Camden in the *Annals*, 'jam primum fatis monstratus.' He must have quitted Oriel, perhaps in company with C. Champernoun, for the purpose. Generally it has been supposed that he crossed the Channel with the rest of the troop. But there is some reason for holding that he reached France earlier. The contingent entered the Huguenot camp on October 5, 1569, two days after the defeat at Moncontour. Ralegh alludes to himself in the *History of the World* as of the beaten army. Praising Count Lewis of Nassau for his skilful conduct of the Huguenot retreat, he remarks: 'Of which myself was an eye-witness, and was one of them that had cause to thank him for it.' The passage proves that he was in the Huguenot camp after Moncontour. Nothing in the remark is inconsistent with his earlier arrival, if there be, as there is, evidence to support it. Elsewhere in the History he says: 'I remember it well, that, when the Prince of Condé was slain after the battle of Jarnac,' the Huguenots consoled themselves for his death. Jarnac was fought on March 13, 1669. If, then, the phrase, 'I remember,' refer to Ralegh's personal experiences of Huguenot sentiment on the field, he must have joined the army at least half a year before the retreat after Moncontour. The only way of avoiding that conclusion is to take the violent course of supposing that he was recalling French criticisms delivered some time after the actual event.

A haze of uncertainty shrouds his original advent among the Huguenots. It lifts for a moment to show him there; and that is all. As soon as he has

Ferocities *of*

Civil War. ridden within the Huguenot lines the clouds gather once more, and darkness swallows up his individuality. He tells one anecdote in the History of the manner in which the Huguenots chased Catholics in the hills of Languedoc. They tracked the fugitives to caverns half way up precipitous cliffs. Then they smoked them out with their treasures by lighted bundles of straw let down by iron chains opposite the mouth. General Pelissier plagiarised the device, with more murderous details, in Algeria in 1849. It is a specimen of the brutalities of a conflict, which its English assistants, though they had countenanced, would not care to chronicle minutely. To Ralegh's keen sight the struggle would soon have displayed itself shorn of the glamour of religious enthusiasm. He regarded it simply as a civil war, by which 'the condition of no nation,' as he wrote later, 'was ever bettered.' Of one of its prime authors, Admiral Coligny, he has recorded his belief that he 'advised the Prince of Condé to side with the Huguenots, not only out of love to their persuasion, but to gain a party.' English troopers on their return were not likely to dilate on their exploits at the Court of Elizabeth, who audaciously disavowed to the French Catholic Court the auxiliaries she had licensed.

On the authority of an observation of the younger Hakluyt's, that Ralegh had resided longer in France than he, the period is computed to have been not less than six years. As he appears to have been in London at the end of February, 1575, that term would be completed within a fortnight, if he were present at the battle of Jarnac. The time covered the massacre of St. Bartholomew's Day, August 24, 1572. But there is no foundation for the story that he was then in Paris, and was one of the Englishmen sheltered in Walsingham's house. He had enlisted as a lad of seventeen. He emerged a man of twenty-three. Of this long and critical stage in his education we know really nothing, as we know nothing of his youth at school and college. After he quitted France it would appear from allusions by several

- *In the Netherlands.* - contemporary writers that he served, about 1577-78, in

the Netherlands with Sir John Norris's contingent under the Prince of Orange. Modern enquirers have doubted the fact, on the ground of evidence that he was in England between 1576 and 1578. The reasoning is not demonstrative. He may, if a regular combatant, have obtained a furlough to cross over, and see his family; or, from his English home, he may have paid a flying visit or visits to his brother, Sir Humphrey Gilbert, who commanded a regiment of the English auxiliaries. The dates are not incompatible even with a statement that he fought at the battle of Rimenant on August 1, 1578, though, had he been present on so famous an occasion, it would have been more like him to refer somewhere to the circumstance. But if there is no sufficient ground for questioning the belief in his participation in the war of the Low Countries, there is yet less for disputing his residence in England from 1576. His signature to a family deed, already

mentioned, in - *The Middle Temple.* - April, 1578, testifies that in 1578 and in

ensuing years he was for a time in Devonshire. Evidence exists that in 1576, if not earlier, he was living in London. For 1576 itself the proof consists of some commendatory verses by 'Walter Rawely of the Middle Temple' prefixed to the *Steele Glasse* by Gascoigne, published in that year. Upon the description Wood has based a distinct assertion that Ralegh went from Oxford to the Middle Temple to improve himself in the intricate knowledge of the municipal laws. Oldys says he had searched the Registers of the Inn and they yielded no sign of a Walter Rawely or Ralegh. Moreover, if Ralegh had ever been formally a law student, it has been argued he could scarcely have solemnly declared at his trial in 1603 that he had never read a word of law or the statutes. On the other hand, doubts of the identity of the Rawely of the poem with Ralegh always involved intrinsic difficulties. Ralegh would have known Gascoigne through Humphrey Gilbert, with whom Gascoigne served in Flanders; and there is not a trace of the existence of a namesake acquainted with Gascoigne, or able to compose the verses. Now, at any rate, no room for serious dispute remains. A list in two manuscript volumes of all members of the Middle Temple from the commencement of the sixteenth century has lately been completed by order of the Benchers. In it, under the date 157 $^4/_5$, February 27, appears an entry 'Walter Rawley, late of Lyons Inn, Gent. Son of Walter R. of Budleigh, Co. Devon, Esq.' The specification of parentage is useful. Without it a hypothesis would have been possible, that the traditions both of Oxford and of the Temple had been concurrently and equally at fault, and that some inglorious William or Walter had been personating the future hero alike in 1572 and in 1575. As for Ralegh's assertions in later years that he had read no law, as large a disclaimer might have been conscientiously made by many students at Inns of Court beside him. But it is evident that he intended to follow the profession of the law, and took the orthodox steps towards initiation into it, having commenced, as was usual, with admission into an Inn of Chancery, the bygone little collection of brick tenements in Newcastle-street. There is no reason to suppose that he was ever called to the Bar.

In the year following the publication of the *Steele Glasse* he undoubtedly was living in London, though in a different quarter. William and Richard Paunsford, two servants of his, as appears from the Middlesex Registers edited by Mr. Jeaffreson, were in December, 1577, taken up for defying the watch. They had to be bailed out. In the recognizance for one Ralegh was

About the Court. described as 'Walter Rawley, Esq. of Islington,' and in the other as 'Walter Rawley, Esq. de Curia,' that is of the Court. Young men of good family and ambition were in the habit of obtaining an introduction to the Court. They used it as a club, though they might not advance beyond the threshold. Ralegh on his return from France had pursued the regular course. He sought for opportunities of advancement where they most abounded; and, while he waited for them, he enjoyed the pleasures of life. In the use of his leisure he may not always have been more discreet than his riotous dependents. His wife is reported to have remarked of a censure upon their elder son's addiction to equivocal society, that she had heard Ralegh in his youth showed similar tastes. Aubrey, whom nobody believes and everybody quotes, the 'credulous, maggotty-headed, and sometimes little better than crazed' antiquarian, as Wood, his debtor for much curious unsifted gossip, courteously characterizes him, relates how, at a tavern revel, Ralegh quieted a noisy fellow, named Charles Chester. He sealed up his mouth by knotting together the beard and moustache. It is on record that in the February of 1580 he was in trouble for a brawl with Sir Thomas Perrot, who afterwards married the sister of Lord Essex, Lady Dorothy Devereux. Ralegh and Perrot were committed by the Council to the Fleet for six days. The affray is not creditable; but it indicates that Ralegh associated with courtiers.

The company he kept was not all of Chester's or of Perrot's kind. His later correspondence proves that at this early period he must have become known to Walsingham and Burleigh, and have found means for allying himself with Leicester. He can have been no absolutely obscure adventurer now, any more than was his family at the time of his birth the utterly fallen stock it has been the fashion to suppose it. Whence he derived the resources for the _Maritime adventures._ maintenance of an establishment, and for social extravagances, is not as clear. He may have brought spoil from France; or, more probably, he had already begun to cultivate the West country art of privateering. Assistance would be furnished at need by his helpful half brother, Humphrey, his 'true brother,' as Ralegh called him. When at last the employment Ralegh desired came, the opening was made by Gilbert. Gilbert had in 1577 formed a plan for the capture, without warning, of the foreign ships, especially the Spanish and Portuguese, which resorted to the Newfoundland coast for the fisheries. His prizes he proposed to bring into Dutch ports, where they could be sold. With the proceeds he would have fitted out an expedition sufficiently strong, he hoped, to conquer the chief Spanish possessions in America. A main feature of the scheme was that the Queen's name should not be compromised. The leaders were to represent themselves as servants of the Prince of Orange. The English Government might, in proof of good faith, punish any naval officers who had abetted the project. Mr. St. John, a former biographer of Ralegh, has fancied that Ralegh's hand can be detected in the design as laid in writing before Elizabeth. Mr. Spedding is inclined to agree, on account of the extraordinary resemblance he traces between it and the Guiana expedition of 1617-18. The parallel is imaginary, as is the supposition that Gilbert's bold and inventive intellect needed inspiration from any one. But undoubtedly, had the Queen's wary counsellors given their sanction, Ralegh would have been among the adventurers. The next year he accepted a command in the expedition Gilbert was equipping for 'Norimbega,' in search, it was said, for the North-West passage to Cathay. By a Royal charter Gilbert had been authorized for six years from 1578 to discover and occupy heathen territory not actually possessed by any Christian prince or people. The adventure was retarded. A Seville merchant complained of the seizure of his cargo of oranges and lemons at Dartmouth by some of Sir Humphrey's company. At his suit the Privy Council ordered Gilbert and Ralegh to remain until he should be compensated. The County authorities were directed to stop the fleet. How the demand was settled, and whether the embargo were formally taken off, is not recorded. A memorandum in the Privy Council books stating the imposition of fines upon Ralegh and several other West countrymen, and their payment in 1579, may perhaps relate to the injunction, and imply that it was disregarded. At any rate, before the end of 1578 the fleet sailed, though curtailed in strength through quarrels among the adventurers. In an encounter with a Spanish squadron it lost a ship. Ralegh's name is not mentioned in the narrative in Hakluyt. Hooker, however, speaks of him as engaged in a dangerous sea-fight wherein 'many of his company were slain.' Battered and dispirited the expedition returned.

From an allusion in Holinshed it would appear that Ralegh held on his course for a time by himself, though finally he too was compelled, early in 1579, to turn back through want of victuals. The year 1579 came and went, and his fortune remained unmade.

In Ireland.

From Humphrey Gilbert came his second chance of distinction. Sir Humphrey in 1569-70 had been appointed President of Munster. With many noble qualities he was unruly. His friends admitted his liability to 'a little too much warmth and presumption.' He had administered his Irish province with a vigour somewhat in excess even of the taste of his age. Consequently, he had been replaced by Sir John Perrot, father of Ralegh's recent opponent. Sir John acted more leniently to the natives. The collision between his son and Ralegh may have arisen out of controversies on the proper policy to be pursued in the island. In any case to Humphrey Gilbert's favour with the Queen, and to his continuing interest in Irish affairs, Ralegh owed his regular entrance into the public service. In 1580 he was commissioned as captain of a hundred foot-soldiers raised to fight the insurgents of Munster, and their Spanish and Italian confederates. From July 13, 1580, he drew allowances in that capacity. The appointment was not lucrative. His pay was four shillings a day. Sir Robert Naunton, who rose to be Secretary of State to King James, and was connected with a crisis in Ralegh's fate, compiled some biographical notes, entitled *Fragmenta Regalia* on Queen Elizabeth's favourite counsellors. Fuller describes the work, which was not published till after the author's death, as a fruit of Naunton's younger years. Allusions to events which occurred after the death of James I prove that part or all was composed, or revised, when he had already risen, and had access to authentic sources of information. Ralegh's career is one of his themes, though he does not continue it nearly to its close. He sketches it with a generosity which contrasts strangely with the subsequent relations of the two men. Of Ralegh's Irish appointment he speaks as 'not leaving him food and raiment, for it was ever very poor.' The employment afforded abundance of hard work. He gathered confidence in himself, if *'Thorough.'* he ever lacked it. An untried, if not wholly unknown, subordinate, he exhibited the spirit and sense of responsibility of a viceroy. 'Thorough' was as much his motto as Stafford's, and he acted upon it from the first. Towards American Indians he could be gentle and just. His invariable rule with Irishmen and Anglo-Irishmen of every degree was to crush. A characteristic story is told of the outset of Ralegh's Irish career. A kerne was caught carrying a bundle of withies on the outskirts of the English camp. Ralegh asked their destination. 'To hang up English churls!' 'Well,' retorted Ralegh, 'they will do for an Irishman;' and the prisoner was strung up by them accordingly. It is a savage legend which deserves to be remembered in justice to the audacity of the nameless peasant. Probably invented to glorify a renowned Englishman's inflexibility, it illustrates at all events the temper in which the war was waged. Ferocity to Irishmen was accounted policy and steadfastness. Every advantage was taken of the superiority of English steel and ordnance. Writing in 1603 for the information of King James, Ralegh says that, when he was a Captain in Ireland, a hundred foot and a hundred horse would have beaten all the force of the strongest provinces, for 'in those days the Irish had darts.' Towards the end of the Queen's reign they had bought good English arms, and fought on even terms.

One of his first public acts was to join Sir Warham St. Leger in trying and executing at Cork in August, 1580, Sir James Fitzgerald, the Earl of Desmond's brother. Fitzgerald was drawn, hanged, and quartered. His immediate superior was the Earl of Ormond, the Lieutenant of Munster, who showed occasional tenderness to his fellow-countrymen. The Lord Deputy was Lord Grey of Wilton, whose views were generally as stern as Ralegh's. Edmund Spenser was assistant secretary to Grey, and held as austere a theory of Irish government. Ralegh in November, 1580, was with

Lord Grey's : *The SmerwickMassacre.* : army. With the assistance of an

English fleet under Admiral Winter it blockaded at Smerwick in Kerry a mixed Spanish and Irish garrison. On November 10 the garrison capitulated without conditions. Thereupon Grey sent in Ralegh and Macworth, who had the ward of the day. They are stated by Hooker, in his continuation of Holinshed, to have made a great slaughter. Four hundred Spaniards and Italians were put to the sword. All the Irishmen and several Irish women were hanged. An Englishman and an Irish priest, who suffered the same doom, had their legs and arms first broken. Only the foreign officers were held to ransom. The act was that of the Deputy. Afterwards it was discovered that the massacre excited general horror through Europe. Attempts were made to repudiate sympathy with it on the Queen's part. Bacon wrote that she was much displeased at the slaughter. Her own letters to Grey comment on the whole proceeding as greatly to her liking. She expresses discontent only that she had not been left free to kill or spare the officers at her discretion. Personally Ralegh cannot be accounted amenable for the atrocity. He is not named in Grey's despatch to the Council. But it would be folly to pretend that he disapproved it. Hooker, his eulogist, claims it for him as an eminent distinction. He cordially sympathized with Grey's ideal of a Mahometan conquest for Ireland.

His Irish service gave him opportunities of a nobler order. He ventured his life in a score of hazardous feats. On one occasion his horse was desperately wounded. He must have been slain but for the aid of his servant Nicholas Wright, a trusty Yorkshireman. Another time the Seneschal of Imokelly with fifteen horsemen and sixty foot lay in wait for him at a ford between Youghal and Cork. He had crossed in safety when Henry Moile, one of a few Downshire horsemen he had added to his foot soldiers, was thrown in the middle of the stream. Back rode Ralegh, and stood by his comrade in the face of tremendous odds. The Seneschal, though his men outnumbered Ralegh's by twenty to one, was intimidated. He let Ralegh accomplish his purpose, which was the occupation of Barry's Court, the seat of Lord Barry. Barry was one of the Irish nobles whose loyalty was not fixed. Ralegh desired to convince the class of the futility of resistance by sudden blows. His courage in this instance was more apparent than his wisdom. He had with difficulty obtained the Deputy's consent to the enterprise. The result justified Grey's hesitation. Barry had escaped before Ralegh's arrival at his castle. He became, and remained for years, an open enemy. At last he seems to have been reconciled to the Government. In 1594 Ralegh was interceding for him against the grant of a favour at his expense to another veteran malcontent, Florence MacCarthy. Ralegh's vigour had fuller success against another suspected noble, Lord Roche, of Bally. Roche's castle, twenty miles from Cork, was strong, and his retainers devoted and many. With a petty detachment Ralegh set off on a dark night. He foiled two bands, one of eight hundred, the other of five hundred, which endeavoured to block his way. During a parley he contrived to introduce first a few and then all his followers. Lord Roche professed much loyalty, and entertained the intruders courteously at dinner. He refused to accompany Ralegh on his return till he was shown that the castle was in the hands of the English soldiers. Reluctantly he yielded, and Ralegh conveyed him and his family across the rugged hills into Cork by night. Roche proved an excellent subject.

Ralegh was indefatigable. He shunned no toil or danger. He did not care if the enemy were five or twenty to one. But he was not a workman who never complains of his tools, or an ox content to be muzzled while treading out the corn. He spoke of his soldiers as such poor and miserable creatures as their captains did not dare lead them into battle. Wellington sometimes was as uncomplimentary to his. He bitterly criticized Ormond. Grey had granted him the custody of Barry's Court. He wrote in February, 1581, to Sir Francis Walsingham, with whom he had established a correspondence. He asked the Secretary to obtain from the Deputy Grey his confirmation in the post. He accused Ormond of compelling so long a delay before Ralegh could enter, that Barry had been able to dismantle the castle. He imputed the blunder either to covetousness, or to unwillingness that any Englishman should have anything. He contrasted the multiplication of traitors in Munster by a thousand in the two years of Ormond's rule with Gilbert's suppression of a previous rising in two months. 'Would God Sir Humphrey Gilbert's behaviour were such in peace it did not make his good service forgotten, and hold him from the preferment he is worthy of!' He was ashamed to receive her Majesty's pay, though but a poor entertainment, and see her so much abused. Walsingham wrote to Grey, and the Lord Deputy assigned to Ralegh the Barry's Court domain from Rostellan Castle to Fota. It comprised one side of Cork harbour, with the island now occupied by Queenstown. The Queen, through the influence, it is said, of Burleigh, refused her sanction. Next year Ralegh was writing again to Grey in vehement censure of Ormond. He repudiated any complicity in the defencelessness of the great wood of Conoloathe, and the country between the Dingle and Kilkenny. The commissariat of Cork, he charged, had been recklessly neglected; and Desmond's and Barry's wives were being encouraged to gather help for their traitor lords.

Discontent.

Denunciations of a general by his officer have an evil sound. Ralegh's apology, such as it is, must be sought in his just sense of a masterly capacity. He knew he was right; from the point of view of the prevalent Elizabethan policy towards Ireland, though not from Burleigh's, he was right. He raged at his want of official authority to correct the wrong. He fretted, moreover, at being left in Ireland at all. Ormond quarrelled with Grey, and was recalled in the spring of 1581. The lieutenancy of Munster was assigned jointly to Ralegh, Sir William Morgan, and Captain Piers. Ralegh continued discontented. He sighed for a wider sphere. From his quarters at Lismore he wrote in August, 1581, to Lord Leicester. He desired 'to put the Earl in mind of his affection, having to the world both professed and practised the same.' Incidentally he intimated more than readiness to return to England. 'I have spent,' he writes, 'some time here under the Deputy, in such poor place and charge as, were it not for I knew him to be one of yours, I would disdain it as much as to keep sheep.' His tone implied that he understood he had come on probation for more exalted functions elsewhere, and that he had a claim upon Leicester's patronage. How he had established it is unknown. Probably the intimacy began in London before he received his Irish commission. He was at any rate sufficiently intimate to be able to recommend a man of some eminence, as was Sir Warham St. Leger, to the Earl's protection.

He did not wish to stay in Ireland. The immediate success of his hardness and resoluteness, when he was given a free hand, would have deprived him of the option, if he had wished it. After Ormond's dismissal the pacification of Munster went rapidly on under him and his fellow lieutenants. Captain

Return to England. - John Zouch, an officer as ruthless to Irishmen as himself, who was appointed Governor of the province in August, 1581, worked on the same lines. It became practicable to disband part of the English forces. Ralegh's own company was paid off without apparent dissatisfaction on his part. Being needed no longer in Ireland he was sent home by Grey in December, 1581, with despatches. For his expenses he was paid on December 29, at the liberal rate of £20, which may be roughly reckoned as equivalent to £100.

CHAPTER III.

Ralegh and Grey.

This visit of Ralegh's to the Court was the turning-point in his career. How it became that has been explained in different ways. According to Naunton a variance between him and Grey drew both over to plead their cause. Naunton goes on to say that Ralegh 'had much the better in telling of his tale; and so much that the Queen and the lords took no slight mark of the man and his parts; for from thence he came to be known, and to have access to the Queen and the lords.' It is natural to suppose that Ralegh's Irish campaigns were concerned with his sudden rise at Court. Thenceforward he was a high authority on Irish policy. His Irish experience continued to be the sheet-anchor of his ascendency with the Queen. Naunton's tale, too, is supported by evidence from the Hatfield and the Irish State papers of Ralegh's disposition to form and push Irish plans of his own, and of Grey's keen jealousy of the habit. Burleigh on January 1, 1582, in a letter to the Lord Deputy, mentioned that Mr. Rawley had informed her Majesty how the charge of five or six hundred soldiers for the garrison of Munster might be shifted from the Queen to the province without umbrage to Ormond, its most powerful land-owner. To this the Lord Deputy speedily replied, vehemently criticising 'the plot delivered by Captain Rawley unto her Majesty.' He condemned it as a plausible fancy, 'affecting credit with profit,' but 'framed upon impossibilities for others to execute.' To Walsingham he complained bitterly of misrepresentations at Court in the same January, and, in the following April, declared that he 'neither liked Captain Rawley's carriage, nor his company.' On the other hand, Grey is not known to have returned from Ireland till August, 1582; and the Council Register contains no reference to a personal controversy between Ralegh and him. But Ralegh may well have privately expounded to the Queen and some Privy Councillors his views, which would then have been transmitted to Grey to answer. Naunton's mistake in confronting the Deputy and the self-confident Captain directly at the Council board does not seriously affect the value otherwise of his statement. Still, the account of Ralegh's admittance to the Queen's favour, with its particular circumstances, rests, it must be remembered, on Naunton's own not unimpeachable authority. Other authors who tell the same story, have simply and unsuspiciously borrowed it from him. Students of Ralegh's history have to accustom themselves to the use by successive biographers of the same hypothetical facts with as much boldness as if they had been the fruit of each writer's independent research.

Another account attributes to Leicester Ralegh's sudden favour on his return from Ireland. A few months before he was, we have seen, soliciting the Earl for a change of employment. His introduction at Court may have been the answer. Sir Henry Wotton, adopting the view, cynically surmised that Leicester wished to 'bestow handsomely upon another some part of the pains, and perhaps of the envy, to which long indulgent fortune is *Fuller's Tale.* obnoxious.' By others, whom Scott has partly followed, the Earl of Sussex has been credited with the elevation of Ralegh, as a counterpoise to Leicester. Neither the one noble nor the other, it was supposed, could have patriotically desired to enrol in the public service the most effective of recruits. Amongst all the subtle solutions of the mystery of Ralegh's leap into prominence, Fuller's well-worn story, which is now Scott's, commends itself for comparative simplicity. Everybody has heard how her Majesty, meeting with a plashy place, made some scruple to go on; when Ralegh, *Not Improbable.* dressed in the gay and genteel habit of those times, presently cast off and spread his new plush cloak on the ground, whereon the Queen trod gently over, rewarding him afterwards with many suits for his so free and seasonable tender of so fair a footcloth. Fuller, again, it is who vouches for the sequel of the incident. Ralegh, he says, having thus attracted notice, wrote on a window, which Elizabeth was to pass—

Fain would I climb, yet fear I to fall

Elizabeth capped it with

If thy heart fails thee, climb not at all

Some of Ralegh's later biographers have felt so intensely the seriousness of their task, that they either omit or ridicule the legend. The whole appeared first in the *Worthies*, published in 1662. No documentary proof can be given of its veracity; and there is no disproof. The opportunity might easily have occurred; and Ralegh was of an eagerness and an adroitness not to have let it slip. Undoubtedly the anecdote has the intrinsic merit beyond the rest of pointing to the final and determining agent in his change of fortune. All the other answers to the enigma may contain an ingredient of truth. Leicester would recognize his capacity, and might have been ready to use him. Sussex would perceive the danger of allowing so redoubtable a free lance to pass to a rival service. Walsingham and Burleigh were manifestly impressed with his extraordinary sagacity and strength of will. His Irish services, which had called forth the admiration of Grey himself so long as Ralegh fought under him, could not fail to be appreciated by the Queen's wise councillors. He was backed by the vast family circles of the Gilberts and Champernouns. In his later life he could speak of 'an hundred gentlemen of my kindred.' He was no novice at the Court itself, which he had studied for years before it recognized him as an inmate. But Leicester and Sussex, like Grey, and even Burleigh and Walsingham, though they might have employed him, and have bandied him among them, would have concurred in keeping him in the background. To Elizabeth herself may confidently be ascribed the personal decision that he was to be acknowledged, and not merely used, but distinguished.

The Queen's Choice.

To the Queen he owed his emergence from an obscurity, which posterity wonders to find enveloping him till thirty. His was not a nature which ripens late. As a boy at home, as an undergraduate at Oxford, as an adventurer in France, as a seaman in the Atlantic, as a military leader in Munster, as a commencing courtier, he might have been expected to flash forth from the mass of his comrades. No apathy of contemporary opinion is to blame for the long delay. Rather it was the hurry and the glitter of contemporary life. A nation, like the English under Elizabeth, facing the dawn of a new age, does not pause to mark degrees of individual brightness. All eyes are dazzled with the radiance of the era itself. The few rare and peculiar stars are not discriminated as shining with a lustre of their own. The Queen would not be better able than her subjects to measure the particular mode in which Ralegh overtopped his neighbours. She discerned the special gifts which others discerned, the 'good presence in a handsome and well compacted person; the strong natural wit and a better judgment, with a bold and plausible tongue, whereby he could set out his parts to the best advantage.' She was diverted by his flights of fancy emphasized by the broad Devon accent, which, to the day of his death, he never lost, or tried to lose. She must have been conscious of depths of capacity, to which, whatever the exigency, appeal was never made in vain. But the surpassing attraction for her was the feeling that he and his grandeur were her creature and creation.

Personally she chose him, and she exacted that his service should be personally rendered to her. He understood the conditions of his tenure of influence, and generally fulfilled them faithfully. She knew, and he knew, that he was selected for gifts which made him a valuable servant of the State, as impersonated in its chief. Yet it is not strange that, in an age of coarse feeling, and coarser language, his elevation should have been attributed to mere feminine weakness. It is much more surprising that the warning, 'No scandal about Queen Elizabeth,' should have been disregarded by grave modern historians and biographers. Mr. Edward Edwards, for instance, Ralegh's most thorough and painstaking biographer since the learned but unmethodical Oldys, takes the report for granted, and appears to think it honourable. The belief cannot bear the least examination. Elizabeth was in the habit of requiring all her courtiers to kneel to her as woman as well as Queen, to hail her at once Gloriana and Belphoebe. The fashion was among her instruments of government. By appealing to the devotion of her courtiers as lovers, she hoped to kindle their zeal in serving their Queen. They who mock at her claims to adoration as the Lady of the land are ungrateful to a policy which preserved the tone of English society for a generation romantic, poetical, and chivalrous. In pursuance of her usual system, and in innocence of any vice but vanity, she was sure to invite the language of passion from the owner of genius and looks like Ralegh's. She played upon his Christian name, writing it as she and others pronounced it, Water. She enjoyed the anger her kindness aroused in other admirers, such as Hatton. He was willing to offer the homage for which she thirsted. So were other courtiers by the dozen. Cautious methodical George Carew wrote to her when she was seventy, and nearing the grave, envying 'the blessing others enjoy in beholding your Royal person whose beauty adorns the world.' Of sensual love between her and Ralegh there is not a tittle of evidence which will be accepted by any who do not start by presuming in her the morals of a courtesan. In support of the calumny, passages of the *Faerie Queene* have been cited, in which the poet has been interpreted as literally and as illiberally as the courtier. Fastidious Spenser would have shuddered to imagine the coarse construction against his Queen to which his delicate allegories were to be wrested. Had there been ground for the legend, we may feel tolerably certain that Lady Ralegh would have known of it. She could not have refrained from hinting at a motive for the wrath with which, it will hereafter be seen, her mistress visited her transgression.

Ralegh's Versatility.

Ralegh himself may not have been sufficiently careful to guard against a fable flattering to his charms, if injurious to his independence. He furthered malignant humours in his own time by his fondness for personal adornment. His lavish vanity seems to have been taken as proof of his and his Sovereign's amours. He must in any case, by no fault of his own, but by the excessive bounty of nature in heaping courtly graces upon him, have been exposed to the liability of misconstruction by later ages. Measured by his force of character and his acts he has as little as possible in common with a Leicester or a Hatton. Yet posterity, misled by tradition, has never been sure whether his distinctive vocation were not that of a fine gentleman. Contemporaries, partly from misapprehension, partly from admiration, and partly from jealousy, tried to fasten him to that. When the splendour of his exploits by sea and land demonstrated him to be more than a courtier, they ranked him as seaman or swordsman. His versatility lent itself to the error, and operated to the disappointment of his real aim. His constant effort was to be accepted and trusted as a serious statesman. He might have attained his end more completely if his absorption in it had dimmed the brightness of his marvellous intelligence, or deadened his delight in its gymnastics. But he had to live his life according to his nature. The multiplicity of his interests separates him from others of his mental level. He loved power, both the contest for it and its exercise. He coveted money for its uses, and equally for the inspiring experiences involved in its acquisition. He liked to act the patron, and was content in turn to play the client. He loved toil, and he could enjoy ease. He revelled in the strifes of statesmanship and the physical perils of battles and travel. He resembled his period, with its dangers and glories, its possibilities of Spanish dungeons and Spanish plunder, its uncertainties of theology and morality. He had a natural gift for deriving pleasure from his actual circumstances, a dull and brutal civil war, or a prison, though none could utter more dismal groans. By predilection he basked in a Court, where simultaneously he could adore its mistress and help to sway her sceptre.

His Aspect.

Hitherto his career had been run outside the verge of chronicles. Its early stages left few direct records. They have to be pieced together by retrospective allusions proceeding from himself or others, after he had already risen. The difficulties of his biographers are not at an end when he has mounted into the full blaze of publicity. His name thenceforth was in a multitude of mouths; yet much in his character, position, and motives always remains shadowy and uncertain. His appearance at the time it was winning an entrance for him at Court can only be conjectured. He was tall and well-proportioned, with thick curly locks, beard, and mustache, full red lips, bluish-grey eyes, and the high forehead and long bold face, remarked in a contemporary epigram. Aubrey describes him by report similarly, with the addition that he was sour eye-lidded. His characteristic features, and the 'general aspect of ascendency,' were the same in youth and in later life. They are vividly represented by several extant portraits, by Zucchero's, somewhat wanting in repose and dignity, at Longleat; by another of Zucchero's, now in the National Gallery of Ireland, the original of the print in Sir Henry Ellis's collection of letters, representing Ralegh at forty-four, with a map of Cadiz; by that at Knole, from which Vertue's print in Oldys's Life probably was engraved; by that of 1588, formerly in Sir Carew Ralegh's house at Downton, and now in the National Portrait Gallery; by one belonging to Mr. J.D. Wingfield Digby; by one, dated 1618, in the possession of Mr. T.L. Thurlow; and by the best, in Mr. George Scharf's decisive judgment, the picture in possession of Sir John Farnaby Lennard, at Wickham Court, Kent. The last, the original of Houbraken's engraving, was painted in 1602 for the Carews of Beddington. Young Walter, then eight years old, stands by Ralegh's side, a handsome boy, richly dressed, with features, as they remained in later life, like his father's, Dates of

Portraits. and the same air of command. A picture, described as by Cornelius Janssen, sold at Christie's rooms in December, 1890, represents a visage worn and sombre, the hair on the head thin. As the artist's first commonly acknowledged portraits taken in England are dated 1618, the work, if by Janssen, must have been executed after Ralegh's second Guiana expedition, and might naturally exhibit these traits. There are also several contemporary miniatures, one, in particular, at Belvoir Castle. This is of especial interest, on account of the age inscribed, sixty-five, and the year, 1618, which imply a belief that he was born later than 1552. From the date, 1618, and the representation of a battle, on the companion miniature of young Walter, apparently by the same hand, it may be inferred that the portrait of the father was, as that of the son must have been, painted after the second voyage to Guiana. Probably, to judge from the combination of Lady Ralegh's and her husband's initials on the back, it was executed for her. In it, to a degree even beyond the portrait attributed to Janssen, the hair of the head is pathetically white. Though elsewhere the marks of age have not been so openly betrayed, all the extant portraits, unless that in the National Portrait Gallery be an exception, were executed after he had reached middle life. He may be beheld in most of them as he appeared to his rivals and partisans, the veteran knight in magnificent apparel, pearls, and silver armour, haughty and subtle, tanned, hardened, and worn with voyages to the Spanish Main and fighting at Cadiz, 'Ralegh the witch,' the 'scourge of Spain,' the 'soldier, sailor, scholar, courtier, orator, historian, and philosopher.' We do not see the daredevil trooper of Languedoc and Munster, the duellist, the master of the roistering watch-beating Paunsfords. He is not visible as pictured to the vivid fancy of the author of *Kenilworth*, the youthful aspirant, graceful, eager, slender, dark, restless, and supercilious, with a sonnet or an epigram ever ready on his lips to delight friends and sting enemies.

The spelling of his name for the first thirty-two years of his life was as vague and unsettled as his acts. There was no standard of orthography for surnames till the latter part of the seventeenth century. Neither the owners, nor others, were slaves to uniformity. Posterity has used its own liberty of selection, often very arbitrarily. Robert Cecil, for instance, signed his name Cecyll, and nobody follows him, not even his descendants. For Ralegh's name his contemporaries never had a fixed rule to the end of him. Transcribers with the signature clear before them would not copy it; they could not keep to one form of their own. His correspondents and friends followed the idea of the moment. Lord Burleigh wrote Rawly. Robert Cecil wrote to him as Rawley, Raleigh, and Ralegh. A secretary of Cecil wrote Raweley and Rawlegh. King James, for whom in Scotland he had been Raulie, wrote once at any rate, and Carew Ralegh commonly, Raleigh. Carew's son Philip spelt his name both Raleigh and Ralegh. Lady Ralegh signed one letter Raleigh, but all others which have been preserved, Ralegh. The only known signature of young Walter is Ralegh. The Privy Council wrote the name Raleghe, Rawleighe, and Rawleigh. George Villiers spelt it Raughleigh, and Cobham, Rawlye. In Irish State Papers he is Rawleie. Lord Henry Howard wrote Rawlegh and Rawlie. The Lord Admiral called him Rawlighe. For some he was Raileigh, Raughlie, and Rauleigh. In a warrant he was Raleighe, and in the register of Stepney Church, Raylie. Naunton wrote Rawleigh and Raghley, and Milton, in a manuscript commonplace book, Raugleigh. Sir Edward Peyton in his book spelt the name Rawliegh. Stukely in his Apology spelt it Raligh. The name to his verses printed in Gascoigne's volume is Rawely, and in a manuscript poem it is Wrawly. In another manuscript poem it is Raghlie. Puttenham printed it Rawleygh. In the wonderful mass of manuscripts at Lambeth, collected by Sir George Carew, who kept every paper sent him, though his correspondents might beg him to burn their letters, the name, beside forms already given, appears spelt as Ralighe, Raule, Rawlee, Rauley, Rawleye, Raulyghe, | *Seventy-four* | | *Forms.* | Rawlyghe, and Ralleigh. In a letter from Sir Thomas Norreys in the equally wonderful, but less admirable, pile of Lismore papers, he is Raulighe. In the books of the Stationers' Company he is Rawleighe, and Rauleighe in the copy in the Harleian MSS. of the discourse of 1602 on a War with Spain. In Drummond's Conversations with Ben Jonson he is Raughlie. References occur to him in Mr. Andrew Clark's *Oxford Register*, as Rallegh, Rawlei, Rauly, Raughley, Raughly, Raughleigh, Raylye, and Rolye.

Foreigners referred to him as Ralle, Rallé, Raleghus, Raleich, Raleik, Raulaeus, Rale, Real, Reali, Ralego, and Rhalegh. In addition, I have found in lists compiled by Dr. Brushfield the name spelt Raley, Raleye, Raleagh, Raleygh, Raleyghe, Ralli, Raughleye, Rauleghe, Raulghe, Raweleigh, Raylygh, Reigley, Rhaleigh, Rhaley, Rhaly, and Wrawley.

Ralegh himself had not kept the same spelling throughout his life. Down to 1583 his more usual signature had been the phonetic Rauley. But in 1578 he signed as Rawleyghe a deed which his father signed as Ralegh, and his brother Carew as Rawlygh. A letter of March 17, 1583, is the first he is known to have signed as Ralegh; and in the following April and May he reverted to the signature Rauley. From June 9, 1584, he used till his death no other signature than Ralegh. It appears in his books when the name is mentioned. It is used in a pedigree drawn up for him in 1601. Of the hundred and sixty-nine letters collected by Mr. Edward Edwards, a hundred and thirty-five are thus signed. Six signed Rauley, one Raleghe, and one Rauleigh, belong to an earlier date. The rest are either unsigned or initialled. The reason of his adoption of the spelling Ralegh from 1584, unless that it was his dead father's, is unknown. Of the fact there is no doubt. The spelling Raleigh, which posterity has preferred, happens to be one he is not known to have ever employed.

CHAPTER IV.

Employment.

His promotion, when it commenced, was liberal; it was not meteoric. He had won his full entry at Court before he gained permanent offices and emoluments. For a time he continued dependent upon the long-suffering Irish Exchequer. In February he received an order for £200 upon the entertainment due to him in Ireland. That, however, seems to have been payment of arrears for previous and actual service. Notwithstanding an angry protest by the Lord Deputy, already alluded to, a fresh commission was issued to him in April, 1582, as Captain of the late Captain Appesley's band of footmen in Ireland. The reason assigned was that he might be required for some time longer in that realm for his better experience in martial affairs. He had leave to appoint a lieutenant, while he was 'for some considerations by Us excused to stay here.' He did not want for employment, though he was given no fixed duties. A system of personal government like that of the Tutors demanded extraordinary services of various degrees of importance. Any and all Ralegh could excellently render. Frequently he acted as the Queen's private secretary. Sometimes he had to escort a foreign envoy. Negotiations were pending for the marriage of Elizabeth to the Duke of Anjou. Leicester was jealous of the Duke and of Simier, his dexterous and personally fascinating agent. Simier was returning to France in the autumn of 1581. He had to be protected, it was rumoured, from Flushing pirates known to be in Leicester's pay. Ralegh's professed adhesion to Leicester did not prevent his appointment as one of the escort. In the publication by an anonymous contemporary, called *Leicester's Commonwealth*, it is related that the vessel containing the returning escort was chased for several hours: 'Master Ralegh well knoweth it, being there present.' Anjou himself quitted England in February, 1582, to assume the sovereignty of the Netherlands. Ralegh again was of the company sent to introduce the Duke to the Queen's allies. *Envoyand Counsellor.* He stayed behind the rest, and was entrusted by the Prince of Orange with letters to the Queen. He has recorded that the Prince confided to him a private, if not very particular, message to her: 'Sub umbra alarum tuarum protegimur.' Probably that was only a text upon which the Prince's communications enabled him to enlarge. He was consulted much concerning Ireland, both by the Council and by the Queen. In March, 1582, articles were exhibited against Ormond for alleged indulgence in his government of Munster towards Irish rebels. He was suspected, for example, of having apprised the Seneschal of Imokelly that 'two choice persons' had stolen into the Seneschal's camp to murder him. Ralegh was named among those who were to be called upon to prove the charges. Burleigh himself, who did not approve of the fierceness of Ralegh's method of dealing with Irish turbulence, respected his experience. In October, 1582, the Lord Treasurer is said to have taken careful notes of his advice how to secure the adhesion of some Munster lords. Lord Grey's reception of a letter from the Treasurer in the preceding January citing an opinion of 'Mr. Rawley' on the mode of levying Irish taxes for the support of the English troops, has already been described. Use was made also of his engineering ability. There are references to reports by him on estimates for the repair of the fortifications of Portsmouth, and to his discussion of the question with Burleigh and Sussex in the Queen's presence. He is even found sitting on a commission with Sir Thomas Heneage to investigate a complaint against Lord Mayor Pullison, of having attached, to satisfy a debt to himself, the ransom of a Barbary captive.

Not till after a probation of years did he obtain definite official rank. In 1584 he had been elected one of the members for Devonshire, with Sir William Courtenay. Apparently in the early part of the same year he was knighted; for in his colonizing patent of March, 1584, he is styled 'Mr.

Walter Ralegh, Knight.' In 1585 he succeeded the Earl of Bedford as Warden of the Stannaries. He had as Warden to regulate mining privileges in Devon and Cornwall, to hold the Stannary Parliament on the wild heights of Crockern Tor, and judicially to decide disputes on the customs, which, though written, he has said, in the Stannary of Devon, were unwritten in Cornwall. Long after his death the rules he had prescribed prevailed. As Warden he commanded the Cornish militia. He had a claim, which was resisted by the Earl of Bath, the Lord Lieutenant of Devonshire, to military powers there also. His prerogatives were strengthened by his appointment shortly afterwards to the Lieutenancy of Cornwall, and to the Vice-Admiralty of the two counties. The Vice-Admiralty was a very convenient office for a dealer in privateering. He nominated as his deputies in the Vice-Admiralty Lord Beauchamp for Cornwall, and his eldest half-brother, Sir John Gilbert, for Devon. Beside his other offices, he is supposed to have held the post of a Gentleman of the Privy Chamber. Later he received a more signal token than any of royal confidence. He was appointed Captain of the Yeomen of the Guard. For several years Sir Christopher Hatton had united the offices of Captain and Vice-Chamberlain. On April 29, 1587, by a preposterous exercise of royal patronage, he became Lord Chancellor. He had already ceased to command the Guard, though the actual date of his retirement is not specified. His immediate successor, appointed perhaps as a stop-gap, was Sir Henry Goodier. Sir Anthony Paulett also is sometimes mentioned in connexion with the post. But the office was permanently filled by the nomination of Ralegh in the early summer of 1586. The Captain's pay consisted of a yearly uniform. Six yards of tawney medley at 13s. 4d. a yard, with a fur of black budge rated at £10, is the warrant for 1592. The cost in the next reign was estimated at £14. Ralegh had to fill vacancies in his band of fifty. He was known to have a sharp eye for suitable recruits, young, tall, strong, and handsome. The regular duty was to guard the Queen from weapons and from poison; to watch over her safety by day and night wherever she went, by land or water. At the Palace the Captain's place was in the antechamber, where he could almost hear the conversations between her and her counsellors. To share them he had but to be beckoned within. Naturally the command seemed to be a stepping-stone to a Vice-Chamberlainship at least, if not to the Keepership of the Queen's conscience.

Royal Parsimony.

None of these offices were in themselves lucrative. A maintenance for the new favourite and the new public servant had otherwise to be found. His endowment came from the usual sources. Naunton says that, 'though he gained much at the Court, he took it not out of the Exchequer, or merely out of the Queen's purse, but by his wit and the help of the prerogative; for the Queen was never profuse in delivering over her treasures, but paid most of her servants, part in money, and the rest with grace.' He adds, it may be hoped, before October 29, 1618: 'Leaving the arrears of recompense due for their merit to her great successor, who paid them all with advantage.' Ralegh himself, after a similar compliment to James, laments in his History the Queen's parsimony to her 'martial men, both by sea and land,' none of whom, he remembers, 'the Lord Admiral excepted, her eldest and most prosperous commander,' did she 'either enrich, or otherwise honour, for any service by them performed.' Notices in official documents of pecuniary grants to himself are rare. An order in September, 1587, for a payment of £2000 to be spent according to her Majesty's direction appears to have been for works at Portsmouth. No meagre substitute was supplied by forfeitures, by enforced demises of collegiate, capitular, and episcopal estates, by monopolies, and by letters of marque.

To All Souls College, Oxford, belongs the honour of having been the first to help to make his fortune. In April, 1583, he wrote to Egerton, then

Solicitor-General, mentioning a grant of two beneficial leases of lands which the Queen had extorted from the college after her manner. On May 4, : *Farm of Wines.* · 1583, he received a more lucrative gift, the farm of wines. By his patent every vintner was bound to pay him for his life an annual retail licence fee of a pound. To save himself trouble, he underlet his rights to one Richard Browne for seven years at £700, or, according to another account, £800, a year. Browne promoted a large increase in the number of licensed taverners. Ralegh had reason to believe that he had not his fair share of profits. Egerton advised him that the demise was disadvantageous, but that it might be hard to terminate it without Browne's concurrence. Ralegh, to compel a surrender from Browne before the expiration of the term, obtained a revocation of his own patent in 1588. On August 9, 1588, a new patent for thirty-one years was granted. It does not seem to have freed him wholly from Browne's claims. This licence again he leased. The lessee was William Sanderson, the husband of his niece, Margaret Snedale. At a later period he had disputes with Sanderson also on the profits. By an account of 1592, he estimated them at a couple of thousand a year. It was never a very popular office to be chief publican. The year after the original grant, it involved Ralegh in a troublesome quarrel. He or Browne had licensed a vintner, John Keymer, at Cambridge, in defiance of the Vice-Chancellor's jurisdiction. The undergraduates loyally beat the intruder, and they frightened his wife nearly to death. The Vice-Chancellor sent him to gaol. The University also invoked the aid of its Chancellor, the Queen's Minister, against the Queen's favourite. Burleigh procured an opinion of the two Chief Justices against the licence. Ralegh was obliged in the end to give way to his assured loving friend the Vice-Chancellor. In the second patent the privileges of Oxford and Cambridge were expressly saved. In other respects it was wider. It allowed Ralegh a moiety of the penalties accruing to the Crown. The controversy with Cambridge may have been due only to Browne, and his eagerness for fees. In general, Ralegh appears to have exercised his powers moderately. A grantee who succeeded commended him for having 'ever had a special care to carry a very tender hand upon the business for avoiding of noise and clamour, well knowing it to be a thing extracted from the subject upon a nice point of a statute law.' A year after the first patent of wines he received

: *Broadcloths.* : a similar boon. This was a licence in March, 1584, to export for a twelvemonth woollen broadcloths. A payment to the Crown was reserved. In 1585, 1587, and 1589 the same privilege was conferred and enlarged. One grant authorized him to export overlengths. Burleigh protested. He declared the conditions too beneficial to the grantee. Probably they were. The privilege brought him into collision with several bodies of merchants. Soon after the earliest of the licences had been granted, in June, 1584, we read of a petition, backed by Walsingham, for the release of ships which had infringed his patent. The Queen would not consent unless upon the terms that the offenders compounded with him. In 1586 the Merchant Adventurers of Exeter obtained a commission of inquiry whether his officers did not levy excessive fees upon certificates. He is represented by a local antiquary as less popular in that city than elsewhere in Devonshire. His patent rights as well as his official duties caused ill-will between it and him.

A gift in appearance much more magnificent, though the gains eventually were meagre, was the Irish grant of 1586. At last the Earl of Desmond's insurrection had been quelled, at the cost of the utter devastation of a province. The curse of God was, it was lamented, so great, and the land so barren, that whosoever did travel from one end to the other of all Munster, even from Waterford to Limerick, about six score miles, he should not meet man, woman, nor child, save in cities or towns, nor yet see any beast, save foxes and wolves, or other ravening creatures. The few survivors fed upon weeds and carrion, robbing the graves and gibbets of their dead. It was determined to repeople the 574,268 forfeited acres. Ralegh retained his Irish captain's commission. In 1587 his name occurs at the head of the list. He, Ormond, Hatton, and Fitton were among the principal Undertakers for the resettlement. By the scheme nobody was to ⠄ *An Irish Seigniory.* ⠄ undertake for more than twelve thousand acres. On each portion of that size eighty-six families were to be planted. In Ralegh's favour, by express words and warrant in a special letter from her Majesty, the Crown rent was fixed at a hundred marks, calculated subsequently as £60 13*s.* 4*d.*; and the limitation of acreage was relaxed. Seigniories varied in extent from twelve to four thousand acres. Possibly in order to avoid too gross an appearance of indulgence to him, Sir John Stowell and Sir John Clyston, according to the Boyle-Lismore papers, were associated or named with him as joint undertakers. A Privy Seal warrant in February, 1586, confirmed by letters patent in the following October, awarded to the three three seigniories and a half in Waterford, Cork, and perhaps Tipperary. A certificate of March, 1587, stated that, if the lands assigned to them and their tenants should not be found to amount to 'three seigniories of twelve thousand acres apiece, and one seigniory of six thousand acres, then other lands should be added.' The patronage of the Wardenship of Our Lady's College of Youghal was added to Ralegh's share with several other lucrative privileges. Three centuries afterwards the House of Lords decided that an exclusive salmon fishery in the tidal waters of the Blackwater was among them. The domain stretched along both banks of the river from Youghal harbour. The soil was rich; but the royal commissioners for the survey reported it waste from neglect. Generally it was overgrown with deep grass, and in most places with heath, brambles, and furze.

English Forfeitures.

In 1587 he added English estates to his Irish. The Babington conspiracy had been detected the year before. By a grant which passed the Great Seal without fee in March, 1587, he acquired much of the principal plotter's property. He obtained lands in Lincolnshire, Derbyshire, and Notts, together with all goods and personalty, except a curious clock reserved to the Queen's own use. According to modern taste, the pillage of confiscated estates is not an honourable basis for a great man's prosperity. In the reign of Elizabeth it was still the orthodox foundation. It was give and take, as Ralegh had to experience. That the unfortunate Babington had rested some hope of life on Ralegh's known Court influence is but a coincidence. He wrote on the 19th of September, 1586, the day before his execution, of 'Master Rawley having been moved for him, and been promised a thousand pounds, if he could get his pardon.' There was a traffic in pardons at Court. Odious and suspicious as was the practice, and liable to the grossest abuse, the presentation of money in return did not necessarily mean that the leniency had been bought. The Sovereign levied fines thus for the benefit of favourites on men too guilty to be let off scot-free, and not guilty enough to be capitally punished. Ralegh himself appears in after years to have received large sums from two pardoned accomplices of Essex, Sir Edward Bainham and Mr. John Littleton. From Littleton he is said to have had £10,000. But in the present instance no evidence has been discovered that Babington's overtures were countenanced in the least by Ralegh, or that he accepted money for urging them.

Five years separated the needy Munster Captain from the Lord Warden of the Stannaries, the magnificent Captain of the Queen's Guard, the owner of broad lands in England, and Irish seigniories. He had climbed high, though not so high as the insignificant Hatton. He had progressed fast though another was soon to beat him in swiftness of advancement. He had gathered wealth and power. He was profuse in his application of both. Much of his gains went in ostentation. He was fond of exquisite armour,

gorgeous

Luxury and splendour. raiment, lace, embroideries, furs, diamonds, and great pearls. As early as 1583 he must have begun to indulge his taste. On April 26 in that year the Middlesex Registers show that Hugh Pewe, gentleman, was tried for the theft of 'a jewel worth £80, a hat band of pearls worth

£30, and five yards of damask silk worth £3, goods and chattels of Walter Rawley, Esq., at Westminster.' Pewe was enough of a gentleman to read 'like a clerk,' and thus save his neck. Later Ralegh was satirized by the Jesuit Parsons as the courtier too high in the regard of the English Cleopatra, who wore in his shoes jewels worth 6600 gold pieces. Tradition speaks, with exaggeration as obvious, of one court dress which carried £60,000 worth of jewels. He loved architecture and building, gardens, pictures, books, furniture, and immense retinues of servants. In his taste for personal luxury he resembled the entire tribe of contemporary courtiers. It was a sumptuous age everywhere. England, which had suddenly begun to be able to gratify a love of splendour, seemed in haste to make up for lost time. Elizabeth encouraged the propensity at her Court. Her statesmen, warriors, and favourites enriched themselves with sinecures, confiscations, and shares in trading and buccaneering adventures. They spent as rapidly. They were all extravagant, and mortgaged the future. Almost all were continually straitened for money. Impecuniosity rendered them rapacious. The Lord Admiral received, as Ralegh has intimated, enormous gains from the Queen and from prizes, and was perpetually in need. Robert Cecil had to supplement his vast legitimate revenues from illicit sources, and died £38,000 in debt. Essex, whose disinterestedness is eulogized, had £300,000 from the Queen, in addition to most lucrative offices. The whole was insufficient for his wants. All alike, old friends and old foes, fed on one another, when there was nobody else to spoil. Prodigality and greediness in money matters were, it is to be feared, common traits of Elizabethan heroes. They were far from perfect; their defects differed from those of their modern descendants in the ethical consequences; they did not make offenders ashamed of themselves, and afraid of being found out; they did not necessarily vitiate the substance of their characters, and destroy their self-respect.

CHAPTER V.

Ralegh was not freer from the faults of his class than the rest. Beyond the rest, he showed public spirit in his expenditure. By arguments, by his influence, by his example, he fanned the rising flame of national enterprise. From the first he devoted a large part of his sudden opulence to the promotion of the maritime prosperity of the nation. Among his earliest subjects of outlay was the construction in 1583 of the Ark Ralegh. It was, according to a probable account, of two hundred tons burden, and cost £2000. Mr. Payne Collier gives its burden as eight hundred tons, and its worth as £5000. None understood better than Ralegh the ship-building art. Ten years of prison, it will be hereafter noticed, did not deaden his

Gilbert and Ralegh. instinct. Humphrey Gilbert was again preparing for a voyage to 'the Unknown Goal.' Two-thirds of the six years of his patent for discoveries had run out. He was anxious to utilize the residue. Ralegh would gladly have accepted his invitation to accompany him as vice-admiral. The Queen had tried to hold back Gilbert 'of her especial care, as a man noted of no good hap by sea.' By earnest representations that he had no other means of maintaining his family, he prevailed upon her, through Walsingham, to give him leave. In a letter from Ralegh, she sent him a token, an anchor guided by a lady, with her wish of as great good-hap and safety to his ship, as if herself were there in person. She prayed him to be careful of himself, 'as of that which she tendereth,' and to leave his portrait with Ralegh for her. Ralegh she peremptorily forbade to go. He had to content himself with lending his ship. It had not been more than two days out from Plymouth when a contagious sickness attacked the crew. It returned on June 13, 1583. Gilbert did not know the cause. He only saw the ship run away in fair and clear weather, having a large wind. So home he wrote denouncing the men as knaves. How he took possession of Newfoundland, and how, on his return, he died, with his memorable last words, are matters belonging to his history, though incidentally that crosses Ralegh's. But his companionship, example, and affection had contributed to form his brother, whom his courage fired, and his fate did not daunt.

Ralegh's Patent.

Ralegh immediately sought and obtained a royal licence corresponding to that bestowed on Gilbert. March 25, 1584, is an eventful date in the annals of colonization. On that day was sealed a patent for him to hold by homage remote heathen and barbarous lands, not actually possessed by any Christian prince, nor inhabited by Christian people, which he might discover within the next six years. A fifth of the gold and silver acquired was reserved to the Crown. His eyes were bent on the region stretching to the north of the Gulf of Florida, and of any settled Spanish territory. In 1562 a French Protestant settlement had been attempted in Florida. Laudonnière reinforced it a couple of years later. But the jealousy of Spain was aroused. Pedro Melendez de Avila pounced down in 1565. He captured the forts. Eight or nine hundred Huguenots he hanged on the neighbouring trees as heretics, not as Frenchmen. Dominique de Gorgues, of Gascony, avenged their fate by hanging their Spanish supplanters in 1567, not as Spaniards, but as assassins. There the experiment at colonization ended. Neither Spain nor France had repeated the attempt. The whole land was vacant of white men.

Ralegh's fancy was inspired with visions, destined to be more than realized ultimately, of an English counterpart in the north to the Spanish empire in the south. He had already begun to equip a couple of vessels. He despatched them to America on April 27, 1584, under Captains Philip Amadas and Arthur   Barlow. They took the roundabout route by the Canaries and West Indies. In July they were saluted with a most fragrant gale from the land they were seeking. Sailing into the mouth of a river they saw vines laden with   *The Discovery.*   grapes, climbing up tall cedars. On July 13 they proclaimed the Queen's sovereignty, afterwards delivering the country over to the use of Ralegh. It was the isle of Wokoken, in Ocracoke Inlet, off the North Carolina coast. In the neighbourhood were a hundred other islands. One of the largest was named Roanoke. They were visited by Granganimeo, father or brother to King Wingina, who lay ill of wounds received in war. The visit was returned by them. They bought of Granganimeo twenty skins, worth as many nobles, for a tin dish which he coveted as a gorget. His wife offered a great box of pearls for armour and a sword. After some stay with the friendly and timid people, they returned to England about the middle of September. They brought to Ralegh chamois and other skins, a bracelet of pearls as big as peas, and two Indians, Manteo and Wanchese.

Elizabeth herself devised for the virgin land discovered in the reign of a virgin queen the appellation of Virginia. Possibly the name was favoured by some resemblance to a native phrase Wynganda coia. This means, writes Ralegh, in the *History of the World*, 'You wear good clothes,' which the settlers supposed to be the reply to their question of the name of the country. The similarity of the king's name may have assisted the choice. Spenser entitles Elizabeth, in the dedication of his great poem, 'Queen of

England, France, and Ireland, and of Virginia.' Ralegh had a seal of his arms cut, with the legend, 'Walteri Ralegh, militis, Domini et Gubernatoris Virginiae propria insignia, 1584, amore et virtute.' He hastened to realize his lordship, which was still somewhat in the air. He obtained a fair amount of support, though his brother, Carew Ralegh, could not prevail upon the Exeter merchants to become partners. They were not moved by his catalogue of the merchantable commodities which had been found. They stigmatized the undertaking as 'a pretended voyage,' which certainly it was not. On April 9, 1585, 'at the pleasant prime,' says Holinshed, a fleet of seven sail set forth from Plymouth, under Ralegh's cousin, Sir Richard Grenville, as general of the expedition. Mr. Ralph Lane was Governor of the colony, and Captain Philip Amadas was his Deputy. Lane had an Irish commission. Elizabeth ordered that a substitute should be found for him, that he might go to Virginia for Ralegh. Ralegh drew up rules, which have been lost, for the political government. Thomas Cavendish, a future

- *Colonization.* - circumnavigator of the globe, and Thomas Hariot, or Harriot, were among the colonists. Hariot, who describes himself as 'servant to Sir Walter Ralegh,' was commissioned to survey and report. He published a remarkable description of the territory in 1588. Manteo and Wanchese returned to America with the expedition. On the way out, by Hispaniola and Florida, Grenville took two Spanish frigates. He reached Wokoken in June, and visited the mainland. He was not happy in the conduct of the expedition, being reported by Lane, writing to Walsingham on September 8, 1585, to have exhibited intolerable pride and ambition towards the entire company. Already, on August 25, not a day too soon, he had sailed for England. He had, he reported at his return to Walsingham, peopled the new country, and stored it with cattle, fruits, and plants. He left Governor Lane and 107 colonists. On the homeward voyage a third Spanish ship was captured. Stukely, a kinsman both of Grenville and of Ralegh, was with Grenville on board the Tiger. For some unintelligible reason he thought himself entitled to £10,000 of the booty. According to his estimate, as reported by his mendacious son, Sir Lewis, the whole was worth £50,000. Much of the treasure consisted of a cabinet of pearls. Sir Lewis Stukely alleged that Ralegh charged Elizabeth with taking all to herself 'without so much as even giving him one pearl.' The Queen was as fond of large pearls as he.

Grenville had promised he would bring supplies by the next Easter at latest. Lane and his companions occupied themselves meanwhile with surveys of the goodliest soil under the cope of heaven, as they described it. They had planted corn, and perceived signs of pearl fisheries and mines. Hariot, observing the native use of tobacco, had tried and liked it. The nutritious qualities of the tubers of the potato had been discovered.

Unfortunately the planters quarrelled with the natives, whom they found, though gentle in manner, cunning and murderous. Their friend, Granganimeo, died, and they slew King Wingina and his chiefs without warning, for alleged plots. At this crisis Sir Francis Drake arrived with a fleet of twenty-five sail, fresh from the sack of St. Domingo and Cartagena.

He gave Lane a bark of *Failure.* seventy tons, pinnaces, and provisions, and lent him two of his captains. But a storm sank the bark. The colonists, losing courage, insisted on being taken home. On June 19, 1586, they set sail, on the eve of the arrival of a ship laden with provisions, which Ralegh had sent. A fortnight later came Grenville with three ships, also well stored. He could do nothing but leave fifteen men with supplies on Roanoke and return. Not even now was Ralegh disheartened. In the spring of 1587 he fitted out a fourth expedition. He had meant to conduct it himself. The Queen would not let him go. It comprised 150 householders. Some were married, and brought their wives with them. Agricultural implements were taken. Captain John White was in command. He and eleven others of the company were incorporated as the Governor and Assistants of the City of Ralegh in Virginia. Ralegh had fixed upon Chesapeake Bay as the site of the settlement. Roanoke was preferred. White could detect no trace of Grenville's fifteen men, and Lane's fort had been razed to the ground. Vainly the new colonists endeavoured to conciliate or awe the natives by baptizing and investing Manteo with the Barony of Roanoke. Jealousies arose between them and the tribes. They aggravated their difficulties by murdering in error a number of friendly Indians. Misfortunes of various kinds beset them. Supplies failed, and Governor White came home for more. At his departure the colony included eighty-nine men, seventeen women, and two children. Among them were White's daughter, Eleanor Dare, and her child. The time was inopportune. An embargo had been laid on all shipping, in expectation of the Spanish invasion. By Ralegh's influence it was raised in favour of a couple of merchantmen, equipped for a West Indian voyage, on condition that they transported men and necessaries to Virginia. They broke the compact. Though they embarked White, they took no colonists. They chased Spanish ships, fought with men-of-war from Rochelle, and came back to England shattered.

Ralegh's persistency.

Ralegh had other calls upon his resources. For the present he could do no more for Virginia. He reckoned he had spent £40,000 on the plantation. As Hakluyt wrote, 'it demanded a prince's purse to have the action thoroughly fulfilled without lingering.' Elizabeth was not willing to play the part of godmother in the fairy-tale sense. For a substitute, the founder, being in difficulties, had recourse to the very modern expedient of a company. In March, 1589, as Chief Governor, he assigned a right to trade in Virginia, not his patent, to Thomas Smith, John White, Richard Hakluyt, and others. He reserved a fifth of all the gold and silver extracted. The Adventurers were not very active. Ralegh still felt himself responsible for the colony, if it could be described as one. Such expeditions as sailed he mainly promoted. Southey's accusation that he 'abandoned the poor colonists' is ludicrously unjust. If, as has without due cause been imputed to Bacon, the charge in the essay on Plantations of the sinfulness of 'forsaking or destituting a plantation once in forwardness' refer to Ralegh, Bacon would be as calumnious. In 1590 White prosecuted the search for his daughter and grandchild, and the rest of the vanished planters. Ralegh despatched other expeditions for the same object, and with as little success. One, under Samuel Mace, with that purpose sailed in 1602 or 1603. By the time Mace returned, the Chief Governor was attainted, and his proprietorship of Virginia had escheated to the Crown.

Ralegh never relinquished hope in his nursling. 'I shall yet live,' he wrote just before his fall, 'to see it an English nation.' In 1606 a new *Reward of an idea.* and strong colony was sent out, and his confidence was justified. From an old account of the career of his nephew, Captain Ralph Gilbert, a son of Sir Humphrey, it would seem he still considered in 1607 that his connexion with the country continued. In that year Ralph Gilbert is said to have voyaged to Virginia on his behalf. Though his direct exertions were confined to the region of the James and Potomac, his jurisdiction in the north was recognized. The term Virginia covered a very wide area. It included, not only the present Virginias, but the Carolinas and more besides. New England itself originally was supposed to be comprised. Captain Gosnold, Captain Bartholomew Gilbert, and others, when they planned the occupation of Martha's Vineyard in 1602, described it as 'the north part of Virginia,' and sought and obtained Ralegh's permission and encouragement. Posterity has rewarded his faith and perseverance. He never set foot anywhere in the country called generally Virginia. His expeditions by deputy were themselves confined to the part which is now North Carolina. All his experiments at the colonization of that were failures. His £40,000, his colonists, and the polity he framed for them, had disappeared before any white settlement took root. But he will always be esteemed the true parent of North American colonization. An idea like his has life in it, though the plant may not spring up at once. When it rises above the surface the sower can claim it. Had the particular region of the

New World not eventually become a permanent English settlement, he would still have earned the merit of authorship of the English colonizing movement. As Humboldt has said, without him, and without Cabot, North America might never have grown into a home of the English tongue.

Ralegh's Virginian scheme cost much money, and brought in little. It gave him fame, which he craved still more, and kept the town talking. His distant seigniory excited the English imagination. He was believed to have endowed his Sovereign with a new realm. He had the glory of having enriched his country with new fruits, plants, and flowers. The nature of the man was that he could touch nothing but immediately it appropriated itself to him. *Potatoesand Tobacco.* He is fabled to have been the first to import mahogany into England from Guiana. He set orange trees in the garden of his wife's uncle, Sir Francis Carew, at Beddington; and he has been credited with their first introduction. The Spaniards first brought potatoes into Europe. Hariot and Lane first discovered them in North Carolina. He grew them at Youghal, and they became his. Hariot discoursed learnedly on the virtues of tobacco, and Drake conveyed the leaf to England. Ralegh smoked, and none but he has the repute of the fashion. He gave the taste vogue, teaching the courtiers to smoke their pipes with silver bowls, and supplying them with the leaf. Sir John Stanhope excuses himself in 1601 from sending George Carew in Ireland any 'tabacca, because Mr. Secretary and Sir Walter have stored you of late.' Till he mounted the scaffold, having first 'taken tobacco,' the kingdom resounded with legends, doubtful enough, of his devotion to this his familiar genius. It was told how his old manservant deluged him at Sherborne with spiced ale to put out the combustion inside him; how he won wagers of the Queen that he could weigh vapours; how he smoked as Essex died. Society stared to see him take a pipe at Sir Robert Poyntz's. His gilt leather tobacco case was a prize for a Yorkshire museum. For words, ways, and doings, he was the observed of all observers. He was active in twenty different directions at once. He was always before the eyes of the world. His name was on every lip.

Among his constant motives of action was a fiery indignation at the spectacle of the Spanish monopoly of the New World. No sentiment could stir more of English sympathy. The people heartily shared his determination to rival Spain, and to pillage Spain. He had the Viking spirit, and he burnt with a freebooter's passion for the sea. But he had an intuition also of *Pioneer and Privateer.* the national capacity for colonization, in which the purest patriot must have concurred. He was resolved to direct the maritime enthusiasm of his countrymen and their age to that definite end. He succeeded, though destined to the lot rather of Moses than of

Joshua. His outlay on Virginia did not bound his expenditure in these ways. Adrian his half-brother, and his habitual associate, had resumed Sir Humphrey Gilbert's old project for the discovery of a North-West Passage to India and China. A patent was granted him in 1583. He established a 'Fellowship' to work it. Ralegh joined. Captain John Davys was appointed commander, and two barks were equipped. Davys discovered Davis's Straits. Mount Ralegh, shining like gold, he christened after one of his most celebrated patrons. Hakluyt in 1587 stated that Ralegh had thrice contributed with the forwardest to Davys's North-West voyages. From a mixture of patriotism, maritime adventurousness, and the love of gain, he employed his various opportunities to engage in privateering as a regular business. Privy Council minutes for 1585 mention captures by him, through his officers, of Spanish ships, with 600 Spaniards, at the Newfoundland fisheries. He sent forth in June, 1586, his ships Serpent and Mary Spark, under Captains Jacob Whiddon and John Evesham, to fight the Spaniards at the Azores. In a battle of thirty-two hours, against twenty-four Spanish ships, they failed to capture two great caracks which they coveted. They brought home three less valuable, but remunerative, prizes. Don Pedro Sarmiento de Genaboa, Governor of the Straits of Magellan, and other captives were worth heavy ransoms. Ralegh repeats in the History, 'a pretty jest' told him 'merrily' by the worthy Don Pedro, on whom he clearly did not allow thraldom to weigh heavily, how the draftsman of the chart of the Straits invented an island in them at his wife's instance, that she might have something specially her own in the chart. In the same year, 1586, he contributed a pinnace to a plundering expedition of the Earl of Cumberland's to the South Sea. Though he was not allowed to be often at sea in person, he vindicated by his eager promotion of maritime adventures a full right to be entered, as we find him in January, 1586, in an official list of 'sea captains.'

As Vice-Admiral of the South-West, he possessed advantages beyond most for private raids upon Spanish commerce. When he was not on the spot, his faithful and affectionate deputy in Devonshire, Sir John Gilbert, was at hand to look after his ships' stores. Doubtless outrages were committed

- *Charges of Piracy.* - under shelter of his Court favour. He joined the evil experiences of the sailor with those of the soldier and courtier in his dying regrets. Occasionally the Privy Council had to expostulate energetically. In 1589 a ship of his took two barks of Cherbourg. He and his officers were charged to minister no cause of grief to any of the French king's subjects. In the same year, Albert Reynerson was lodging complaints against Ralegh's captain of the Roebuck. Another of his captains, John Floyer, in 1592, was accused of having captured a ship of Bayonne with a load of cod, beside a waistcoat of carnation colour, curiously embroidered. Filippo Corsini sued him in that year for a ship his people had seized. In 1600 the Republic of Venice was aggrieved at the capture of a Venetian merchantman by Sir John Gilbert, junior, eldest son of Sir Humphrey, in command of one of Ralegh's vessels. At other times Venice claimed the surrender of Venetian goods in Spanish bottoms, though Ralegh stoutly argued against the claim. Sometimes the Government could not but interfere when neutrals had been pillaged. It was always reluctant to discourage the buccaneering trade, which it knew to be very lucrative. For instance, Ralegh and eleven other adventurers in 1591 equipped, at a cost of £8000, privateers which brought home prizes worth £31,150. The profit to the partnership was £14,952, which must be multiplied five times to express the present value. In high places no repugnance to the pursuit was felt. The Queen not rarely adventured, and looked for the lion's share of the spoil. Robert Cecil, after he had succeeded to his father's ascendency, was willing to speculate, if his association might be kept secret: 'For though, I thank God, I have no other meaning than becometh an honest man in any of my actions, yet that which were another man's *Pater noster,* *His Defence.* would be accounted in me a charm.' Ralegh's views and character obliged him to no bashful dissimulation of the practice. To him privateering seemed strictly legal, and unequivocally laudable. He boasted in 1586 that he had consumed the best part of his fortune in abating the tyrannous prosperity of Spain. He acted as much in defence and retaliation as for offence. He stated in the House of Commons in 1592 that the West Country had, since the Parliament began, been plundered of the worth of £440,000. In 1603 he wrote that a few Dunkirk privateers under Spanish protection had 'taken from the West Country merchants within two years above three thousand vessels, beside all they had gotten from the rest of the ports of England.' He himself, as the State Papers testify, had often to lament losses of ships through Spanish and French privateers. Public opinion entirely justified the vigour with which he conducted his retaliation. If he were unpopular among his countrymen, or any section of them, the fact is not to be explained by the employment of his riches and influence in onslaughts upon foreign commerce. As he has written in his History, Englishmen never objected to the most fearful odds, when 'royals of plate and pistolets' were in view. They might have been expected to be grateful to a leading promoter of lucratively perilous enterprises; and in the West they were.

CHAPTER VI.

In social and private as well as public life Ralegh was open-handed and liberal in kind offices. Those are not unpopular characteristics. He was a patron of letters. His name may be read in many dedications. Few of them can have been gratuitous. Martin Bassanière of Paris inscribed to him very appropriately his publication of Laudonnière's narrative of the French expedition to Florida. Richard Hakluyt, junior, during his residence in France, had lighted upon Laudonnière's manuscript. From him Bassanière

Hakluyt. received it. He translated the volume in 1587, and dedicated his

version to Ralegh. Hakluyt had to thank Ralegh also for material assistance both with money and with advice in the compilation of his celebrated collection of voyages. The manuscript, for example, of the Portuguese narrative of de Gama's voyage in 1541 to the Red Sea had been bought for £60 by Ralegh, who presented it to him. Ralegh again was 'at no small charges' towards the production by the French painter, Jacques Morgues, of a series of coloured illustrations of Florida, whither he had accompanied Laudonnière. In 1586 the publisher of John Case's *Praise of Music* dedicated it to Ralegh, as a virtuoso. In 1588 Churchyard dedicated to him the *Spark of Friendship.* Hooker, the antiquary, introduced the continuation of the Irish history of Giraldus Cambrensis with a fervent encomium on the illustrious Warden of the Stannaries, who was 'rather a servant than a commander to his own fortune.' A medical treatise was inscribed to him as an expert. A list which has been preserved of his signs for chemical substances and drugs, shows that as early as 1592 he had paid attention to medicine. He appears to have kept amanuenses to copy interesting manuscripts. Thus, John Peirson who, in 1585, was in trouble in connexion with a tract entitled *Reasons why the King of Scots is unacceptable to the People of England,* deposed that he delivered one of the five copies he made to 'Sir Walter Ralegh, my master.'

Hariot.

Throughout life he befriended Hariot, the universal philosopher, as he has been called. Hariot has been credited with the invention of the system of notation in Algebra. He discovered the solar spots before, and the satellites of Jupiter almost simultaneously with, Galileo. Hariot, who numbered Bishops among his admirers, was accused by zealots of atheism, because his cosmogony was not orthodox. They discerned a judgment in his death in

1621 from cancer in the lip or nose. His ill repute for freethinking was reflected on Ralegh who hired him to teach him mathematics, and engaged him in his colonizing projects. Ralegh introduced him to the Earl of Northumberland, who allowed him a liberal pension. But new ties did not weaken the old. Hariot and he remained constantly attached. Hariot was the friend whose society he chiefly craved when he was recovering from his wound in the Tower. During his long imprisonment Hariot was the faithful companion of his studies. Hariot brought to his notice another Oxford man, Lawrence Keymis. Keymis is described by Wood as well read in geography and mathematics. I am indebted to Professor Jowett for a confirmation from the Register of Balliol, which Keymis entered in 1579, graduating Master of Arts in 1586, of Wood's statement that he was elected a probationer Fellow in November, 1582. He was then nineteen years old, and an undergraduate. Five Bachelors of Arts were elected with him. To him also, of whom there will be much, too much, hereafter to say, Ralegh was a generous patron. Ralegh was equally ready to spend his court interest in the service of a pious theologian like John *Udal.* Udal the Hebraist.

Udal in 1590 published of the Bishops, that they 'cared for nothing but the maintenance of their dignities, be it the damnation of their own souls, and infinite millions more.' He was tried for treason, since the Bishops, it was averred, governed the Church for the Queen. A jury convicted him of authorship of the book. The Judges iniquitously held that to amount to a conviction of felony. They therefore sentenced him to death. He prayed Ralegh to intercede with the Queen to commute his punishment to banishment, 'that the land might not be charged with his blood.' Ralegh accepted the office, and Essex combined with him. Retailers of court gossip conjectured that his kindness was policy. They imagined that he and Essex were secretly allied, and that Essex was employing him as 'an instrument from the Puritans to the Queen upon any particular question of relieving them.' A simpler and more generous motive is the more probable. He fought for Udal against the same lying spirit of legal casuistry which was to destroy himself. King James to his honour joined subsequently in mediating. Among them they saved the enthusiast's neck; but he died in the Marshalsea, pending a dispute whether he could safely be permitted to carry his anti-prelatic zeal and immense learning into a chaplaincy in Guinea.

Other instances could be mentioned of Ralegh's disposition to pass his favour on. 'When, Sir Walter,' asked Elizabeth of him, as he came with a petition from a friend, 'will you cease to be a beggar?' 'When your gracious Majesty,' was the answer, 'ceases to be a benefactor.' He has had attributed to him, though obscurely, the project of an institution, described as an 'office of address,' a species of entrepôt at which either information and useful services, or both, might be exchanged. Southey interprets it in the former sense, and regards it as an anticipation of the Royal Society. That was the view of Evelyn, who says that Ralegh put this 'fountain of communication in practice.' How is not remembered. At any rate, in the second sense he energetically applied the principle in his *Good Offices* own conduct. Not less from kindness than from the wish to secure personal adherents, he was generally helpful. Now, his client was a poor wounded officer, whose arrears of pay he was praying the Treasury to discharge; partly, for love of him; partly, for honest consideration. Now, it was some prosperous placeman, his equal, or his superior in rank. As he boasts, in claiming a return from an Irish law officer, 'I assure you, on mine honour, I have deserved it at his hands in places where it may most stead him.' He used like language of the Lord Deputy Fitzwilliam. Before he rose he had ranked himself among Leicester's followers. Leicester speedily grew jealous of his prosperity. Sir Henry Wotton, who imputed the beginning of Ralegh's rise to Leicester, has stated in his Parallel between Essex and George Villiers, that the Earl soon found him such an apprentice as knew well enough how to set up for himself. Ralegh never withheld due marks of deference from his elder. Churchyard the poet described, or undertook to describe, a grand Shrovetide show prepared by Ralegh, in which the gentlemen of the Guard represented the Earl's exploits in Flanders. Ralegh was ever at pains to remove any specific grievance. On March 29, 1586, he writes to assure Leicester that he had urged the Queen to grant the request for pioneers in the Netherlands. He seems to have been accused, as he was to be accused seventeen years later, of intrigues on behalf of Spain, which he had constantly been attacking. He could not have had much difficulty in defending himself from the charge, about which he remarks he had been 'of late very pestilent reported.' It was not so clear that he recognized the Earl's paramount title as Queen's favourite. To disarm suspicion on that score he adds a postscript: 'The Queen is in very good terms with you, and, thank be to God, well pacified; and you are again her Sweet Robyn.' He cannot have esteemed Leicester. A stinging epitaph, attributed to him with the usual scarcity of evidence, may express his real view of the poor-spirited soldier, the deceitful courtier, the statesman and noble 'that all the world did hate.' But he was no backbiter. Elizabeth vouched for his claim to Leicester's friendliness. She bade Walsingham declare to Leicester, upon her honour, that the gentleman had done good offices for him in the time of her displeasure.

He could be useful to the greatest; whether only great, or great and deserving too. He had been always solicitous of Burleigh's goodwill. As a rival at Court of Leicester, he had it. Burleigh loved no Court favourites. 'Seek not to be Essex; shun to be Ralegh,' was his warning to his son. Robert Cecil, awkward and deformed, was in no danger. Favourites represented a side of the Queen's nature which continually troubled the wise Minister. Their accomplishments were not his. They were costly. While he cannot have failed to perceive something admirable in Ralegh, he would not value the majority of his merits. The poetry and imaginativeness he despised. Still he always preserved amicable relations. He condescended to use Ralegh's personal influence as well as Hatton's. In the spring of 1583

The Earl of Oxford. he solicited the mediation of both those favourites with the Queen for his son-in-law, Edward Vere, Earl of Oxford. Oxford was in disgrace on the charge, not very heavy in those days as against an Earl, of having slain Long Tom, a retainer of Mr. Knyvett's. The Queen had rejected Burleigh's own intercession. She appears to have granted forgiveness at Ralegh's suit. Oxford's arrogance had provoked Sir Philip Sidney. It had not spared Ralegh, who, Aubrey says, had been 'a second with him in a duel.' Ralegh pretended no kindliness for the Earl; he avowed to Burleigh that as a mediator he acted for the Minister's sake alone: 'I am content to lay the serpent before the fire, as much as in me lieth, that, having recovered strength, myself may be more in danger of his poison and sting.' Eighteen years after, not that he cared, he found the venom was not exhausted.

Ralegh did not hoard or keep to himself the wealth and power conferred upon him. His was an age of patronage. Other successful courtiers had, like him, their trains of dependants. He was at least as bountiful as any and as sympathetic. His followers believed in and worshipped him. Posterity he has captivated. Yet throughout his active career he aroused bitter hatred, unless in the West, and in his own home circle. The fact requires to be noted for the purpose of appraising contemporary comments upon his acts.

His Unpopularity. Apologists and impartial chroniclers are as distinct as enemies in intimating that he was a constant mark for 'detraction' and 'envyings.' He was unpopular on account alike of his demeanour, of the Queen's favour, and of the monopolizing energy in the public service by which to posterity he has justified it. All students recollect Aubrey's description of him as one whose blemish or 'næve it was that he was damnably proud.' In serious illustration of the charge, Aubrey repeats a tale related by an old attendant, who had seen the Lord High Admiral in the Privy Garden wipe with his cloak the dust from Ralegh's shoes 'in compliment.' Aubrey's description of Ralegh is all hearsay; since he was not born till 1627. He may have been told anecdotes by members of the family; for his grandfather was a Wiltshire neighbour of Sir Carew Ralegh, and he was himself a schoolfellow of Sir Carew's grandchildren. But he was utterly uncritical, and his bare assertion would carry little weight. The testimony of a sworn foe, like Lord Henry Howard, to Ralegh's extraordinary haughtiness, may be regarded even with more suspicion. An old acquaintance, however, and a political ally, the Earl of Northumberland, similarly describes Ralegh as 'insolent, extremely heated, a man that desired to seem to be able to sway all men's courses.' That this was the current opinion, due, as it was, more or less to misconception, is borne out by a mass of authority. Ralegh must have profoundly impressed all about him with a sense that he felt himself better fitted than themselves to regulate their lives. His air of conscious superiority silenced opposition, but was resented. Neither a mob, nor Howards and Percies pardoned his assumption of an infinite superiority of capacity. His gaiety and splendour were treated as proofs of arrogance. His evident contempt of 'the rascal multitude' added to the odium which dogged his course. He never condescended to allude to the subject in writing or in authenticated speech. Though he courted occasions for renown, he did not seek applause. His position as a Queen's favourite in any case must have brought aversion upon him. Tarleton, as he half acted, half improvised, is said to have shuffled a pack of cards, and pointed at him, standing behind the Queen's chair, an insolent innuendo: 'See, the knave commands the Queen.' The comedian, if the story be true, could reckon upon the support of a vast body of popular malevolence. *An Excess of Capability.* Still, as a favourite, Ralegh only shared the lot of his class. The same privileged player is alleged to have proceeded to satirize Leicester as well. Hatton was a frequent butt for fierce sarcasms upon royal favouritism. The phenomenon in Ralegh's unpopularity is that proof absolutely irrefutable of the grandeur of his powers, and all the evidence of his exploits, should never have won him an amnesty for the original sin of his sovereign's kindness. Pride itself, it might have been thought, would have been pardoned at last in the doer of such deeds. His inexpiable offences really were his restless activity, and his passion for personal management. He was a born manager of men. Whatever was in hand, he saw what ought to be done, and was conscious of ability to arrange for the doing. He could never be connected with an enterprise which he was not determined to direct. He could endure to be a subordinate only if his masters would be in leading-strings.

CHAPTER VII.

As a favourite Ralegh was certain to have originally been hated by the people. His favour might have been tolerated by courtiers, or by a sufficient section of them, if he had been content to parade and enjoy his pomps, and had let them govern. His strenuous vigour exasperated them as much as his evident conviction of a right to rule. They never ceased to regard him on that account as a soldier of fortune, and an upstart. So poor a creature as Hatton had his party at Court. When he retired to the country in dudgeon at a display of royal grace to Ralegh, his friends, as Sir Thomas Heneage, were busy for him so late as April, 1585. Elizabeth was persuaded by them to let them give him assurances on her behalf, that she would rather see

Popularity of sex.

Ralegh hanged than equal him with Hatton, or allow the world to think she did. When Hatton was out of date the courtiers combined to set up Essex against him, and had the assistance of the multitude in their tactics. The popular attitude towards Essex is the solitary exception to the rule of the national abhorrence of favourites. It is explained as much by the dislike of Ralegh as by Essex's ingratiating characteristics. Animosity against Ralegh stimulated courtiers and the populace to sing in chorus the praises of the stepson of the detested Leicester. No anger was exhibited at the elevation of a lad of twenty to the Mastership of the Horse. Stories of the Queen's supposed infatuation, how she 'kept him at cards, or one game or another, the whole night, and he cometh not to his own lodgings till birds sing in the morning,' amused, and did not incense. Meanwhile the approved soldier, the planter of Virginia, was in the same May, 1587, truthfully described as 'the best hated man of the world in Court, city, and country.'

For the crowd Essex may have had the merit of being of an ancient nobility, which needed no intricate demonstration by antiquaries and genealogists. He had enough patrimonial wealth to justify the Sovereign in showering largess upon him. He was not one of the irrepressible west countrymen who brought their nimble wits, comeliness, and courage to the market of the Court. He was more bright than stately. His petulance did not produce an impression of haughtiness. For the courtier class he possessed the yet higher virtue of willingness to be at once a centre and

watchword and an instrument. From *His Antipathyto Ralegh.* the first he was manipulated as an engine against Ralegh. In a letter to one of his many confidants he shows the readiness with which he accepted the office. In 1587 Elizabeth was on a progress, and was staying at North Hall in Hertfordshire. Ralegh, as Captain of the Guard, and Essex both attended her. Essex writes to his friend, Edward Dyer, that he reproached the Queen for having slighted his sister, Lady Dorothy Perrot, the wife of Ralegh's old antagonist, Sir Thomas. He declared to her 'the true cause of this disgrace to me and to my sister, which was only to please that knave Ralegh, for whose sake I saw she would both grieve me and my love, and disgrace me in the eyes of the world. From thence she came to speak of Ralegh, and it seemed she could not well endure anything to be spoken against him; and taking hold of the word "disdain," she said there was "no such cause why I should disdain him." This speech did touch me so much that, as near as I could, I did describe unto her what he had been, and what he was. I did let her know whether I had cause to disdain his competition of love, or whether I could have comfort to give myself over to the service of a mistress which was in awe of such a man. I spake, what of grief and choler, as much against him as I could, and I think he, standing at the door, might very well hear the very worst that I spoke of himself. In the end I saw she was resolved to defend him, and to cross me. For myself, I told her I had no joy to be in any place, but was loth to be near about her, when I knew my affection so much thrown down, and such a wretch as Ralegh highly esteemed of her.' When he called Ralegh a wretch the Queen expressed her disgust at the impertinence by turning away to Lady Warwick, and closed the interview.

Essex spoke, and perhaps thought, thus of Ralegh in 1587. So the nation at large spoke and thought of him then, and for many years afterwards. If he had only been such as he had as yet shown himself, posterity might have found it difficult to prove the condemnation unjust. He had risen in virtue of a handsome person and a courtly wit. He had equipped expeditions of discovery, in which he took no share of the perils, and the whole of the glory. He had fought and spoiled the Spaniards, chiefly by deputy, risking his own person as little as 'the noble warrior' of his reputed epigram, 'that never blunted sword.' The hardships and dangers he had sturdily ¦ *Ralegh's* ¦ ¦ *cline.* ¦ braved in France and Ireland were for his contemporaries simple myths, as they would have been for us, had he died at thirty-five. Had he retained the Queen's favour uninterrupted, had she not been capricious, had there been no Essex, had there been no Elizabeth Throckmorton, he might have died at sixty, at seventy, or at eighty, and a verdict hardly less severe been pronounced. It is not certain. Possibly in any event, the vigour inherent in the man, his curiosity, his instinct for stamping his will on the world outside, his eagerness to impel his nation to empire westwards, might have had their way. They might have mastered the contradictory ambition to be victorious in a contest of factions. While he was still absorbed in Court strifes, and in the seductive labour of building up a fortune, he had proved that he was no mere carpet knight. But it was well that his natural tendencies towards a life of action were braced by the experience of a chill in the ardour of royal benevolence. From 1587, as the star of Essex rose, and his was supposed to be waning, his orbit can be seen widening. It became more independent. As reigning favourite he had vicariously explored, colonized, plundered, and fought. Henceforth he was to do a substantial part of his own work.

Essex, at the period of the North Hall scene, was new to the Court. He must soon have discovered that Ralegh was not to be spurned as a clown, or to be stormed out of the Queen's graces by insolence. He did not grow therefore the less hostile. He rejected Elizabeth's inducements to him to live on terms of amity with a rival in all essential respects infinitely his superior. Persuaded that she could not dispense with himself, he persisted in putting her to her option between them. The rank and file at Elizabeth's *Antedated.* Court had a keen scent for their Sovereign's bias. They foresaw the inevitable end, though they antedated by several years the actual catastrophe. In 1587 Arabella Stuart, a girl of twelve, was at Court. She supped at Lord Burleigh's. The other guests were her uncle, Sir Charles Cavendish, and Ralegh. Cavendish mentions the entertainment in a letter to a friend. He relates that Burleigh praised to Ralegh 'Lady Arbell,' who had been congratulating herself that 'the Queen had examined her nothing touching her book,' for her French, Italian, music, dancing, and writing. Burleigh wished she were fifteen years old. 'With that he rounded Sir Walter in the ear, who answered, it would be a very happy thing.' Cavendish goes on to observe that Sir Walter was in wonderful declination, yet laboured to underprop himself by my Lord Treasurer and his friends. He inferred from the contrast between Ralegh's former pride and his present too great humility, that he would never rise again. My Lord Treasurer and his friends were not given to the support of discarded favourites. Ralegh's presence at so intimate a gathering, and the confidence vouchsafed him, are signs that he was still potent. The stream of the royal bounty continued to flow. The Babington grant was in 1587. For several years to come other similar tokens of regard were accorded him. Towards the close of 1587 itself signal testimony was offered of the trust of the Queen and her counsellors in his wisdom and martial skill.

In February, 1587, Queen Mary Stuart was executed. It is the one important event of the period with which Ralegh's name is not connected. He does not appear to have been consulted, nor to have spoken on the matter either in or out of Parliament. Its consequences concerned him. The act quickened the : *A Council of War.* : Spanish preparations for the invasion of England. King Philip had no thought of concealment. He published his designs to all Europe. The menaced kingdom had full notice. In November, 1587, a council of war was instructed to consider the means of defence. Its members were Lord Grey, Sir Thomas Knolles, Sir Thomas Leighton, Sir Walter Ralegh, described as Lieutenant-General of Cornwall, Sir John Norris, Sir Richard Grenville, Sir Richard Bingham, who had been Ralegh's early comrade in Ireland, Sir Roger Williams, and Mr. Ralph Lane. They advised that Milford Haven, the Isle of Wight, the Downs, Margate, the Thames, and Portland should be fortified against Spanish descents. They thought it improbable the King of Spain would venture his fleet far within the Sleeve before he had mastered some good harbour. Consequently they recommended the defence of Plymouth by strong works, and a garrison of 5000 men from Cornwall and Devon. Portland they reported should be guarded by 2700 from Dorset and Wilts. If the enemy landed, the country was to be driven so as to leave no victuals for the invader. Ralegh separately petitioned Burleigh for cannon for Portland and Weymouth. Thence some have inferred that he was now Governor of the former.

In December, 1587, he was employed, in concert with Sir John Gilbert and Lord Bath, in levying a force of 2000 foot and 200 horse in Cornwall and Devon. Exeter claimed exemption on account of its heavy expenses for the defence of its trade against Barbary corsairs. By the beginning of 1588 the immediate fear of attack had abated. The invasion was thought to have been put off. Ralegh took the opportunity to visit Ireland. There he had both public and private duties. He retained his commission in the army. Moreover, he was answerable, as a Crown tenant, for twenty horsemen, though his charges for them were refunded. Thus, in March, 1588, an order was made for the payment to him of £244 for the previous half year. Always he had his estate to put in order, and functions connected with it to perform. According to the local records, he served this year the office of Mayor of - *The Armada.* - Youghal. During a considerable portion of the term he must have been an absentee. In Ireland the news reached him that the Armada had started or was starting. Hastening back he commenced by mustering troops in the West, and strengthening Portland Castle. But his own trust was in the fleet. In his *History of the World* he propounds the question whether England without its fleet would be able to debar an enemy from landing. He answers by showing how easily ships, without putting themselves out of breath, will outrun soldiers marching along the coast. The Spaniards in July, 1588, could, in his opinion, but for the English ships, have chosen a landing-place with no sufficient army at hand to resist them. The Armada might have failed, he admits, against the choice troops gathered about the Queen. He did not believe in the ability of the remainder round the coast to encounter an army like that which the Prince of Parma could have landed in England. His advice had its weight in inducing Elizabeth to fit out the fleet, which did noble service under Howard of Effingham.

He acted upon his own doctrine. On July 21 the Defiance assailed a Spanish ship near the Eddystone. On the 23rd the Spaniards were over against Portland. Thereupon Ralegh gave over his land charge to others. With a body of gentlemen volunteers he embarked, and joined in the universal rush at and about the enemy. All day the battle raged. Ships started out of every haven, to the number of a hundred. All hurried to Portland, 'as unto a sea-field where immortal fame and glory was to be attained, and faithful service to be performed unto their prince and country.' It was for the _Against 'Grappling'._ Englishmen 'a morris dance upon the waters.' We may be sure he applied his principle of the worse armed but handier fleet, not 'grappling,' as 'a great many malignant fools' contended Lord Howard ought, but 'fighting loose or at large.' 'The guns of a slow ship,' he observes, 'make as great holes as those of a swift. The Spaniards had an army aboard them, and Howard had none; they had more ships than he had, and of higher building and charging; so that had he entangled himself with those great and powerful vessels he had greatly endangered this Kingdom of England. But our admiral knew his advantage, and held it; which had he not done he had not been worthy to have held his head.' Camden reports advice given to Howard by one of his officers to grapple on July 23. It has been surmised that Ralegh dissuaded him. It may be so; and Ralegh can be construed as wishing it to be so understood.

Next day the Spaniards lay by to breathe. The English had leisure to send ashore for powder and shot. These for the great guns had, he has recorded, been unduly stinted. On July 25 the battle was resumed, as the enemy sailed towards the Isle of Wight. A Portuguese galleon was captured. On moved both fleets to the Straits of Dover. Many fresh English volunteer ships kept streaming in till the English fleet numbered 140 sail. Here Camden alludes to Ralegh by name. So does a correspondent of Mendoza, describing him as 'a gentleman of the Queen's Privy Chamber.' He must have been at the decisive struggle before Calais; 'Never was seen by any man living such a battery.' He was present at the desperate stand of the Spaniards opposite Gravelines. He helped to hunt the enemy into the northern seas. In a passage, attributed by Strype to Drake, of his _Report of the Truth of the Fight_ *about the Isles of the Azores,* he writes: 'The navy of 140 sail, was by thirty of the Queen's ships of war and a few merchantmen, beaten and shuffled together, even from the Lizard Point, in Cornwall, to Portland, where they shamefully left Don Pedro de Valdez with his mighty ship; from Portland to Calais, where they lost Hugo de Monçada, with the galleys of which he was captain; and from Calais, driven with squibs from their anchors, were chased out of the sight of England round about Scotland and Ireland; where, for the sympathy of their barbarous religion, hoping to find succour and assistance, a great part of them were crushed against the rocks; and those others who landed, being very many in number, were, notwithstanding, broken, slain, and taken, and so sent from village to village, coupled with halters, to be shipped into England; where her Majesty, of her princely and "invincible" disposition, disdaining to put them to death, and scorning either to retain or entertain them, they were all sent back again to their own country, to witness and recount the worthy achievements of their "invincible navy".'

Ralegh had much to do with the preliminary arrangements for the repulse of the Armada. He advised on the manner in which the victory might be improved. Several of the noble Spanish prisoners were committed to his charge. A plan was formed, which the completeness of the Spanish overthrow rendered unnecessary, for the despatch of Sir Richard Grenville and him to Ireland for the suppression of any armed body of Spanish fugitives. His part in the actual Channel fighting had been that simply of

one among many : *Retaliation on Spain.* : gallant captains. When next the State made a naval demonstration he continued to play a secondary character. In April, 1589, an expedition, under Drake and Norris, of six Queen's men-of-war and 120 volunteer sail, started to restore Don Antonio to the throne of Portugal. It was retaliation for the Armada. Ralegh sailed in a ship of his own, as a volunteer without a command. Lisbon was assailed and Vigo burnt. Otherwise the chief result of the attempt was spoil. In the Tagus 200 vessels were burnt. Many of them were easterling hulks laden with stores for a new invasion of England. Disease, arising from intemperate indulgence in new wine, crippled the fleet, and led to a quarrel between Ralegh and another Adventurer. Colonel Roger Williams had lent men to bring home one of Ralegh's prizes. Williams treated ship and cargo as therefore his in virtue of salvage. Ralegh, always tenacious of his rights, resisted, and the Privy Council upheld him. The expedition, which ended in June, though it did not gain much glory, was profitable. He, for example, effected some lucrative captures, and was paid £4000 as his share of the general booty.

CHAPTER VIII.

Ralegh would have been happier if he could have gone on fighting Spain instead of returning to the discord of Court rivalries. Before the summer was over he was again immersed in bickerings with Essex. The Earl was prone to take offence. After the defeat of the Armada he had challenged Ralegh to mortal combat. The unknown grievance was probably not more serious than the title to a ribbon of the Queen's, for which, a little later, he provoked a duel with Blount, Lord Mountjoy. Between him and Ralegh the Council interposed. It averted a combat, and endeavoured to suppress the fact of the challenge. The two could be bound over to keep the peace. They could not be reconciled. Too many indiscreet or malignant partisans were interested in inflaming the conflict. Elizabeth tried with more or less *Out of Favour.* success to adjust the balance by a rebuff to each. She rejected Ralegh's solicitation of the rangership of the New Forest for Lord Pembroke. She gave the post to Blount, Essex's recent antagonist. Still, on the whole, there appears to have been some foundation for the gossip of courtiers that Ralegh was more really in the shade. Soon after his return from Portugal he had quitted the Court, first, for the West, and then for Ireland. Captain Francis Allen wrote, on August 17, 1589, to Francis Bacon's elder brother, Anthony, who subsequently conducted Essex's foreign correspondence: 'My Lord of Essex hath chased Mr. Ralegh from the Court, and hath confined him into Ireland.' The statement was not accurate. Ralegh was able practically to contradict it by his return, after a visit to Munster of a few months. In a letter of December, 1589, he assured his cousin Carew, 'noble George,' then Master of the Ordnance in Ireland: 'For my retreat from Court, it was upon good cause to take order for my prize. If in Ireland they think I am not worth the respecting, they shall much deceive themselves. I am in place to be believed not inferior to any man, to pleasure or displeasure the greatest; and my opinion is so received and believed as I can anger the best of them. And therefore, if the Deputy be not as ready to stead me as I have been to defend him—be it as it may. When Sir William Fitzwilliams shall be in England, I take myself for his better by the honourable offices I hold, as also by that nearness to her Majesty which I still enjoy.'

He could truly deny any permanent manifestation of a loss of royal goodwill. He had been receiving fresh marks of it. He was about to receive more. His Irish estate afforded sufficient ground for absence from Court, though no less agreeable motive had concurred. He had rounded off his huge concession by procuring from the Bishop of Lismore, in 1587, a lease of Lismore Manor at a rent of £13 6s. 8d. He was building on the site of the castle a stately habitation, which his wealthy successors have again *At oughal.* transformed out of all resemblance to his work. He had conceived an affection for the Warden's house attached to the Dominican Friary at Youghal, Myrtle Grove, or Ralegh's House, as it came to be styled. Its present owner, Sir John Pope Hennessy, who has made it the occasion of a picturesque but bitter monograph, thinks he liked it because it reminded him of Hayes Barton. Other observers have failed to see the resemblance. At present it remains much as it was when Ralegh sat in its deep bays, or by its carved fire-place. The great myrtles in its garden must be almost his contemporaries. He had his experiments to watch, his potatoes and tobacco, his yellow wallflowers, in the pleasant garden by the Blackwater. He had to replenish his farms with well affected Englishmen whom he imported from Devon, Somerset, and Dorset. In 1592 it is officially recorded that, beside fifty Irish families, 120 Englishmen, many of whom had families, were settled on his property. He was developing a mineral industry by the help of miners he had hired from Cornwall. He was conducting, at a cost of some £200 a year, a lively litigation with his Lismore neighbours, of which he wrote in a few months to his cousin: 'I will shortly send over an order from the Queen for a dismiss of their cavillations.' It was the short way of composing law proceedings against Court favourites. He was planning the confusion by similar means of the unfriendly Fitzwilliam's 'connivances with usurpers of his land.' Yet a cloud there seems to have been, if only a passing one. A memorable incident of literary history, connected with this sojourn in Ireland, verifies the talk of the Court, and lends it importance. It may even point to a relation between the haze dimly discernible now, and the tempest which burst three years later.

Edmund Spenser.

Edmund Spenser had been with Lord Deputy Grey when Ralegh was a Munster captain. But, if the poet be taken literally, they were not acquainted before 1589. His Irish services, as Ralegh's, were rewarded out of the Desmond forfeitures. He received 3028 acres in Cork, with Kilcolman Castle, two miles from Doneraile. The estate formed part of a wide plain, well watered, and, in the sixteenth century, well wooded. The castle is now a roofless ivy-clad ruin. The poet was turning it into a pleasant residence.

Ralegh came to see it and him. Spenser has described the visit in the tenderest and least artificial of his poems. *Colin Clout's Come Home Again*, printed in 1595, was inscribed to his friend in 1591. The dedication was expressed to be in part payment of an infinite debt. The poet declared it unworthy of Sir Walter's higher conceit for the meanness of the style, but agreeable to the truth in circumstance and matter. Lines in the poem corroborate the hypothesis that Elizabeth had for a time, perhaps in the summer of 1589, been estranged from Ralegh:—

> His song was all a lamentable lay
> Of great unkindness, and of usage hard,
> Of Cynthia, the Ladie of the Sea,
> Which from her presence faultlesse him debard.

They equally imply that, before Colin Clout's lay was indited, great Cynthia had been induced by his complainings to abate her sore displeasure—

> And moved to take him to her grace againe.

The circumstances of Spenser's own introduction to Court indicate that

. *The Faerie Queene.* . Ralegh had recovered favour. He read or lent to

Ralegh during the visit to Kilcolman the first three books of the *Faerie Queene*. According to Ben Jonson he also delivered to him now or later 'the meaning of the Allegory in papers.' The poem enchanted the visitor, who offered to become the author's sponsor to Elizabeth. Together, if Colin Clout is to be believed, they crossed the sea, and repaired to the Court. There—

> The Shepheard of the Ocean—quoth he—
> Unto that Goddesse grace me first enhanced,
> And to my oaten pipe enclin'd her eare.

The first three books of the *Faerie Queene* were published early in 1590, with an expository letter from the most humbly affectionate author to the Right Noble and Valorous Sir Walter Ralegh. First of all the copies of commendatory verses prefixed to the poems stood two signed W.R.

Spenser, in *Colin Clout*, lauded Ralegh as a poet:—

> Full sweetly tempered is that Muse of his,
> That can empierce a Princes mightie hart.

Ralegh must have shown him part of a poem addressed to Elizabeth as Cynthia, and estimated to have contained as many as 15,000 lines when completed, if ever. This prodigious elegy was never published by Ralegh, and no entire manuscript of it is known to exist. Some years ago a paper was found in the Hatfield collection, endorsed as 'in Sir Walter's own hand.' The handwriting resembles that of Ralegh in 1603. It comprises altogether 568 verses. Two short poems, of seven and fourteen lines, come first; and the manuscript terminates with an unfinished poem of seven *Cynthia.* stanzas in a variety of terza rima. The body of the contents consists of 526 elegiac verses, described in the manuscript as 'The twenty-first and last book of the Ocean, to Cynthia.' Archdeacon Hannah, in his *Courtly Poets from Ralegh to Montrose*, concludes, with some hesitation, that the whole was composed as a sequel, between 1603 and 1612, to a much earlier poem. He sees in it allusions to the death of the Queen, which would more or less fix the date. Mr. Edmund Gosse, in the *Athenaeum*, in January, 1886, has contested that hypothesis. He thinks, in the first place, that the twenty-one lines which precede, and the twenty-one which follow, the so-called twenty-first book, have no relation to the poem of *Cynthia*. The rest he holds to be not a continuation of *Cynthia*, but an integral portion of the original work. That work, as a whole, he has convinced himself, was produced during the author's transient disgrace, between August, 1589, and its end, which may be taken to have been not later than December in the same year. That no part of *Cynthia*, as we have it, was written later than 1603 scarcely admits of doubt. Ralegh would not have sat down in the reign of James to write love ditties to Elizabeth. His repinings and upbraidings are manifestly all pointed at a dead heart, not at a dead queen. Mr. Gosse is, however, more successful in his argument that the main Hatfield poem was written in the lifetime of Elizabeth, than in his attempt to date it in 1589. He assumes that the poem was a finished composition when Ralegh read from it to Spenser. It is not likely that it ever was finished. Spenser's allusions to it point to a conception fully formed, rather than to a work ready for publication. In the latter case it is improbable, to the verge of impossibility, that Ralegh should not have communicated it to his circle. An initial objection to the view that the twenty-first book was penned in 1589 is its reference to the—

Twelve years entire I wasted on this war,

that war being his struggle for the affection of Elizabeth. This Mr. Gosse ingeniously, but not satisfactorily, appropriates as the main support of his chronology. In the Paunsford recognizance Ralegh is set down as of the Court in 1577. On no other evidence Mr. Gosse infers that he was laying siege to Elizabeth's heart before he went to Ireland. Thus the dozen years of the campaign would be conveniently over by the autumn of 1589. A simpler solution seems to be to assign the rough-hewing of the entire project of *Cynthia*, and its partial accomplishment, to the term of Ralegh's short occultation in 1589. He might well have disclosed to Spenser his project, and read out passages. They would be melancholy for their sorrow's crown of sorrow, their recalling of former undimmed felicity—

> Of all which past the sorrow only stays.

They would exaggerate royal unkindness. They would hardly have descanted on the tenderness as absolutely extinct. Even before Spenser extolled the *Cynthia* in *Colin Clout* in 1591, the harshness was softened, and had melted back to the playing at love in which Elizabeth was wont to indulge with her courtiers. When he resumed the theme on his banishment from Court in 1592, he would feel that he had solid cause for lamentation. By 1594 his disgrace seemed definite; the royal kindness won by years of devotion—

> Twelve years of my most happy younger days—

appeared to have been utterly killed; and he was preparing to sail away into space. The twenty-first book might have been written at any time between 1592 and 1595, and its most dismal groans be fairly explicable. Looking back to his regrets in 1589 for an episode of neglect, he could wonder at himself—

> At middle day my sun seemed under land,
> When any little cloud did it obscure.

Had Spenser seen the twenty-first book of *Cynthia* in 1591, with its real or unreal blackness of despair, he would not have spoken of Ralegh as basking in the renewed radiance of happy prospects. So *Cynthia*, as far as it was ever composed, may be considered one poem, to which the extant twenty-first book essentially belongs. There is not, therefore, necessarily any hope, or fear, that the whole exists, or ever existed, in a perfect shape. Ralegh would nurse the idea for all the years in which the Queen's withdrawal of the light of her countenance gave him comparative leisure. The twenty-first book itself would be written with the direct purpose of softening his mistress's obduracy. The explanation of its preservation among the Hatfield papers may be that, on the eve of his departure, forsaken, withered, hopeless, for Guiana, it was confided, in 1594 or 1595, to Cecil, then a good friend, for seasonable production to the Queen. Viewed as written either in 1589, or in the reign of James, much of the twenty-first book is without meaning. Its tone is plain and significant for the years 1592 to 1595. If traced to that period, it tells both of the bold coming adventure of 1595,

> To kingdoms strange, to lands far-off addressed,

and of the irresistible power of 'her memory' in 1592

> To call me back, to leave great honour's thought,
> To leave my friends, my fortune, my attempt;
> To leave the purpose I so long had sought,
> And hold both cares and comforts in contempt.

Concurrent testimony in favour of a date for the book later than 1589, though much prior to 1603, is afforded by the use in it of the name Belphoebe:

> A queen she was to me—no more Belphoebe;
> A lion then—no more a milk-white dove;
> A prisoner in her breast I could not be;
> She did untie the gentle chains of love.

> *Belphoebe.*

Belphoebe was a word coined apparently by Spenser. To the poem of *Cynthia* Spenser had said he owed the idea of the name, implying that it was of his coinage. It was fashioned, he stated, 'according to Ralegh's excellent conceit of Cynthia, Cynthia and Phoebe being both names of Diana.' Ralegh, by the introduction of the name into his *Cynthia*, at once has dated the canto in which it occurs as not earlier than 1591, or, perhaps, than 1595, and indicated his desire to link his own verses to the eventful meeting

> among the coolly shade
> Of the green alders, by the Mulla's shore.

Spenser referred again to the poem of *Cynthia*, and to Ralegh's poetic greatness, in the most beautiful of the sonnets offered to his several patrons at the end of his surpassing romance and allegory:

> To thee, that art the Summer's Nightingale,
> Thy Sovereign Goddess's most dear delight,

Why do I send this rustic Madrigal,
That may thy tuneful ear unseason quite?
Thou only fit this argument to write,
In whose high thoughts Pleasure hath built her bower,
And dainty Love learned sweetly to indite.
My rhymes I know unsavoury and sour,
To taste the streams that, like a golden shower,
Flow from the fruitful head of thy Love's praise;
Fitter perhaps to thunder martial stowre,
Whenso thee list thy lofty Muse to raise;
Yet, till that thou thy Poem wilt make known,
Let thy fair Cynthia's praises be thus rudely shown.

Ralegh's Sonnet.

It was his return for tribute in kind. By the side of Ralegh's sonnet its flattery hardly seems extravagant:—

Methought I saw the grave where Laura lay,
Within that temple where the vestal flame
Was wont to burn; and passing by that way,
To see that buried dust of living fame,
Whose tomb fair Love and fairer Virtue kept,
All suddenly I saw the Fairy Queen,
At whose approach the soul of Petrarch wept;
And from thenceforth those graces were not seen,
For they this Queen attended; in whose stead
Oblivion laid him down on Laura's hearse.
Hereat the hardest stones were seen to bleed,
And groans of buried ghosts the heavens did pierce:
Where Homer's spright did tremble all for grief,
And cursed the access of that celestial thief.

Before this, or Spenser's eulogy on him, was printed, Ralegh had acquired the reputation at Court of a poet. Puttenham, a critic of high repute, had,
Poetic Gifts. in *The Art of English Poesy*, printed in 1589, pronounced 'for ditty and amorous ode, Sir Walter Ralegh's vein most lofty, insolent, and passionate.' By 'insolent,' not 'condolent,' as Anthony Wood quotes, Puttenham meant original. His first public appearance as a poet was in

1576, when in grave and sounding lines he maintained Gascoigne's merits against envious detractors, as if with a presentiment of his own fate—

> For whoso reaps renown above the rest,
> With heaps of hate shall surely be oppressed.

His flow of inspiration never dried up till his head rolled in the dust. But the years between 1583 and 1593 seem, so far as dates, always in Ralegh's career distracting, can be fixed, to have been the period of his most copious poetic fruitfulness.

Throughout his life he won the belief of men of letters and refinement in his poetic power. Their admiration has never failed him in the centuries which have followed. He has not been as fortunate in gaining and keeping the ear of the reading public. For that a poet has not only to be born, but to be made. Ralegh had a poet's gifts. He had music in his soul. He chose to think for himself. He possessed the art of the grand style. The twenty-first book of the *Cynthia* errs in being overcharged with thought. It abounds in noble imagery. There is pathos as well as dignity. Its author, had he lived in the nineteenth century, in default of new worlds to explore, or Armadas to fight, might have written an *In Memoriam*. In previous English poetry no such dirge is to be found as his Epitaph on Sir Philip Sidney. A couple of stanzas will indicate its solemn music:—

> There didst thou vanquish shame and tedious age,
> Grief, sorrow, sickness, and base fortune's might;
> Thy rising day saw never woeful night,
> But passed with praise from off this worldly stage.

> What hath he lost that such great grace hath won?
> Young years for endless years, and hope unsure
> Of fortune's gifts for wealth that still shall dure:
> O happy race, with so great praises run!

He had as light a touch. He understood how to play with a conceit till it glances and dances and dazzles, as in his, for probably it is his, *Grace of Wit, of Tongue, of Face*, and in *Fain would I, but I dare not*. Praed was not happier in elaborate trifling than he in his *Cards and Dice*. Prior might have envied him *The Silent Lover*. His *Nymph's Reply to the Passionate Shepherd*, if it be his, as Izaak Walton without suspicion assumes, and, if it did not compel comparison with Marlowe's more exquisite melody, would assure his place among the poets of the age. He was able to barb a fierce sarcasm with courtly grace. How his fancy could swoop down and strike, and pierce as it flashed, may be felt in each ringing stanza of *The Lie*—

> Say to the Court, it glows
> And shines like rotten wood;
> Say to the Church, it shows
> What's good, and doth no good:
> If Church and Court reply,
> Then give them both the lie.

His fancy could inspire in his *Pilgrimage* one of the loftiest appeals in all literature to Heaven from the pedantry of human justice or injustice.

Their Limitations. He could match Cowley in metaphysical verse, as in *A Poesy to prove Affection is not Love*. But the Court spoilt him for a national poet, as it spoilt Cowley; as it might, if it had been more generous, have spoilt Dryden. He desired to be read between the lines by a class which loved to think its own separate thoughts, and express its own separate feelings in its own diction, sometimes in its own jargon. He hunted for epigrams, and too often sparkled rather than burned. He was afraid not to be witty, to wrangle, as he himself has said,

> In tickle points of niceness.

Often he refined instead of soaring. In place of sympathising he was ever striving to concentrate men's regards on himself. Egotism is not inconsistent with the heat of inspiration, when it is unconscious, when the poet sings because he must, and bares his own heart. Ralegh rarely loses command of himself. He is perpetually seen registering the effects his flights produce. Apparently he had no ambition for popular renown as a poet. He did not print his verses. He cannot be said to have claimed any of them *Disputed Authorship.* but the *Farewell to the Court*. His authorship of some, now admitted to be by him, has been confidently questioned. A critic so judicious as Hallam, for reasons which he does not hint, and a student as laborious as Isaac D'Israeli, have doubted his title to *The Lie*, otherwise described as *The Soul's Errand*, which seems to demonstrate his authorship by its scornful and cynical haughtiness embodied in a wave of magnificent rhythm. Verses, instinct with his peculiar wit, like *The Silent Lover*, have been given away to Lord Pembroke, Sir Robert Ayton, and others. Its famous stanza—

> Silence in love bewrays more woe

Than words, though ne'er so witty;
A beggar that is dumb, you know,
Deserveth double pity!

was in the middle of last century boldly assigned to Lord Chesterfield. His compositions circulated from hand to hand at Court. They were read in polished coteries. So little did they ever become a national possession that, complete or incomplete, the most considerable of them has vanished, all but a fragment. Small as is the whole body of verse attributed to him, not all is clearly his. Dr. Hannah, and other ardent admirers of his muse, have been unable to satisfy themselves whether he really wrote *False Love and True Love*, with its shifting rhythm, and its bewitching scattered phrases; the Shepherd's fantastically witty *Description of Love*, or *Anatomy of Love*—

It is a yea, it is a nay;

or the perfect conceit, which Waller could not have bettered in wit or equalled in vivacity, with the refrain—

What care I how fair she be!

Twenty-seven other poems, among them, the bright sneering *Invective against Women*, have been put down to him on no other ground than that they cannot be traced to a different source. He might have been the author of the graceful *Praise of his Sacred Diana*. He might have sighed for a land devoid of envy,

Unless among
The birds, for prize of their sweet song.

From him might have come the airy melody of the charming eclogue *Phyllida's Love-call to her Corydon*, which invites the genius of a Mendelssohn to frame it in music. He might have penned in his prison cell the knell for the tragedy of human life, *De Morte*. He might have been the shepherd minstrel of the flowers—

You pretty daughters of the earth and sun.

But, unfortunately, the sole pretext for affirming his title, as the editors of the 1829 collection of his works affirmed it, is that the poems are found in the *Reliquiae Wottonianae*, in Davison's *Poetical Rhapsody*, or in *England's Helicon*, and are there marked 'Ignoto.'

- 84 -

The assignment, often, as Mr. Bullen shows in his editions of *England's Helicon*, and *A Poetical Rhapsody*, without the slightest authority or foundation, of poetic foundlings of rare charm and distinction to Ralegh is

- *Carelessness of Literary Renown.* - a token of the prevalent belief in the

unfathomed range of his powers. At the same time it implies that he had never been adopted, and identified, by the contemporary public specifically as a poet. He would not be discontented with the degree and kind of the poetic fame conceded to him. Had he coveted more he would have been at more pains to stamp his verses. His poetic gift he valued merely as a weapon in his armoury, like many others. It held its own and a more important place in his career. Imagination, which might have made a poet, elevated and illuminated the captain's and the courtier's ambition and acts. If it put him at a disadvantage in a race for power with a Robert Cecil, it carried him to Guiana, and gave him the palm in the glorious struggle at the mouth of Cadiz harbour; it inspired him in the more tremendous strife with judicial obliquity; it supported him on the scaffold in Palace Yard.

CHAPTER IX.

THE REVENGE. (September, 1591).

Long after Ralegh began to be recognized in his new circle as a poet, he first showed himself a master of prose diction. The occasion came from his loss of an opportunity for personal distinction of a kind he preferred to literary laurels. The hope and the disappointment alike testify that, whatever had been the Queen's demeanour in 1589, she frowned no longer in 1591. Essex's temporary disgrace, on account of his marriage with Lady Sidney in 1590, had improved Ralegh's prospects. So much in favour was he that, in the spring of 1591, he had been commissioned as Vice-Admiral of a fleet of six Queen's ships, attended by volunteer vessels and provision *Sir Richard Grenville.* boats. Lord Thomas Howard, second son of the Duke of Norfolk beheaded in 1572, commanded in chief. The object of the expedition was to intercept the Spanish plate fleet at the Azores. Ralegh's cousin and friend, the stern and wayward but gallant Sir Richard Grenville, finally was substituted for him. There is no evidence that the change was meant for a censure. Much more probably it was a token of the Queen's personal regard. He sent with the squadron his ship, the Ark Ralegh, under the command of Captain Thynne, another of his innumerable connexions in the West. The English had to wait for the plate galleons so long at the Azores that news was brought to Spain. A fleet of fifty-three Spanish sail was despatched as convoy. Ralegh was engaged officially in Devonshire. The Council directed him in May to send off a pinnace to tell Howard that this great Spanish force had been descried off Scilly.

The warning arrived too late. The Spaniards surprised the fleet on September 10, when many of its men were ashore. Grenville in the Revenge covered the embarkation. Thus he lost the wind. He mustered on board his flagship scarce a hundred sound men. Soon he was hemmed in. The Foresight *The Fight.* stayed near him for two hours, and battled bravely, but finally had to retire. For fifteen hours he fought the squadron of Seville, five great galleons, with ten more to back them. Crippled by many wounds, he kept the upper deck. Nothing was to be seen but the naked hull of a ship, and that almost a skeleton. She had received 800 shot of great artillery, some under water. The deck was covered with the limbs and carcases of forty valiant men. The rest were all wounded and painted with their own blood. Her masts had been shot overboard. All her tackle was cut asunder. Her upper works were razed and level with the water. She was incapable of receiving any direction or motion, except that given her by the billows. Three Spanish galleons had been burnt. One had been run aground to save her company. A thousand Spaniards had been slain or drowned. Grenville wished to blow up his shattered hulk. A majority of the handful of survivors preferred to accept the Spanish Admiral's terms. They were that all lives should be spared, the crew be sent to England, and the better sort be released on payment of ransom. Grenville was conveyed on board a Spanish galley, where he was chivalrously treated. He lingered till September 13 or 14 in sore pain, which he disdained to betray. Jan Huygen van Linschoten, a Dutch adventurer, who was at the time in the island of Terceira, heard of the struggle both from the Spaniards and from one of the English prisoners. He describes it briefly in a diary he kept. He was told how the English admiral would amaze the Spanish captains by crushing wine-glasses between his teeth, after he had tossed off the contents. The fragments he swallowed, while the blood ran out of his mouth. It is Linschoten, not Ralegh, who has preserved Grenville's dying words: 'Here die I, Richard Grenville, with a joyful and quiet mind, for that I have ended my life, as a true soldier ought, that hath fought for his country, Queen, religion, and honour.'

Ralegh might have met Grenville's fate. He took up the pen to celebrate his

Ralegh's Narrative. kinsman's heroism, and to point the moral for

England of the feats valour like his could accomplish against Spain. His *Report of the Truth of the Fight about the Isles of Azores* was first published anonymously in November, 1591. Hakluyt reprinted it, as 'penned by Sir Walter Ralegh,' in his Collection of Voyages in 1599. Few finer specimens of Elizabethan prose diction exist. It is full of grandeur, and of generosity towards every one but Spaniards. Of the commander-in-chief, Thomas Howard, he spoke with especial courtesy. Ralegh's relations to the Howards, though always professionally intimate, were not always very friendly, either now or hereafter. About the period of Grenville's death, in particular, there had been some sharp dispute with the High Admiral. A letter written in the following October by Thomas Phelippes to Thomas Barnes, alludes to a quarrel and offer of combat between Ralegh and him. Ralegh was only the more careful on that account to do justice to a member of the family. Howard, it seems, had been severely criticised for a supposed abandonment of his comrade. Ralegh vindicated him from the calumny. The admiral's first impulse had been to return within the harbour to succour Grenville. It was a happy thing, in Ralegh's judgment, that he suffered himself to be dissuaded. 'The very hugeness of the Spanish fleet would have crushed the English ships to atoms; it had ill sorted with the discretion of a General to commit himself and his charge to assured destruction.' But the real aim of the narrative was to preach a crusade against Spanish predominance in the Old and New Worlds. Towards Grenville personally the behaviour of the Spaniards, it could not be denied, was magnanimous. Ralegh saw nothing but perfidy in their conduct otherwise. They broke, he declares, their engagement to send the captives home. Morrice FitzJohn of Desmond was allowed to endeavour to induce them to apostatize and enter the service of their enemy. That was the Spanish system, he exclaims: 'to entertain basely the traitors and vagabonds

of all : *An Indictment of Spain.* : nations; by all kinds of devices to gratify covetousness of dominion,' 'as if the Kings of Castile were the natural heirs of all the world.' Yet 'what good, honour, or fortune ever man by them achieved, is unheard of or unwritten.' 'The obedience even of the Turk is easy, and a liberty, in respect of the slavery and tyranny of Spain. What have they done in Sicily, Naples, Milan, and the Low Countries?' 'In one only island, called Hispaniola, they have wasted three millions of the natural people, beside many millions else in other places of the Indies; a poor and harmless people, created of God, and might have been won to his knowledge, as many of them were.' 'Who, therefore, would repose trust in such a nation of ravenous strangers, and especially in these Spaniards, who more greedily thirst after English blood than after the lives of any other people in Europe;' 'whose weakness we have discovered to the world.' Historians, with whom Ralegh has never been a favourite, treat as merely dishonest rhetoric the compassion he now and again expressed for the millions of innocent men, women, and children, branded, roasted, mangled, ripped alive, by Spaniards, though as free by nature as any Christians. There is no just reason to think him insincere. The pity gave dignity and a tone of chivalry to his more local feeling, Protestant, political, commercial, of hatred and jealousy of Spain. Spain, he declared, was ever conspiring against us. She had bought the aid of Denmark, Norway, the French Parliament-towns, the Irish and Scotch malcontents. She threatened the foundations of English liberty of thought. She tried to starve the rising English instinct for territorial expansion. He summoned Englishmen eager for foreign trade to protest against the Spanish embargo, which everywhere they encountered. He pointed out to them, as they began to feel the appetite for wealth, the colonial treasury of Spain glittering in full view before them.

A multitude of Englishmen, especially in Ralegh's own country of the West, were conscious of all this. Ralegh gave the sentiment a voice in his story of his cousin's gallant death. Henceforth he never ceased to consecrate his energies and influence directly to the work of lowering the flag of Spain, and replacing it by that of England. From the beginning of his career he had been a labourer in this field. He now asserted his title to be the champion of his nation. Previously he had usually striven by deputy. Now he was to display his personal prowess as a warrior and a great captain. For years he was to be seen battling with Philip's empire by sea and land, plundering his merchantmen, storming his strongholds, bursting through his frontiers, and teaching Englishmen to think that sheer usurpation which for Spaniards was right divine. His own countrymen did not at first accept his leadership. They affirmed his principle, but preferred that others than he should have the primary honour of applying it. Gradually competitors dropped off; and he remained. Through popular odium, popular curiosity, and, finally, popular enthusiasm, he grew to be identified with the double idea of English rivalry with Spain and of English naval supremacy. The act in which he appears challenging the right to be its representative is about to open. But previously the curtain has to fall upon the courtier. The conqueror at Cadiz, the explorer of Guiana, steps from behind a veil of darkness and disgrace which would have overwhelmed other men utterly, and served him as a foil.

Philip replied to Lord Thomas Howard's unfortunate expedition by the

- *Proposed Expeditionto Panama.* - equipment of a fleet of sixty ships. Plymouth was understood to be their object. Ralegh persuaded the Queen to parry the blow by striking at Panama, and at the plate fleet which would be gathered in its harbour. Elizabeth contributed the Garland and Foresight. Ralegh provided the Roebuck, and his elder brother, Carew Ralegh, the Galleon Ralegh. Two ships were equipped by the citizens of London. Lord Cumberland had been arranging for an independent cruise. Ultimately he joined with six vessels. The Queen also invested £1800 in the adventure, and London £6000. Ralegh had been named General of the Fleet. He exhausted all his resources to ensure success. 'I protest,' he wrote, 'both my three years' pension of the Custom-house, and all I have besides, is in this journey.' He had borrowed £11,000 at interest; and in addition was heavily in debt to the Crown. In part discharge of his obligations, he assigned to the Queen the Ark Ralegh at the price of £5000. Calumny asserted that the apparent sale was a mere pretext for a present from the Treasury to him. The preparations were still incomplete in February, 1592. He travelled to the West for additional stores. When all was ready for departure westerly winds set in. For many weeks the fleet was weatherbound in the Thames. Some time before it was able to move his own relation to it was become uncertain. Elizabeth, he was aware, wished to keep him at Court. He was not unwilling to consent to a compromise. He wrote to Robert Cecil from Chatham on March 10: 'I have promised her Majesty, if I can persuade the companies to follow Sir Martin Frobisher, I will, without fail, return, and bring them but into the sea some fifty or threescore leagues, though I dare not be known thereof to any creature.'

Certainly he meant to embark. In May he was angrily complaining of 'this cross weather.' 'I am not _Sails and returns._ able to live to row up and down with every tide from Gravesend to London.' At length on the 6th of May, 1592, the fleet was under sail with him on board. On the 7th, he was overtaken by Frobisher with orders to come back. He was to leave Sir John Burgh, Borough, or Brough, and Frobisher to command as his lieutenants. Choosing to construe the orders as optional in date, Ralegh proceeded as far as Cape Finisterre. Thence, after weathering a terrific storm on May 11, he himself returned. Before his departure he arranged the plan of operations. Half the fleet he stationed under Frobisher off the Spanish coast to distract the attention of the Spaniards. The rest he sent to watch for the treasure fleet at the Azores. For an attack on Panama the season was too late.

CHAPTER X.

Immediately on his return, if not before, he understood the reason of his recall. He had written to Cecil on March 10: 'I mean not to come away, as they say I will, for fear of a marriage, and I know not what. If any such thing were, I should have imparted it unto yourself before any man living; and therefore, I pray, believe it not, and I beseech you to suppress, what you can, any such malicious report. For, I protest, there is none on the face of the earth that I would be fastened unto.' As soon as he reached London in June, he was thrown into the Tower. He had seemed before to be enjoying the plenitude of royal favour. So lately as in January it had been shown by the grant of a fine estate in Dorset. No official record is discoverable of the cause of his imprisonment. Disobedience to the order to quit the fleet would have been a sufficient pretext. It was not mentioned. The imprisonment was a domestic punishment within her own fortress-palace, *Elizabeth Throckmorton.* inflicted by the Queen as head of her household. The true reason was his courtship of Elizabeth, daughter to the Queen's devoted but turbulent servant and confidant, Sir Nicholas Throckmorton. He had died in 1571, at the age of fifty-seven, in Leicester's house. His eldest son, Nicholas, was adopted by a maternal uncle, the last Carew of Beddington, and became Sir Nicholas Carew. Elizabeth Throckmorton, who had as many cousins in high positions as Ralegh, was appointed a maid of honour. Her portrait proves her to have been handsome. She was tall, slender, blue-eyed and golden-haired. Her mental qualities will be in evidence during the rest of Ralegh's life. Never were written more charming letters than hers, in more unembarrassed phonetic spelling.

The Captain of the Guard and she attended on the Queen together. He made her an exception to his rule as to maids of honour, that, 'like witches, they can do hurt, but no good.' He found her only too amiable. Camden, in his *Annals*, published in 1615, explains Ralegh's crime and punishment: 'honorariâ Reginae virgine vitiatâ, quam postea in uxorem duxit.' Wood says the same in his Latinized English, merely translating Camden. A letter from Sir Edward Stafford to Sir Anthony Bacon, with the impossible date, July 30, couples Ralegh's and Miss Throckmorton's names in a burst of exultation, natural to Essex's friends: 'If you have anything to do with Sir Walter Ralegh, or any love to make to Mrs. Throckmorton, at the Tower to-morrow you may speak with them; if the countermand come not tonight, as *Scantiness of Testimony.* some think will not be, and particularly he that hath charge to send them thither.' Stafford does not specify the offence. The sole independent testimony is the single sentence of Camden's. Yet posterity has had no option but to accept the account. The error, if other courtiers had been the culprits, would have excited little surprise. Elizabeth's maids of honour were not more beyond suspicion than Swift asserts Anne's to have been. Essex's gallantries at Court, after as before his marriage, were notorious and many. Lord Southampton and his bride were the subjects of a similar tale a few years later. Palace gossip treated it as a very ordinary peccadillo. Cecil in February, 1601, tells Carew of the 'misfortune' of one of the maids, Mistress Fitton, with Lord Pembroke, as if it were a jest. Both the culprits, he remarks, 'will dwell in the Tower a while.' His phrases show none of the horror they breathed when he spoke of Ralegh, and the Queen was likely to read them. The English Court was pure in the time of Elizabeth for its time. It degenerated greatly under her successor. Harington contrasts manners then with the previous 'good order, discretion, *Hard to believe.* and sobriety.' But no little licence was permitted, and the tales of it commonly excite small surprise. As told of Ralegh, and yet more of Elizabeth Throckmorton, the story startles still. No evidence exists upon which he can justly be pronounced a libertine. How she, refined, faithful, heroic, should have been led astray, is hardly intelligible. She must have now been several years over twenty, probably twenty-eight or twenty-nine, and in her long after-life she bore herself as entitled to all social respect. She was allowed it by every one, except her Mistress, who never restored her to favour. By the Cecils she was treated with unfailing regard. In the whole of her struggle, by her husband's side, and over his grave, for his and her son's rights, not a whisper was heard of the blot on her fair fame. If Camden had not spoken, and if Ralegh and she had not stood mute, it would have been easy to believe that the imagined liaison was simply a secret marriage resented as such by the Queen, as, two years before, she had resented Essex's secret marriage to Sidney's widow. That seems to have been asserted by their friends, at the first explosion of the scandal. A letter, written on the eve of Ralegh's committal to the Tower, by one who manifestly did not hold the benevolent opinion, says, after a spitefully prophetic comparison of Ralegh with his own

Hermit poor in pensive place obscure:

'It is affirmed that they are married; but the Queen is most fiercely incensed.'

That the royal anger had a better foundation than the mere jealousy of affection or of domination, it is to be feared, is the inevitable inference from the evidence, however concise and circumstantial. Had contradiction been possible, Camden would have been contradicted in 1615 by Ralegh and his wife. Cecil alluded to Ralegh's offence in 1592 as 'brutish.' With all

. *Harder to disbelieve.* . his zeal to indulge the Queen's indignation, he could not have used the term of a secret marriage. The prevailing absence of Court talk on the occurrence is not traceable to any doubt of its true character. Courtiers simply believed it dangerous to be outspoken on a matter affecting the purity of the Virgin Queen's household circle. Her prudery may indeed go some way towards accounting for, if not excusing, the fault. It was dangerous for one of her counsellors to be suspected of an attachment. So late as March, 1602, Cecil was writing earnestly to Carew in repudiation of a rumour that he was like to be enchanted for love or marriage. Almost borrowing Ralegh's words to himself of ten years earlier, he declares upon his soul he knows none on earth that he was, or, if he might, would be, married unto. In Elizabeth's view love-making, except to herself, was so criminal that at Court it had to be done by stealth. Any show of affection was deemed an act of guilt. From a consciousness of guilt to the reality is not always a wide step. In Ralegh's references and language to his wife may be detected a tone in the tenderness as though he owed reparation as well as attachment. The redeeming feature of their passion is that they loved with true love also, and with a love which grew. His published opinions, as in his *Instructions to his Son*, on wives and marriage, like those of other writers of aphorisms in his age, ring harshly and coldly. But he did not act on frigid fragments of sententious suspiciousness. He was careful for his widow's worldly welfare. With death, as it seemed, imminent, he trusted with all, and in everything, his 'sweet Besse,' his 'faithful wife,' as scoffing Harington with enthusiasm called her. His constant desire was to have her by his side, but to spare her grieving.

When and where they were married is unknown. So careful were they to avoid publicity that Lady Ralegh's brother, Arthur Throckmorton, for some time questioned the fact, though his suspicions were dissipated, and he became an attached friend of the husband's. Probably the ceremony was performed after the imprisonment and not before. If the threat of detention in the Tower, mentioned by Stafford, were carried into effect against the lady, Ralegh at all events betrayed no consciousness that she was his neighbour. In his correspondence at the time he never speaks of her. His business was to obtain his release. He understood that allusions to the partner in his misdeed would not move the Queen to kindness. Like Leicester, and like Essex, he continued, though married, to use loverlike phrases of the Queen, whenever they were in the least likely to reach her ear. The Cecils were - *A Rhapsody.* - his allies against Essex. In July, 1592, under cover of an account for the Yeomen's coats for an approaching royal progress, he burst into a wonderful effusion to, not for, Robert Cecil: 'My heart was never broken till this day, that I hear the Queen goes away so far off—whom I have followed so many years with so great love and desire, in so many journeys, and am now left behind her, in a dark prison all alone. While she was yet nigher at hand, that I might hear of her once in two or three days, my sorrows were the less; but even now my heart is cast into the depth of all misery. I that was wont to behold her riding like Alexander, hunting like Diana, walking like Venus, the gentle wind blowing her fair hair about her pure cheeks, like a nymph; sometimes sitting in the shade like a Goddess; sometimes singing like an angel; sometimes playing like Orpheus. Behold the sorrow of this world! Once amiss, hath bereaved me of all. O Glory, that only shineth in misfortune, what is become of thy assurance? All wounds have scars, but that of fantasy; all affections their relenting, but that of womankind. Who is the judge of friendship, but adversity? Or when is grace witnessed, but in offences? There were no divinity but by reason of compassion; for revenges are brutish and mortal. All those times past—the loves, the sighs, the sorrows, the desires—can they not weigh down one frail misfortune? Cannot one drop of gall be hidden in so great heaps of sweetness? I may then conclude, Spes et fortuna, valete. She is gone in whom I trusted, and of me hath not one thought of mercy, nor any respect of that that was. Do with me now, therefore, what you list. I am more weary of life than they are desirous I should perish; which, if it had been for her, as it is by her, I had been too happily born.' Did ever tailor's bill, though for the most resplendent scarlet liveries bespangled with golden roses, inspire a like rhapsody! By one writer on Ralegh it has been characterized, so various are tastes, as 'tawdry and fulsome.' To most it will seem a delightful extravagance. To contemporaries the extravagance itself would appear not very glaring. Elizabeth aroused both fascination and awe in her own period which justified high flights. After her goodness and wrath were become alike unavailing this is how a cynic like Harington spoke of her: 'When she smiled it was a pure sunshine that every one did choose to bask in if they could; but anon came a storm, and the thunder fell in wondrous manner on all alike.' Ralegh doubtless was

sincere in - *A Comedy inthe Tower.* - repining for the radiance as in

deprecating the scowls, though he overrated his ability to conjure that back, and these away. In the same July, apparently, on July 26, he played a little comedy of Orlando Furioso,—not the approach to a tragedy of eleven years after. His chamber in the Tower was the scene. The spectators were his Keeper and cousin, Sir George Carew, and Arthur Gorges. Gorges was still, like Carew, his friend in 1614, and was sung by him then as one

> Who never sought nor ever cared to climb
> By flattery, or seeking worthless men.

He now wrote to Cecil that Ralegh, hearing the Queen was on the Thames, prayed Carew to let him row himself in disguise near enough to look upon her. On Carew's necessary refusal he went mad, and tore Carew's new periwig off. At last they drew out their daggers, whereupon Gorges interposed, and had his knuckles rapped. 'They continue,' he proceeds, 'in malice and snarling. But, good Sir, let nobody know thereof.' He adds in a more veracious postscript: 'If you let the Queen's Majesty know hereof, as you think good, be it.'

Ralegh thought he understood his royal Mistress, of whom he had written not very respectfully to Carew himself two or three years before: 'The Queen thinks that George Carew longs to see her; and, therefore, see her.' Like others he perceived her weaknesses; he did not appreciate her strength. To his surprise she remained offended; and none can blame her. His conduct had been treason to her sovereign charms. Her indignation on that ground may be ridiculed. But she had a sincerer love for purity of manners than posterity has commonly believed. Ralegh had set an ill example. He had broken his trust; the seduction of a maid of honour was a personal affront to his sovereign; he properly suffered for it, and not in excess of the offence. His confinement was not rigorous. George Carew since February, 1588, had been Master of the Ordnance in Ireland. He was acting as Lieutenant-General of the Ordnance for England in August, 1592; being confirmed in the post in 1603, and made Master-General in 1609. In virtue of his office he had now _The Brick Tower_ as well as later apartments in the Brick tower, which was considered to be under the charge of the Master of the Ordnance. To the Brick tower Ralegh had been sent, and he was committed to Carew's easy custody. He had his own servants, whom he was allowed to lodge on the upper floor of the tower. His friends were granted liberal access to him. From his window he could see the river and the country beyond. The old Tower story that he was shut up in a cell in the crypt, is a fiction. Not even his offices or their emoluments were taken away. He could perform the duties by deputy. But from June to December he was in confinement; and for long afterwards he was forbidden to come into the royal presence.

He chafed at the light restraint. He affected indignation at the severity of the penalty with which his 'great treasons,' as he called them in mockery, were visited. He did not attempt to dispute its legality, more than questionable as that was. Almost from the first he evinced the extraordinary elasticity of nature, which was to be tried a hundredfold hereafter. While he protested against the inevitable he carved his life to suit it. From his gaol issued messages of despair and of business in the *Anger against the Irish Lord Deputy.* strangest medley. He was much exercised about his Irish estate; and he cast his burden upon Cecil: 'Your cousin, the doting Deputy,' Fitzwilliam, he wrote, had been distraining on his tenants for a supposed debt from himself as Undertaker. A sum of £400 for arrears of rent was demanded, though all Munster had scarce so much money in it. The same Fitzwilliam, he alleges, had been mulcting the Queen £1200 a year for a band of worthless soldiers in Youghal, under 'a base fellow, O'Dodall.' Perhaps his estimate of the Captain may not be unbiassed. A Sir John Dowdall seems to have disputed his title to, and, two years later, to have ejected him from possession of, the manor of Ardmore and other lands demised to him in 1592 by Bishop Witherhead of Lismore. He was aggrieved by Lord Deputy Fitzwilliam's slowness to aid him in his litigations. He thought it, as it was, 'a sign how my disgraces have passed the seas.' At least his warnings of a rising of the Burkes, O'Donells, and O'Neales need not have been neglected. 'I wrote,' he complained, 'in a letter of Mr. Killigrew's ten days past a prophecy of this rebellion, which when the Queen read she made a scorn of my conceit.' Not that it was anything in reality to him. He cared not either for life or lands. He was become, he declared with some zoological confusion, 'like a fish cast on dry land, gasping for breath, with lame legs and lamer lungs.' Still, he felt bound to point out the pity of it. Then too, he reminded the High Admiral, there was the Great Susan, 'which nobody but myself would undertake to set out.' It could hardly be more profitable to punish him than that he 'should either strengthen the fleet, or do many other things that lie in the ditches.' Among them, for instance, was the business of keeping in order, as he alone could, the soldiers and mariners 'that came in the prize.' They ran up and down, he says, exclaiming for pay. So, again, in vain he knew of the warships of the French League lying in wait for English merchantmen, and threatening to make us a laughing-stock for all nations. His information and his zeal were fruitless, through 'this unfortunate accident,' of which neither he nor his correspondents ever state the nature. 'I see,' he cries to the High Admiral, who appears to have been mediating, 'there is a determination to disgrace me and ruin me. Therefore I beseech your Lordship not to offend her Majesty any farther by suing for me. I am now resolved of the matter. I only desire that I may be stayed not one hour from all the extremity that either law or precedent can avow. And if that be too little, would God it were withall concluded that I might feed the lions, as I go by, to save labour. For the torment of the mind cannot be greater; and, for the body,

New Combinations. — would others did respect themselves as much as I value it at little.' He was always impatient, inordinately despairing in misfortunes, till the last extremity. He was always astonished that the world pretended to go on without him, and certain it could not. As constantly he was framing new combinations and keeping straight the old. He let not a clue slip from his crippled hands. Throughout the long interval of disgrace he was as active as in his sunniest prosperity, perhaps more so.

An accident freed him in September from actual duress. His disposition of the fleet of which he continued titular 'General,' though Frobisher and Burgh had royal commissions, proved successful. Already a Biscayan of 600 tons burden, the Santa Clara, had been captured and sent to England. This was the prize of which, and its prize crew, Ralegh wrote to the High Admiral. The squadron under Frobisher deceived and perplexed the Spaniards. Sir John Burgh slipped by and made for the Azores. His ships spread themselves six or seven leagues west of Flores. They were disappointed of the Santa Cruz, of 900 tons, which on July 29 her officers burnt. On August 3 the great Crown of Portugal carack, the Madre de Dios, came in sight. Three engaged her, and she was prevented from running ashore. She was of 1600 tons burden, had seven decks, and carried 800 men. The struggle lasted from 10 a.m. to 1 or 2 a.m. next morning. The captors hotly debated their rival merits. Lord Cumberland argued that the Roebuck and Foresight *The Prize.* were both disabled, and that his soldiers boarded and took the ship. Burgh accused Cumberland's people of plundering. All agreed on the magnificence of the prize. Burgh wrote: 'I hope, for all the spoil that has been made, her Majesty shall receive more profit by her than by any ship that ever came into England.' The purser of the Santa Cruz deposed that the Madre de Dios contained precious stones, pearls, amber, and musk worth 400,000 crusados. She brought two great crosses and a jewel of diamonds, presents from the Viceroy to the King. She had 537 tons of spices. The pepper alone was represented by Burleigh as worth £102,000. It fell to the Crown's share. She carried fifteen tons of ebony, beside tapestries, silks, and satins.

After a stormy voyage she reached Dartmouth on September 8. At once the eagles rushed upon the carcase. The ports of arrival looked like Bartholomew Fair, said an eye-witness. The Council ordered the search of all trunks and bundles conveyed from Plymouth or Dartmouth. It sent Robert Cecil post-haste to hinder more plundering. Sir John Hawkins, next chief adventurer after Ralegh, had written already to Burleigh to say that for the partition of the spoil 'Sir Walter Ralegh is the especial man. I see none of so ready a disposition to lay the ground how her Majesty's portion may be increased as he is, and can best bring it about.' Ralegh was permitted to quit the Tower. After a stay of two days in London, he was despatched westwards. He travelled as a State prisoner in charge of a keeper, Blount. As he went, he wrote, on September 17, of London jewellers who had been buying secretly the fine goods: 'If I meet any of them coming up, if it be upon the wildest heath in all the way, I mean to strip them as naked as ever they were born. For it is infinite that her Majesty hath been robbed, and that of the most rare things.' Cecil was in front, and on September 19 reached Exeter. He had turned back all he met on the road from Dartmouth or Plymouth. He could smell them almost; such had been the spoils of amber and musk among them. 'I fear that the birds be flown, for jewels, pearls, and amber; yet I will not doubt but to save her Majesty that which shall be worth the journey. My Lord, there never was such spoil! I will suppress the confluence of the buyers, of which there are above 2000.' He adds: 'I found an armlet of gold, and a fork and spoon of crystal with rubies, which I reserve for the Queen. Her Majesty's captive comes after me, but I have outrid him, and will be at Dartmouth before him.'

At Dartmouth.

Ralegh never grudged praise. He testified freely to Cecil's zeal. He wrote on September 21 from Dartmouth: 'I dare give the Queen £10,000 for that which is gained by Sir Robert Cecil coming down, which I speak without all affection, or partiality, for he hath more rifled my ship than all the rest.' Cecil in turn, though in a more qualified tone, commended Ralegh's exertions, in a very interesting letter to Sir Thomas Heneage: 'Within one half hour Sir Walter Ralegh arrived with his keeper, Mr. Blount. I assure you, Sir, his poor servants, to the number of 140 goodly men, and all the mariners, came to him with shouts of joy; I never saw a man more troubled to quiet them. But his heart is broken, as he is extremely pensive, unless he is busied, in which he can toil terribly. The meeting between him and Sir John Gilbert was with tears on Sir John's part. But he, finding it is known that he has a keeper, whenever he is saluted with congratulations for liberty, doth answer, "No, I am still the Queen of England's poor captive." I wished him to conceal it, because here it doth diminish his credit, which I do vow to you before God is greater among the mariners than I thought for. I do grace him as much as I may, for I find him marvellous greedy to do anything to recover the conceit of his brutish offence.'

Cecil, Raleigh, and William Killigrew were appointed joint commissioners. They examined even Burgh's chests. They paid the mariners their wages. They gave 20*s.* in addition to each from whom they had taken pillage. On

August 27, Ralegh and Hawkins had jointly written to the High Admiral, asking for convoy for the carack. They computed it worth £500,000. About the middle of September Ralegh wrote to Burleigh from the Tower, that its value he estimated at £200,000. It turned out to be £141,000. Whatever it was, the general rule for distributing the value of privateer prizes was a

: *Division of the Spoil.* · third to the owner, a third to the victuallers, a third to the officers and crew. Elizabeth contributed 1100 tons of shipping out of 5000, and £1800 out of £18,000. So she was entitled to a tenth, that is, from £20,000 to £14,000. Ralegh was ready, after negotiation with Sir George Carew, to add £80,000 for the Queen. 'Four score thousand pounds is more than ever a man presented her Majesty as yet. If God have sent it for my ransom, I hope her Majesty of her abundant goodness will accept it. If her Majesty cannot beat me from her affection, I hope her sweet nature will think it no conquest to afflict me.' Finally £36,000 was allowed to Ralegh and Hawkins, who between them had, they said, spent £34,000. To Lord Cumberland, who had spent only £19,000, was awarded £36,000, and £12,000 to the City of London, which had spent £6000. Ralegh, who was, he boasted, 'the greatest adventurer,' grievously complained to Burleigh. He asserted also that, while he had deprived Spain in 1591 of £300,000, he had lost in Lord Thomas Howard's voyage £1600. He reckoned up, besides, the interest he had been paying on £11,000 since the voyage began. The Queen was grasping in such matters. So, too, was her Lord Treasurer. Sir John Fortescue, Chancellor of the Exchequer, had to remonstrate: 'It were utterly to overthrow all service if due regard were not had of my Lord of Cumberland and Sir Walter Ralegh, with the rest of the Adventurers, who would never be induced to further adventure if they were not princely considered of.' He added in a courtly strain: 'And herein I found her Majesty very princely disposed.'

CHAPTER XI.

Ralegh generally could hold his own, even in a bargain with his Queen. In 1592 his hands were tied. He had to use his prize, as he said himself, for his ransom; and it effected his purpose. Once more he was a free man, and he had much to render liberty precious and delightful. He had a bride beautiful, witty, and devoted; and in 1594 a son was born to him, whom he named Walter. He had many pursuits, and wealth which should have been abundant, though all Elizabeth's courtiers were impecunious. An important addition had been made to his possessions shortly before his disgrace. For

Negotiation

for Hayes. some time after his rise he had intended to fix his country residence in Devonshire. He is said to have had a house in Mill-street, Ottery St. Mary. In 1584 he had asked Mr. Duke, of Otterton, to sell him Hayes. His written request, which Aubrey copied, with omissions and inaccuracies due to the creases and stains undergone by the paper through careless handling, is, on uncertain authority, said to have been at one time preserved at the farmhouse. Subsequently, if not from the first, it was kept at the residence of the Duke family, Otterton House, between two and three miles off. Polwhele saw it at Otterton House shortly before 1793. Afterwards it disappeared. Dr. Brushfield found the original, as he believes, at Plymouth, in the 1888 collection of Armada and Elizabethan relics. It is the property of Miss Glubb, of Great Torrington. The letter was written from the Court, on July 26, 1584, by Mr. Duke's 'very willing frinde in all I shal be able, W. Ralegh,' and runs as follows: 'Mr Duke—I wrote to Mr Prideux to move yow for the purchase of hayes a farme som tyme in my fathers possession. I will most willingly geve yow what so ever in your conscience yow shall deeme it worth: and if yow shall att any tyme have occasion to vse mee, yow Shall find mee a thanckfull frind to yow and yours. I have dealt wth Mr Sprinte for suche things as he hathe at colliton and ther abouts and he hath promised mee to dept wth the moety of otertowne vnto yow in consideration of hayes accordinge to the valew, and yow shall not find mee an ill neighbore vnto yow here after. I am resolved if I cannot 'ntreat yow, to build att colliton but for the naturall disposition I have to that place being borne in that howse I had rather seat my sealf ther then any wher els thus leving the matter att large unto Mr Sprint I take my leve resting reedy to countervail all your courteses to the vttermost of my power.'

His offer was not accepted, the Dukes, it is conjectured by Polwhele, not *Colaton Ralegh*, choosing to have so great a man for so near a neighbour. According to a local tradition, he carried out his alternative project of building at Colaton Ralegh, on land which he may be presumed to have bought of his father or eldest brother. In the garden of the Place he is said to have planted, as elsewhere, the first potatoes grown in England. But himself he never rooted there, though he was described as 'of Colaton Ralegh' in a deed of 1588. The royal bounty soon tempted him away; and he sold any property which had entitled him to that designation. The estate of Sherborne, which is inseparably connected with his memory, consisted of an ancient castle and picturesque park, together with several adjacent manors. It had belonged to the see of Salisbury since the time of Bishop Osmund, who cursed all who should alienate it, or profit by its alienation. Ralegh was not deterred by the threat. He is rumoured to have been impressed by the charms of the domain as he rode past it on his journeys from Plymouth to London. Towards the close of 1591 the bishopric of Salisbury, which had been vacant for three years, was filled by the appointment of Dr. Coldwell. Dean Bennett of Windsor, and Dr. Tobias Matthew, or Matthews, afterwards Bishop of Durham and Archbishop of York, father to the wit and letter-writer, Sir Toby, had declined it on account of a condition that the new Bishop must consent to part with Sherborne. Ralegh subsequently declared that he had given the Queen a jewel worth, £250 'to make the Bishop.' He not rarely concerned himself about vacant bishoprics for his own purposes. His present fit of ecclesiastical zeal was explained by Dr. Coldwell's execution of a lease to the Crown in January, 1592, of Sherborne and its dependencies for ninety-nine years. A rent was *Sherborne Castle*. reserved to the see of £260, which, according to the Bishop, was not regularly paid. The Queen at once assigned the lease to Ralegh. The manor of Banwell, which lay conveniently for the property, belonged to the see of Bath and Wells. Elizabeth demanded this of Bishop Godwin. The Bishop in his gouty old age had contracted a marriage which offended the Queen's notions of propriety, with a rich city widow. This was employed as a lever to oblige him to one of the forced exchanges for Crown impropriations which, though not illegal, friends of the Church styled sacrilege. Sir John Harington, Elizabeth's witty godson, writing in the reign of James, is fond of the term. He admits that he himself conveyed one of the sharp messages by which Elizabeth tried to obtain Banwell. Finally a compromise was effected. Godwin courageously clung to Banwell, but redeemed it by the grant in Ralegh's favour of a ninety-nine years' lease of Wilscombe.

Ralegh found occupation at Sherborne. We know something of his life there. We know, though not nearly enough, much more of it than when Gibbon assigned the absence of the 'details of private life' as a principal reason for the abandonment of his original decision to take Ralegh for his literary theme. It was varied and animated. He pursued amusement and business with equal earnestness. In his *Farewell to the Court*, which foreshadows the sentiment of this period, though probably written earlier, he mourns for his 'sweet spring spent,' his 'summer well-nigh done;' but he had energy for other matters than repining at 'joys *Falconry.* expired like truthless dreams.' He built. He planted. He diverted himself with rural pastimes, especially with falconry. Throughout his career he always was ready for a hawking match or a bargain for falcons. He once offered the reversion in fee of an Irish leasehold for a goshawk. An incident of his Munster estate, which doubtless he valued highly, was his title to half the produce of an eyrie of hawks in the wood of Mogelly. Amidst the anxieties of his final expedition he found spirits and strength for a trial of hawks at Cloyne. The leisure and opportunities of Sherborne stimulated his ardour for the sport. Cecil kept falcons. In August 1593, Ralegh wrote to him from Gillingham Forest, of which he and his brother Carew were joint rangers: 'The Indian falcon is sick of the backworm, and therefore, if you will be so bountiful to give another falcon, I will provide you a running gelding.' He chased another sort of game than herons. In April, 1594, he boasted that he had caught in the Lady Stourton's house a notable stout villain, with his copes and bulls. 'He calls himself John Mooney; but he is an Irishman, and, I think, can say much.' Both his wife and he soon grew fond of Sherborne, 'his fortune's fold,' as he called it alike in verse and in a letter of 1593 to Cecil. Thither they always gladly returned, though they were often called elsewhere. The plague dislodged the family in 1594. It was, he wrote in September, 1594, raging in the town of Sherborne 'very hot.' 'Our Bess,' he added, 'is one way sent, her son another way; and I am in great trouble therewith.' Less alarming occasions were constantly taking him away. He had to be in Devonshire and Cornwall, discharging the duties of his Wardenship and Lieutenancy. Every year he went to Bath for the waters. He resorted to Weymouth for sea bathing for his wife and child. He was much at all seasons in London.

Though banished from the Court he went on frequenting its neighbourhood. He had more than one London residence. As a student of the law, he may have lived in Lyon's Inn and the Middle Temple. In the early period of his attendance on the Queen he had been lodged in the Palace, at Greenwich, Whitehall, Somerset House, St. James, and

Richmond. Since 1584 he possessed ⸱ *Durham House.* ⸱ a London house of his own. The Church supplied him, as at Sherborne and Lismore. Durham House, strictly called Duresme Place, was the town house of the see of Durham. It covered nearly the whole site of Adelphi Terrace, and the streets between this and the Strand. In the reign of Edward VI the Crown seized it, and granted it successively to the Princess Elizabeth and to Dudley, Duke of Northumberland. There, the year after Ralegh's birth, Lady Jane Grey had been wedded to Dudley's son. Mary restored it to Bishop Tunstall. Elizabeth resumed it. In 1583 or 1584 she gave the use of a principal part of the spacious mansion to Ralegh. The remainder she permitted Sir Edward Darcy to inhabit. At Durham House the famous Dr. Dee, mathematician, astrologer, and spiritualist, who, in his diary for 1583, mentions him gratefully, records that he dined with him in October, 1593. There he held on various occasions his Court as Lord Warden of the Stannaries, and heard important suits. Aubrey speaks of Ralegh as living there 'when he came to his greatness.' He knew well his study, in a little turret looking over the Thames, with a prospect now, as in Aubrey's day, 'as pleasant perhaps as anything in the world.' Ralegh is reported to have owned other dwellings also in and about London. Probably he already possessed, though, till he left Durham House, he is not likely to have occupied, a house in Broad Street. It may be presumed to have been part of his wife's share in the Throckmorton property. Several residences have been put down to him, without sufficient evidence. Ralegh House, at Brixton Rise, has been assigned to him, in mistake perhaps for his nephew, Captain George Ralegh, who lived in Lambeth parish. Because he visited his wife's relatives at Beddington Park, he is alleged to have occupied the mansion. He is rumoured to have lived at West Horsley, which his son, Carew Ralegh, first acquired in 1643 from the Carews of Beddington. On testimony so far more substantial that Lady Ralegh had inherited a small estate in the parish from her father, he is said to have lived at Mitcham. The house his wife owned seems to have been Ralegh House, at the corner of Wykford Lane, ⸱ *Mile Endand Islington.* ⸱ though two other houses at Mitcham have pretended to the honour. More certainly he lived in a villa at Mile End in 1596. That is known through the entry of the burial at Stepney of a manservant who died at Mile End in 1596, and from the addresses of two letters of his dated within two and four months of the same time. Dr. Brushfield thinks the house may have been hired for a season for the sake of country air. Mile End is described in 1597 as a common where penny-royal grew in great abundance. Ralegh would find its vicinity to Stepney, the general resort of seamen, convenient. The publication of the Middlesex Registers has corroborated the tradition, which gave him a suburban abode at Islington, on a site possibly afterwards occupied by the Pied Bull. For the local belief that he built, or patronized, and smoked in, the Old Queen's Head, Dr. Brushfield considers there is no foundation. His choice of any part of Islington for residence would have been determined by its contiguity to the vast royal chase in which the Queen delighted to hunt. But his occupancy of a house there commenced before the days of his grandeur, and probably had ceased before them.

His dwellings were not more numerous than his avocations. Never was his activity more various than during this interval of royal disfavour. He overflowed with public spirit. He had been sitting in the House of Commons in the spring of 1592. He was a frequent and effective speaker. His voice is reported to have been small. That would be after sickness, toil, and imprisonment had enfeebled him. He omitted no opportunity of proclaiming his hostility to Spain. Before his disgrace he had argued for a declaration of open war. He knew, he said, of many who held it not lawful in conscience, as the time was, to take prize from the Spaniards. Of those weak brethren he was never one. After his liberation from the Tower, when the House met he again attended. He was not so strangely in advance of

his ˙ *In Parliament.* ˙ protectionist age as not to support a Bill for prohibiting

Dutch and German aliens from retailing foreign wares in England. His view of Dutchmen would have satisfied Canning: 'The nature of the Dutchman is to fly to no man but for his profit. They are the people that maintain the King of Spain in his greatness. Were it not for them he were never able to make out such armies and navies by sea.' While politically he was attached to Holland, he was persistently jealous of her commercially. In the next reign he drew up an elaborate plan for abstracting her lucrative carrying trade. On questions of liberty of thought he was far beyond his time. He stoutly opposed a cruel capital measure against the Brownists: 'That law is hard that taketh life, and sendeth into banishment, when men's intentions shall be judged by a jury, and they shall be judges what another means.' He prevailed to have the Bill handed for revision to a Committee of Members. On the Committee his name stands first. His disgrace had left him sufficiently prominent to be thought worth libelling by Robert Parsons the Jesuit, 'Andraeus Philopater.' Parsons described him as keeping a school of atheism, wherein the Old and New Testaments were jested at, and scholars taught to spell God backwards.

In the shade though he was, he would abide no wrong to his official authority. In February, 1592, before his disgrace, he had found leisure in the midst of the preparations for his expedition to reprove the Devon justices of the peace for the application of their 'foreign authority' to compel his tinners to contribute to the repair of a private bridge. Still under a cloud in May, 1594, he was not afraid to protest highly to Lord Keeper Egerton against an encroachment by the Star Chamber on his Stannary jurisdiction. A year later the county magistrates do not seem to have thought his continuing obscuration exonerated them from defending themselves against the charge of 'intermeddling' with his prerogatives. He regarded himself as holding a commission to watch and warn against all danger by sea. In June, 1594, he was informing the Lord High Admiral that Spain had an armed fleet in the Breton ports. He prayed the Admiral to ask her Majesty's leave that his 'poor kinsman' might serve as a volunteer soldier or mariner in an attack upon it. Apparently he had his wish and was allowed to embark. But his advice had been followed tardily. He writes from the Foreland on August 25, that the season was too late. The only hope was that the enemy might approach the Thames. When he was not at sea he was contracting for the victualling and equipment of ships of war. That was *Irish Policy.* among his frequent occupations. At all periods he had his eye upon Ireland. Neither royal coldness nor bodily ailments could force him to be silent on Irish affairs. In May, 1593, sick, and 'tumbled down the hill by every practice,' he would go on exclaiming against the administrative blunders which had let England be baffled and 'beggared' by a nation without fortifications, and, for long, without effective arms. 'The beggarly, the accursed kingdom,' had cost a million not many years since. 'A better kingdom might have been purchased at a less price, and that same defended with as many pence, if good order had been taken.' Though he was not admitted to the Queen's presence, she seems to have read memorials he drew up on the subject of Ireland. It is impossible not to reprobate his sentiments on the treatment of the native Irish. His correspondence with Cecil shows, that he was as willing to connive at their treacherous murder as other contemporary English statesmen, though not Burleigh, or perhaps Burleigh's son. But he believed honestly in the rectitude of his doctrines. He was patriotic in insisting upon their application for the benefit of a Government which, he thought, persecuted him. It may even be acknowledged that the resolute and consistent despotism he advocated might have been more tolerable, as well as more successful, than the spasmodic and fitful violence which discredited the Irish policy of the reign. He was indisputably right in condemning a system under which the island was 'governed neither as a country conquered nor free.'

CHAPTER XII.

GUIANA (1594-1595).

Continuance of Disgrace.

Had not history preserved the memory of Ralegh's exile from Court, his public life was so animated that the displeasure of the Queen need hardly have been remarked. To himself the blight on his prospects was always and dismally visible. The Queen had raised him from obscurity, and afforded his genius scope for shining. Well as he understood the value of his powers, he knew they derived still from her, as ten or a dozen years before, their opportunity of exercise. He was not blind to the jealousy of competitors, or to popular odium. As by an instinct of life, of the working life which alone he prized, he was continually striving to retrieve his fall by the ordinary devices of courtiers, and not without gleams of hope. Nicholas Faunt had been private secretary to Walsingham, and was therefore naturally of the Essex faction. He wrote to Anthony Bacon in January, 1594, that Ralegh was expecting to be nominated a Privy Councillor: 'And it is now feared of all honest men that he shall presently come to the Court; yet it is well withstood. God grant him some further resistance!' The further resistance came, whether from rivals, or from the rankling anger in Elizabeth's breast. Nowhere does it appear that he had speech of her. He continued to be forbidden to perform in person the duties of Captain of the Guard. Between 1592 and 1597 they seem to have been discharged by John Best, described as Champion of England. His disappointment was fortunate for his fame, if not for his future tranquillity. In his enforced retirement he brooded on schemes of maritime adventure. He determined to prove the impossibility of suppressing him. His Panama project had been imputed to his discovery that 'the Queen's love was beginning to decline.' That could not then have been truly asserted. Naunton has similarly explained the

Guiana expedition:—'Finding his favour declining, he undertook A

Project, andits Motive. a new peregrination to leave that terra infirma of the Court for that of the wars, and by declining himself, and by absence, to expel his and the passion of his enemies; which in Court was a strange device of recovery, but that he knew there was some ill office done him, that he durst not attempt to mend any other ways than by going aside, thereby to teach envy a new way of forgetfulness, and not so much as to think of him; howsoever, he had it always in mind never to forget himself;

and his device took so well, that, at his return, he came in, as rams do by going backwards, with the greater strength; and so continued to the last in the Queen's grace.' Nothing, it is certain, ever was farther from Ralegh's thoughts than a wish to be forgotten, whether by enemies or by friends; yet Naunton's theory is true at bottom. The persistency of the shadow at Court was as plain to Ralegh as to others. Its own merits might else have recommended to him the Guiana expedition. But at this especial juncture it was his engine for storming his way back into his Sovereign's kindness.

Guiana had one important merit as a field for enterprise. It was known to be free from European occupation, as well as reputed to be rich. Camden describes it as 'aurifera Guiana ab Hispanis decantata.' Many Spanish expeditions, from the year 1531 onwards, had been fitted out to find the King el Dorado, who loved to anoint his body with turpentine, and then roll in gold dust. Neither he nor his city, called by the same name, had been discovered. Attempts to penetrate into the interior had all failed. The Indians were warlike and united; the country was a jungle, environed with vast waters not easily navigated; and the invaders had quarrelled among themselves. The latest effort had been made in 1582 by Don Antonio de Berreo. Berreo was son-in-law to Quesada, who had annexed New Grenada to ⌐ *Difficulties.* ⌐ Spain. Berreo alleged that he spent 300,000 ducats, and journeyed 1500 miles, before he arrived within Guiana. He seems never to have actually entered. From a tribe on the confines he received gifts of gold images and ornaments which he sent to King Philip by his officer Domingo de Vera. But other Indians on the borders blocked further progress by firing the savannahs. He was forced to retire to Trinidad, of which he was appointed Governor. From Trinidad he concerted raids on the mainland. One of his captains ascended the Orinoko for some distance, and on April 23, 1593, took formal possession of the country for Spain. Ralegh's own subsequent experience proved that individual Spaniards had stolen in, searching for gold. He questioned seamen who had been in or near this wonderful land. He studied every published narrative which touched upon it. A treatise, never printed, and now lost, which he had himself composed on the West Indies, may have embodied the results of his enquiries. The information he collected filled him at once with admiration for the invincible constancy, as he described it, of the Spaniards, and with hatred of their rapacity and cruelty. He abhorred their barbarous treatment of the native owners of the New World. As always, he could not comprehend by what right they claimed a monopoly of its sovereignty for themselves against the rest of Europe.

Lady Ralegh perceived the bent of his thoughts. She wrote in February, 1594, to invoke the aid of Cecil, in diverting her husband from the perilous temptation. I reproduce her letter in the original spelling: 'I hope for my sake you will rather draw sur watar towardes the est then heulp hyme forward touard the soonsett, if ani respecke to me or love to him be not forgotten. But everi monthe hath his flower and everi season his contentement, and you greate counselares ar so full of new councels as you are steddi in nothing; but wee poore soules that hath bought sorrow at a high price desiar, and can be plesed with, the same misfortun wee hold, fering alltarracions will but multiply misseri, of wich we have allredi felte sufficiant. I knoo unly your parswadcions ar of efecke with him, and hild as orrekeles tied to them by Love; therfore I humbelle besiech you rathar stay him then furdar him. By the wich you shall bind me for ever. As yet you have ever geveng me caus.'

If Cecil tried dissuasion, he did not succeed. In the course of 1594 Ralegh sent out as a pioneer his 'most valiant and honest' old officer, Captain Whiddon, to explore the Orinoko and gather information. Whiddon sailed to Trinidad. There Berreo received him amicably, as it seemed, though Whiddon thought the imprisonment of some of his crew implied treachery. Berreo, with the assistance of de Vera in Spain, was promoting an expedition of his own, and was not likely to be communicative. Whiddon was back before 1595. *A Royal Commission.* Ralegh forthwith began preparations for an expedition to be conducted by himself. He procured a Royal Commission to 'our servant Sir Walter Ralegh,' neither 'trusty' nor 'well-beloved,' to offend and enfeeble the King of Spain and his subjects in his dominions to the uttermost; to discover and subdue heathen lands not in the possession of any Christian prince, nor inhabited by any Christian people; to resist and expel by force of arms all persons who should attempt to settle within 200 leagues of the place where he or his people might fix their habitations within the six following years; and to capture all ships trading within the limits aforesaid. He speedily equipped several ships. The cost was such that, as he said at his trial, if he had died in Guiana, he had not left 300 marks a year to his wife and son. Captain Laurence Keymis was in command of a galley. Captain Whiddon sailed again, to his grave as it happened in Trinidad. Believers in Ralegh assisted. Thus, the High Admiral lent the Lion's Whelp, which Anthony Wells King commanded. Two barks joined the expedition, one under Captain Crosse, the other under Captain Caulfield. There were 100 officers, gentlemen volunteers, and soldiers. In the number was John Gilbert, Sir Humphrey's son. He was a close ally of Ralegh's in maritime adventures, notwithstanding occasional disagreement on their respective proportions of the profits. Cecil contributed money. Two ships, under Captains Amias Preston and Sommers, or Summers, which were expected to unite in the undertaking, never came. The squadron when collected was detained by contrary winds. Ralegh boasted to Cecil that he was indifferent to good fortune or adversity. But in another letter he confessed: 'This wind breaks my heart.' The delay was the more exasperating that other ships had run out, 'bound to the wars, a multitude going for the Indies.' He was afraid the chiefest places of his enterprise might be attempted, and he should be undone. Others would reap no advantage; for he knew 'they would be beaten, and do no good.'

The Voyage.

However, at last, on February 6, 1595, he was off. He had bequeathed to Cecil the charge of staying litigation against him. He was especially afraid of a suretyship suit instituted by Widow Smith. The widow 'hath a son that waits on the keeper, and a daughter married to Mr. Wilkes, so it will be harder to clear.' He captured a Spanish ship at the Canaries with firearms, and a Fleming with wine. At Teneriffe he paused in vain for Preston and Sommers. They had assumed that he would have quitted Teneriffe before they could arrive. At least that was their explanation. So they were gone on an adventure of their own. Finally Ralegh set sail. He reached Trinidad on March 22. He stayed a month for the Lion's Whelp, and also for Preston and Sommers. He employed his leisure in a careful survey of the coast. On the shore he found clumps of mangroves bearing oysters. He satisfied his mind that the Indian fig-tree is not the Tree of Knowledge, its only fruit being oysters, which adhere to its pendulous fibres. Terrible tales were told him of the Spanish habit of chaining and torturing native chiefs. He heard also that five months before Berreo had sent to Spain for reinforcements. It seemed dangerous to leave an enemy behind him. He had, moreover, a grievance for the maltreatment of Whiddon's men the year before. A combination of motives induced him to lead a hundred of his company in a night attack on Berreo's new city of St. Joseph. By dawn he took it. He burnt it down, having first released from a dungeon five caciques fastened together with a single chain. The proceeding was high-handed and summary. Now it would be criminal. It did not bear that character then. Lingard has stigmatised Ralegh as a murderer, on account of the Spanish lives lost during the assault. Berreo and the Spanish Government were less particular. They saw nothing in his conduct adverse to the laws of war and nations. If their soldiers had arrived in time, they would have anticipated him in the aggression. Throughout this whole period Spaniards and Englishmen, on the ocean and in the Indies, fought or fought not, as suited not merely their mutual, but their several, convenience. *Capture of Berreo.*

Neither side held it treachery to be assailed without a solemn declaration of war. Berreo, as there is no real reason to doubt, though Southey has questioned it, was captured in the town. Ralegh speaks of him as a well descended gentleman, of great assuredness, and of a great heart. He had his defects. He tortured natives, and was so ignorant as not to know east from west. These blemishes of feeling and education did not prevent Ralegh from behaving as a polished English gentleman to a polished Spanish hidalgo. They lived together in great amity, and conversed much. Berreo was so far from showing rancour that he told all he knew of previous attempts upon Guiana. He did not under-rate the difficulties, partly because he had reason to believe in them, partly from a wish to put his captor off a project he hoped hereafter to accomplish himself. Among other impediments to an entrance he mentioned that the main land was 600 miles farther from the sea than Whiddon had understood it to be. Ralegh concealed the disquieting fact from his men.

He assembled a conclave of island chiefs. His Sovereign, a virgin Queen, he informed them, had commissioned him to free them from the Castilian yoke. Then he set forth from Curiapan in an old gallego boat cut down to draw but five feet of water. It was fitted with banks of oars. Sixty officers and gentlemen volunteers embarked with him. A boat, two wherries, and a barge carried forty more. They were victualled for a month. The ships anchored near los Gallos in the Gulf of Paria. Twenty miles of sea were

A Maze of Waters. crossed 'in a great billow' to Guanipa Bay, where dwelt savages who shot poisoned arrows. Then the expedition was entangled in a labyrinth of rivers. These were the eight branches of the Orinoko. 'All the earth,' wrote Ralegh, 'doth not yield the like confluence of streams.' That is hardly an exaggeration statement about the Orinoko, which is fed by more than 436 rivers, and a couple of thousand rivulets. A young Indian pilot, whom Ralegh had brought, named Ferdinando, became bewildered. The boats might have wandered a whole year had not, partly by force, and partly by good treatment, the services of an old native been secured. Though often sorely perplexed, he piloted them along a succession of narrow reaches of the Caño Manamo. By Ralegh's orders he and the other Indian promised an outlet by every next day, to cheer the crews. All were, however, on the verge of utter despair, when suddenly the tangled thickets on the banks opened up into a lovely champaign country. It was a paradise of birds and beasts. The turf was diversified by groves of trees, disposed in order as if by all the art and labour in the world. Still as the oarsmen rowed the deer came down feeding by the water's side, as if they had been used to a keeper's call. On an excursion off the route they were following they overtook two canoes laden with bread. Among the bushes they found a refiner's basket. In it were quicksilver and saltpetre, prepared for assay, and the dust of ore which had been refined. It belonged to some Spaniards who escaped; but the natives, their companions, were caught. One of them, called Martino, proved a better pilot than Ferdinando and the old man.

Naturally the refining apparatus suggested a hunt after gold. Ralegh was of a different opinion. The attempt, he considered, would give notice to other nations of the riches of the country. To the present expedition it could not have been very profitable from lack of tools. He had no mind to dig with his nails. Had he wanted gold he might, he says, have obtained much in actual bullion from the Indians. But he 'shot at another mark than present profit.' He decided to advance, his men being of good courage, and crying out to go on, they cared not how far.

On the fifteenth day they discovered afar the Guiana mountains. Towards evening they entered the main channel of the Orinoko. No Englishman had preceded them. Consequently Captain Keymis afterwards re-named the river, after his commander, Raleana. Now they were in a more populous region. But the natives did not obstruct their advance. Ralegh had the art of impressing them with faith and admiration. Hard as it was, he hindered his

Friendly Chiefs. men from robbing the villagers, insulting their women, or,

like the Spaniards in Peru, ransacking their hallowed graves for treasure. A border prince, Toparimaca, regaled Ralegh's captains with pine-apple wine till some of them were 'reasonable pleasant.' He also lent his elderly brother for pilot. Under his guidance a branch of the river, edged with rocks of a blue colour, like steel ore, was explored. On the right bank were seen the plains of the Sayma, reaching to Cumana and Caraccas, 120 leagues to the north. There dwelt the black smooth-haired Aroras, accustomed to use poisoned arrows. No Spaniard knew how to cure hurts from urari, which seems to be strychnine. 'Yet they taught me,' writes Ralegh, 'the best way of healing as well this as all other poisons.' Humboldt speaks of the Guaikas, who still use poisoned darts, and by the terror of them have repelled intruders.

On they voyaged as far as Aromaia and its port, Morequito, 300 miles from the sea. Here Ralegh was visited by wise Topiowari, King of Aromaia, 110 years old. His nephew and predecessor, Morequito, had been murdered by the Spaniards. He himself had been dragged for seventeen days in a chain, like a dog, till he ransomed himself with a hundred plates of gold and several chains of spleen stones. The old chief, who walked to and fro, twenty-eight miles, brought a present of flesh, fish, fowl, Guiana pine-apples, the prince of fruits, declares Ralegh, bread, wine, parakeets, and an armadillo, which Ralegh afterwards ate. Ralegh told him he had been sent by his Queen to deliver the Indians from Spanish tyranny. Thence he would have ascended the Caroni, but his men could not row a stone's throw in an hour. So he pushed on by land to view the falls, ten or a dozen in number, each as high above the other as a church tower. Deer flitted across every path. Birds at evening sang a thousand different tunes. Cranes and herons, white, crimson, carnation, perched on the banks. Fresh easterly breezes blew. Every stone they stooped to take up promised either gold or silver by its complexion. A Captain George, who had been captured with Berreo, had told them a rich silver mine was near the Caroni. Topiowari's only son, Caworako, informed him of the Carolians. He said they were foes to the Spaniards. They had a feud also with the Epirumei, subjects of the Inca of Manoa, who abounded in gold. The Carolians and three tribes at the head of _Indigenous Marvels._ the Caroni, he asserted, would help Ralegh against both Spain and the Inca. He spoke too of the Ewaipanomas, with eyes in their shoulders and mouths in their breasts, living on the Caora. He was sure of the eyes and mouths, for they had lately fought and slain many hundreds of his father's people. Ralegh vouches neither for the Amazons in the province of Topago, nor for these Ewaipanomas, 'For my part I saw them not, but am resolved that so many people did not all combine, or forethink to make the report.' Nineteen years later he took occasion in his History to justify by the Greek belief in Amazons 'mine own relation of them, which was held for vain and improbable.'

By this time the summer was over. Winter in the Tropics is the rainy season. It shows itself less by any sensible change of vegetation than by floods, gusts, thunder and lightning. The streams rose and raged; the men were wetted to the skins ten times a day, and had no dry clothes to put on. The fleet was some hundred miles away. Ralegh set his face homewards. The boats glided down the Orinoko at a rate, though against the wind, of little less than 100 miles a day. On his arrival at Morequito Topiowari came on a parting visit. He brought a plentiful supply of provisions, which Ralegh bought at fair prices. Every day, said the old man, had death called for him; but he was animated by a sagacious anxiety for his country, which the Spaniards threatened. Ralegh's noble courtesy was as unstinted to the patriarchal savage as to the Queen of England. He had infused the like temper into his officers, and Topiowari's confidence was won. Already they had talked freely on the politics and nature of Guiana, and how to obtain access to its heart. Now the chief definitely offered to join in a march upon golden Manoa if Ralegh would leave fifty Englishmen to defend him from the vengeance of the Inca and Spain. Ralegh was timid for his men. He

Sparrow and Goodwin. compromised by engaging to return next year. Topiowari sent with him his son, who was christened in England Gualtero. Ralegh left in Aromaia Francis Sparrow, or Sparrie, to sketch and describe the country and travel to Manoa with merchandise. Sparrow trafficked in Indian slaves. At last the Spaniards captured him and forwarded him to Spain, from which he made his way home in 1602. A boy, Hugh Goodwin,

remained by his own wish to learn the language. Ralegh found him at
Caliana in 1617. He had almost forgotten his native tongue. When these
arrangements were being made Ralegh steadfastly purposed to come back
shortly. For the moment his plan rather was to lay the foundation of
friendships, and to acquire information, than to conquer territory or open
mines. For example, he gave away, he states, more money's worth in gold
guineas than he received in gold plates. He had seen enough to be
persuaded the region was a land of gold. He was shown specimens of gold
wrought by the Epirumei, and the process had been explained to him. In
Aromaia itself he observed all the hills spread with stones of the colour of
gold and silver. At first he had conjectured they were marquesite. He tested
them and ascertained they were *el madre del oro*. Where that is, the presence
of gold below was supposed to be indicated. He remarked also the outside
of many mines of white spar, from which he drew as flattering a
conclusion.

From Aromaia a cacique Putijma accompanied him towards Mount
Iconuri, which *Keymis's Gold Mine.* contained a gold mine. 'Being a very
ill footman,' he soon gave in. He sent Keymis on, arranging that they
should meet at the Cumaca. Putijma conducted Keymis to the mine. On his
own route Ralegh passed many rocks like gold ore, a round mountain of
mineral stone, and a mountain of crystal. The crystal mountain he did not
find crowned with the diamond, which, according to Berreo, blazed afar.
Its true diadem was a mighty river, rushing down with a noise as of a
thousand enormous jangling bells. Near Mount Roraima the natives were
solemnizing a festival, 'all as drunk as beggars.' They pressed upon the
strangers abundance of delicate pine-apple wine. On the Cumaca Keymis
rejoined Ralegh. They bade adieu to sorrowing Putijma. They were
themselves downcast. 'Their hearts were cold to behold the great rage and
increase of Orinoko,' 'the sea without a shore,' as Humboldt has termed its
mouth. The Caño Manamo too, by which they had entered Guiana, was
now violently in flood. They had to follow the Capuri branch. At its mouth
a fierce gale was blowing, and the galley was near sinking. Ralegh,
embarking in his barge with Gifford, Caulfield, and his cousin, Grenville,
thrust into the sea at midnight. The galley he left to come by day. 'Thus,
faintly cheering one another in show of courage, it pleased God about nine
o'clock the next morning we descried the Isle of Trinidad.' The ships were
riding at anchor at Curiapan on the south-west of the island. 'Never was
there to us a more joyful sight.' Only one man had perished, a very proper
young negro, who, leaping into the river of Lagartos to swim, was instantly
devoured before them all by a crocodile. The rest, in spite of wet, heat,
want of sleep, clean clothes, and shelter, and a diet of rotting fruit,
crocodile, sea-cow, tapir, and armadillo, all survived. They had suffered

from no pestilence. Schomburgk thinks Ralegh coloured too highly the mineral riches of Guiana. He attests the veracity of the praises both of its prodigious vegetable and animal fruitfulness, and of its healthiness away from the malaria of the coast. His opinion was formed on an experience of eight years of exploration.

Voyage Homewards.

Ralegh had intended to sail to Virginia, and endeavour to relieve his settlers. Extremity of weather forced him to abandon the design. He demanded supplies at Cumana, where he left Berreo, at St. Mary's, and at Rio de la Hacha. Being refused them, he sacked and burnt all three. Incidentally he mentions that he found 'not a real of plate.' But he had punished the settlements for their churlishness, not for the sake of booty. He did not care to look out for spoil. 'It would have sorted ill,' he wrote, 'with the offices of honour which by her Majesty's grace I hold this day in England, to run from cape to cape for the pillage of ordinary prizes.' On July 13, off Cuba, Preston and Sommers met, as states their chronicler, the Honourable Knight Sir Walter Ralegh returning from his painful and happy discovery of Guiana, and his surprise of the Isle of Trinidad. Their two ships and his three remained in company for twenty days. In August, 1595, he is understood to have been back in England, 'a beggar,' as he expressed it, 'and withered.' His wife had been watching over his interests. Her letter to Cecil of March 20, 1595, is pleasantly characteristic. She explained in it her urgency in a suit against Lord Huntingdon: 'I rather choose this time to follow it in Sir Walter's absence, that myself may bear the unkindness, and not he.' The subject of the proceedings was a refusal by the Earl to surrender for Ralegh's use Lady Ralegh's portion, which was in his hands, and had become payable through her mother's death.

The return did not excite much popular sensation. Cecil seems to have doubted the genuineness or value of the minerals. He cannot have profited by his investment in the adventure, and was not disposed to be fervent in its praise. Hakluyt remarks how careful the cold Secretary of State was not to be overtaken with any partial affection for the planting of Guiana. Even in Devonshire there seem to have circulated 'slanderous and scoffing speeches touching Sir Walter's late occasion at sea.' His enemies before he went predicted he would never return, but would become 'a servant to the Spanish King.' Now that he was back, they depreciated the importance of the enterprise, and especially his part in it. Very absurdly they contended that he was too easeful and sensual to have undertaken a journey of so great travail, and had been hiding in Cornwall. Some gold he had helped to dig out with his own dagger. A London alderman persuaded an officer of the Mint to report this worthless; but Westwood, a refiner of Wood Street, and Dulmar Dimoke, and Palmer, Controllers of the Mint, pronounced it very rich. Calumniators, taking up a different position, alleged that the whole had been imported from Barbary into Guiana. Ralegh himself wrote to Cecil on November 21, 1595: 'What becomes of Guiana I much desire to hear, *Ralegh's Book on Guiana.* whether it pass for a history or a fable.' He had to take pen in hand, and defend himself from slanders by his *Discovery of the large, rich, and beautiful Empire of Guiana, with a relation of the great and golden city of Manoa.* The volume was published in 1596, with a grateful dedication to his friends in adversity, his kinsman, the Lord Admiral, and Cecil. Hume characterizes the account as 'full of the grossest and most palpable lies.' The sole apparent ground for the accusation is that Ralegh quoted Indian tales of strange creatures, giving the Indian narrators as his authorities. It is not necessary to deny that he may have been prone to believe in them too. The legend of a nation of Amazons is of venerable antiquity. His was an age of faith in portents, in witches, and wizards. If he did not sternly refuse credence even to the shoulder-eyed Ewaipanomas, it must be remembered that a world of 'stranger things than are to be seen between London and Staines,' as he has said, was being opened up to wondering Europe. Ralegh's personal evidence, as I have mentioned, Schomburgk has tested; and he certifies that it is not open to Hume's condemnation. *Vindication of his Veracity.* Humboldt concurs. In particular, the geographical knowledge exhibited in Ralegh's narrative has been proved to be, for the period, curiously wide and accurate. His observations on the natural phenomena of the region are equally faithful and sagacious. The trust he reposed in its metallic riches is being now demonstrated to have been more solidly founded than even Sir Robert Schomburgk thought it. International disputes have recently arisen out of the discovery of gold in the country still known as Guiana. Of the gold field in Venezuela, which was comprised in Ralegh's Guiana, a Government Inspector of Mines stated in 1889 that he believed we had in it Sir Walter's el Dorado itself.

Contemporaries were captivated by the charm of the narrative. It suffered from no dearth of readers at home. Abroad it was admired almost more warmly. Four German editions appeared between 1599 and 1602, the first three being published at Nuremberg. It was translated into Dutch in 1598, and again in 1605, 1617, 1707, 1727, and 1747. Latin versions were issued at Nuremberg and Frankfort in 1599. Ralegh's comrade, Keymis, glorified the author and discoverer in Latin verse. George Chapman sang the exploit in English. The Queen continued obdurate. Ralegh's friends in vain interceded for his recall to Court. In vain he waited for a summons, 'living about London,' as was said in December, 1595, perhaps at Mitcham or Mile End, 'very gallant.' He would not have minded his toil had it brought his pardon. If he could thereby have appeased the Queen's 'so powerful displeasure,' he would for a year more have 'held fast his soul in his teeth.' But he imagined himself not at all advanced towards forgiveness by his feat. Elizabeth, he complained, persisted in 'the ungrateful custom of making one failing eclipse the merit of many virtuous actions.' Personal resentment, he supposed, closed her ears to his eloquent entreaties that she should keep a small army afoot in Guiana marching towards Manoa. In that event, he was certain, the Inca would yield to her Majesty so many hundred thousand pounds yearly as should both defend her from all enemies abroad and defray all expenses at home. She would have the means of foiling the wiles by which, through his American gold, Philip 'crept into councils, and set loyalty at liberty in the greatest monarchies.' Guiana contained, he asserted, all things precious. Its lord would possess as many diamonds *The Gold of Guiana.* as the princes of India, and more gold, a more beautiful empire, more cities and people than either the King of Spain or the Great Turk. He understood the temper of his age. He was aware that 'where there is store of gold, it is in effect needless to remember other commodities for trade.' Therefore he dilated on the gold and diamonds of Guiana rather beyond measure, though not without reason. But he had a quick eye for its other and more permanent advantages. Throughout his career, to its end, and in all his writings, he differed from other Elizabethan statesmen and explorers in regarding war with Spain not merely in its retaliatory, defensive, and plundering aspects, but as a means of enlarging the national boundaries. He desired to endow England with a colonial empire. He pointed out that the new country had everything which could render it habitable for Europeans. It was only a six weeks' voyage from England. It was free from white occupants, and had escaped spoliation. It was a region in which, he was convinced, Englishmen could thrive and be happy. With his military instinct he had truly discerned how easily it might be guarded by a couple of forts on sites commanding the entrance into the Orinoko.

He trusted she who was the lady of ladies would be inspired to accept the direct dominion. If not, he was ready to judge those men worthy to be its kings who by her grace and leave should undertake the task of themselves. Unlicensed Undertakers were not wanting, much to his disgust. He wrote to Cecil in November, 1595, that he heard Mr. Dudley and others were sending ships. He besought that none be suffered to soil the enterprise, and that *Spanish Plantation of San Thome.* he should be thought worthy to govern the country he had discovered. The whole duty of sovereignty properly, he held, appertained to the State. If it could not afford the requisite funds, he expounded in an unpublished essay how a few hundred English artificers might teach the Indians to arm themselves against the Spaniards. By an able and generous argument he reconciled the indefeasible right of the natives to their territory with the industrial colony he was planning. As the State could in no shape be induced to interest itself, he maintained the English connexion with Guiana at his private charge. In the January of 1596 he despatched Keymis with the Darling and Discovery. They were laden with merchandise to comfort and assure the people that they should not yield to any composition with other nations. Burleigh and Robert Cecil were joint adventurers with Ralegh. Burleigh advanced £500, and his son lent a new ship bravely furnished. Keymis learnt they had been forestalled. King Philip, perturbed by the tidings of Ralegh's enterprise, had granted Berreo's application by de Vera for troops. On May 16, 1595, before Ralegh's own return, Sir John Gilbert heard from a Frenchman that the King had sent forces to el Dorado. A powerful force for the conquest of Manoa arrived in Trinidad in 1596. Finally, it is true, the majority miserably perished, and the expedition effected nothing. But a village had already been planted near the port of Topiowari, who, Keymis heard, was dead. This settlement, known as San Thome, Santo Thomè, San Tomè, Santo Tomas, or St. Thomas, did not owe its actual beginning to Berreo. It was first founded by Jesuits in 1576, close to the confluence of the Caroni and Orinoko. At the period of Ralegh's voyage it had become deserted. Berreo reoccupied the site; and Keymis found the mouth of the Caroni blocked, and guarded by a battery. 'Thus,' wrote Lady Ralegh indignantly to Cecil, on Keymis's return, Ralegh being away in Spain, 'you hear your poor absent friend's fortune, who, if he had been as well credited in his reports and knowledges as it seemeth the Spaniards were, they had not now been

possessors of that place.' Keymis had to alter *Another of Keymis's Gold Mines.* his route. His passage to the mine from which the ores and white stones had been taken the year before was intercepted. He went in the direction of Mount Aio. Putijma had pointed out a gold mine in that neighbourhood to a pilot. Even this mine, however, he did not actually reach, though he was within fifteen miles of it. He was afraid, he said, that he and his men might be cut off in the attempt, and the secret of the treasure be buried with them.

He was content to foster the amity of the Indians, to remark additional signs of gold and spleen stones, and to discover above fifty fresh rivers and tribes. After an absence of five months, he arrived off Portland at the end of June. In a published narrative of his expedition he apologised for having emptied Ralegh's purse in the prosecution of patriotic designs thwarted by 'envy and private respects.'

CHAPTER XIII.

CADIZ. THE ISLANDS VOYAGE. (1596-1597).

Ralegh, like his wife and Keymis, may have thought his labour and his money thrown away. They had not been. Guiana, after all, rehabilitated him. His advice that England should not let herself be constrained to a defensive war by the power of the Indian gold of Spain, was followed. Again he emerged into official prominence as a warrior. He had never ceased to carry himself as one who owed it to the State to counsel and to lead. In November, 1595, he was warning Cecil of a fleet of sixty sail preparing in *A Policy of Offence.* Spain for Ireland. He was urging the necessity for the quality, 'not plentiful in Ministers,' of despatch. 'Expedition in a little is better than much too late. If we be once driven to the defensive, farewell might.' Within the same month he was admonishing the Council by letter of the imminent danger of a Spanish invasion of England from Brittany. Disasters themselves favoured his advice and projects. An expedition conducted by Hawkins and Drake against Panama had been unsuccessful. The commanders died, Hawkins in November, 1595, Drake in the next January; both, Ralegh has written, broken-hearted from disappointment and vexation. Spain was encouraged by the failure. A Spanish league with the Earl of Tyrone frightened and exasperated Elizabeth. She equipped ninety-six sail, and the Dutch added twenty-four. They carried 14,000 Englishmen, 1000 being gentlemen volunteers, and 2600 Dutchmen.

Lord Admiral Howard and Essex were joint Generals. They had a council of *Distribution of Commands.* war of five members. Lord Thomas Howard and Ralegh served for the seas. Sir Francis Vere and Sir Coniers Clifford represented the troops. The fifth on the council was Sir George Carew. All five were charged, as they would answer before God, to give their counsels to both Generals without any private respect to either, for love or fear. The English fleet was divided into four squadrons. Ralegh commanded twenty-two ships, manned by 1352 mariners and 1875 soldiers. As usually happened, the expedition was detained by cross weather, which caused Ralegh, he declared, deeper grief than he ever felt for anything of this world. His anguish did not wholly occupy him. Some of his enforced leisure he employed in petitioning for the appointment to the bishoprics of Lismore and Waterford of the very learned Hugh Broughton. The ground partly was the comfort Broughton would be to all the English nation thereabouts. Partly, he wished to requite old Archbishop Magrath, who was usurping the two sees, for having dealt badly with him touching divers leases and lands. He was less successful in pleading for learning than for folly. Broughton was not given the mitre. But four years later Cecil, writing to Carew of a nominee for the Kerry Bishopric, described him significantly as 'another manner of man than Sir Walter Ralegh's last silly priest.' Now Ralegh was busy also begging a grant of 'concealed lands' in Ireland for a former servant, and an Exeter prebend for Mr. William Hilliard. He was inducing Cecil to be 'bound for me for the £500, which I stand in danger to the Widow Smith for.' At last the wind became more accommodating. Ralegh, whom carping gouty Anthony Bacon pretended to suspect of having contributed to the delay from underhand motives, collected the truant ships and seamen. On June 1, 1596, the armament quitted Plymouth.

Until the fleet was at sea its destination had been kept secret. On June 20 it anchored half a league from Cadiz. A council was held from which Ralegh was absent, being engaged in intercepting runaway Spanish ships. It was resolved to attack the town first. On his return, he found Essex in the act of putting soldiers in boats on a stormy sea. One barge had sunk. First he dissuaded the Earl from prosecuting that plan. Next, he won over the Lord Admiral. When he came back from Howard's ship, crying out 'Entramos!

Ralegh's Strategy. Entramos!' Essex in exultation threw his plumed hat into the water. Again by Ralegh's counsels, the attack was postponed till the morning for the sake of the light. He drew up a scheme of operations and sent it to the Lord Admiral, who and Essex, he says, were willing to be 'advised by so mean an understanding.' His project was to batter the galleons first, and to appoint to each two great fly-boats to board afterwards. The Generals were to stay with the main body of the fleet. Ralegh obtained permission to lead the van in the Warspright, which had a crew of 290. He was to be seconded by five other ships. Carew commanded the Mary Rose, named after the ill-fated ship which foundered at Portsmouth in the presence of Henry the Eighth, with its crew and captain, another Sir George Carew, the present George's cousin. Marshal Vere was in the Rainbow, Southwell in the Lion, Conyers Clifford in the Dreadnought, and Lord Thomas Howard in the Nonparilla. An anonymous contemporary writer, supposed to be Sir William Monson, who, it must be admitted, says little of Ralegh's extraordinary prominence in the action, states that Lord Thomas Howard challenged the leadership of the van by right of his place as Vice-Admiral, and was granted it. Ralegh was in this, at all events, not to be thwarted.

At dawn he started, well in advance of all. Thereupon the St. Philip, St. Matthew, St. Andrew, and St. Thomas, all mighty galleons, sailed into the strait of the harbour towards Puerto Real. They moored under the fort of Puntal, with a fringe of galleys, three about each, to assist. The Warspright was cannonaded on her way by the fort and by the galleys, which she esteemed but as wasps in respect of the powerfulness of the others. She made no answer except by 'a blare with a trumpet to each discharge.' Sailing on she anchored close against the St. Philip and St. Andrew, the biggest ships in the Spanish navy. They had overpowered Grenville's ship at the Azores. Ralegh determined 'to be revenged for the Revenge, or to second her with mine own life.' He at once cannonaded them while waiting for the

The Attack. fly-boats, which were to board. The five supporting ships were at hand, but behind. Essex in his flagship now came up. He was eager to join, and anchored beside him. After a struggle of three hours the Warspright was near sinking. Ralegh was rowed to Essex's ship. He told the Earl he meant, in default of the fly-boats, to board from his ship: 'To burn or sink is the same loss; and I must endure one or the other.' 'I will second you upon my honour,' cried Essex. Ralegh, on his return after a quarter of an hour's absence, found that the Nonparilla and the Rainbow had headed the Warspright. Thomas Howard had on board his ship the Lord Admiral. Nevertheless, Ralegh would not yield precedence, 'holding mine own reputation dearest, and remembering my great duty to her Majesty.' Determined to be 'single in the head of all,' he pushed between the Nonparilla and Rainbow, and 'thrust himself athwart the channel, so as I was sure none should outstart me again for that day.' Vere pulled the Rainbow close up by a hawser he had ordered to be fastened to the Warspright's side. But Ralegh's sailors cut it; and back slipped into his place the Marshal, 'whom,' writes Ralegh, 'I guarded, all but his very prow, from the sight of the enemy.' At length he proceeded to grapple the St. Philip. His companions were following his example, when a panic seized the Spaniards. All four galleons slipped anchor, and tried to run aground, 'tumbling into the sea heaps of soldiers, so thick as if coals had been poured out of a sack.' The St. Matthew and the St. Andrew, of ten to twelve hundred tons burden, were captured before there was time for their officers to burn them. In his wonderfully vivid letter, undated and unaddressed, known as *A Relation of Cadiz Action*, he does not name the captor. But a note in his own hand, in his copy of a French account, *Les Lauriers de Nassau*, affirms, 'J'ay pris tous deux.' The St. Philip and the St. Thomas were blown up by their captains. A multitude of the men were drowned, or horribly scorched. 'There was so huge a fire, and such tearing of the ordnance, as, if any man had a desire to see Hell itself, it was there most lively figured.' The English, Ralegh says, spared the lives of all after the victory; the Flemings, who did little or nothing in the fight, slaughtered mercilessly, till Ralegh first, and then the Lord Admiral, beat them off.

Towards the close of the three hours' struggle, Ralegh received from a spent shot a grievous wound, 'interlaced and deformed with splinters,' in the leg.

So stunned were the Spaniards by the naval disaster that the English troops when they landed had an easy victory. They routed eight hundred horsemen

. Occupation of Cadiz. . who met them. Then, hotly pursuing, they forced their way in under Essex along with the fugitives. Before 8 o'clock that night the English were masters of the market-place, forts, town, and all but the castle. It held out till break of day. Ralegh was carried ashore on his men's shoulders; but his wound was painful, and he was anxious for the fleet. That was practically deserted. The superior officers had all run headlong to the sack. So he retired on board. A promise was made him of a full share of the spoil. He wrote on his copy of *Les Lauriers* that the engagement was not kept. Cadiz agreed to pay a hundred and twenty thousand crowns as ransom for the persons of the citizens. All the rich merchandise in the town, and forty thousand ducats in cash, were spoil of war. A grander booty might have been gained if the Generals had been guided by him, though Sir William Monson arrogates to himself the honour of the suggestion. At daybreak he had sent his step-brother, Sir John Gilbert, and his brother-in-law, Sir Arthur Throckmorton, who were in his ship, to ask authority to follow the Indian fleet into Puerto Real road. The cargoes were worth eight million crowns. The Generals demurred. He says in their excuse that 'the confusion was great; it was almost impossible for them to order many things at once.' They declined also an offer by the Cadiz and Seville merchants in the afternoon to redeem the ships for two million ducats. Ralegh himself preferred capture first, and ransom afterwards. Essex desired to take the vessels; but he wished to employ his land officers, Blount and others, not Ralegh and his sailors. The Lord Admiral was against any composition. 'We came,' he said, 'to consume them, and not to compound with them.' The Spanish commander, the Duke of Medina, settled the difficulty. On the following morning, June 23, he set fire to the whole, galleons, frigates, and argosies. Among them were several ships which had been fitted out for Guiana. The galleys escaped both Spanish and English fury.

. The Spoil.

To the English leaders were allotted many rich prisoners. 'Some,' wrote Ralegh, 'had for them sixty-six, or twenty, thousand ducats, some ten thousand, beside great houses of merchandise.' Had it not been for his wound, he avows with candour that he also should have possessed himself of 'some house.' As it was, his part of the spoils was 'a lame leg and deformed. I have not been wanting in good words, or exceeding kind and regardful usage, but have possession of nought but poverty and pain.' His complaint was an exaggeration. It is inconsistent with the report of the royal commissioners. They drew up an inventory subsequently at Plymouth of the spoil appropriated by the chiefs, except Essex and the two Howards. In their tables Ralegh's plunder is valued at £1769, which he was allowed to keep. But he fared ill in comparison, for example, with Vere, who secured an amount of £3628. He appears also to have been disappointed in an expectancy he had of £3000 prize-money from the proceeds, among other booty, of those two well-furnished Apostles aforesaid, as he familiarly terms the St. Matthew and St. Andrew. Another and more generous grievance was the inferiority of the gains of his seamen to those of the soldiers. With other principal officers of the fleet he offended Vere by backing the sailors in their demand for a search of the soldiers' chests. Throughout there had been ill-will between Vere and him. Before they set out they disputed precedence. The contention was compromised on the terms that Vere should have priority on land, and Ralegh on water. During the voyage the strife was inflamed by Sir Arthur Throckmorton's hot temper. On the return to England a fresh outburst of professional jealousy fretted the sore.

Essex was for holding Cadiz; and Vere engaged for its retention if he might keep four thousand men. But it was known the measure would be disliked at Court. The owners of booty, moreover, wanted to convey it home. Consequently, most of the town was demolished, and its fortifications were dismantled. As Ralegh writes in the *History of the World*, describing Cadiz as one of the three keys of the Spanish Empire, bequeathed by Charles the Fifth to Philip: 'We stayed not to pick any lock, but brake open the doors, and, having rifled all, threw the key into the fire.' On July 5 the *Return of the Expedition.* army embarked. A descent was made upon Faro; and the noble library of Bishop Osorius was taken. It became the nucleus of the commencing Bodleian. Then the fleet set off homewards. This was against the wishes of Essex, but accorded with those of Ralegh. Provisions were scarce. In his own ship sickness had broken out, and his wound troubled him. Sir William Monson adds an insinuation gratuitous and baseless in respect of him, that 'riches kept them who got much from attempting more.' Preceding the rest he reached Plymouth Sound on August 6. He went up to London, whither his praises had preceded him. Sir George Carew had written to Cecil on June 30: 'Sir Walter Ralegh's service was so much praiseworth as those which were formerly his enemies do now hold him in great estimation; for that which he did in the sea service could not be bettered.' As warm testimony was furnished by friends of Essex. Sir Anthony Standen, a very close adherent of the Earl's, who, however, in the next reign was one of Ralegh's fellow-prisoners, had looked upon him with extreme suspicion. At the commencement of the expedition he had written to an acquaintance: 'Sir Walter Ralegh's carriage to my Lord of Essex is with the cunningest respect and deepest humility that ever I saw.' He could not resist the evidence of Ralegh's conduct. He wrote to Burleigh from Cadiz on July 5: 'Sir Walter Ralegh did in my judgment, no man better; and his artillery most effect. I never knew the gentleman until this time, and I am sorry for it, for there are in him excellent things beside his valour; and the observation he hath in this voyage used with my Lord of Essex hath made me love him.'

Ralegh's real reward.

Ralegh murmured at the scantiness of his spoil. His real reward was his restoration at Court. He sent a letter by Sir Anthony Ashley to Cecil on July 7. After extolling Essex for having behaved both valiantly and advisedly in the highest degree, without pride and without cruelty, he expressed a hope that her Majesty would take his own labours and endeavours in good part. His prayer was granted. Elizabeth finally was induced to abate her wrath. It can never have been vindictive, or she would have deprived him of his Captaincy. He was reported in May, 1597, to be daily at Court, and to be likely to be admitted to the execution of his office before he should go to sea. The rumour was well founded. His deeds at Cadiz gave the Queen an excuse for showing indulgence, of which she would be glad to avail herself on another account also. She felt an obligation to him for his part in smoothing the relations between her young favourite and her young Minister. Already, in February, 1597, Essex and Ralegh were known to be holding frequent conferences. Ralegh was acting as a mediator between the Earl and Cecil. Their reconciliation was an object ardently desired by Elizabeth. He succeeded, and they combined to requite him.

On June 1, 1597, Cecil obtained leave to bring him to the Palace. _On Guard._ Elizabeth, writes a courtier, Whyte, used him very graciously, and gave him full authority to execute his place as Captain of the Guard. This he immediately undertook, and swore many men into the void places. In the evening he rode abroad with the Queen, and had private conference with her. From that time, the same indefatigable observer noted, he came boldly to the Privy Chamber, as he had been wont. Though on June 1

Essex was away from Town, it is especially remarked by Whyte that the re-establishment of Ralegh was due to a large extent to him. Ralegh, he, and Cecil were in league to gain the consent of the Queen to a fresh foray upon Spain and its commerce. That was a main object of the consultations which stirred the wonder of courtiers. The victualling of the expedition was confided to Ralegh. He contracted to provision 6000 men for three months at the rate of ninepence a head. He complained that he was out of pocket, which was not believed, though it was acknowledged that the work was very well done. It was sure to be. He appreciated fully Coligny's advice, as quoted by himself, that 'who will shape that beast war must begin with his belly.' If he made a good bargain with the State, he executed its conditions honestly. Not all of the profit could he retain on this, or probably on other occasions. He had to supply Essex with much for his private consumption. None of Elizabeth's courtiers objected to such irregular gains. But Essex was chiefly anxious for the glory he expected from the enterprise. His mind was said to be 'full of conquering and overcoming the enemy;' and he had learnt at Cadiz the value of Ralegh as a colleague. The triumvirate, it was noticed, dined together one day at Essex House and conversed for three hours after. Another day, early in July, Cecil was host. In return Essex again, and Ralegh, entertained Cecil. An allusion to this festivity in a letter of Ralegh's has furnished his biographers with a pet puzzle. 'I acquainted the Lord General,' wrote Ralegh to Cecil on July 6, 1597, 'with your kind acceptance of your entertainment; he was also wonderful merry at *The Islands Voyage.* your conceit of Richard the Second. I hope it shall never alter, and whereof I shall be most glad of, as the true way to all our good, quiet, and advancement, and most of all for Her sake, whose affairs shall thereby find better progression.' Commentators have been tempted to discern some shadow before of the fatality four years later, when the patronage by Essex and his partisans of the play of *Henry IV* at the Globe Theatre became an article of indictment. The passage forms a conundrum to which the clue has not yet been found. If the reference be to Shakespeare's drama which Essex, Cecil, and Ralegh may have seen acted in this July, it constitutes the only ascertained association of the hand which could do all and the brain which could conceive all.

Evidence of the amity of the three was afforded by the liberal scale of the expedition, which started on July 10. A fleet of 120 vessels sailed from Plymouth. Twenty were Queen's ships. Ten were contributed by the Low Countries. The rest were volunteers. Essex commanded in chief, as lieutenant-general and admiral. Lord Thomas Howard was vice-admiral. Ralegh was rear-admiral. Lord Mountjoy was lieutenant of the land forces.

Vere was marshal, and George Carew master of the ordnance. The serjeant-major was Sir Ferdinand Gorges. Sir Arthur Gorges was captain of Ralegh's flagship. Essex feared that Vere and Ralegh might harbour a mutual grudge on account of the strife over the Cadiz spoil. He persuaded them to shake hands at Weymouth. 'This,' chronicles Vere, 'we both did, the more willingly because there had nothing passed between us that might blemish reputation.' Ralegh, in the *History of the World*, has spoken in the same spirit of Vere, as constituting with Sir John Norris 'the most famous' pair of captains by land, and is indignant that he should have left behind him neither title nor estate.

The object of the expedition was to destroy the navy at *Weather-bound.* Ferrol, and capture the Indian treasure ships. It was intended also to take and garrison Terceira, and any others of the Azores. Hence it has been known as the Islands or Island Voyage. The enterprise commenced ill. Four days of storm drove the armament back to Plymouth. There it lay for a month. Essex was in despair. Ralegh suggested to Cecil that the Queen might send a comforting message. A truer man, he said, there could not be upon the earth; but God having turned the heavens with such fury against the fleet, it was a matter beyond human power, valour, or wit to resist. The programme had to be revised. Essex and Ralegh rode post to Court to consult the Queen and Council. The decision was that all the soldiers but a thousand Dutchmen should be disbanded. The attack on Ferrol was to be limited to an attempt by Ralegh to fire the ships in the harbour. Essex was forbidden to participate, whether from regard for his safety, or to secure to his subordinate a free hand. The modification was in conformity with Ralegh's advice. He had expressed to Cecil his doubt of the prudence of prosecuting the original design. The Spanish force at Ferrol he thought too strong, and the season too advanced. He and Essex returned together to Plymouth, where the Earl was his guest on board the Warspright. 'Her Majesty may now be sure his Lordship shall sleep the sounder, though he fare the worse, by being with me; for I am an excellent watchman at sea,' wrote Ralegh. The fare would not be extremely rough. Ralegh could bear hardships, if necessary, anywhere. He was ready at any moment, and in any weather, to go to sea, though, like Lord Nelson, he was liable to visitations of sea-sickness. But at sea, as elsewhere, he liked comfort, refinement, and even luxury, if compatible with duty. He had many servants. He took chests of books. He hung his walls with pictures, and furnished his cabin sumptuously. Among the treasures of the Carews of Beddington was a bedstead, reputed to have been part of his ship furniture, with upholstery of green silk, and with gilt dolphins for legs. The stately chair, which was in the late Mr. Godwin's collection of the chairs of great men, may have been its companion.

At Plymouth the fleet delayed weather-bound till August 18. It had not been five days at sea before another tempest arose off Cape Ortegal. Carew in the St. Matthew was driven into Rochelle. Eventually he had to return to Plymouth. The wind blew out of Ferrol, and the curtailed scheme for an assault on it, and on Terceira too, had to be abandoned. All that remained was to intercept the Indian ships. The fleet was divided by stress of weather. Ralegh wrote to Cecil on September 8 that in ten days he had never come so much as into bed or cabin. He did not rejoin the main body till *Mischief-making*. Essex had been ten days at the Island of Flores. Essex 'seemed to be the joyfullest man living for our arrival,' says Arthur Gorges. Some had tried to persuade him that Ralegh had kept away intentionally with the victuallers; but Essex told Ralegh he saw through 'their scandalous and cankered dispositions.' Gorges believed he spoke sincerely; 'for though the Earl had many doubts and jealousies buzzed into his ears against Sir Walter, yet I have often observed that both in his greatest actions of service, and in the times of his chiefest recreations, he would ever accept of his counsel and company before many others who thought themselves more in his favour.'

At Flores it was determined at a council of war that Essex and Ralegh should lay waste Fayal. Essex sailed away. Ralegh following arrived first. The forts fired; and the islanders began carrying off their goods to the interior. Ralegh still paused. The officers, except a few of Essex's sycophants, like Sir Guilly Meyricke, chafed. Delay, as Monson, no admirer of Ralegh, has intimated in his narrative of the affair, might have enabled the Spaniards to provide themselves better. Ralegh's own patience was not inexhaustible. He cannot have been sorry to be afforded a reasonable pretext for separate action. He states in the *History of the World* that his delay was in deference to the desire of some in the company who would have 'reserved the title of such an exploit, though it was not great, for *Attack on Fayal*, a greater person.' When the difficulty of the enterprise was urged, he felt bound to prove by example that the 'defence of a coast is harder than its invasion.' On the fourth day he landed. He took no soldiers, but only 260 seamen and gentlemen volunteers, with some ordnance, in pinnaces. They were met by double the number of Spaniards, and by a sharp fire. So staggered were his men that Ralegh had to order his own barge to be rowed full upon the beach. Other boats followed. Landing, the invaders waded through the water, clambered over rocks, and forced their way up to and through the narrow entrance. The town itself, called Villa Dorta, was four miles off, and a fort guarded it. Up to the front deliberately marched Ralegh, with his leading staff in his hand. He wore no armour except his collar. His men were less serenely indifferent to the shot, especially the Low Countries soldiers, who were now come ashore to his help. The garrison, driven from the lower works, mounted to the higher. Ralegh, perceiving a disinclination in his force to go on, preceded with Gorges and eight or ten servants. Amidst a hail of ball and stones, he in his white, and Gorges in his red, scarf, presented excellent marks. They discovered the best passage, and then their men came up. But by the time they reached the fort and town both had been deserted.

Early next morning, September 22, the rest of the fleet, which had been roving after the treasure ships, was descried bearing in. Essex was grievously disappointed at having missed the one opportunity of glory on this unlucky expedition. Pernicious counsellors like Blount, Shirley, and Meyricke, recommended him to bring Ralegh before a court-martial. Some actually asserted he deserved to be executed. Not unconscious of the Earl's mood he paid him a state visit in his barge. He was at once taxed with breach of discipline. He was reminded of an article that none, on pain of death, should land any of the troops without the General's presence or his order. His reply was that the provision was confined to captains. It could

Essex's Jealousy. not apply to him, a principal commander, with a right of succession to the supreme command, in default of Essex and Thomas Howard. Most of all, he protested against orders which he heard had been given for the arrest of the officers who accompanied him in the landing. He insisted that whatsoever his Lordship conceived to be misdone he must take it wholly on himself to answer, being at that time commander-in-chief. Essex seemed so far impressed by his arguments as to visit him at his lodgings, though he graduated the return to good humour by declining to stay and sup. In the morning he paid Essex a second visit, though not without hesitation. At one moment the prospect of ill treatment was so threatening that he was disposed to go off to his squadron and prepare to repel force. Lord Thomas Howard hindered extremities by pledging his honour to make himself a party if wrong or violence were offered. Essex could not overcome his mortification. He evinced it in a puerile manner by omitting all mention of the capture of Fayal from his official reports. Monson, who was with the expedition, expresses an opinion that if Essex, being 'by nature timorous and flexible, had not feared how it would be taken in England, Sir Walter Ralegh would have smarted for it.' In appearance the Earl ultimately allowed himself to be pacified by a solemn discussion of Ralegh's conduct, and a severe censure voted by a majority of the principal officers. According to one incredible account, Ralegh was gravely declared on the occasion to have rendered himself, by his assumption of independent power, liable to a capital penalty. Posterity will be inclined to transfer the actual condemnation to the commander-in-chief, whose freakish pique stopped only short of an outrage. But Essex had the fortune or misfortune to have all his errors popularly accounted virtues. In relating this occurrence, for instance, Vere, though he admits the matter was 'grievously aggravated by the most,' speaks of Ralegh's act as a 'crime,' which it was very good of the General to visit simply 'with a wise and noble admonition.' Sir Henry Wotton later mentions, as if it were an act of heroic self-denial, that the Earl replied to advice to send Ralegh before a court-martial: 'I would if he were my friend.'

Caracks captured and missed.

To cement the hollow reconciliation, Villa Dorta was burnt, after the kindly usage, and the fleet went prize hunting. Three Spanish ships from the Havannah were captured. The largest, of 400 tons, was laden with gold, cochineal, indigo, civet, musk, and ambergris, beside many valuable passengers. Enough of cochineal and indigo was taken 'to be used in this realm for many years,' according to an official report. Ralegh was its captor. He expressed his pleasure either magnanimously or contemptuously: 'Although we shall be little the better, the prizes will in great measure give content to her Majesty, so that there may be no repining against this poor lord for the expense of the voyage.' They missed forty India-men, which escaped into the strong harbour of Terceira. The colonels bragged they were ready to storm the forts. Howard and Ralegh, who thought the enterprise impracticable, offered as a test of the sincerity of the soldiers to back them with 3000 seamen. Thereupon the project was dropped. At St. Michael's, Essex, according to Gorges, who it must be remembered was Ralegh's officer, wasted precious days at Villa Franca. He let his men revel in fruit and wine, and lost the moment for surprising the capital. Ralegh meanwhile, in the road, took a Brazil ship, which, when sold in England, paid the wages of the whole of the 400 sailors and soldiers of the Warspright. Through a Dutch captain's over-haste, an 1800 ton carack 'of infinite wealth, laden with the riches of the East and West,' eluded him. She ran herself aground, and was burnt by her crew. He in his barge crossed the furious surf too late to put out the flames. Very speedily she was all over thunder and lightning. Her ordnance discharged from every port, and the clouds exhaled from her spicy entrails perfumed the air for many hours. By this time autumn was come. Not too soon, the fleet, which had assembled off Villa Franca, set sail. The town was spared the customary flames, for

causes unknown to Gorges. After *Historian of the Expedition.* suffering

from want of water, and from tempests, in which the skill of John Davys,

Essex's famous pilot, proved inferior to that of Broadbent, who was Ralegh's, St. Ives was reached. Ralegh's return rejoiced Cornwall, which had been alarmed by descents of Spanish caravels. The whole tale was set forth vividly by Sir Arthur Gorges in his *Relation of the Island Voyage*, written in 1607, and printed, it is said, at the request of Prince Henry.

CHAPTER XIV.

A Busy Life.

The Islands Voyage was the last for many years of Ralegh's personal adventures at sea. After it he found enough, and too much, to occupy him at home. He speaks of himself as 'mad with intricate affairs and want of means.' As soon as he returned he had to take precautions against an expected attack on Falmouth by a Spanish fleet of 110 or 160 sail. Only the tempest which had troubled Essex and him prevented its arrival while he was away. He was arranging for the journey into Spain of a spy, who had a pass from Philip, whereby he might safely look into the ports. He was urging on the Council the despatch of light warships against the Spanish treasure fleet. He represented it as a complement to the preceding expedition, less hazardous and likely to be much more lucrative. The squadron would be absent only in the dead of winter, and could be back by spring, 'sufficient timely to answer any attempt from Spain.' He was provisioning Western ports, paying their garrisons, and reckoning the cost of maintenance of captive Spaniards. He was scolding a presumptuous nephew, John Gilbert. He was upholding the ancient tenures of the Duchy of Cornwall, and resisting the exaction of obsolete licences for drying and packing fish. He was relieving miners from extortions by merchants. He was advocating an Irish policy of terrorism, in the course perhaps of a visit to Munster, as Mr. Payne Collier has inferred from the language of his letter itself, rather more confidently than it warrants, though a current rumour that he was out of heart at the moment with his Court prospects favours the hypothesis of self-banishment. At any rate, in October, 1598, he was writing to shame-faced Cecil in defence, it is sad to say, of official connivance at the assassination of Irish rebels: 'It can be no disgrace if it were known that the killing of a rebel were practised. But, for yourself, you are not to be touched in the matter.' In his History he condemns lying in wait privily for blood as wilful murder. In return for his activity and his fierceness he was recognised as both hostile and important enough to be singled out as a mark for the Ultramontane fury which kindled and fed Irish revolts. That at times assumed strange forms. His name is joined in 1597 with those of Cecil and the Lord Admiral as among the Englishmen whom Tempest the Jesuit destined to destruction. The instrument was a poison, for which the sole antidote was the utterance of the word Eguldarphe three times before drinking. Then the glass would break, or the wine, if in a silver cup, would froth and fume.

Public affairs and private affairs, small things and great, filled Ralegh's life to overflowing. They were all transacted at high pressure. Everything he did he did with his whole might. He always 'toiled terribly.' He sat in the House of Commons in the winter of 1597-8, and his name often occurs in reports of debates and committees. He spoke on the infesting of the country by pretended soldiers and sailors, on the cognate subject of sturdy vagabonds and beggars, on the fruitful topic of the Queen's debts. He took part in the burning controversy whether the Lords were entitled to receive, seated, Members sent by the Lower House to confer on a Bill, instead of coming down to the bar. He was being consulted by the Privy Council on the right way of dealing with Tyrone's Ulster rising. He was praying a licence for a translation from the Italian of a history of King Sebastian's and Thomas Stukely's invasion of Morocco, on the ground that he had perused and corrected something therein. He was soliciting and obtaining a Governorship. He was seeking the enlargement out of prison of his cousin Henry Carew's 'distressed son.' He was nursing at Bath his ailments, of which their Lordships of the Council were very sorry to hear, and wished him speedy recovery. He was, through Cecil, and with the Queen's leave, applying pressure to Bishop Cotton of Salisbury, at the end of 1598, for the change of his lease of Sherborne into the fee. He was building there a new mansion. He was playing primero at the Palace with Lord Southampton, and doubtless as eagerly, though he did not, like the Peer, threaten to cudgel the Royal Usher who told them they must go to bed. He was exclaiming at the supineness which suffered Spain to prepare expeditions against Flanders or Ireland, capture 'our small men-of-war,' and send safe into Amsterdam 'the ship of the South Sea of Holland, with a lantern of clear gold in her stern, infinite rich—and none of yours stayed her!'

Never was there a busier existence, or one apparently more evenly occupied. But at this period it had really a single engrossing care, and that was the rivalry with Essex. Once it had looked as if the two might become friends. Before the Islands Voyage, Essex had been closely allied both with him and with Cecil. Afterwards, on an alarm of a Spanish invasion in 1596, Essex and he seem to have been jointly directed to advise on a system of coast defence. Essex drew up a series of questions, to which Ralegh categorically replied. He expressed an opinion that it was not worth while to attempt to fortify aught but 'the river of Thames.' He thought it unwise either to hazard a battle, or to store much ammunition anywhere but in London. His reason was that 'we have few places guardable, Portsmouth excepted.' Essex and he hoped apparently to be given another foreign command. In October, 1597, Ralegh was prompt to report to Cecil the testimony of a Plymouth captain just come from abroad, that 'the Earl our General hath as much fame and reputation in Spain and Italy as ever, and more than, any of our nation had; and that for an enemy he is the most honoured man in Europe.' He appeared to nurse no anger for the reproaches and menaces used at Flores and Fayal. Those were reported by Whyte to Sir Robert Sidney to have been greatly misliked at Court, where

Ralegh was 'happy to have good and _Attempts at Friendship._ constant friends able by their wisdom and authority to protect and comfort him.' He did not take advantage of his influence there to direct attention to his commander's blunders at St. Michael's. On the contrary, he seized every opportunity, with seeming sincerity, of dwelling upon his courage and capacity. He exhibited friendliness in various ways. In December, 1597, he had accepted a mission from the Queen to compromise a question of precedence between Essex and the Lord High Admiral. Towards the beginning of 1598 he, Essex, and Cecil again met often at Essex House and Cecil House in secret conclave. Cecil in February, 1598, was sent to France on a mission to dissuade Henry IV from concluding a separate peace with Spain. His journey was made an occasion for special demonstrations of goodwill among the rival courtiers. Entertainments were given him in which Ralegh with Lady Ralegh, and members of the Essex party, like Lord Southampton and Lady Walsingham, equally participated. Essex accepted favours from Ralegh and Cecil. Ralegh offered him a third of the prizes he had captured. Cecil procured him a grant of £7000 from the sale of the cochineal belonging to the Crown. He was believed to have reciprocated the kindness of each by promising Cecil that in his absence nothing disagreeable to him should be done, and Ralegh, that he would join Cecil in having him appointed a Privy Councillor, if not Vice-Chamberlain. But the show of cordiality was deceptive, and Essex chose to imagine himself continually aggrieved. The Islands Voyage had been a failure. The Queen told him it had been. She blamed him for having accomplished nothing at Ferrol. She reproached him with the escape of the plate fleet. He was discontented with himself. His flatterers consoled him by assurances that others were in fault rather than he. They pointed at Ralegh; and the old jealousy revived with redoubled violence.

Ralegh was no longer an object for generosity. He was become again a power at Court. He was perpetually consulted on maritime and Irish affairs. Conferences were held between him and the Council in 1599 concerning Ireland, and his advice for the victualling of the garrisons was adopted in the January of the same year. His Western command, at a time when Spanish incursions were from moment to moment possible, brought him into peculiar prominence. When his hopes in 1598 either of the Vice-Chamberlainship, or *Tolerance of Disappointments.* of a seat at the Privy Council, were frustrated, he was disappointed; unlike his adversary, he could bear disappointment. He was at once the most patient and the most impatient of men. His was the healthy form of disappointment, which, if an outlet in one quarter be closed, incites to the discovery of another. The gossip of the town reported in October, 1598, that he was meditating a voyage to Guiana in company with Sir John Gilbert: 'He is discontented he thrives no better.' It was one of a Court life's passing clouds, and he treated it so that it should pass. To the diseased mind of Essex he appeared prosperous and triumphant at all points, and beyond all deserving. Even the few laurels of the late expedition had been gathered by him. When they had been at variance, Ralegh had put him in the wrong. Ralegh could not tolerate an insolent superior. Essex could endure no equal. He was ever sulking at Wanstead, or raging. Ralegh's name was the established text for his outbursts of wrath. An anecdote told by the anonymous author, said to be Lord Clarendon, of *The Difference between George Duke of Buckingham and Robert Earl of Essex*, is supposed to illustrate the humiliations to which his temper exposed him. On the Queen's birthday, November 17, 1598, the accustomed tournament was being held in the Tilt-yard before her Majesty. Ralegh, not brooding on late rebuffs, led a gallant retinue in orange-tawny plumes. Essex had heard of Ralegh's preparations. He entered with his visor down, at the head of a larger and more magnificent troop flaunting 2000 feathers of the same colour. It must be admitted that, as Horace Walpole remarks, 'the affront is not very intelligible at present.' Apparently, he wished to produce an impression by his glorious feather triumph that Ralegh and his followers were a company of esquires or pages. But the two bodies tilted, and Essex 'ran very ill.'

Essex in Ireland.

In chagrin, and almost despair, Essex at the end of March, 1599, went over to Ireland as Lord Deputy. The vacancy had been a theme of much dispute at Court. In 1598, Ralegh, Sir Robert Sidney, and Sir Christopher Blount, Essex's step-father, had been mentioned by rumour for the appointment. In March, Rowland Whyte had written positively to Sir Robert Sidney that it had been decided to nominate either Sir William Russell or Ralegh, but Russell had absolutely declined, and 'the other doth little like it.' Perilous as the post was, 'a fair way to destruction,' as Whyte described it, a refusal of it by Ralegh, had the choice been given him, is incredible. Essex in any case preserved enough influence to have hindered his nomination. At last, to exclude others, and to keep himself before the world, Essex consented to be appointed. As soon as he had landed in Ireland he began to bemoan his 'banishment and proscription into the cursedest of all islands.' So loud was his discontent as to give rise to extraordinary popular fancies. London was in the August of 1599 barricaded for a fortnight. A fleet was put in commission under Lord Thomas Howard as Admiral. Ralegh was Vice-Admiral, and 'took leave at Court of all the ladies' about August 18. He stayed in the Downs for three weeks or a month. The ostensible, and doubtless the true, reason was the threat of a Spanish descent upon the Isle of Wight. But not a few believed that it was a precaution, less against the Spaniard than against an apprehended invasion by Essex from Ireland. Wild as was the rumour, it was favoured by the reckless talk of Essex and his companions. Sir Christopher Blount on the scaffold confessed to Ralegh that some had designed the transport of a choice part of the army of Ireland to Milford, and a march upon London.

Essex before this, on June 25, 1599, had been writing to Elizabeth: 'Is it not lamented by your Majesty's faithfullest subjects, both there and here, that a Cobham and Ralegh—I will forbear others for their places' sakes—should have such credit and favour with your Majesty, when they wish ⌐ *Attacks* ⌐

⌐ *on Ralegh.* ⌐ the ill success of your Majesty's most important action, the decay of your greatest strength, and the destruction of your faithfullest servants?' His fury against Ralegh seems too excessive to have been genuine. In part it may be explained by his knowledge, on which Sir John Pope Hennessy has laid inordinate stress, that Ralegh was the most strenuous opponent of his Irish policy. He would detect the voice and hand of Ralegh in all the hindrances to, and in every criticism upon, his measures. He would imagine he heard him arguing adversely at sittings of the Council, to which he was informally admitted, and in the Queen's chamber. Sympathy may reasonably be felt now both with his special difficulties, and with his general tendencies in Irish administration, rather than with his rival's doctrines. His, however, were only tendencies. His conduct both in Ireland and in England proves that he thought of Irish administration as a weapon of combat for Court ascendency, not as a means of correcting the wrongs of ages. The tone of his tirades upon his condemnation to residence in Ireland is wholly inconsistent with the romantic theory that he had undertaken the government as a humanitarian mission of peace and benevolence to the Celt.

His abrupt return was but the climax in a series of extravagances which had terrified the Queen. He was indignant at any delay in a restoration of the old royal kindness. At first he condescended to a few overtures for forgiveness. His friends could not believe that he would not be welcomed back. They were persuaded that, if Elizabeth saw him, all would be as it had been. Leave was importuned for him to run again in the ring at Whitehall on the Queen's birthday. He was induced to affect penitence. It was noted hopefully that the royal favour to Ralegh was not without breaks. He had wished to be a Commissioner for the peace negotiations with Spain at Boulogne. The Queen refused, as his appointment would have confirmed his title to a Privy Councillorship. In June he was said to have been scolded worse than cat and dog, and dismissed into the country bag and baggage. Obediently he went over to his Cork estate, where he aided Carew in his Munster Presidency with his 'strong counsel' in July. As before, he kept his temper, and the Queen relented. She sent comforting messages when he fell ill from vexation, as was said, and recalled him to Court. Essex was not content to work upon her compassion. He grew contemptuously impatient. He was much more resentful than grateful when his pardon came without a renewal of his farm of sweet wines. Everybody has heard of his rude taunt thereupon at Elizabeth, that 'her conditions were as crooked as her carcase.' Ralegh in his *Prerogative of Parliaments* applies it as an illustration how 'undutiful words of a subject do often take deeper root than the memory of

ill deeds.' He asserts that the saying 'cost the Earl *Despair and Cabals.* his head, which his insurrection had not cost him, but for that speech.' Essex did not stop at sneers. He caballed with persecuted Papists and Puritans alike, and with various desperados. He alarmed King James with fantastic accounts of conspiracies for the Infanta's succession. In the plot were, he intimated, Ralegh potent in the West and Channel Islands; Cobham, Warden of the Cinque Ports; the Lord Treasurer; the Lord Admiral, Burleigh, Cecil's brother, President of the North; and Carew, President of Munster. All were persons, he alleged, well affected to the King of Spain. He urged James to require a public recognition of his title. He 'pretended,' wrote Cecil to Carew, 'an intention to remove me from the Queen, as one who would sell the kingdom of England to the Infanta of Spain, with such other hyperbolical inventions.' He desired to replace Ralegh in the Captaincy of the Guard by Sir William Russell.

On Sunday, Feb. 8, 1601, came the explosion. Very little secrecy had been preserved, and the guard at Court was doubled. In the morning Ralegh invited Sir Ferdinando Gorges, Governor of Plymouth Fort, to come by water to him at Durham House. Essex was willing Gorges should meet Ralegh on conditions: he must take a couple of companions for his protection, and the meeting must be on the river, not at Ralegh's lodgings. Ralegh consented. Gorges, some time later, during his confinement at the Gate-house, on June 14, 1601, wrote an account of the interview. At his examination by several Privy Councillors he had stated that Sir Christopher Blount tried to persuade him to seize or kill Ralegh. He refused, 'unless Sir Walter had given me the first occasion by violent deeds or unkind words, for either of which I was both resolved and prepared.' He admitted the 'intent was particular against Sir Walter Ralegh and others.' He thought this a proof that 'it was no matter of treason against her Majesty, but rather a manifestation of the contrary.' Essex gave out that his rising was prompted by a discovery that there was an ambuscade of musketeers placed upon the water by the device of Lord Cobham and Ralegh, to murder him in the way as he passed. Blount, at his trial, confessed there was no foundation for the allegation. In reply to Cecil, who asked if he thought Cobham and Ralegh had projected the murder of the Earl, he said he did not believe they ever meant any such thing, nor that the Earl himself feared it; only it was a word cast out to colour other matters. Essex himself subsequently made a similar admission with respect to his charges against Ralegh and Cobham of treason to the Queen and State. Blount, it is said, being unable to induce Gorges to commit the crime, himself from a boat fired four shot at Ralegh. Ralegh was present officially at his execution, and interposed on his behalf when the Sheriff would have forbidden him to go on speaking. Blount reciprocated the courtesy by asking Ralegh's forgiveness, 'both for the wrong done you, and for my particular ill intent towards you.' Ralegh was a witness at the trial of Essex, on February 19. When he was called, Essex rudely cried: 'What booteth it to swear this fox!' He insisted upon the oath being administered upon a folio, not upon a small, Testament. Ralegh was not to be irritated into retorting angrily. He calmly explained that on the river Gorges said this would be the bloodiest day's work that ever was, and wished Ralegh would speed to Court for the prevention of it. Gorges admitted the accuracy of the account. Essex denied its agreement with the report made by Gorges to him at Essex House.

Essex was a popular idol. Ralegh, till his fall, never was. A contemporary said that Essex's reverses endeared him, and Ralegh's successes seemed to deepen the public dislike. The populace deluded itself with the fancy,

absolutely groundless, that Essex's ruin

was due to Ralegh, and that Ralegh must have exulted at it. Malignant anecdotes were current of his demeanour at his rival's last moments. He was said to have snatched at the pleasure of conveying to the Lieutenant of the Tower the instructions for the execution. He was described as, on February 25, standing in a window over against the scaffold, and puffing out tobacco smoke in defiance. After his own death, Sir Lewis Stukely alleged him to have said that the great boy died like a calf, and like a craven; to have vaunted to one who asked if in the Islands Voyage the Earl had not brought him to his mercy, that he trusted they were now quits. Against such gross tales Ralegh needs no defence. He could not have behaved like a boorish ruffian to an adversary in the death agony. He could not have spoken unmannerly words of his dead Cadiz comrade. He had been present at the Earl's trial as Captain of the Guard. In spite of taunts, he had given his evidence with dignity and moderation. As Captain of the Guard he had escorted several of the insurgents, though not Essex himself, to prison. In his official capacity he carried the order for the execution. In the same character he was present in the Tower. At first he had stood near the scaffold, supposing that Essex might wish to speak to him. To avoid misconstruction by lookers-on he soon withdrew. He stationed himself in the distant Armoury, where he could see without being seen. Afterwards he was sorry, he said, for it; since he heard that the Earl had inquired for him, desiring to have been reconciled.

His Part in the Catastrophe.

His aspect is reported to have been sad and gloomy, as he was rowed back to Durham House. With his nature, and his gifts of imagination, he could not but have been awed by the consummation he had witnessed of a tragic doom. Later he believed he had always lamented the fate of Essex as the beginning of a new peril to himself from those who before had needed his support against a powerful rival. He may already have had a presentiment. He could rightly declare that the death was not his work. Essex was his own undoer. A time had been at which Ralegh would gladly have become his firm friend. His emphatic concurrence, recorded by Rowland Whyte, with Lady Ralegh's wish that there were 'love and concord amongst all' was not hypocritical. In all sincerity he had written twice in that spirit in the spring of 1600 to Lady Essex. He had found it of no use; and a period came when he rejoiced in an inveterate enemy's discomfiture. It is fanciful to affirm that he would have been pleased to assist in turning aside the final shock of ruin. His sentiments towards Essex at the end, unhappily, are too certain for the precise meaning of his enigmatical undated letter to Cecil, discovered among the Hatfield papers, to be of much consequence. Of its authenticity there is no real doubt, though Mr. Charles Kingsley, whose enthusiasm for Ralegh is delightful and unmixed, chooses to question it on the slender ground that it is signed by initials, and that the style is, to his taste, unlike Ralegh's. Its exact meaning is much more open to dispute. Here it is:—

'I am not wise enough to give you advice; but if you take it for a good counsel to relent towards this tyrant, you will repent it when it shall be too late. His malice is fixed, and will not evaporate by any your mild courses. For he will ascribe the alteration to her Majesty's *Advice to Cecil.* pusillanimity, and not to your good nature: knowing that you work but upon her humour, and not out of any love towards him. The less you make him, the less he shall be able to harm you and yours. And if her Majesty's favour fail him, he will again decline to a common person. For after revenges fear them not; for your own father, that was esteemed to be the contriver of Norfolk's ruin, yet his son followeth your father's son and loveth him. Humours of men succeed not, but grow by occasions and accidents of time and power. Somerset made no revenge on the Duke of Northumberland's heirs. Northumberland, that now is, thinks not of Hatton's issue. Kelloway lives that murdered the brother of Horsey; and Horsey let him go by all his lifetime. I could name you a thousand of those; and therefore after-fears are but prophecies, or rather conjectures, from causes remote. Look to the present, and you do wisely. His son shall be the youngest Earl of England but one, and if his father be now kept down, Will Cecil shall be able to keep as many men at his heels as he, and more too. He may also match in a better house than his; and so that fear is not worth the fearing. But if the father continue, he will be able to break the branches, and pull up the tree, root and all. Lose not your advantage; if you do, I rede your destiny. Yours to the end, W.R. Let the Queen hold Bothwell while she hath him. He will ever be the canker of her estate and safety. Princes are lost by security; and preserved by prevention. I have seen the last of her good days, and all ours, after his liberty.' By Bothwell is meant Essex. The real Bothwell was a natural son of James V. of Scotland, who had plotted against the reigning king, and been pardoned, and had plotted again.

On the date of the letter depends whether it signify doing to death, or grinding into obscurity. It is endorsed in Cecil's hand, 'Sir Walter Ralegh,' and in a later hand, '1601.' That is hardly a possible date. The civil, ecclesiastical, and legal year in England, by which a secretary at Hatfield is likely to have reckoned, closed on March 24. Consequently '1601' had not begun when Essex was already dead. The only question is, when in the legal year 1600 the letter was written. If at the end, when *Difficulties of* accomplishment of the capital sentence. If it were written early in 1600 its more probable purpose would be to induce Cecil to urge the Queen to strip Essex of all his dignities and offices. Ralegh's apologists can adduce for the less bloodthirsty interpretation the passage: 'If her Majesty's favour fail him, he will again decline to a common person.' The words naturally refer to disgrace, not to death. It has been imagined that the plan was to incapacitate him by law for employment, and to hold him a State prisoner. The remark, 'His son shall be the youngest Earl of England but one,' remains equally puzzling on either construction. Advocates of that which treats the letter as a plea for imprisonment and disqualification for office have to show how he could have been kept a State prisoner for life for offences he had committed before the rising of February, and, moreover, how the imprisoned living father was to make way in his peerage for the son. On the other theory which presumes it to have been an argument for sending Essex to the scaffold, it is as unintelligible how the father's fate, with its necessary attainder of blood, could legally transmit his dignity.

The inherent inconsistencies of the document are scarcely more perplexing than the circumstances of its origin. It has been suggested that the idea of the letter was Cecil's, and that he plotted to deceive posterity by inducing Ralegh to hold the pen. In the crude shape, that is an incredible hypothesis. But Cecil was of a nature to discuss questions of policy with his confidants, and extract their views, while he revealed only half his own. Very possibly the letter may have arisen out of a conversation in which the Minister had canvassed the question of acting with prudent magnanimity towards the fallen favourite. He may have requested Ralegh to repeat in writing objections urged orally by him to such a course for the exposition of the case on both its sides. At all events, it would be convenient for Cecil to have the document if in future it should be doubted which of the confederates had been the more vindictive. Ralegh could easily be drawn to try his hand, between fancy and earnest, at an academic theme on the lines of fashionable Italian statecraft. If the paper be indeed nothing but an exercise in pleading, the author deserves to be applauded for the artistic assumption of an air of sincerity which chills the reader's blood.

CHAPTER XV.

From Essex's execution to the death of Elizabeth, on March 24, 1603, is a period of two years wanting a month. It constitutes another stage in Ralegh's career. No more fascinating Court favourite, no Leicester, Essex, or mere Hatton, stood now in his way. If even Elizabeth's vivacious temperament may have ceased to require attentions as from a lover, she never grew insensible to wit, grace, versatility, and valour like his. The

- *Lord Oxford.* jealousy he continued to arouse was a tribute to his power.

To this time belongs the story, contained in Bacon's *Apophthegms*, of Lord Oxford's insolence. The malicious Earl had returned, the Mirror of Tuscanismo, from his seven years' self-inflicted exile at Florence. He had gone thither to spite his father-in-law, Burleigh, by deserting his wife, and squandering his estate. The Queen was playing on the virginals before him and another nobleman, while Ralegh was on duty near at hand. The ledge in front happened to have been taken away, so that the jacks were seen. Oxford and his companion smiled and whispered. Elizabeth inquired the reason. They were amused, answered Oxford, to see that when jacks went up heads went down. The point of the sarcasm is presumed to have been the connexion of Ralegh's influence with the decapitation of Essex. That the reference was to Ralegh might have seemed rather dubious had not Bacon taken it for granted. The fact of the favour of the Queen is certain.

Courtiers wrote to one another how 'good his credit with the Queen had lately grown.' He had a multiplicity of Court duties thrown upon him. His acquaintance with other lands and their languages brought him forward whenever intercourse had to be held with foreigners. As Sir John Harington said of him, he was 'especially versed in foreign matters, his skill therein being always estimable and praiseworthy.' When Prince Maurice was endeavouring to relieve Ostend, which the Archduke and Infanta were besieging, Ralegh and Cobham paid his camp a visit. They were stated by Cecil to have no charge, and to have 'stolen over, having obtained leave with importunity to see this one action.' The English envoy wrote to Cecil that the two gallants had been entertained with much honour and extraordinary respect, but had seen little. Sir Henry Neville, however, told Winwood their journey was not for curiosity only. They 'carried some

- *Sully and Biron.* message, which did no harm.' In March, 1601, Ralegh, by the Queen's order, had been escorting a Spanish envoy, sent to negotiate a truce, round London. Later, during the Queen's summer progress to Dover, he, with Cobham and Sidney, received Sully. As Captain of the Guard he playfully took Sully into custody, and conducted him to the Queen. The great Minister had been privately sent over by King Henry, who was at Calais. On September 5, the Duc de Biron arrived, to announce to Elizabeth the marriage of Mary de Medici to Henry. Several noblemen had been directed by the Council to provide for the Marshal's solemn reception in London. By some accident they were absent. Ralegh, who had not been especially commissioned, happened to be in town. Apparently Sir Arthur Savage and Sir Arthur Gorges, who spoke French fluently, came to his help. Among them they amused the Frenchmen till horses were ready to convey them to Hampshire. The Queen was at Basing House. Ralegh wrote to Cecil: 'We have carried them to Westminster to see the monuments; and this Monday we entertained them at the Bear Garden, which they had great pleasure to see. I sent to and fro, and have laboured like a mule.' On the Wednesday he rode with the Marshal and his numerous company to the Vyne. The fair and large house of Lord Sandys has formed the subject of an interesting volume by its present owner, Mr. Chaloner Chute. It had been furnished from the royal apartments at the Tower, Hampton Court, and neighbouring country houses, for the accommodation of the foreign visitors. The Hampshire gentry lent seven score beds. Not when Ralegh had seen all housed were his cares over. He told Cobham, 'The French wear all black, and no kind of bravery at all.' His wardrobe, plentiful as assuredly it was, had not been equipped in unison with such demureness. So, 'this Saturday night, late,' he wrote on September 12 to Cobham from Basing, 'I am now going to London to provide me a plain taffeta suit, and a plain black saddle.' Elizabeth rewarded his exertions in rendering the stay of the Frenchmen agreeable by knighting his brother, Carew Ralegh, on her departure from Basing House. Mr. Benjamin Tichborne received the same honour.

Ralegh was a patron of literature, and had to devote evenings to the wits.

The Mermaid. To him has been ascribed the institution, at the beginning of the seventeenth century, of the Mermaid Tavern meetings in Bread Street, Shakespeare's, Jonson's, Beaumont's, Fletcher's, Selden's, Cotton's, Camden's, and Donne's club. It is very likely; so likely that the intrinsic probability of the fact might be a motive for a fiction. Whether as founder or guest it is more than likely he would take occasional part in the wit combats of which Beaumont has sung. We may lament that there was no Boswell, or even a Drummond, to report an encounter between Ralegh and Shakespeare. Ralegh abhorred drunkenness. 'It were better,' he has said, 'for a man to be subject to any vice than to drunkenness.' But teetotalism had not been invented in the days of Elizabeth. Not wholly unconnected with the social evenings at the Mermaid may have been the frequent trouble he experienced from bodily ailments. On September 19, 1601, he pronounced himself too grievously ill to be able to travel to Bath for his annual cure. His ailments did not prevent him from warning Cecil of a powerful Spanish fleet held ready, with 6000 or 7000 soldiers, to descend either upon Ireland or the Low Countries. Fresh intelligence, which on September 26 he despatched to Cecil for transmission to the Lord Admiral, led him to believe the expedition was designed for Cork or Limerick. He inferred from the presence of many women on board that a 'Plantation' was meant. It was no false alarm. He announced to Cecil, on October 13, 1601, the landing of a strong body of Spaniards, and their intrenchment, as he had prognosticated, outside the town of Kinsale. His readiness to accept responsibility was met in the same spirit, particularly when Ireland was concerned. Later, Cecil admitted that Ralegh, though no Privy Councillor, was often invited to confer with the Council. Only three months before Elizabeth was seized with her mortal sickness, in 1602, he, with Cecil, was consulted by her on the treatment of Cormac McCarthy, Lord of Muskerry. Cecil was for leniency. Ralegh advised that no mercy should be shown, Cormac McCarthy's country being worth the Queen's keeping. Elizabeth accepted his frankly selfish advice.

In Parliament.

He sat as senior member for the County of Cornwall in the Parliament which met on October 27, 1601. He had been previously a Cornish representative, as member for Michell, in the House which was elected in 1593. In November, 1601, he obtained the rejection of a Bill to compel the sowing of hemp for cables and cordage. 'I do not like,' he said, in a spirit much in advance of his age, 'this constraining of men to manure or use their ground at our wills; but rather let every man use his ground to that which it is most fit for, and therein use his own discretion.' The Tillage Act he held up for a warning. It ordered every man to plough a third of his land, often to great loss. The land, 'if unploughed, would have been good pasture for beasts.' Later in the Session he supported a motion for the repeal of that Statute. He pleaded for a subsidy. The Queen wanted it urgently, having in vain raised money by the sale of her own jewels, by loans, and by savings out of her purse and apparel. He argued for its equal payment by every class. The burden he acknowledged was not the same to all, as Bacon had contended, *dulcis tractus pari jugo*. 'Call you this *par jugum*,' cried Ralegh, 'when a poor man pays as much as a rich, and peradventure his estate is no better than it is set at, while our estates are £3 or £4 in the Queen's books, and it is not the hundredth part of our wealth?' But he knew all must be taxed, in order that the necessary sums might be levied. In his *Prerogative of Parliaments* he mentions that he once moved an exemption 'by commandment of Queen Elizabeth, who desired much to spare the common ¦ *Monopolies.* ¦ people.' On calculation, it was found that the exemption reduced the subsidy to a trifle. He delivered a 'sharp speech' in his own defence, in a debate against monopolies. The Crown in May, 1599, had arrogated a right of preemption of tin in the Duchy of Cornwall, and had committed the management of the business to the Warden of the Stannaries. Deliverance of the miners from the oppression of the merchants was alleged as the motive. The real object was popularly believed to be the increase of Ralegh's emoluments. In Parliament he took the other ground. Previously, whether tin were 17s. or 50s. a hundred, the workman, he argued, had only 'two shillings a week, finding himself.' Since the grant of his patent, every miner, be tin at what price soever, had 4s. a week truly paid. Yet, if other patents were cancelled, he would, he said, freely consent to the abrogation of his. A great and uncommon silence is reported to have followed this speech. Other patentees in the House were probably not inclined to be as self-denying. He supported a proposal to prohibit the exportation of ordnance, notwithstanding the rise, under the existing law, of the duty to £3000 a year. He said: 'I am sure heretofore one ship of her Majesty's was able to beat ten Spaniards; but now, by reason of our own ordnance, we are hardly matched one to one.' He supported the continuance of the tax for the improvement of Dover harbour. The amount was 1000 marks a year. Mr. Swale objected that the port was never the better. Ralegh thought it one of the best and most necessary harbours in England. The debate might have been held in any of the last dozen Sessions, with as much practical effect. He obtained the rejection, by 106 to 105, of a Bill against recusants. The measure was designed to enforce a more regular attendance in Church on Sundays. Its loss vexed Cecil, who gibed at very flexible consciences.

Whatever the work in hand, legislation, public administration, or private maritime enterprise, he laboured at it as zealously as if it were his sole business. All his desire was for more and more work. He was not always

Governorship of Jersey. disappointed in that pursuit. Though his frequent hopes of appointment to the Vice-Chamberlainship or a seat at the Privy Council were constantly foiled, he had been consoled in 1600 with the Governorship of Jersey. On Sir Anthony Paulett's death, the post was conferred upon him, with the lordship of St. Germain. Out of the emoluments he had to pay a rent of £300 to the Crown for the benefit of

Lord Henry Seymour. Seymour had been a rival candidate for the Governorship. Ralegh's appointment was one of the irritations of Essex, who befriended another suitor. He speedily visited the island. The passage from Weymouth took him two days and nights at sea. The islanders 'royally entertained him with joy,' wrote Lady Ralegh in October to Cecil. He had told her, she said, that he never saw a pleasanter island; but he protested unfeignedly his post was not in value the very third part that was reported, or that indeed he believed. Without delay he undertook the completion of the fort Isabella Bellissima, 'for the name sake,' he wrote from the island to Cecil on October 15, 1600. He would not think of 'any penny receipt till that piece of work were past the recovery of any enemies.' He deprecated the demolition of Mont Orgueil, 'a stately fort of great capacity,' which had cost more than 20,000 marks. He had left, he said, some men in it at his own charge. He criticised the late Governor's 'immeasurable reckoning' of her Majesty's moneys. In July, 1602, he went again over, and spent several weeks. He saw that the castles were defensible enough, and the country reasonably well provided. The tradition is that he promoted a profitable trade between Jersey and Newfoundland. With Newfoundland he had a near family connexion through Humphrey Gilbert. He instituted a register of Jersey lands, and abolished compulsory service of the inhabitants of the district in the Mont Orgueil garrison. During his visits he sat as judge in the island Court. Faculties and energy with him were elastic. He always had leisure for new labours.

Maritime Enterprises.

Above all, his schemes of colonization were never intermitted. Down to 1603 he went on sending expeditions to Virginia. He was as solicitous for Guiana. In October, 1596, he had despatched from Limehouse his pinnace, the Watt, under Captain Leonard Berry. Mr. Thomas Masham's account of the voyage is in Hakluyt. Berry further explored the country. He collected fresh evidence of its fertility, salubrity, and riches, and of the goodwill of the natives towards Englishmen. He returned in June, 1597. His departure from Guiana was accelerated by the importunities of his Indian friends for an alliance with them against a hostile tribe. He feared such a league might prove embarrassing on Ralegh's next visit. Before the Queen's death Ralegh equipped yet another expedition, under Captain Samuel Mace, to look after both his potential dominions of Virginia and Guiana. It effected nothing; but the failure was powerless to impair Ralegh's faith in the value and feasibility of his discoveries.

In addition to his many public or semi-public toils, he was busy with a host of private affairs. Until a short time before the Queen's death he owned an extensive Irish as well as an English estate. Property was always for him an incentive to labour. While he had his Irish property he developed it in every possible way. Lismore Castle, which he rented from the See and Chapter of Lismore, he rebuilt. In 1589 he had written to George Carew: 'I pray, if my builders want, supply them.' His factory employed a couple of hundred men in the fabrication of hogsheads. By his influence with the Privy Council he often obtained, in favour of ships which he freighted, a waiver of the restraint of 'the transportation of pipe staves out of the realm of Ireland into the Islands,' that is, the *Irish Pipe Staves.* Canaries, and to Seville. The thinnings, he said, of his vast woods sufficed for the supply of materials. He denied that he denuded the land of timber. Against that wasteful and impoverishing practice he constantly remonstrated. There had not been taken, he stated to the Lords of the Council, the hundredth tree. Sir John Pope Hennessy holds a different view, and asserts that no man cut down more timber, to the irreparable hurt of the land. His principle of moderation may, it is possible, have been observed by himself, and not by his agents. Latterly he founded a company to work the property. With his chief partners, Bathurst, and a foreign merchant, Veronio Martens, he complained in 1601 to the English Council that the Undertakers were being robbed by the managing director, Henry Pine or Pyne. A sum of £5000 had, it was affirmed, been expended. Not half had been returned in profits, though Ralegh had received no payment for his wood. The Privy Council listened to the prayer of 'our loving friend, Sir Walter Ralegh,' and instructed Carew, the President of Munster, to forbid Pine to export more pipe staves. Ralegh had other disputes with Pine. At one time he even questioned if Pine had not conspired with his Sherborne bailiff to palm off a forged lease for a long term of the lands of Mogelly. He was involved also in endless disputes with other farm tenants, as an absentee landlord might have expected to be. Ultimately he resolved, by the advice of Carew and of Cecil, to free himself from the burden. In December, 1602, he sold his interest in all, except the old castle of Inchiquin Ralegh. Of that, Katherine, dowager Countess of Desmond, fabled to have been born in 1464, was, and remained till 1604, tenant for life. Boyle, since distinguished as the Great Earl of Cork, bought the rest, lands, castles, and fisheries, with Ralegh's ship Pilgrim thrown in as a make-weight. The *Sale of Lismore.* amount paid, according to Boyle's assertion, fifteen years later, in reply to Lady Ralegh, and thirty years later, in reply to Carew Ralegh, was a full price for a property at the time, it is admitted, woefully dilapidated. Boyle declared that it was not worth nearly the amount he paid. He complained of having been forced to an expenditure, for which the vendor was liable, of £3700 to clear the title. So shrewd a man of business would hardly have thus defrauded himself. He is sure to have had an excellent bargain. But it does not follow that the arrangement was unfair to a speculative absentee like Ralegh. In his hands the land was notoriously unprofitable. Lady Ralegh's estimate of it as worth £2000 a year at the time cannot be accepted.

Ralegh never parted with a scheme before he had another ready to occupy him. Sherborne more than replaced Lismore as an object of affection, and as a subject of care and anxiety also. He had not spared trouble and outlay on it since the Queen in the height of his favour first gave him a foothold as a lessee. We have seen how, to develop his term into the fee, he created and transplanted Bishops. His assiduity was rewarded in 1598 by Bishop Cotton's accommodating acceptance of a surrender of the lease, and grant of the fee to the Crown, subject to the old rent of £260. From the Crown the fee was conveyed to him. The transfer comprised the lordship of the Hundred of Yetminster, with the manor of Sherborne, five other manors in Dorset and Somerset, and the Castle, lodge, and parks of Sherborne and Castleton. Ralegh added to the estate by buying out leases with his own money, and by the purchase of several adjacent properties. Then he set himself seriously to the perfecting of the whole. He did not stint his expenditure. Sir John Harington says that with less money than he bestowed in building, drawing the river into his garden, and buying out leases, he might, without offence to Church or State, have compassed a much better purchase. He had begun by trying to improve the existing castle. In 1594 he altered his plan, and designed a new house at some distance. Only the centre of the present Sherborne Castle, a four-storied edifice with hexagonal towers at the ends, *Sherborne Castle.* was erected by him. Aubrey described it as a delicate lodge of brick, not big, but very convenient for the bigness, a place to retire to from the Court in summer time, for contemplation. Digby, when he became its owner, added four wings with a tower to each. Pope visited Lord Bristol there, and has sketched the place in one of his graceful letters to Miss Blount. He dwells particularly on the lofty woods clothing the amphitheatre of hills, the irregular lovely gardens, the masses of honeysuckle, the ruins of the old fortress, the sequestered bowling-green, and the grove Ralegh planted, with the stone seat from which he overlooked the town and minster, and dreamt and smoked. The spirit of Ralegh still dominates Sherborne, after all the efforts of the first Lord Bristol to lay it by swelling the lodge into a sumptuous castle, and of the sixth by turning Capability Brown loose into his pleasure grounds.

He loved Sherborne, and his wife was perhaps still more attached to it. In October, 1601, he wrote: 'My wife says that every day this place amends, and London to her grows worse and worse.' He had his worries there, as was his self-imposed fate wherever he was. He was premature in reposing confidence. He has written that he had lost more than he was worth by trusting dependents with his purse and delaying to take their account. He was almost excessively resentful of frauds on his trustfulness when he detected them. He was masterful in small things, as in great. While in the Tower in August, 1592, he had appointed his 'man, John Meere,' Bailiff of the manor of Sherborne, with extensive powers of management. He had invested him with copyhold lands. Several years later, in 1596, Adrian Gilbert took up his regular abode at Sherborne, and superintended his brother's improvements, under the title of Constable of Sherborne Castle. Meere quarrelled with him about the rival prerogatives of Constable and Bailiff to license the killing of animals for meat in Lent. Ralegh nominated another Bailiff, but Meere refused to retire. The family had interest with one of the Howards, Viscount Bindon, of whose 'extortions' and 'poisoning of his wife' Ralegh takes merit to himself for not having spoken. Mrs.

Meere, too, was a kinswoman of Lady Essex. Long strife had | *Strife with* |

| *Meere.* | prejudiced Ralegh so bitterly against both Meere and Essex that

he believed either capable of any monstrosity. He did the Earl's memory the injustice of fancying that he secretly had meant to use the Bailiff for a malicious forgery; 'for,' said Ralegh, 'he writes my hand so perfectly as I cannot any way discern the difference.' Colour is given to the charge against him of the forgery of an Irish lease, by the fact that Digby afterwards prosecuted him for the forgery of Ralegh's signature to a conveyance of English lands to Captain Caufeilde. Meere in August, 1601, arrested the opposition Bailiff. For this Ralegh put him in the stocks in Sherborne market-place, and had him bound over to good behaviour by the county justices. Thereupon Meere served upon Ralegh and others twenty-six subpœnas. Next year the conflict went on raging. Meere succeeded at the assizes in sustaining his right to the bailiwick. As Ralegh kept him out nevertheless, he petitioned the Star Chamber Ralegh on his part complained loudly that, through Lord Bindon's influence, Meere, at once 'a notorious cowardly brute, and of a strong villainous spirit,' had been allowed to sue him, though out of the land in Jersey.

Yet these vexations only made him cling the more fondly to his Sherborne home. He hoped to dwell happily and splendidly there himself, to be buried in its minster, and to leave it to a long line of descendants. While he had only a ninety-nine years' lease, he had conveyed his term to trustees for his son Walter. He had done this by two conveyances. These he revoked in 1598. His motives, he explained later, were several: 'I found my fortune at Court towards the end of her Majesty's reign to be at a stand, and that I daily expected dangerous employments against her Majesty's enemies, and had not in the former grants made any provision for my wife.' He re-settled the property on his son, reserving £200 a year to Lady Ralegh for her life. After he had acquired the fee, he conveyed it by deed at Midsummer, 1602,

Sir AmiasPreston's Challenge.
to himself for life, with successive

remainders to his son Walter, to any future sons, and to his brother Carew Ralegh. The deed had been drawn by Doddridge, afterwards a judge, many months before it was sealed. The reason of the date chosen for its formal execution was stated by himself at his trial to have been a challenge from Sir Amias Preston in the summer of 1602. Preston was the captain who, being too late to join the Guiana expedition, went off with Sommers on an independent quest. He had signalized himself at Cadiz, where Essex knighted him. The challenge may have arisen out of the Essex feud, for Sir Ferdinando Gorges, Essex's vehement partisan, is known to have been concerned in it. No duel was fought. Fuller, who errs in describing Ralegh as a Privy Councillor, says in his *Worthies*: 'Sir Walter Ralegh declined the challenge without any abatement to his valour; for having a fair and fixed estate, with wife and children, being a Privy Councillor, and Lord Warden of the Stannaries, he looked upon it as an uneven lay to stake himself against Sir Amias, a private and single person, though of good birth and courage, yet of no considerable estate.' Fuller's account is not to be rejected because the ground assigned may not seem very heroic. Duelling was governed by prosaic laws. Nobody was expected to risk his life on unequal terms. There had to be a parity of ranks; and the same principle might well apply to fortunes. Ralegh himself had no such fondness for the fashionable mode of adjusting quarrels as to waive any orthodox right of refusal. In his History he denounces 'the audacious, common, and brave, yet outrageous vanity of duellists.' Men who die in single combat he styles 'martyrs of the Devil.' He derides the victor's honours, 'where the hangman gives the garland,' and the folly of the duellist's principle, that rudeness 'ought to be civilized with death.' In the essay entitled *Instructions to his Son*, he declares a challenge justifiable only if the offence proceed from another; it is not, he says, 'if the offence proceed from thyself, for if thou overcome, thou art under the cruelty of the law; if thou art overcome, thou art dead or dishonoured.'

Its consequences.

At any rate, whatever the origin or issue of the dispute, he thought he was going to fight. In consequence, as he stated subsequently, he resolved to leave his estate settled. An incident of his preparations, which seemed trivial at the time, assumed preposterous gravity later on. He had spread out his loose papers, and among them a book by one Snagge, which he had borrowed from the dead Lord Burleigh's library. In it the title of the King of Scots to the succession was contested. Cobham, who may well have been Ralegh's intended second, happened to see and carry off the volume. It was found at a critical moment in his possession, and was traced to Ralegh. That was an affair of the future. For the present Ralegh probably associated Sir Amias Preston's challenge chiefly with the definite disposition of his property in a manner consonant with the creation of an affluent and permanent county family.

CHAPTER XVI.

COBHAM AND CECIL (1601-1603).

He did not know it, but he was now at the culmination of his prosperity. His kinsman, the learned Richard Carew, dedicated to him at the beginning

Impatience of Subordination. of 1602 the *Survey of Cornwall*, in terms, which, however exalted, were not exaggerated. He had a noble estate, his sovereign's renewed confidence, and many important offices. In politics he was still among those who followed rather than led, who executed, and did not direct. Of constant subordination he was become impatient. He was not content to be nothing more than 'a swordsman,' an instrument, though highly distinguished and favoured. His aim was to force his entrance within the citadel of administrative power. As a counsellor he exerted commanding weight on two main branches of national policy, Ireland and armaments. His Irish policy has been refuted by events. It is open to all the accusations which have been brought against it of cruelty and remorselessness. But its temper was that of a large body of English statesmen; and he understood much better than the rest the true method of putting it in practice. Had he been a Minister, and not only a royal confidant, he might have succeeded for a time in establishing in Ireland a peace of silence. He held as fixed and more generous views on the subject of national defences, and on the proper strategy in dealing with Spain. He fretted at being condemned to urge them from the outside instead of within. His exclusion from partnership in responsible authority was, he felt, perpetual, unless he could break in. Probably at no period did he aspire after supremacy, or expect to dispossess Cecil. His ambition, though restricted to the hope of admittance to association, would not the less bring him into collision with the jealous Secretary. He was reported in 1598 to be ambitious of a peerage. He cared more for power than titles, and his ancient friends, like his ancient rivals, thwarted his plans. We know | *The* |

Privy Council. that Cecil could not bear even so moderate an approximation for him to official trust as his regular introduction into the Privy Council. For that he had so long been craving and looking, that, according to Henry Howard's taunt, he by this time 'found no view for Paradise out of a Council board.' In June, 1601, there had been, as in 1598, a prospect of his nomination. Lords Shrewsbury and Worcester instead were sworn in. Cecil intimated his satisfaction. He told Sir George Carew that Ralegh should never have his consent to be a Councillor, unless he surrendered to Carew the Captaincy of the Guard.

Ralegh's efforts for a line of his own in statesmanship, and Cecil's consequent antagonism, are the special features of the coming chapter in his biography. His relations to the Cecils had always been intimate. Lord Burleigh, notwithstanding differences concerning Ireland, encouraged him as a counterpoise to Leicester. He repaid the kindness, it will be recollected, by interceding for the Lord Treasurer's son-in-law. He was a guest at the entertainment Burleigh gave to Arabella Stuart. With Robert Cecil Ralegh's connexion was much closer. Cecil valued his help at Court, and his society. In February, 1598, during his mission to France, he mentions him to Burleigh as one 'with whose kindness he has been long and truly fastened.' 'If some idle errand,' he writes word, 'can send over Sir Walter, let us have him.' With seeming sincerity he wrote in 1600 of him as one 'whose judgment I hold great, as his person dear.' He was a companion of Ralegh in several of his privateering speculations. Lady Ralegh wrote of Lady Cecil as of a sympathetic friend. Perpetually she was appealing to her 'cousin' Cecil as a support against Sir Walter's tribulations and hers. He is 'a comfort to the grieved.' She 'presumes of his honourable favour ever.' She confided to him her view of her Mistress the Queen as, like herself, 'a great believer.' In January, 1597, Ralegh condoled as a most loving comrade with Cecil on gracious Lady Cecil's death. His letter exhorting to implacability testifies to the closeness of their league against Essex. The Earl's fiery anger had burnt against both alike. Had his mad freak of treason succeeded, both would have been sacrificed in company.

Intimacy with Robert Cecil.

After Essex succumbed the alliance appeared as strict as before. The two households, as well as the masters, were affectionately familiar. Cecil's son, William, was a most welcome guest at Sherborne. No stronger proof of trust, it might have been thought, could be given by the father. There is talk how 'the beloved creature's stomach is altogether amended, and he doth now eat well and digest rightly;' how 'he is also better kept to his book.' As one intimately conversant with Cecil's affairs, Ralegh undertook in August, 1601, the supervision of his recently purchased estate at Rushmore. Pleasant postscripts are interposed on Lady Ralegh's behalf: 'Bess returns you her best wishes, notwithstanding all quarrels.' 'Bess says that she must envy any fingers whosoever that shall wear her gloves but your own.' There are threats from her that for the breach of a recent engagement he shall on his next visit have plain fare. Ralegh relied on Cecil to protect his monopoly of Virginian trade under his patent against unlicensed Adventurers. They cheapen, he complained, by their imports sassafras from its proper price of 20s. to 12s. a pound; they 'cloy the market;' 'they go far towards overthrowing the enterprise' of the plantation of Virginia, 'which I shall yet live to see an English nation.' In addition they introduced contraband cedar-trees. These, if the Lord Admiral would order their seizure, Ralegh intended to divide 'into three parts—to ciel cabinets, and make bords, and many other delicate things.' He asked for Cecil's aid; 'but what you think unfit to be done for me shall never be a quarrel either internal or external. If we cannot have what we would, methinks it is a great bond to find a friend that will strain himself in his friend's cause in whatsoever—as this world fareth.'

Throughout Elizabeth's reign, and beyond it, Ralegh's language to Cecil keeps the same tone of implicit faith. In words Cecil was not behind his

: *Cecil's Sentiments.* : more fluent and continuous correspondent. At heart he

would appear, from his communications to others, to have come to regard Ralegh as a dangerous rival before the Queen's death. Shrewd observers detected the growth of the sentiment, in spite of the alliance against the common foe, and even, for reasons which are not obvious, in consequence of it. 'Cecil,' wrote Harington, who had been a trusted comrade of Essex, in his *Nugae*, 'doth bear no love to Ralegh in the matter of Essex.' An important letter found among the Burleigh papers, without date or signature, but for good cause attributed to Lord Henry Howard, and probably written towards the end of Elizabeth's reign, shows how eagerly Cecil and Ralegh were regarded by their respective partisans as hostile competitors. Probably its genesis resembled that of Ralegh's argument for the thorough overthrow of Essex. It seems to have been an elaborate written embodiment of a policy which the Minister may have heard before from its author's mouth. It differs from Ralegh's letter in being absolutely in harmony with Howard's conduct at the time and after. In it the writer, with the 'Asiatic endless' prolixity which James himself ridiculed, propounded a plan for arranging that 'Cobham, the block all mighty that gives oracles, and Ralegh, the cogging spirit that prompteth it,' should be set in responsible positions in which they would be sure to fail. There is no reason to suppose that Cecil accepted the particular advice. He would be inclined to doubt the certainty of Ralegh's failure, should an opportunity of distinction be afforded him. But the document could not have been written unless its author had been positive of Cecil's sympathy with its object, the reduction of Ralegh, by whatever means, to a condition of confirmed obscurity and dependence.

As the termination of the Queen's reign more manifestly approached, the interests of Cecil and Ralegh seemed to grow more and more widely

Rival Camps. separated. Researches into the secret history of the final year or two reveal Ralegh and Cobham on one side, and Cecil and Lord Henry Howard on the other, as chiefs of opposite camps, with a converging outlook upon King James. Cecil, like his father, had been regarded by James as hostile to his proclamation as Elizabeth's heir. The death of 'my martyr Essex' increased his dislike. He was not assured of the baselessness of Essex's cry as he rode through the city: 'The crown of England is sold to the Spaniard!' He may have suspected the existence of schemes for the elevation of Arabella Stuart. Henry Howard brought him and Cecil to a mutual understanding. Howard, now remembered chiefly as the builder of Northumberland House, took a leading part in the machinations of Elizabeth's and James's reigns. As a Catholic, though at times conforming, and as brother of the hapless Duke of Norfolk, he had hated the Cecils. His dislike of Robert Cecil had been inflamed by partizanship for his kinsman Essex; notwithstanding, with his insatiable love of intrigue, he is said to have played off the two against one another. Now, convinced that Cecil was too strong, or too necessary, to be discarded, and possessing James's full confidence, he set himself to the cure of the King's distrust. Finally Cecil became for James 'my dearest Cecil.' James accepted him so entirely as to promise that Cecil's friends and foes should be his. Thenceforward a league was formed, and a correspondence was opened, between the King on one side and Cecil and Howard on the other, which are equally discreditable to all three.

The compact was not the work of a moment, and Cecil's rivals do not appear to the end to have understood how absolute it was. Neither was it of very old standing. For long Elizabeth's councillors hesitated to throw in their lot with the Scottish claim to the succession. They could not read clearly the national inclination. The country had been undecided. As Cecil *The Succession.* confessed he had once said, there were several competitors for whose right it was possible to argue. The Suffolk family possessed some sort of Parliamentary title. Arabella Stuart was not, like James, an alien, or a foreign sovereign. Discussion, or even advocacy, of either title, whether by Cecil, Ralegh, or Cobham, was, till the actual proclamation of James, not treasonable. But after the death of Mary Stuart, and, more plainly still, after that of Essex, it became manifest that the English people meant to crown the King of Scots. Cecil and Ralegh equally discerned the certainty. Both acted accordingly, and each suspected the other's procedure. Both started evenly with the same stain, in James's eyes, of enmity to Essex. Cecil, however, had the advantage of partnership with Henry Howard, and Ralegh the disadvantage of partnership with Cobham.

He had to overcome the more invincible obstacle of his possession of a character, demeanour, and policy, in good features as well as bad, essentially distasteful to the Prince he had to conciliate.

Without Elizabeth's knowledge, Cecil kept up an active correspondence with the Scottish Court. Ralegh had his concealed relations with it too. Neither is to be severely blamed for feeling an attraction to the nearest heir to the throne. Something even of personal enthusiasm at the prospect was not so absurd a sentiment as it seems to posterity. The nature of James was not well understood, and hope was placed in his youth. Contrasts were drawn, as Ralegh expressed it at his trial, between a lady whom time had surprised, and an active king. Ralegh had recognised that no other successor was possible. Lord Northumberland, writing to persuade James to be courteous to him, declared that he 'must allow Ralegh's ever allowance of the King's right.' Ralegh indeed had never favoured any rival candidate, Arabella Stuart as little as the Infanta. About Arabella there is no cause to doubt the veracity of his assertion, reported by Dudley Carleton, that 'of all women he ever saw he never liked her.' Simply he had opposed, as Elizabeth herself opposed, and in his character of her faithful servant, the termination of the abeyance of the dignity of heir presumptive. In the interest of her tranquillity he had addressed to Elizabeth a written argument against the announcement of a successor. Eventually, some time before Elizabeth's death, he had perceived that it was useless to act as if any successor but James were possible. With his sanguine temperament he acquiesced in the inevitable as if it were positively advantageous. He saw his way to render as excellent service to the State under King James as he was rendering now. He was conscious of the obstacles in his path; he was

Prejudices of King James. unconscious that they were insuperable. He knew

he had been always ranked as of the anti-Scottish party. He knew the specific meaning James would put upon his resistance to the formal declaration of a successor. His antagonism to Essex, he was aware, had created a strong repulsion against him in the King's mind. But he overrated the amount of the resources at his disposal for his protection from the weight of aversion he had excited. He equally underrated the inveteracy of the dislike, and the degree of additional suspicion which his measures of self-defence would awaken. James had long looked forward to a day when he should 'have account of the presumption of the base instruments about the Queen who abused her ear.' That was his way of thinking of the Queen's favourite councillors. Cecil knew how to purchase his pardon. Ralegh, gathering strength about him to render his friendship worth buying, only deepened the king's conviction that he could be mischievous; he did not implant a conviction that he was a desirable auxiliary. The 'consultations of Durham House' became notorious. They alarmed both

Howard and James just sufficiently to induce them to temporise. They fixed the resolution sooner or later to ruin the promoter. The Duke of Lennox came to London in November, 1601. He cultivated Ralegh's acquaintance through Sir Arthur Savage. James characterized Savage in a letter of 1602 to Howard as 'trucheman,' or interpreter, 'to Raulie, though of a nature far different, and a very honest plain gentleman.' Terms were offered by the Duke which Ralegh boasted he had rejected. To Cecil he protested that he had been over-deeply engaged and obliged to his own mistress to seek favour anywhere else. According to Howard, Ralegh asked Cecil to divulge this to the Queen; but Cecil, with good sense, represented to him that the Queen 'would rather mark a weakness than praise his resolution.'

Lord Henry Howard.

Whatever he had done or left undone, whatever promises had been made, and however they had been entertained, the end would have been the same. Henry Howard inflamed the instinctive aversion which James had long felt for Ralegh. Howard hated Ralegh with a virulence not easily explicable, which appeared to be doubled by its abatement towards Cecil. He had resolved to destroy both Ralegh and Cobham. On the testimony of his own letters it is clear he did not mind how tortuously and perfidiously he worked. He calculated upon Cobham's weakness, and upon the inflammation of Ralegh with 'some so violent desire upon the sudden as to bring him into that snare which he would shun otherwise.' He poisoned James's mind incurably against 'those wicked villains,' 'that crew,' and its 'hypocrisy,' the 'accursed duality,' or 'the triplicity that denies the Trinity.' By the triplicity he signified Ralegh, Cobham, and Northumberland. Ralegh had other enemies besides. Among them was Cobham's new wife, Frances Howard, Countess dowager of Kildare, daughter of the Lord Admiral. Henry Howard, who did not like her, admitted that she had helped in persuading Cecil to side with King James. She and Lady Ralegh had 'an ancient acquaintance,' which had resulted in mutual detestation.

Lady Ralegh in March, 1602, reminded Cecil how 'unfavourable my Lady Kildare hath dealt with me to the Queen. I wish she would be as ambitious to do good as she is apt to the contrary.' Lady Kildare had infused her own animosity into her father, whose official 'weakness and oversights' it is very likely Ralegh was, as Henry Howard had said, given to 'studying.' 'My Lord Admiral,' wrote Howard to Mar, James's ambassador, 'the other day wished from his soul he had but the same commission to carry the cannon to Durham House, that he had this time twelve months to carry it to Essex House, to prove what sport he could make in that fellowship.' In its larger sense the alleged fellowship comprised the Earl of Northumberland, who played fast and loose with it, Lady Shrewsbury, known as Lady Arabella's custodian, and Lady Ralegh, in addition to her husband and Cobham. Howard honoured Lady Ralegh with his particular hostility. 'She is a most dangerous woman,' he exclaims, 'and full of her father's inventions.' He was much alarmed at the possible success of some project for bringing her to her old place in the Privy Chamber. To its failure he ascribed her determination to 'bend her whole wit and industry to the disturbance of the possibility of others' hopes since her own cannot be settled.' He urged Cecil to arrange that it should be brought to Elizabeth's knowledge 'what canons are concluded in the chapter of Durham, where Ralegh's wife is president.' Ralegh himself and Cobham were, however, the universal objects of his copious invectives: 'You may well believe,' he wrote, 'that hell did never vomit up such a couple.' Cecil's own language to James was almost as vituperative. He was furious at the bare notion that any should vie with him for the heir's confidence. He represented Cobham and Ralegh, who were trying to obtain a share of James's favour, as mere hypocrites who hated the King at heart. If they held themselves out as his friends, or he held himself out as theirs, James was not to believe it. He excused himself for 'casting sometimes a stone into the mouth of these gaping crabs' to prevent them from 'confessing their repugnance to be under his Majesty's sovereignty.' He hoped to be pardoned if from ancient 'private affection' he had the semblance of supporting Ralegh in particular, 'a person whom most religious men do hold anathema,' who had, moreover, shown 'ingratitude to me.' He could not imagine that he

owed as much to Ralegh as Ralegh to him. But that was natural. If James should hear that he had not checked demonstrations by Ralegh, in his 'light and sudden humours,' against the King, he prayed James to ascribe it to a desire to retain sufficient influence over him 'to dissuade him, under pretext of extraordinary care of his well doing, from engaging himself too far.' He warned James especially against being beguiled into thinking Ralegh a man of a good and affectionate disposition. If 'upon any new humour of kindness, whereof sometimes he will be replete,' he should write in Cecil's favour, 'be it never so much in my commendation,' James was not to believe it. The correspondence of Howard and Cecil with James breathes throughout a jealous terror that Cobham and Ralegh, and chiefly Ralegh, might either supersede them in James's kindness, or steal into his confidence under the pretext of fellowship with them, and claim a share in the advantages. Ralegh's correspondence with the King, as theirs implies, has no such malignant, envious features. The King, however, was already incurably prejudiced.

Howard's and Cecil's imputations only confirmed an impression of long standing.

Against two enemies of this force and animosity Ralegh had no actual ally except Lord Cobham. Henry Howard had mentioned Northumberland as a confederate. How far the Earl, who had married Essex's sister, Dorothy, widow of Sir Thomas Perrot, could be reckoned upon may be judged from his description of Ralegh to James as 'a man whose love is disadvantageous to me in some sort, which I cherish rather out of constancy than policy.' Cobham was Cecil's brother-in-law, and their interests had long been inseparable. Ralegh would originally have desired his friendship as a means of cementing the intimacy with his potent connexion. He had been of the league against Essex. In opposition to Essex's solicitations for Sir Robert Sidney he had obtained the Lord Wardenship of the Cinque Ports. Essex had joined him with Cecil and Ralegh in the charges of perfidy. His personal favour with Elizabeth had been useful to the family compact. He was wealthy, and Cecil valued wealth in his domestic circle. Houses and lands brought him in £7000 a year; and he had woods and goods worth a capital sum - *Character of Cobham.* - of £30,000 besides. His furniture was as rich as any man's of his rank. One piece of plate was priced at £3500, and a ring at £500. He spent £150 at a time upon books. He was not devoid of good instincts; for he could repent of a misdeed or unkindness, and, after repeating it, repent again. But he was garrulous, puffed up with a sense of his own importance, full of levity and passion, and morally, if not physically, a coward. Ralegh, whom some social brilliancy in the man, as well as his rank and fortune, may have dazzled, can at no time have been wholly unconscious of the defects which later he resentfully characterized: of the 'dispositions of such violence, which his best friends cannot temper', 'his known fashion to do any friend he hath wrong, and then repent it', and 'his fashion to utter things easily.' Cecil regarded a nature like this scornfully. Infirmities might be tolerated in a brother-in-law who was a trusty ally. They could not be endured in a competitor.

Neither Ralegh nor Cobham appears to have detected the growth of rancour in Cecil. Ralegh maintained confidential intercourse with him on affairs of state. Together they were, as has been seen, conferring privately with Elizabeth on the policy to be adopted towards Munster rebels a few months before her death. Ralegh's correspondence with him betrays no suspicion of estrangement. It keeps throughout the old amiable style. There is talk of the price of timber at Rushmore. Salutations were sent so late as July 20, 1602, to 'my Lord Cobham and you, both in one letter,' with vows to 'do you both service with all I have, and my life to boot.' Ten weeks before Elizabeth's death Cecil was writing to Ralegh about partnership in a privateer. Ralegh in a memorable letter to his wife in July, 1603, spoke of the business association as still subsisting. It is difficult to believe that Cecil reciprocated, unless from complaisance and policy, the ferocity against Ralegh and Cobham, or either, which inspired Henry Howard's *Cecil's Jealousy.* venomous canting mystifications, and was echoed by James. His correspondence with Ralegh's cousin, George Carew, countenances the view that his hostility had something in it of hurt affection. He was capable of tenderness for men who were willing to be his auxiliaries, who at all events would not be, and could not be, his rivals. But he was mistrustful. He readily confused any increased intimacy between friends of his with enmity to himself. He wrote to Carew in Ireland in June, 1601, to excuse himself, in his enigmatical manner, for an appearance of unkindness: 'If I did not know that you do measure me by your own heart towards me, it might be a doubtfulness in me that the mutinies of those I do love and will—howsoever they do me—might incite in you some belief that I was ungrateful towards them. But, sir, for the better man, the second always sways him, and to what passion he is subject who is subject to his lady, I leave to your judgment and experience.' Later, in 1602, he complained to Carew: 'Our two old friends do use me unkindly. But I have covenanted with my heart not to know it. In show we are great. All my revenge shall be to heap coals of fire on their heads.' He carried out his promise, and his coals scorched. Yet it may be questioned if he were conscious of a virulent humour towards his friend and his brother-in-law. Merely they were in his way, and threatened to embarrass the career which was his life. They were presuming to act independently. They pursued schemes which, if successful, would disturb his monopoly of power. If unsuccessful, they might, through his connexion with them, compromise him. He would not be sorry if circumstances combined against them, and brushed them as politicians from his path.

CHAPTER XVII.

THE FALL (April-June, 1603).

Elizabeth died on March 24, 1603. In the previous September Howard had reported her 'never so gallant many years, nor so set upon jollity.' James set out from Scotland on April 5. Ralegh at the Queen's death was in the West. He returned hastily to London. There is a legend, countenanced by Sir John Hawles, that, with Sir John Fortescue and Cobham, he tried a movement for 'articling' with James before proclaiming him. Unsuspicious Aubrey narrates that at a consultation at Whitehall he went to the length of recommending the establishment of a 'commonwealth.' His object, he is said to have explained, was to save Englishmen from being subject to a needy, beggarly nation like the Scotch. Neither story rests on any foundation, except some possible light taunt of his. His name was not appended to the Proclamation, as he was not a Privy Councillor; but he was present at a meeting in the evening, when a loyal letter of welcome to the King was drawn up, and he signed it. Immediately afterwards he started, like many others, northwards, and met the King at Burleigh House. Cecil had taken credit for having stayed, he said, the journey of the Captain of the Guard, who was conducting many suitors to James. Ralegh did not suffer himself to be stopped either by Cecil's advice or by a Proclamation against the resort to the King of persons holding public offices, to the injury of public business. He assigned as the cause of his arrival the need of

a royal letter to authorize the continuance of legal process in the Duchy of Cornwall, and to check the waste of

royal woods and parks within it. Unmannerly James is said by Aubrey to have received him with a poor rude pun on his name: 'Rawly! Rawly! true enough, for I think of thee very rawly, mon.' Isaac D'Israeli credits the story. He superfluously thinks it settles, as without better authority than the King's broad Scotch it certainly could not, the proper pronunciation of the name. In itself it may be rather more plausible than Aubrey's tale of Ralegh's reply to the King's boast that he could have won the succession by force: 'Would God,' cried Ralegh, 'that had been put to the trial!' 'Why?' asked James. 'Because,' was the oracular answer—'never,' says Aubrey, 'forgotten or forgiven'—'your Majesty would then have known your friends from your foes.' It is much easier to agree with the apparent meaning of

Aubrey's interrupted general reflection on the first meeting of King and subject: 'Sir Walter Ralegh had that awfulness and ascendency in his aspect over other mortals that the K—— '. At all events, the King ordered the speedy delivery of the authorization, that Ralegh might have no excuse for delay. The unwelcome guest took the hint. Acting-Secretary Sir Thomas Lake reported to Cecil that he was gone, having 'to my seeming taken no great root here.'

At a council held by James at Cecil's seat of Theobald's, monopolies granted by Elizabeth were called in. The measure was based by its authors upon the need of popularity for the new reign. They were not sorry to hit Ralegh with the same stone. A question was raised at the Board whether the office of wine licenser were not a monopoly. Until the Council should have decided, the levy of all dues was suspended. A large part of Ralegh's income was at once cut off. He was summoned a few days later to the Council Chamber at Whitehall, to be informed that the King had appointed Sir Thomas Erskine, afterwards Earl of Kellie, Captain of the Guard. To this he is related to have in very humble manner submitted himself. His enemies knew they could in this as in other ways wound him with a certainty of applause for the gratification of their spite. Within a month of the Queen's decease a prayer of 'poor men' had been addressed to James against monopolies. The manifesto contained an especial allusion to Ralegh, of whom it wildly spoke as about to be created Earl of Pembroke. So, on the occasion of the dismissal from the command of the Guard, Beaumont, the French Ambassador, informed his Court that Cecil had induced the King to ⌐ *Odium.* ⌐ make the change on the ground of Ralegh's unpopularity, which would render his removal highly acceptable to the country. Henry Howard, before the demise of the Crown, when the effect of Ralegh's blandishments upon James was feared, had preached to the King on the same text. He reported a refusal by Elizabeth of the command of a regiment to Northumberland, for the reason that 'Ralegh had made the Earl as odious as himself, because he would not be singular, and such were not to be employed by princes of sound policy.'

For the present a semblance of consideration was preserved. The loss of the Captaincy was apparently sweetened by the elimination from his patent for the Governorship of Jersey of the reservation of £300 a year to the Crown or Seymour, and by the condonation of some arrears due from him. His fall elicited from him no symptom of anger against the King. If a letter purporting to be addressed by him to James be genuine, though the evidence for it is not strong, he was not as placid with respect to others. There the loss of his captaincy is angrily imputed to Cecil, who is accused of having brought about the deaths both of Essex and Queen Mary.

Chronology must have forbidden James to attach weight to the latter allegation, if he had cared for it. On the former he would be better inclined to credit Howard, who asserted that Cecil had worked for Essex's deliverance. Cecil himself could produce the letter of 1600-1, signed 'W.R.' Soon Ralegh experienced a fresh proof of his helplessness, in a notice of ejectment from Durham House. Bishop Tobias Matthew of Durham met James at Berwick, and gained his ear. He used his influence and Ralegh's odium to procure an order for the restoration of the London episcopal residence. It was retaliation for his loss of the See of Sarum through Ralegh. On May 31 a royal warrant was issued for the removal of the present occupants, Ralegh and Sir Edward Darcy. Ralegh wrote on June 8 or 9, asking permission to stay till Michaelmas. He pleaded the £2000 he had spent on the structure during the twenty years of his tenancy. He recounted his outlay on autumn and winter provisions for a household of forty persons and twenty horses. He complained to no purpose. He was ordered to quit by Midsummer.

Inopportune Advice.

Notwithstanding rebuffs, he continued to frequent the Court. He was at Beddington Park when the King on his Progress visited Sir Francis Carew, Lady Ralegh's uncle. Ralegh previously had laid before James a *Discourse touching a War with Spain, and of the Protecting of the Netherlands*. It is a most forcible, and, from its own point of view, sagacious disquisition in favour of persistency in the war with Spain, and the alliance with Holland, as well for offensive purposes against the Spaniards, as for defence, whether against Spain or France. As a controversial pamphlet it evinces none of the want of judgment with which Hallam charges Ralegh, though the defect appears plainly in his obtrusion of such views upon James. At Beddington he had an opportunity of clenching his argument, and the King's suspicions, by an offer, of which he subsequently boasted, to invade the Spanish dominions, at no cost to the King, with 2000 men. In the treatise he opposed the conclusion of any hasty peace with Spain. He referred to another essay, now lost, and never published, in which he had indicated *How War may be made against Spain and the Indies*. Spain was anxious for peace, and desired to consolidate it by separating England from France and Holland. The negotiations had begun in the lifetime of Elizabeth. They had excited much party spirit at Court, where Cobham already was conspicuous as their advocate, and Ralegh as their opponent. James's accession infused additional keenness into the contest. France was apprehensive of the King's proclivity towards an alliance, not merely peace, with Spain. Henry IV was not disinclined to the restoration of tranquillity in Europe. He was afraid of an Anglo-Spanish pacification of a character so cordial as to affect the league between the French and English Governments as it had existed in the late reign. He sent Sully over to cement the good understanding of the two States by arguments and gifts to the leading courtiers. Sully found the new Court honeycombed with intrigues. His fixed idea was that Spain was meditating much beyond the simple alienation of England from her ancient allies; 'qu'il se tramait quelque chose de bien plus important.' By means of the competing factions he tried to discover this great secret design. His researches were not confined to statesmen in authority, like Cecil, whom he

characterizes in his candid *Memoirs* as 'tout mystère,' caring for *The*

Fourth Party. no combination except so far as it might serve his individual political interests. He pursued his inquiries also among politicians out of power. They composed, he says, a 'Fourth Party,' with no basis of agreement, unless that its members could agree with no other party. He names as its leaders Northumberland, Southampton, Cumberland, Cobham, Ralegh, and Griffin Markham. They are described by him as 'gens seditieux, de caractère purement Anglais, et prêts a tout entreprendre en faveur des nouveautés, fut-ce contre le Roi.' Northumberland he induced by a large pension to collect for him secret intelligence, though he did not believe it. All he obtained from 'Milords Cobham et Raleich' was that, when he broached to them his notion of the dark schemes of Spain, they replied 'conformement à cet avis.'

His communications with Ralegh were limited to the extraction of this expression of assent. Nowhere does he assert or imply that Ralegh accepted any present from him, or entered into any compact. Yet Hume founds on the bald statement of sympathy a formal allegation that Ralegh offered his services to France, and that the offer was repulsed. It is a sample of the way in which he has been traduced. Sully's evidence exhibits him in his invariable attitude of an adversary of Spain and Spanish pretensions. It does

not indicate the smallest tendency *Ralegh's Egotism.* in him to further his own policy by means of illegitimate foreign influences. His mistake was the belief that he could by perseverance impose his doctrines and himself upon the sovereign. In theory he understood, as he lays down in his History, that it is not sufficient to be wise with a wise prince, valiant with a valiant, and just with a just; a courtier, who would have an estate in his prosperity, must, he teaches, live altogether out of himself, study other men's humours, and change with the successor to the throne. In practice none ever disobeyed this law of advancement more signally than Ralegh in relation to James. His egotism often before had blinded him to the idiosyncrasies of others. He seems to have been more than ordinarily incapable of comprehending those of his present ruler. He presumed eagerness in a young King to signalize his accession by feats of arms. The high spirit of James was the source from which he hoped to draw the motive force necessary for the accomplishment of his vast designs against the colonial empire of Spain. An accidental conjunction of circumstances enabled him to see speedily the effect of his attempt to storm the royal confidence by displaying his own martial propensities.

CHAPTER XVIII.

Awaiting Trial (July-November, 1603).

The Plots.

We now enter the period of the plot and plot within plot in which Anthony Copley, the priests William Watson and Francis Clarke, George Brooke and his brother Cobham, Sir Griffin Markham and his brothers, the Puritan Lord Grey of Wilton, and Sir Edward Parham were variously and confusedly implicated. The intrigue, 'a dark kind of treason,' as Rushworth calls it, 'a sham plot' as it is styled by Sir John Hawles, belongs to our story only so far as the cross machinations involved Ralegh. His slender relation to it is as hard to fix as a cobweb or a nightmare. Even in his own age his part in it was, as obsolete Echard says, 'all riddle and mystery.' Cobham had an old acquaintance with the Count of Arenberg, Minister to the Archduke Albert and the Infanta Isabel, joint sovereigns of the Low Countries. The Infanta was that daughter of Philip II whose claims to the English throne Jesuits had asserted, and Essex had affected to fear. During the late reign Cobham had been in the habit of corresponding with the Count both openly and secretly. De la Fayle and an Antwerp merchant, la Renzi or de Laurencie, carried letters and messages to and fro. In November, 1602, the Count had invited Cobham to come over and confer about peace, of which Cobham was a strong advocate. After James's accession he wrote again. Cobham inquired of Cecil and the King how he was to reply. James answered that Cobham should know his pleasure on the meeting of the Council. To Lennox he remarked angrily that Cobham was more busy in it than he needed to be. Cobham meanwhile thought of going abroad; but Cecil dissuaded him. In May, 1603, Arenberg sent a third letter by de la Fayle.

Cobham's Projects.

During this period Cobham frequently met Ralegh. He was negotiating the purchase of a fee farm from the Crown, and trusted much to Ralegh's advice. He had confided to Ralegh £4000 worth of jewels to complete the contract. Their talk, Ralegh admitted later, though commonly about private affairs, would sometimes turn upon questions of State. Before the Queen's death, it must be repeated, Ralegh would have committed no crime, or even impropriety, in listening, if he ever listened, without disapproval to Cobham's most intemperate assertions in favour of the title of Arabella, and against that of James. The evidence adduced of their talk on politics after the King's accession contains no reference to any such topic. Even if its subject then had been improper, nothing worse than passive complicity was proved against Ralegh. Thus, one day at dinner, in Cobham's house at Blackfriars, Cobham declared that the Count, when he came, would yield such strong arguments for peace as would satisfy any man. He specified great sums of money to be given to certain Councillors for their aid. Cecil and Lord Mar were instanced by him. On the same occasion he held out liberal offers to Ralegh. Ralegh, by his own account, which was not contradicted by other testimony, only listened. When he was taxed at his trial with having given ear to matters he had not to deal in, he exclaimed: 'Could I stop my Lord Cobham's mouth!' The teaching of adversity showed him that in prudence he should have removed himself from the possibility of hearing. 'Venture not thy estate,' he wrote in his *Instructions to his Son and to Posterity*, 'with any of those great ones that shall attempt unlawful things, for thou shalt be sure to be part with them in the danger, but not in the honour. I myself know it, and have tasted it in all the course of my life.' But the application of the warning, and the regret, to the hearing of Cobham's vague after-dinner flights might have seemed, unless for the result, impossibly remote.

Negotiations with Arenberg.

Early in June the Count arrived in London, under the escort of Henry Howard. Cobham, with la Renzi, visited him on June 9. At night Cobham supped with Ralegh at Durham House; or Ralegh supped with Cobham at Blackfriars, being accompanied by him back to Durham House afterwards. From Durham House Cobham was alleged to have gone privily with la Renzi to obtain a promise of money from the Count. According to Cecil's narrative in the following August to Sir Thomas Parry, the Ambassador at Paris, Cobham had told Arenberg that if he would provide four or five hundred thousand crowns, 'he could show him a better way to prosper than by peace.' Scaramelli, the Secretary to the Venetian Legation, wrote home on December 1, 1603, that Arenberg promised 300,000 ducats in cash, and an equal sum when he should have returned to Flanders. Ralegh subsequently was accused of having on this occasion been offered money by Cobham to be a promoter of peace. Cobham, in the written statement read at the trial, alleged that Ralegh had bargained for £1500 a year for divulging Court secrets. How Ralegh, out of favour and wholly eclipsed, was to learn them, Cobham did not indicate. Ralegh mentioned subsequently he had noticed from a window of Durham House that Lord Cobham once or twice after visiting him was rowed past his own mansion at Blackfriars. He went to St. Saviour's, on the other side of the river. There la Renzi was known to be residing. This is the sum of the facts out of which the large fabric of Ralegh's guilt was to be constructed.

He had attended the Court to Windsor. There he heard of the arrest of Anthony Copley in Sussex on July 6. From Copley, according to Cecil at the trial, the first discovery of the Bye or Surprising Treason came. By letter from Windsor, Ralegh informed Cobham. On July 12 Copley was examined. George Brooke was arrested on the 14th, and the arrests of Lord Grey of Wilton and Sir Griffin Markham were ordered. One day between the 12th and the 16th Ralegh was on the Terrace at Windsor. The King was preparing to hunt, and Ralegh was waiting to join the cavalcade. Cecil came out, and bade him, as from the King, stay. The Lords in the Chamber, Cecil said, had - *The 'Surprising Treason.'* - some questions to put to him. How far he was interrogated on the intercourse of Cobham with the Count, and how much he disclosed, is obscure. At his trial he gave his story of the transaction. He said he was examined at Windsor touching the conspiracy to surprise and coerce the King; next, about plotting for Arabella; thirdly, about practices with the Lord Cobham. He added: 'It is true I suspected that Lord Cobham kept intelligence with Arenberg. For long since he held that course with him in the Low Countries, as was well known to my Lord Treasurer and to my Lord Cecil. La Renzi being a man also well known to me, I, so seeing him and the Lord Cobham together, thought that was the time they both had been to Count d'Arenberg. I gave intimation thereof. But I was willed by my Lord Cecil not to speak of this, because the King at the first coming of Arenberg would not give him occasion of suspicion. Wherefore I wrote to the Lord Cecil that if la Renzi were not taken the matter would not be discovered. Yet, if he were then apprehended, it would give matter of suspicion to the Lord Cobham. This letter of mine being presently shown to the Lord Cobham, he spake bitterly of me; yet, ere he came to the stairs' foot, he repented him, and, as I hear, acknowledged that he had done me wrong.'

Ralegh's account of the matter, in a court of honour, might have been that Cobham's understanding with Arenberg did not seem to him of much importance. As it perplexed the Council he, not perceiving the possible prejudice to his friend, volunteered his services in clearing it up. When it was discovered to be deadly, or had been inflated into an appearance of capital criminality, his letter to Cecil was employed to represent to Cobham an act, it must be admitted, at best of not very friendly officiousness as black treachery. His suggestion to Cecil is in any case inconsistent with consciousness of a guilty connexion with treason, if there were treason. Nobody of the least sagacity, much less the 'master of wiles,' such as contemporaries accounted Ralegh, if he had been concerned in a plot, and if his implication in it had been known to a single person, would have been so foolish as to provoke his one accomplice to retaliate by accusing him.

From the examination at Windsor he returned a prisoner, confined to his own house. Some intercourse was then held between him and Cobham, through Captain Keymis. He said he sent Keymis to explain to Cobham that, being under restraint, he could not come himself, and to mention what he had done with Mr. Attorney in the matter of a great pearl and diamond given him by Cobham in order to arrange the business of the fee farm Cobham was purchasing from the Crown. He had added that he 'had cleared him,' which was, he asserted, true, as he had remarked to Cecil that he believed Cobham had no concern with the plot of the priests. Cecil's statement disagrees both as to Ralegh's examination, and as to the message to Cobham. According to Cecil, Ralegh was not examined at Windsor on any matter concerning Cobham. Yet, though Cobham was not then suspected, and though Ralegh had been examined about himself alone, he immediately, it is alleged, sent Keymis to tell Cobham that he had been examined concerning him, and that he had cleared him of all to the Lords. Keymis is stated, though not by Cecil, to have added verbally, as if from Ralegh, an exhortation to Cobham to be 'of good comfort, for one witness could not condemn a man for treason.' Ralegh denied positively that any such message came from him. Mr. S.R. Gardiner, in his *History of England from the Accession of James I to the Disgrace of Chief Justice Coke*, condemns this as 'an unlucky falsehood.' His reason for the violent charge is that he does not suppose so loyal a friend as Keymis would have invented a damaging calumny. Keymis would not have invented it to injure; he may, in the hope

that the effect would be beneficial, · *The Message by Keymis.* · have repeated

to Cobham casual expressions he had heard from Ralegh; or Cobham may have himself imagined the message was from Ralegh without any authority to that purport from Keymis. The former hypothesis is not inconsistent with the character of the messenger. Keymis could endure much for his leader. Without flinching he bore imprisonment in the Tower and Fleet, from which he was not released till December 31, 1603. He was a brave and loyal follower, but not very prudent, as after-events evinced. If the prosecution thought it could prove that he really used the words as from Ralegh, it is strange that it did not venture to produce him in court to testify to it.

Cobham could not have escaped suspicion. Ralegh's allusion to his dealings with Arenberg was not needed to direct it against him. He was notoriously reckless in his language. It had been remarked by Beaumont, the French Ambassador, in the previous May that he could scarcely mention Cecil without abusing him as a traitor. He was not likely to have been reticent on his relations with the Archduke's envoy. He was examined before the Privy Council several times at Richmond after July 15. On July 20 he confessed that he had asked Arenberg to procure five or six hundred thousand crowns for distribution among English malcontents. He had purposed to go on, after an interview with the Archduke in the Netherlands, and seek the money from the King of Spain. From Spain he intended, if the report of his examination can be credited, to return home by way of Jersey, where he expected to meet Ralegh. With him he meant to discuss the application of the money. So far his statement indicated reliance on his power of persuading Ralegh to abet the design. It showed no present complicity on Ralegh's part. At this point, according to the official narrative, 'a note under Ralegh's hand was shown to Examinate. Examinate, when he had perused the same, brake forth, saying, "O, Traitor! O, Villain! I will now tell you all the truth." And then said that he had never entered into these courses but by Ralegh's instigation; and that he would never let him alone.' He referred to suggestions by Ralegh of plots and invasions, and said he feared when he had him in Jersey, he would send him to the King. Convinced believers in Ralegh's duplicity will accept as satisfactory confirmation of that extraordinary apprehension an opinion attributed by Aubrey to Lord Southampton, an old enemy, that Ralegh joined the conspiracy in order to buy his peace by betraying it, and had schemed to inveigle Cobham and others over to Jersey, where he might secure them for the Government.

By this time various circumstances supposed to criminate Ralegh had been collected from the answers of the other accused persons. Each had been given over to one or more Commissioners to worry into confessions. Sir William Waad, or Wade, had charge of Ralegh, as of others. It was Waad who had broken open Queen Mary's cabinet at Chartley Hall. He was fitted for *Weaving a web for Ralegh.* any dirty work. Keymis also had been arrested, and was examined by Waad and the Solicitor-General on Ralegh's communications with Cobham. They told him he deserved the rack. Waad hereafter denied that they ever 'threatened him with it.' La Renzi was examined, and deposed that Ralegh had been in Cobham's company when Cobham received letters from Arenberg, and sent others to him. The contents of the voluminous inquisitorial dust-heap were perpetually being sorted, and distributed, or, reluctantly, discarded. Any answers reflecting on another, particularly if reflecting on Ralegh, were carefully put aside, to fill gaps in the direct evidence against him. Thus, Brooke, according to Sir

William Waad, 'confidently thinketh what his brother knows was known to the other.' On July 17, Brooke said that the conspirators among themselves thought Sir Walter Ralegh a fit man to be of the action. No account was made of the report by Markham of an express warning given him by Brooke himself against communications to Cobham, on the ground that whatever Cobham knew, Ralegh the witch would get out of him. In August, Brooke affirmed that both Ralegh and Cobham had resolved to destroy the King 'with all his cubs.' Watson mentioned that he and Brooke, and apparently Copley, had consulted concerning Sir Walter's surprising of the King's fleet. Copley reported a remark by Brooke that the project of causing stirs in Scotland came out of Ralegh's head. Watson had said of an

assembly at Cobham's house reported to ⦂ *Extorted Evidence.* ⦂ him by

Brooke, that, beside Brooke and Cobham, my Lord Grey and Sir Walter Ralegh were there, and showed every one of them great discontent, but especially the two Lords. My Lord Cobham discovered his revenge to no less than the depriving of his Majesty and all his Royal issue both of crown, kingdom, life, and all at once; and my Lord Grey, to use Master Brooke's own words, uttered nothing but treason at every word. At a subsequent examination Watson stated to Sir William Waad that from Brooke's words it was evident the great mass of money reported to be at the disposal of the Jesuits was, most of it, from the Count of Arenberg. It was impossible for all the Catholics in England to raise so much of themselves. Brooke, moreover, it was recorded, had stated that his brother, Cobham, told him Lord Grey and others were only on the Bye, but he and Ralegh were on the Main. By the Main was signified the dethronement of James in favour of Arabella.

Such second or third hand tales were to be used to point and colour the particle of direct testimony. This was Cobham's allegation that Ralegh had instigated the dealings with Arenberg. Otherwise, as Cecil almost officially admitted in a letter of August 4 to Parry, the only ground for proceedings against him was that he had been discontented *in conspectu omnium* ever since the King came. Without Cobham's charge it would have been impossible to prosecute him with any show of justice. Immediately after Cobham's examination he was committed to the Tower. He was conveyed thither from Fulham Palace, where he had been examined before Bishop Bancroft, one of the Royal Commissioners. He believed his doom decided. He found himself treated as convicted before he was tried. A resignation of the Wardenship of the Stannaries had been extorted from him. 'He underwent,' Sir John Harington wrote, 'a downfall of despair as his greatest enemy could not have wished him so much harm as he would have done himself.' Sir John spoke of a period before 1618. He did not know how Ralegh's enemies could accumulate hate. Ralegh never put any faith in the equity of

English criminal procedure. He was resolved, if the story about ⌐*Attempt*¬ ⌐*at Suicide.*¬ to be related is to be credited, to disappoint it of some of its cruel fruits. Very soon after his arrival at the Tower, it has been supposed on July 20, he is said to have attempted his life. He was lodged in two small rooms in the Bloody tower. A couple of servants of his own waited on him. He dined with the Lieutenant, Sir John Peyton. Being at table, he was reported to have suddenly torn his vest open, seized a knife, and plunged it into his breast. It struck a rib and glanced aside. Being prevented from repeating the blow, he threw the knife down, crying, 'There! An end!' The wound appeared at first dangerous, though it turned out not very serious. For the details of the occurrence we have to rely upon Cecil's correspondence, together with a few words from Scaramelli, Secretary to the Venetian Legation. Cecil wrote of it to Parry, at Paris, on August 4: 'Although lodged and attended as well as in his own house, yet one afternoon, while divers of us were in the Tower, examining these prisoners, Sir Walter Ralegh attempted to have murdered himself. Whereof when we were advertised, we came to him, and found him in some agony, seeming to be unable to endure his misfortunes, and protesting innocency with carelessness of life. In that humour he had wounded himself under the right pap, but no way mortally; being, in truth, rather a cut than a stab.' Cecil adds: 'He is very well cured both in body and mind.' Several days earlier, on July 30, Peyton had written to Cecil that the hurt was nearly well. James had been informed of the event by Cecil. His comment was that Ralegh should be well probed by a good preacher, and induced to wound his spirit, not his body. Beaumont, the French Ambassador, observed on the matter to Henry IV: 'Sir Walter Ralegh is said to have declared that his design to kill himself arose from no feeling of fear, but was formed in order that his fate might not serve as a triumph to his enemies, whose power to put him to death, despite his innocency, he well knows.' Confiscation was the triumph of which he wished to deprive his persecutors, if he really contemplated suicide. His motive would be the rescue of Sherborne for his wife and child from forfeiture through attainder, the sure result, as he truly foresaw, of a trial for treason.

A Disputed Letter.

'After he had hurt himself,' it is stated on the extant copy of the letter, though more probably, if at all, on the eve of the attempt, he is alleged to have written to apprise his wife of his approaching death. In 1839, in an edition of Bishop Goodman's *Court of King James the First*, the late Professor John Brewer printed an unsigned paper, purporting to be such a letter, which had been found in All Souls College Library. Mr. Brewer describes it as in Sir Henry Yelverton's Collection, for no other apparent reason than that the document is in a commonplace book, which includes three speeches by Yelverton. The contents are miscellaneous, ranging from satirical verses to State papers, and of dates from 1500 to 1617. Mr. Oman, of All Souls, considers that the hand, the same throughout, of the copyist is of ordinary seventeenth century character. The volume came to the college from the collection of Narcissus Luttrell. The name of the original owner, for or by whom the matter was compiled and transcribed, is not known. Consequently, belief in the authenticity of the supposed letter from Ralegh depends on its own intrinsic probability.

In the course of it, Ralegh, 'for his sake who was about to be cruel to himself, to preserve' his wife, begged her to be charitable 'to my poor daughter, to whom I have given nothing,' and to 'teach my son to love her for his father's sake.' Nowhere else is an allusion to this daughter discoverable. Nothing is known of her or her mother. Almost a necessary presumption is, that, if she existed, she was an illegitimate *An pocryphal Daughter.* child. One benevolent writer has suggested, without a shadow of evidence, a prior marriage to that with Elizabeth Throckmorton. The manner in which she is commended to Lady Ralegh's compassion excludes the explanation that Lady Ralegh was her mother, whether before or after marriage. Ralegh proceeded to ask his wife's 'kindness for his brother Adrian Gilbert,' and for Keemis, 'a perfect honest man who hath much wrong for my sake.' He advised her to marry, not to please sense, but to avoid poverty, and in order to preserve their son. Very bitterly he cries: 'That I can live never to see thee and my child more! I cannot. I have desired God, and disputed with my reason, but nature and compassion hath the victory. That I can live to think you are both left a spoil to my enemies, and that my name shall be a dishonour to my child—I cannot. I cannot endure the memory thereof. For myself, I am left of all men, that have done good to many. All my good turns forgotten; all my errors revived and expounded to all extremity of ill. All my services, hazards, and expenses for my country—plantings, discoveries, fights, councils, and whatever else— malice hath now covered over. I am now made an enemy and traitor by the word of an unworthy man. He hath proclaimed me to be a partaker of his vain imaginations, notwithstanding the whole course of my life hath approved the contrary, as my death shall approve it. Woe, woe, woe be unto him by whose falsehood we are lost. He hath separated us asunder. He hath slain my honour, my fortune. He hath robbed thee of thy husband, thy child of his father, and me of you both. O God! Thou dost know my wrongs. Know then, thou my wife and child; know then, thou my Lord and King, that I ever thought them too honest to betray, and too good to conspire against. But, my wife, forgive them all, as I do. Live humble, for thou hast but a time also. God forgive my Lord Harry, for he was my heavy enemy. And for my Lord Cecil, I thought he would never forsake me in extremity. I would not have done it him, God knows. But do not thou know it, for he must be master of my child, and may have compassion of him. Be not dismayed that I died in despair of God's mercies. Strive not to dispute it. But assure thyself that God hath not left me, nor Satan tempted me. Hope and despair live not together. I know it is forbidden to destroy ourselves; but I trust it is forbidden in this sort, that we destroy not ourselves despairing of God's ¬ *Apology for Self-Destruction.* ¬ mercy. The mercy of God is immeasurable; the cogitations of men comprehend it not. In the Lord I have ever trusted; and I know that my Redeemer liveth. Far is it from me to be tempted with Satan; I am only tempted with Sorrow, whose sharp teeth devour my heart. O God! Thou art goodness itself; Thou canst not but be good to me. O God! that art mercy itself; Thou canst not but be merciful to me!

'Oh, what will my poor servants think at their return, when they hear I am accused to be Spanish, who sent them, at very great charge, to plant and discover upon his territory. Oh, intolerable infamy! O God! I cannot resist these thoughts. I cannot bear to think how I am derided, to think of the expectation of my enemies, the scorns I shall receive, the cruel words of lawyers, the infamous taunts and despites, to be made a wonder and a spectacle! O Death! hasten thou unto me, that thou mayest destroy the memory of these, and lay me up in dark forgetfulness. O Death! destroy my memory, which is my tormentor; my thoughts and my life cannot dwell in one body. But do thou forget me, poor wife, that thou mayest live to bring up my poor child. The Lord knows my sorrow to part from thee and my poor child. But part I must, by enemies and injuries; part with shame, and triumph of my detractors. And therefore be contented with this work of God and forget me in all things, but thine own honour, and the love of mine.

'I bless my poor child, and let him know his father was no traitor. Be bold of my innocence, for God—to whom I offer life and soul—knows it.'

The obstacles to the acceptance of this composition as authentic are almost insuperable. It does not ring truly. Hard as it may be to distinguish rhetoric and passion in the death-bed ¦ *Doubts.* ¦ phrases of men who have lived before the world, the contrast here with the natural pathos of the other, and undisputed, farewell of December, is too irreconcilably vivid. Then there is the extraordinary apparition of an otherwise invisible daughter. It is not the more intelligible for the opposite difficulty that few forgers would have been likely to venture upon so surprising an invention. The total disappearance of the original manuscript, and the absence for more than two centuries of all knowledge of its contents, are still stronger elements of doubt. Together, the circumstances fully justify the scepticism of Mr. Hepworth Dixon in the copious compilation styled by him a *History of the Tower*, though it is not requisite to adopt his amusing surmise that a document allowed to repose in the dark till the present age was fabricated to taint the credit of Ralegh as a virtuous husband. Probably the epistle was innocently concocted as a literary exercise by an admirer, who wished to explain or apologise for his temporary loss of self-control.

Notwithstanding a fire and indignation, occasionally approaching grandeur, which, it must be admitted, raise another perplexing question, who, if not Ralegh, had the wit to pen the epistle, it seems necessary to surrender the letter. But it is too great a leap from repudiation of it to the disbelief, first insinuated by Mr. Tytler, and more boldly and absolutely enunciated by Mr. Dixon, in the attempt itself at suicide. Their theory is that the whole was an invention of Ralegh's enemies. It may be admitted that the stab, like the letter, has its difficulties. If he tried to kill himself, it is strange that a practised swordsman should not have succeeded. Whether he meant death or not, the reserve of the Crown advocates at Winchester is equally mysterious. They were, it might have been thought, sure to dwell upon the act in the one case as contemptible, in the other as presumptive proof of a sense of guilt. The latter is the obvious way in which it would strike the mind. Sir Toby Matthew, son of the Bishop who had lately ejected Ralegh from his London house, described it as *Reasons for Silence.* 'a guilty blow.' Two centuries later, it suggested to Hallam, 'a presumption of consciousness that something could be proved against him.' Why did Ralegh's contemporary and official adversaries not press the presumption home, if they could? On the other side, there is the yet weightier evidence of Ralegh's own conduct. He and his wife and friends must have heard the rumour, and their tongues were not tied. Whatever reasons counsel and judges had for reticence, the town had none. If Ralegh could have contradicted the discreditable tale, it is, as in the case of an earlier scandal, inconceivable that he should not. The explanation of his absolute silence, and the partial, not entire, silence of his adversaries, is that he was ashamed of his despair, and they were ashamed of having brought him to it. Cecil, after the trial, referred to the matter, after the fashion of Matthew and of Hallam, as 'suspicious.' At the time of the occurrence he mentioned it to Sir Thomas Parry in a tone more of apology. He appeared to be afraid

European opinion might imagine that Ralegh had been driven mad by merciless treatment. Had death ensued, a worse suspicion, however in this instance unjust, was to be feared. Cecil would remember that there had been Tower suicides before, and that they had been interpreted as evidence rather against the gaolers than the prisoners.

For a moment it seemed as if Ralegh had been superfluously mistrustful of English justice. A mass of tremendous charges had been rolled together. To Waad's hopeful fancy they appeared, he told Cecil, to have gravely implicated Ralegh, as well as Cobham. Investigated with a view to a positive arraignment, the pile broke up and evaporated. Watson's and Brooke's stories proved as unsubstantial as the astonishing romance adopted by grave de Thou. According to the French annalist, Ralegh, in disgust at the loss of his Captaincy of the Guard, had joined in a plot to kill the King, started by a band of Englishmen incensed at the Scottish irruption. He had accepted the post of assassin. But his sister's report of his agitation, of which she misapprehended the cause, induced inquiry. *Improbability of Ralegh's Complicity.* Arrested, he confessed the whole to James, and bought his life by the betrayal of Grey, Cobham, and Markham. Silly as is that tale, there was almost a more obvious dearth of motive for the prominent part assigned to him in the most circumstantial of the extorted depositions. Evidence was given that the other conspirators had agreed upon the apportionment among themselves of the high offices of State. No one testified that any had been reserved for the most competent, the most distinguished, and the most ambitious of the company. Ralegh's sole reward for the alleged terrible risk was, by Waad's report of Brooke's and Watson's admissions, to be some such sum of eight or ten thousand crowns as was to be offered to Cecil and Northumberland, who incurred no danger.

Soon it must have become apparent that success in a prosecution of Ralegh depended solely on the plausibility and consistency of Cobham's accusations. They were peculiarly deficient in those qualities. Ralegh has recorded that Cobham's remorse for the evil wrought by his charges of July 20 commenced within the building in which they had been uttered. At any rate, on the 29th he retracted them more or less completely. By a letter of that date, addressed to the Lords of the Council, he admitted he had pressed Arenberg for four or five hundred thousand crowns, though nothing was decided about their application. He had expected, he said, a general discontentment, and the money was to be expended as occasion offered. At his oral examination on the same day he is stated by Cecil, in a letter to Parry, to have 'cleared Sir Walter in most things, and to have taken all the burden to himself.' It may be inferred from an allusion by him in a letter that some of the Lords who had been interrogating him allowed their indignation at his apparent calumnies against Ralegh to be perceptible. The result was a growing impression that the proceedings against Ralegh would have to be abandoned. Lord Grey, an austere Protestant, and Sir Griffin Markham, a Catholic, already, it was rumoured, had denied that he had been a conspirator. They had affirmed they would have given up their project upon any suspicion that he was mixed up with it. Now Cobham also was become a broken reed. M. de Beaumont wrote to King Henry that the Lords found it difficult in consequence to sustain Ralegh's prosecution. 'God forgive Sir Walter Ralegh,' Cobham had exclaimed in August to Sir John Peyton's son; 'he hath accused me; but I cannot accuse him.'

Cobham's Remorse.

Cobham's awakened sense of justice prompted him in the autumn to a step which might have been decisive. Peyton was no longer at the Tower. Ralegh's guilt had so far been presumed, as early as August, that his patent as Governor of Jersey had been declared forfeited through his grievous treason intended against the King. The office was conferred on Peyton, in some measure, perhaps, that he might be removed from the charge of Ralegh. The current belief was that his preferment was disgrace for connivance at communications between him and Cobham. To his successor, Sir George Harvey, Cobham wrote on October 24, desiring the grant of facilities to him to address the Council on Ralegh's behalf: 'Mr. Lieutenant, If that I may write unto the Lords I would, touching Sir Walter Ralegh; besides my letter to my Lord Cecil; God is my witness, it doth touch my conscience. As you shall send me word so I will do, that my letter may be ready against your son's going. I would very fain have the words that the Lords used of my barbarousness in accusing him falsely.' Harvey received this brief and not very coherent, but significant, epistle, and locked the request up in his own bosom. He did worse. From the language of his tardy explanation to Cecil it is plain that he effectually discouraged Cobham's disposition to be Ralegh's apologist to the Council. He underrated, however, Ralegh's energy and dexterity. Cecil imagined that Ralegh had solicited from Cobham the original retractation. Messages, he suspected, had passed between the two in which Ralegh had 'expostulated Cobham's unkind using of him.' The correctness of his conjecture for the past is unknown. It was true of the present. Ralegh managed to have a letter, inclosed in, or fastened to, an apple, thrown, in November, four nights before they came to Winchester, into Cobham's window in Wardrobe tower. At the time the Lieutenant was at supper. In it he entreated Cobham to do him justice by his answer, and to signify to him that he had wronged him in his accusation. He added: 'Do not, as my Lord of Essex did, take heed of a preacher. By his persuasion he confessed, and so made himself guilty.' Cobham, though later he forgot the fact, appears to have duly replied in a letter, which was pushed under Ralegh's door. In it he admitted the wrong he had done to Ralegh. The language was not distinct enough. It was 'not to my contenting,' as afterwards said Ralegh, who wrote

again. He did not ask for another written confession. *Written etractations.*

Instead, he besought Cobham to declare his innocence when he should himself be arraigned. Thereupon Cobham sent a letter described by Ralegh as 'very good,' a complete and solemn justification, of which Howell in his *State Trials* adopts the following transcript: 'Seeing myself so near my end, for the discharge of my own conscience, and freeing myself from your blood, which else will cry vengeance against me, I protest upon my salvation I never practised with Spain by your procurement. God so comfort me in this my affliction, as you are a true subject for anything that I know. I will say, as Daniel, *Purus sum a sanguine hujus.* So God have mercy upon my soul as I know no treason by you.' According to another version, differing in language, not in tenor, the letter ran: 'To free myself from the cry of blood, I protest upon my soul, and before God and His angels, I never had conference with you in any treason, nor was ever moved by you to the things I heretofore accused you of; and, for anything I know, you are as innocent and as clear from any treasons against the King as is any subject living. And God so deal with me and have mercy upon my soul, as this is true.' Ralegh seems to have kept to himself the knowledge of the existence of this letter for the present, as Sir George Harvey, with less excuse, concealed the fact of Cobham's prayer to himself.

The correspondence was arranged partly through Edward Cottrell, a Tower servant who waited upon Ralegh. Partly it was through the Lieutenant's son, George, whom Ralegh had won over, as he had won over Sir John Peyton's son, John. It was on account of the discovery by the Council, through Ralegh's production at the trial of Cobham's letter to him, of George Harvey's mediation, and of the youth's imprisonment for it, that on

December 17, *Sir George Harvey's Disclosure.* several weeks after the end of the trial, at which it might have benefited Ralegh, the Lieutenant gave Cecil the letter of October 24. In the confidence that the infraction of discipline by his son, as well as by his two prisoners, would be extenuated by his own confession of an excess of official zeal, he acknowledged his suppression of the October letter. Incidentally he testified to the sincerity of Cobham's remorse. Cobham's 'great desire to justify Sir Walter,' he admitted to Cecil, 'having been by me then stopped, he diverted it, as I conceive, and it is very likely, unto Sir Walter himself.' In this penitent mood Cobham had confessed his misdeeds to others besides. He is reported to have told the vicar of Cobham parish that Ralegh 'had done him no hurt, but he had done Ralegh a great deal.' At last Ralegh might think that Cobham had ceased to be his accuser. Prepared as he was for his companion's 'fashion of uttering things easily,' he could scarcely have anticipated the layers of retractation still latent in that voluminous repository.

His trust in the return of Cobham's veracity would not blind him to the peril he continued to incur from the 'cruelty' of the law of treason; from its willingness, in jealousy for the sovereign's safety, to have an innocent scapegoat rather than no example. He knew that the people took his guilt for granted, and that a jury would reflect popular opinion. He could look for no real help in any quarter. To honest, but unimaginative, politicians, he was an enigma and a trouble with his ideas. They simply wished him out of the way. He was sure of the hatred of the new men, 'very honourable men,' like the Tissaphernes of his History, 'if honour may be valued by greatness and place in Court.' He could calculate on no *Animosity of the Howards* benevolence from the old courtiers. His claims of equality had always been an offence to the ancient nobility, which held itself entitled to precedence in glory as in its rewards. One from whom better things were to have been expected, the Lord Admiral, though he did not actively join in the prosecution, had his personal reasons for rejoicing in the downfall of a sharp censor of his naval administration. Between him and the Howard interest in general there had been frequent feuds, and they were opposed on many important questions. Lord Henry was not the only Howard who bore him ill-will, though the rest were not equally malignant.

Henry Howard's confederate in the Scottish intrigues, Robert Cecil, had no family grievances to avenge. If he once feared Ralegh's rivalry, he could fear it no more. It is very difficult now, as before, to believe that he entertained sentiments of positive animosity or vindictiveness against Ralegh. Canon Kingsley's description of him as one of the most 'accomplished villains in history,' as the archplotter, who had managed the whole conspiracy against Ralegh, though Ralegh knew nothing of it till after the trial, is extravagant. Even Hallam's reference to 'the hostility of Cecil, so insidious and implacable,' seems exaggerated and unjust. The Minister was conscious of no malice. He took no pleasure in the present prosecution. But moral cowardice and incapacity to dispense with power now, as formerly, explain an attitude, which, it must be admitted, is hardly to be distinguished from that of an inveterate enemy. He could not afford, having, after a struggle, clambered on board the new ship of State, to identify himself with wrecked comrades known to be distasteful to his present master. It was convenient for him to assume an air of reluctant conviction that his friend was guilty, and that the only question was whether sufficient evidence could be collected to prove it judicially. On October 3 he wrote that Cobham's original accusation was 'so well fortified with other demonstrative circumstances, and the retractation so blemished by the discovery of the intelligence which they had, as few men can conceive Sir Walter Ralegh's denial comes from a clear heart.' He who knew well the habits of judges and juries in trials for treason, affected to think Ralegh could desire no fairer opportunity. 'Always,' he wrote in October to Winwood, 'he shall be left to the law, which is the right all *Cecil's Coldness.* men are born to.' His elaborate statements of the charges and proceedings to Parry, which were intended for circulation through Europe, convey the same impression of willingness to warp facts under cover of a cold concern for nothing but the truth. He did not deceive foreigners. M. de Beaumont, whose diplomatic interest it was to abet a prosecution which implicated Spain, spoke of him, in language already quoted, as undertaking the affair with so much warmth that it was said he acted more from interest and passion than for the good of the kingdom. He did not deceive unbiassed Englishmen. Harington wrote in 1603: 'I doubt the dice not fairly thrown, if Ralegh's life be the losing stake.' He has not deceived posterity.

To the new Court, its head, and his Scotch favourites, Ralegh necessarily was an object of aversion. He was not the less odious that he was incomprehensible. For years he and his designs had been subjects of suspicion and dread at Holyrood. Now, when he was no longer directly dangerous, he was an obstruction and a perplexity. In spite of the current charges against him, he represented hatred of Spain, with which James was eager to be on terms of amity. He represented the spirit of national unrest and adventurousness, which James abhorred. The obstinate calumny of his scepticism served as a pretext to the King's conscience for the unworthier instinct of personal dislike. His wisdom, learning, and wit were no passports to the favour of the one privileged Solomon of these isles.

He understood all he had to face. Vehemently as he fretted and complained, he was equal to the ordeal. He may *Compensations for · Ralegh's Sufferings.* be said to have been happy in undergoing it. Unless for it, neither his contemporaries nor posterity could have fully comprehended the scope and strength of his character. Unversed in law, he was more than a match for the incomparable legal learning of Coke and for his docile bench of judges. His trial, which is the opprobrium of forensic and judicial annals, makes a bright page in national history for the unique personality it reveals, with all its wealth of subtlety, courage, and versatility. Figures of purer metal have often stood in the dock, with as small chance of safety. Ralegh was a compound of gold, silver, iron, and clay. The trial, and all its circumstances, brought into conspicuous relief the diversity which is no less the wonder of the character than it is of the career. The Ralegh who has stamped himself upon English history, who has fascinated English imagination, is not so much the favourite of Elizabeth, the soldier and sailor; it is the baited prey of Coke and Popham, the browbeaten convict of Winchester, the attainted prisoner of the Tower. Against the Court of James and its obsequious lawyers he was struggling for bare life, for no sublime cause, for no impersonal ideal. Yet so high was his spirit, and his bearing so undaunted, that he has ever appeared to subsequent generations a martyr on the altar of English liberties.

CHAPTER XIX.

THE TRIAL (November 17).

The Indictment.

On September 21 Ralegh had been indicted at Staines for having, with Cobham and Brooke, compassed in the Parish of St. Martin in the Fields to deprive the King of his crown, to alter the true religion, and to levy war. The indictment alleged that Cobham had discoursed with him on the means of raising Arabella Stuart to the crown; that Cobham had treated with Arenberg for 600,000 crowns from the King of Spain, and had meant to go to Spain in quest of support for Arabella. It alleged that Ralegh and Cobham had agreed Arabella should by letter promise the Archduke of Austria, the King of Spain, and the Duke of Savoy, to maintain a firm truce with Spain, to tolerate Papistry, and be guided by the three princes in her marriage. It alleged the publication and delivery by Ralegh to Cobham of a book traitorously devised against the King's title to the crown. Finally, it alleged that Cobham had agreed, when he should have received the money from Arenberg, to deliver eight or ten thousand crowns to Ralegh to enable him the better to effect the intended treasons. Jurors were summoned in September for the trial of this indictment. But for some reason the hearing was deferred till November.

The plague raging in London and the neighbourhood may account for the delay. Pym relates in his *Diary* that it killed 2000 a week. The Tower was reported in September, 1603, to be infected. The King's Bench kept the next term at Winchester. So to Winchester their respective custodians conveyed Brooke, Sir Griffin Markham, Sir Edward Parham, who finally was acquitted, Brooksby, Copley, Watson, Clarke, Cobham, and Grey. They were escorted by under-wardens of the Tower, the Keeper of the Westminster Gate-house, and fifty light horse. Ralegh set out on November

10 in his own coach, under Mob Judgments. the charge of Sir Robert Mansel and Sir William Waad. Waad wrote to Cecil that he found his prisoner much altered. At Wimbledon a group of friends and relatives had assembled to greet him as he passed. Generally he encountered none but looks of hatred. Precautions had to be taken to steal the planter of Virginia, the hero of Cadiz, the wit and poet, the splendid gentleman, the lavish patron, from the curs of London, without outrage, or murder. It was 'hob or nob,' writes Waad to Cecil, whether or not Ralegh 'should have been brought alive through such multitudes of unruly people as did exclaim

against him.' He adds, that it would hardly have been believed the plague was hot in London in presence of such a mob. Watches had to be set through all the streets, both in London and the suburbs. 'If one hare-brain fellow amongst so great a multitude had begun to set upon him, as they were near to do it, no entreaty or means could have prevailed; the fury and tumult of the people was so great.' Tobacco-pipes, stones, and mud were, wrote Cecil's secretary, Mr. Michael Hickes, to Lord Shrewsbury, thrown by the rabble, both in London and in other towns on the road. Ralegh is stated to have scorned these proofs of the aversion of base and rascal people. Mr. Macvey Napier, in his thoughtful essay, attributes to him 'a total want of sympathy with, if not a dislike of, the lower orders.' His disgust, perhaps, was rather evoked by the want of discrimination in all masses. He was habitually good to his dependents, and was beloved by them. A multitude, whatever the rank of its constituents, he regarded as 'dogs who always bark at those they know not.' He had never flattered a mob. He did not now cower before it. To manifestations of popular odium his nature rose, as to every peremptory call upon his powers. He foresaw that posterity would understand him, and would right him.

Two days were taken to reach Bagshot, and three more to traverse the

Chief

Justice Popham. remaining thirty miles to Winchester. Ralegh and others of the accused were lodged in the Royal Castle of Winchester, built by Bishop Henry, Stephen's brother. A King's Bench Court had been fitted up in Wolvesey Castle, the old episcopal palace, now a ruin. There the trial opened on November 17. Sir John Popham was Lord Chief Justice of England. He was not prepossessing in appearance, 'a huge, heavy, ugly man,' and he had an uncouth history. As a child he had been stolen by gipsies. In early manhood he was a notorious gamester and reveller. He took purses, it is stoutly affirmed, on Shooter's Hill, when he was a barrister, and thirty years of age. Then he reformed his morals, read law, and entered the House of Commons. In 1581 he was elected Speaker, and in 1592 was appointed Chief Justice. Essex had imprisoned him in Essex House on the day of the rising, but protected his life from his crazy followers. He had the generosity to requite the favour by venturing to advise the Queen to grant a pardon. He amassed a vast estate, part of it being Littlecote, which he was fabled to have wrested, together with an hereditary curse, from a murderer, Sir Richard Dayrell. With Popham, Chief Justice Anderson, and Justices Gawdy and Warburton, there sat as Commissioners of Oyer and Terminer, Lord Thomas Howard, since July Earl of Suffolk and Lord Chamberlain, Charles Blount, Lord Mountjoy and

Earl of Devonshire, Lord Henry Howard, Robert Cecil, now Lord Cecil, Lord Wotton, Vice-Chamberlain Sir John Stanhope, and Sir William Waad. That the King, with his personal knowledge of Henry Howard's fierce hatred of Ralegh, as evinced in the whole private correspondence with Holyrood, should have appointed him a judge was an outrage upon decency. Attorney-General Coke, Serjeant Hele, who had been Ralegh's counsel against Meere, and Serjeant Phillips, prosecuted. The law allowed no counsel to ¦ *The Jury.* ¦ prisoners. Sir Michael Stanhope, Sir Edward Darcy, Ralegh's neighbour in Durham House, and Sir William Killigrew, had been, it was rumoured, on the jury panel, but were 'changed overnight, being found not for their turn.' The report of a sudden modification in the list is not necessarily untrue, though the jury, it is said, was a Middlesex jury, and had been ordered long before to attend at Winchester. Other Middlesex men, of whom many were at Winchester, may have been substituted. At any rate, Ralegh did not except to any names. 'I know,' said he, 'none of them. They are all Christians and honest gentlemen.' Sir Thomas, or John, Fowler was chosen foreman.

Ralegh asked leave to answer the points particularly as they were delivered, on account of his failing memory and sickness. Coke objected to having the King's evidence dismembered, 'whereby it might lose much of its grace and vigour.' Popham was more considerate. He promised to let Ralegh, after the King's counsel should have produced all the evidence, answer particularly what he would. Hele opened. I cull a few flowers of his eloquence and logic: 'You have heard of Ralegh's bloody attempt to kill the King, in whom consists all our happiness, and the true use of the Gospel, and his royal children, poor babes that never gave offence. Since the Conquest there was never the like treason. But out of whose head came it? Out of Ralegh's. Cobham said to Brooke: "It will never be well in England till the King and his cubs are taken away." It appears that Cobham took Ralegh to be either a god or an idol. Bred in England, Cobham hath no experience abroad. But Ralegh is a man of great wit, military, and a swordsman. Now, whether these things were bred in a hollow tree, I leave to them to speak of who can speak far better than myself.'

He meant Sir Edward Coke, who then addressed the Court. He started gently: 'We carry a just mind, to condemn no man but upon plain evidence.' Thence he proceeded: 'Here is mischief, mischief *in summo gradu*, exorbitant mischief!' He first explained 'the treason of the Bye.' That was the alleged plot of Grey, Brooke, and Markham to surprise the King, and carry him to the Tower. Ralegh reminded the jury that he was not charged with the Bye. 'No,' retorted Coke, but 'all these treasons, though they consisted of several points, closed in together; like Samson's foxes, which were joined in the tails, though the heads were severed.' He anticipated the objection that the Crown had but one witness, Cobham. It had, he argued, more than two witnesses: 'When a man by his accusation of another shall by the same accusation also condemn himself, and make himself liable to the same punishment, this is by law more forcible than many witnesses, and is as the inquest of twelve men. For the law presumes that a man will not accuse himself in order to accuse another.' That is, Coke chose to confuse an argument for the sufficiency of a man's evidence of his own guilt with its cogency as evidence of another's. After this, he declaimed upon the horror of the treason in the present case. 'To take away the fox and his cubs! To

The Main, and the Bye. whom, Sir Walter, did you bear malice? To the royal children?' Ralegh protested: 'What is the treason of Markham and the priests to me?' Coke burst forth: 'I will then come close to you. I will prove you to be the most notorious traitor that ever came to the bar. You, indeed, are upon the Main; but you followed them of the Bye in imitation.' Ralegh asked for proof. 'Nay,' cried Coke, 'I will prove all. Thou art a monster; thou hast an English face, but a Spanish heart. Your intent was to set up the Lady Arabella, and to depose our rightful King, the lineal descendant of Edward IV.' Coke, it will be seen, did not choose to trace the Stuarts to Henry VII. He treated the Tudors as interlopers. 'You pretend,' he continued, that the money expected from Arenberg was to 'forward the Peace with Spain. Your jargon was peace, which meant Spanish invasion and Scottish subversion.' Cobham, argued Coke, never was a politician, nor a swordsman. Ralegh was both. Ralegh and Cobham both were discontented, and Cobham's discontent grew by Ralegh. Such was Ralegh's machiavellian policy that he would never confer with but one at once. He would talk with none but Cobham; 'because, saith he, one witness can never condemn me.'

Next, Coke turned to the communications between Ralegh and Cobham in the Tower. He exclaimed to the jury: 'And now you shall see the most horrible practices that ever came out of the bottomless pit of the lowest hell.' In reply to a protest by Ralegh as to his liability for some underhand practices of Cobham, as Warden of the Cinque Ports, Coke foamed out: 'All he did was by thy instigation, thou viper; for I thou thee, thou traitor! I will prove thee the rankest traitor in all England.' 'No, Master Attorney,' was the answer: 'I am no traitor. Whether I live or die, I shall stand as true a subject as ever the King hath. You may call me a traitor at your pleasure; yet it becomes not a man of quality or virtue to do so. But I *Master Attorney's zeal.* take comfort in it; it is all that you can do; for I do not yet

- 184 -

hear that you charge me with any treason.' The Lord Chief Justice interposed: 'Sir Walter Ralegh, Master Attorney speaks out of the zeal of his duty for the service of the King, and you for your life; be patient on both sides.' It is hard to see how Ralegh had shown impatience. Some impatience he manifested on the reading of Cobham's declaration of July 20. 'Cobham,' said he, 'is not such a babe as you make him. He hath dispositions of such violence which his best friends could never temper.' He was not of a nature to be easily persuaded by Ralegh. Assuredly Ralegh was not likely to 'conspire with a man that hath neither love nor following,' against a vigorous and youthful King, in reliance on a State so impoverished and weak as Spain, and so detested by himself. He ridiculed the notion that King Philip either could or would freely disburse 600,000 crowns on the mere word of Cobham. Elizabeth's own Londoners did not lend to her without lands in pawn. Yet more absurd was the supposition that Ralegh was in the plot. Thrice had he served against Spain at sea. Against Spain he had expended, of his own property, 40,000 marks. 'Spanish as you term me, I had at this time writ a treatise to the King's Majesty of the present state of Spain, and reasons against the peace.'

When the first or second examination of Cobham was cited, Popham offered himself practically as a witness. He had heard Cobham say of Ralegh, as he signed his deposition: 'That wretch! That traitor Ralegh!' 'And surely,' added the Chief Justice, 'his countenance and action much satisfied me that what he had confessed was true, and that he surely thought Sir Walter had betrayed him.' Upon this Ralegh demanded to have his accuser, who was under the same roof, brought in, and examined face to face. Long before, and equally in vain, had his father-in-law, Sir Nicholas Throckmorton, called, as Sir Michael Foster mentions, for the witnesses against him 'to be brought face to face upon the trial.' Ralegh cited 1 Edward VI, that no man shall be condemned of treason, unless he be accused by two lawful accusers. He referred also to 1 and 2 Phil. and Mary, which ordained that an accuser of another of treason shall, if living and in the realm, be brought forth : *Call for Cobham.* : in person before the party arraigned, if he require it. The Canon of God itself in Deuteronomy, he urged, requires two witnesses. 'I beseech you then, my Lords, let Cobham be sent for. Let him be charged upon his soul, upon his allegiance to the King; and if he will then maintain his accusation to my face, I will confess myself guilty.' Popham's answer was: 'This thing cannot be granted; for then a number of treasons should flourish. The accuser may be drawn by practice while he is in prison.' Again and again Ralegh called for Cobham. Popham objected that he might prevaricate in order to procure the acquittal of his 'old friend.' 'To absolve me,' cried Ralegh sarcastically, 'me, the infuser of these treasons! Me, the cause of all his miseries, and the destruction of his house!' Coke asserted: 'He is a party and cannot come. The law is against it.' 'It is a toy to tell me of law,' was the reply, 'I defy law. I stand on the facts.' At one moment his passionate appeal seemed to have awed the Court into justice. Cecil asked if he would really abide by Cobham's words. 'Yes, in a main point.' 'If he say you have been the instigator of him to deal with the Spanish King, had not the Council cause to draw you hither?' asked Cecil. 'I put myself on it,' answered Ralegh. 'Then, call to God, Sir Walter,' said Cecil; 'and prepare yourself; for I verily believe my Lord will prove it.' Cecil knew of Cobham's recent reiteration of his charge, and supposed he could be trusted to insist upon it in Court. The Lords Commissioners, on consultation, doubted this, and finally decided to keep him back, and rely upon his letter.

Two Witnesses.

The trial pursued its course. Popham laid it down that 1 Edw. VI. c. 12, was repealed by 1 and 2 Phil. and Mary. Mr. Justice Gawdy corroborated this, uttering the solitary judicial dictum recorded of him, that 'the statute of Edward had been found inconvenient, and had therefore been repealed.' The provision cited by Ralegh from Philip and Mary's repealing statute, Popham ruled, applied solely to the specific treasons it mentioned. The Act ordained that the trial of treasons in general should follow common law procedure, as before the reign of Edward VI. But by common law one witness was sufficient. The confession of confederates was full proof, even though not subscribed, if it were attested by credible witnesses. Indeed, remarked Popham, echoing Coke, 'of all other proofs the accusation of one, who by his confession first accuseth himself, is the strongest. It hath the force of a verdict of twelve men.' Coke himself later, when, as Mr. Justice Michael Foster expresses it, 'his disgrace at Court had given him leisure for cool reflection,' intimated in his *Institutes* that the statute of Edward the Sixth had not been repealed, and that the obligation, as specified by it, to produce two witnesses to charges of treason remained in force. That was not the view of Elizabethan Judges. At the trial of the Duke of Norfolk it was laid down that the necessity no longer existed. In fairness it must be admitted that Popham and his brethren were bound to assume the law had then been correctly stated. They were equally bound by a series of precedents to allow written depositions to be treated as valid testimony. Only by the assent of counsel for the Crown was the oral examination of witnesses permitted. Ralegh did not struggle against the ruling. He could but plead, 'though, by the rigour and severity of the law, this may be sufficient evidence without producing the witness, yet, your Lordships, as ministers of the King, are bound to administer the law in equity.' 'No,' replied Popham: 'equity must proceed from the King; you can have only

- 186 -

justice from us.' Coke triumphantly exclaimed: 'This dilemma of yours about two witnesses led you into treason.' Cobham's letter of July 29 to the Council about the money asked of Arenberg was read. In it occurred the expression: 'We did expect the general discontentment.' Coke's comment was: 'The peace pretended by Sir Walter Ralegh is merely jargon; for it is clear the money was for discontented persons. Now Ralegh was to have part of the money; therefore, he was a discontented person, and, therefore, a traitor.' That was the logic thought good enough at a trial for treason. So, to Ralegh's indignant : *A Spider of Hell.* : remonstrance at the use of the evidence of 'hellish spiders,' like Clarke and Watson, concerning 'the King and his cubs' as evidence against him, Coke answered: 'Thou hast a Spanish heart, and thyself art a spider of hell; for thou confessest the King to be a most sweet and gracious Prince, and yet thou hast conspired against him.' With equal relevancy he cited from the depositions: 'Brooke thinketh the project for the murder of the King was infused by Ralegh into his brother's head.' For Coke this was valid evidence against Ralegh.

On rolled the muddy stream of inconsequential testimony, and of reasoning to match; the 'irregular ramble,' as Sir John Hawles has termed it. Snagge's book was discussed; how Ralegh borrowed it from Burleigh's library; and how Cobham had it, whether by gift from Ralegh, or by borrowing it when Ralegh was asleep. To Ralegh the whole appeared the triviality it was. 'It is well known,' said he, 'that there came out nothing in those times but I had it. I believe they will find in my house almost all the libels writ against the late Queen.' As utterly irrelevant against him was the introduction of Arabella Stuart to deny her knowledge of any plots in her pretended interest. Worse than irrelevant was pilot Dyer's gossip with a gentleman at Lisbon, to whom Dyer had observed that the King of England was shortly to be crowned. 'Nay,' saith the Portugal, : *Serjeant Phillips.* : 'that shall never be; for his throat will be cut by Don Ralegh and Don Cobham before he be crowned.' 'What will you infer upon that?' asked Ralegh. 'That your treason hath wings,' replied Coke. Hereupon Serjeant Phillips relieved Coke, and almost outdid him. Phillips argued that the object of procuring money was to raise up tumults in Scotland, and to take the lives of his Majesty and his issue. For those purposes a treasonable book against the King's right to the Crown was 'divulged.' Commencing with the unproved allegation that 'Sir Walter Ralegh confesseth my Lord Cobham guilty of all these treasons,' Phillips proceeded: 'The question is, whether Ralegh be guilty, as joining with or instigating him. If Lord Cobham's accusation be true, he is guilty. If not, he is clear. Ralegh hath no answer. Of as much wit as the wit of man can devise, he useth his bare denial. A denial by the defendant must not move the jury.' Nothing could be more crushing than the calm rejoinder: 'You have not proved any one thing by direct proofs, but all by circumstances. I appeal to God and the King on this point whether Cobham's accusation be sufficient to condemn me.'

So weak was the case for the prosecution that to this stage, by the admission of a reporter of the trial, the result was very doubtful. Coke, however, with the cognizance, it may be presumed, of the Court, had prepared a dramatic surprise. Cobham, the day before, had written or signed a repetition of his charge. Ralegh's account of the transaction at the trial was that Lady Kildare, Lady Ralegh's enemy, had persuaded Cobham to accuse Ralegh, as the sole way of saving his own life. A letter from her to him goes some length towards confirming the allegation. She writes: 'Help

Cobham's

New Statement. yourself, if it may be. I say no more; but draw not the weight of others' burdens.' According to another, and not very likely, story, told by Sir Anthony Welldon in his *Court of King James,* Cobham subsequently stated that Waad had induced him by a trick to sign his name on a blank page, which afterwards was thus filled in. The paper alleged a request by Ralegh to obtain for him a pension of £1500 for intelligence. 'But,' it ambiguously proceeded, 'upon this motion for £1500 per annum for intelligence I never dealt with Count Arenberg.' 'Now,' added the writer, as if it were a conclusion from premises, 'as by this may appear to your Lordships, he hath been the original cause of my ruin. For, but by his instigation, I had never dealt with Count Arenberg. And so hath he been the only cause of my discontentment; I never coming from the Count, or Court, but still he filled and possessed me with new causes of discontentments.' The reading of the statement was set in a more than usually decorated framework of Coke's amenities. Ralegh throughout the trial had been for the King's Attorney an 'odious fellow;' the 'most vile and execrable traitor.' He had been stigmatized as 'hateful to all the realm for his pride,' to which Ralegh had retorted: 'It will go near to prove a measuring cast, Mr. Attorney, between you and me.' With Cobham's deposition in his hand, Coke cried: 'I will lay thee on thy back for the confidentest traitor that ever came to a bar.' When Cecil prayed him not to be so impatient, Coke flew out: 'If I may not be patiently heard, you will encourage traitors.' Sulkily down he sat, and would speak no more till the Commissioners entreated him to go on. Resuming, he criticized Ralegh's letter to Cobham in the Tower, which was next read: 'O damnable Atheist! He hath learned some text of Scripture to serve his own purpose. Essex died the child of God. Thou wast by.

Et lupus et turpes instant morientibus ursae.'

Being asked what he said of Cobham's statement to the Lords, 'I say,' answered Ralegh, 'that Cobham is a base, dishonourable, poor soul!' 'Is he base?' retorted Coke. 'I return it into thy throat on his behalf. But for thee he had been a good subject.'

The document did not amount to a confession by Cobham even of his own treason. At highest it was evidence against him of negotiations with Count Arenberg which might have been 'warrantable,' and of discontent which need *Exaggeration of its Importance.* not have been in the least criminal. If such secondary testimony had been legal when its author was available as a witness, and if its statements had been incontrovertible, it ought to have been held worthless against Ralegh. Nothing, so far as appears even from the paper, was ever done towards the gratification of the desire for a foreign pension imputed to him. Within limits, Cobham's allegation that Ralegh had fomented his anger against the new state of things is plausible enough. It would be strange if the two disgraced favourites did not at their frequent meetings club and inflame their mutual pique. Obviously, apart from acts, of which there was no evidence, no irritation by Ralegh, however envenomed, as it was not shown to have been, of Cobham's discontent, could in him have been treason. Judged by all sound laws of evidence, the testimony of the statement was as flimsy as all the rest of the proofs. To attach importance to it was a burlesque of justice. It was treated as demonstrative by a packed Bench, a Bar hungering for place, and a faint-hearted jury, anxious above all things to vindicate authority, and not caring to discriminate among the prisoners on the charges against them. To the whole court it came like a godsend. The author of the fullest report, that which is preserved in the Harleian MSS., expresses the sentiment of Jacobean lawyers: 'This confession gave a great satisfaction, and cleared all the former evidence, which before stood very doubtful.'

In the reporter's judgment it overwhelmed the defendant himself. Reasonably Ralegh 'was much amazed.' He could not have anticipated Cobham's retractation of his retractation. He perceived the new peril in which he was plunged by the statement that he had solicited, or been offered by Cobham, a Spanish pension, though, as he told the King in January, 1604, so little account had he made at the time of the conversation in which the offer was made, that he never remembered any such thing till it was at his *The Prior Recantation.* trial objected against him. He felt public opinion shaken. His faith in himself was not weakened. 'By and by,' says the reporter, 'he seemed to gather his spirits again.' Pulling out of his pocket the recantation, the second, which Cobham had addressed to him from the Tower, and attested by his hope of salvation and God's mercy on his soul, he insisted upon having it too read in court. Hereupon, says the reporter, 'was much ado, Mr. Attorney alleging that the letter was politicly and cunningly urged from the Lord Cobham,' and that the latest paper was 'simply the truth.' When Ralegh raised the natural objection that a statement written by Cobham on the eve of his own trial might be supposed to have been extorted in some sort by compulsion, Coke appealed to Popham to interrogate the Commissioners. Devonshire, as their mouthpiece, declared to the jury that it was 'mere voluntary,' and had not been written under a promise of pardon. But Cecil supported Ralegh in the demand that the jury should have before it the earlier letter also. Coke, in a report printed in 1648 under the name of Sir Thomas Overbury, is represented as exclaiming: 'My Lord Cecil, mar not a good cause.' Cecil replied: 'Master Attorney, you are more peremptory than honest; you must not come here to show me what to do.' Throughout he had been careful to blend the friend with the judge, so far as professions of regret went. He had spoken of the former dearness between himself and this gentleman, tied upon the knot of his virtues. He had declared that his friendship was not extinguished, but slaked. He had vowed himself still his friend, 'excepting faults, I call them no worse.' Now he strained that friendship to the extent of the simple justice of undertaking the duty, 'because he only knew Cobham's hand,' of reading out the letter, which, if the construction put by the prosecution on the other paper were correct, proved the writer a perjured liar either in the Tower or at Winchester.

Coke need not have feared the consequences. Both judges and jurymen had comfortably made up their minds. They were not to be moved by so slight a thing as a contradiction of Cobham in one place by Cobham in another. So prejudiced were they that the Tower letter does not appear to have produced any effect at all. Ralegh, at all events, could do no more. He had striven for many hours, and was utterly exhausted. Without more words he let the jury be dismissed to consider its verdict.

The Verdict
and Judgment.

In a quarter of an hour it returned into court with a verdict of guilty of high treason. Ralegh received the decision with dignity: 'My Lords,' said he, 'the jury hath found me guilty. They must do as they are directed. I can say nothing why judgment should not proceed. You see whereof Cobham hath accused me. You remember his protestation that I was never guilty. I desire the King should know the wrong I have been done to since I came hither.' Then Popham pronounced judgment. Addressing Ralegh, he said: 'In my conscience I am persuaded Cobham hath accused you truly. You cannot deny that you were dealt with to have a pension of £1500 a year to be a spy for Spain; therefore, you are not so true to the King as you have protested yourself to be.' He lamented the fall of one of 'so great parts,' who 'had showed wit enough this day,' 'who might have lived well with £3000 a year; for so I have heard your revenues to be.' Spite and covetousness he held to have been Ralegh's temptations. Yet the King could not be blamed for wishing to have for Captain of the Guard 'one of his own knowledge, whom he might trust,' or for desiring no longer to burden his people with a wine monopoly for Ralegh's particular good. Popham embellished his confused discourse, partly apologetic, and partly condemnatory, but not intentionally brutal or malevolent, by a glance at Ralegh's reputed freethinking. He had been taxed, said Popham, by the world with the

defence of most heathenish : *Popham's Exhortation.* : and blasphemous

opinions. 'You will do well,' the virtuous Chief Justice exhorted him, 'before you go out of the world, to give satisfaction therein. Let not any devil,' or, according to the Harleian MSS. version, 'Hariot nor any such doctor, persuade you there is no eternity in Heaven; if you think thus, you shall find eternity in Hell fire.' Ralegh had warned Cobham against confessions. Let him not apply the advice to himself. 'Your conceit of not confessing anything is very inhuman and wicked. In this world is the time of confessing, that we may be absolved at the Day of Judgment.' By way of peroration he added: 'It now comes into my mind why you may not have your accuser face to face. When traitors see themselves must die, they think it best to see their fellow live, that he may commit the like treason again, and so in some sort seek revenge.' Lastly, he pronounced the savage legal sentence.

When Popham had ended Ralegh spoke a few words. He prayed that the jury might never have to answer for its verdict. He 'only craved pardon for having concealed Lord Cobham's offer to him, which he did through a confidence that he had diverted him from those humours.' Praying then permission to speak to Lords Suffolk, Devonshire, Henry Howard, and Cecil, he entreated their intercession, which they promised, Cecil with tears, that his death might be honourable and not ignominious. He is alleged further to have requested their mediation with the King for a pardon, or, at least, that, if Cobham too were convicted, and if the sentence were to be carried out, Cobham might die first. The petition was not an ebullition of vindictiveness. It had a practical purpose. On the scaffold he could say nothing for Cobham; Cobham might say much for him. It was possible that, when nothing more was to be gained by falsehoods, his recreant friend would clear his fame once for all. Then he quitted the hall, accompanying Sir Benjamin Tichborne, the High Sheriff, to the prison, according to Sir Thomas Overbury, 'with admirable erection, yet in such sort as a condemned man should.'

CHAPTER XX.

Justice and Equity of the Conviction.

Students of English judicial history, with all their recollections of the strange processes by which criminal courts in Ralegh's age leaped to a presumption of a State prisoner's guilt, stand aghast at his conviction. Mr. Justice Foster, in his book, already cited, on *The Trial of the Rebels in Surrey in 1746*, professes his inability to see how the case, excepting *Exceptionally iniquitous.* the extraordinary behaviour of the King's Attorney, differed in hardship from many before it. He is referring to the legal points ruled by the judges against Ralegh. Possibly previous prisoners had been as ill-treated; and the fact amounts to a terrible indictment of English justice. But one broad distinction separates this from earlier convictions. Other prisoners in general were guilty, though their guilt may have been a form of patriotism, or may not have been logically proved. Ralegh's guilt of the crime imputed to him was not proved at Winchester, and has never been proved since. If to have cherished resentment for the loss of offices, to have incurred popular odium, to be reputed superhumanly subtle, to have been the sagacious comrade of a foolish malcontent, to have been alleged by that man, whom he was not permitted to interrogate, to be disaffected at a time at which strangers to him happened to be plotting rebellion, to have abstained from betraying overtures for the exertion by him of an influence he never used and did not possess on behalf of a pacification which the sovereign was negotiating, be high treason, then it is possible, though even then not certain, that Ralegh was a traitor. If none of these possibilities amount to the crime of treason, then he was not.

He was alleged to have listened to disclosures by Cobham . *The Spanish Pension.* of a scheme for obtaining money from the Archduke, or the King of Spain. He was alleged to have been offered a share. He was alleged to have asked for a pension as the price of the revelation of Court secrets. No other relevant charges were brought. Of the evidence against him, the second or third hand hearsay depositions of Brooke, Watson, Copley, and Clarke, like the gossip of Dyer, had no effect even upon the Lords Commissioners and the jury. The fragments of testimony actually credited were contributed by Cobham alone, himself the principal in the supposed transaction, who had retracted his original statement over and over again, whom the Court refused to confront with the man he accused. Had the allegations been ever so consistent, cogent, credible, and corroborated, they proved nothing, except that Ralegh might, not would, have accepted foreign gold if it had been proffered to him. Cecil accepted it for years to come, and died at once Prime Minister and pensioner of Spain. Northumberland had recently taken a pension to furnish France with secret intelligence. The fact does not abate the admiration of Lingard, who yet thinks it reasonable that a jury should have convicted Ralegh on the bare suspicion of a similar offer by Spaniards to induce him to help them towards peace. James was eager for peace. He placed the utmost faith in the possibility of permanent amity with Spain. He was enthusiastically certain of its importance and value to the kingdom and his dynasty. So little did he object to the agent of Ralegh's alleged intrigue through Cobham with the Spanish Court that he never allowed a symptom of impatience on that side to escape him. Ralegh's guilt at worst depended wholly on the reality of his partnership in Cobham's dealings with Arenberg. In the spring of 1604, Arenberg, who had left England at the end of the previous October, before the Winchester trials commenced, returned as the Archduke's envoy for the negotiation of peace between Spain and this country. He went away finally in the summer. To the Archduke who had commissioned *James and Arenberg.* this suspected plotter of treason James wrote in August, 1604: 'We thank you most affectionately for the sincerity and affection you have shown yourself to bear towards the conclusion of this peace and friendship by the choice you have made of such worthy and eminent instruments as are our cousin the Prince Count of Arenberg and his colleague, who, by their sufficiency, prudence, and integrity, have so conducted this important affair that we have received therein very great satisfaction.' He had used the same benevolent tone with respect to the Count during the Winchester proceedings. Cecil officially informed Sir Thomas Parry that the Count had always been made by Cobham to understand that the combinations and money were to be employed simply for the advancement of the peace. An identical defence might be offered for Ralegh, if not for Cobham himself. But it was convenient for James and his Court to exonerate the envoy; it was convenient for them to use the same transaction for a deadly weapon against Ralegh. Of any care or sense of actual truthfulness in King or counsellors throughout the whole business, not a trace can be found.

All concerned in Ralegh's trial and conviction have a heavy burden of bloodguiltiness to bear. But the Judges were less culpable than their lay colleagues and the Crown counsel; the whole bench of Commissioners and the Bar than the jury; the jury than the King, his Ministers, and courtiers.

Sir John Hawles, afterwards Solicitor-General, in a printed reply in 1689 to Shower's apology, called *The Magistracy and Government of England Vindicated*, for Lord Russell's conviction, censured Popham for dispensing with a second witness, and with the presence of Cobham. He argued from the practice of a later period, that Judges who had deviated from it must have been violating their consciences. That is unreasonable. The course taken by the Chief Justice and his brethren conformed, as we have seen, to the legal usage of their time, however opposed to natural justice. The fault was greater in the lay members of the Court, and in the Attorney-General, who might undoubtedly, as representing more directly the Crown, have produced Cobham. All that the Judges declared was that the Crown need not, not that it must not. Still more heinous was the verdict based upon evidence which, if enough in quantity, was manifestly worthless in quality. Twelve worthy gentlemen awarded a horrible death to a man guilty of no other offence, as they knew, than that he had been offered a sum of Spanish money, which he denied he would have accepted, and certainly never received. Most shameful of all was the conduct of the Government which knew the emptiness of the entire case, yet strained every nerve to extort a conviction.

*Legal and
Moral Innocence.*

The question of Ralegh's moral innocence is not the same as that of his legal innocence. All writers answer the latter unanimously in his favour. On the former they are divided. Hume, indeed, a far from partial critic, who could not sympathise with one of his 'great but ill regulated mind,' pronounces wholly for him. He finds no proof or any circumstance to justify the condemnation, which he roundly stigmatises as contrary to all law and equity. Historians since Hume have commonly been willing to suppose that the Government proceeded upon some solid ground. In Lingard's Catholic eyes, Ralegh was simply an unscrupulous flatterer of Elizabeth, and an immoral adventurer. Not pledging his own judgment to the righteousness of the verdict, he remarks that 'the guilt of Ralegh was no longer doubted after the solemn asseveration of Cobham' on the scaffold. Hallam had no bias. Though he thought Ralegh 'faulty,' 'rash,' destitute of 'discretion,' and not 'very scrupulous about the truth,' he admired him as a bright genius, 'a splendid ornament of his country,' 'the bravest and most renowned of Englishmen.' He has declared the verdict against him contrary to law, but thinks it 'very probable that the charge of plotting to raise Arabella to the throne was partly at least founded in truth.' Mr. Gardiner condemns the particular accusation as 'frivolous and false,' but believes it had some basis in his character, in his habit of 'looking down from the eminence of genius upon the acts of lesser men.'

For such support of the prosecution and verdict, qualified as it is, there *Absence of Evidence of Guilt.* is a difficulty in perceiving any foundation, except the improbability that a Government should have conspired to obtain the capital condemnation of an illustrious Englishman on no better testimony than that which it vouchsafed or dared to offer. That even Cobham had engaged in plots for the deposition of James in favour of Arabella, which the Ambassador of the Infanta, herself a Pretender, would not have been in the least likely to further, no evidence except French hearsay from James's Ministers exists to prove. That he may have intrigued for the exercise of illegitimate pressure in Spanish interests upon the King, is very probable on his own admission, though 'it does not follow,' as Ralegh writes in his History, 'that every man ought to be believed of himself to his own prejudice.' It is not equally clear, but it is credible, that he had sounded Ralegh, and had appealed to his constant pecuniary necessities, with a view to his engagement in the design. Ralegh may well have suspected enough, without direct complicity, to be able, if he had chosen, to deliver up Cobham to the Government some time before his interview with the Council at Windsor. His omission may have been a breach of his legal duty as a loyal subject, as his hint to Cecil of the transactions with la Renzi was a breach of perfect faithfulness to friendship. But there is no sufficient ground for questioning his own apology, that he regarded the scheme as the vapouring it for the most part was. Moreover, it is not impossible, or improbable, that he may, as he stated to the Lords Commissioners, have endeavoured to dissuade Cobham from plotting. He may have used threats for the purpose, though he did not carry them out. This would explain Cobham's alarm, otherwise unintelligible, that Ralegh meant to inveigle him and other agitators into Jersey, and then give them up. That he actively abetted a conspiracy, either with Arenberg, or against James, is in itself as improbable as it is in fact unproved. James, on his side, may have believed that Ralegh was willing to acquiesce *Apologies for Condemnation.* in a treasonable conspiracy, and to enjoy some of its fruits.

In this mode the King, and Cecil also, would lull their consciences, while they availed themselves of law for the ruin of one whom they disliked and dreaded. They acted upon surmises, and historians have followed them. Honest-minded writers have been ashamed to think the State could have persecuted an innocent man as it persecuted Ralegh without other evidence than that it disclosed. They have tried to explain the incomprehensible by the unknown. Forgetting the characters of James and his Minister, they have inferred Ralegh's criminality from his subjection to the treatment of a criminal.

Every effort was made at the time to demonstrate his capital guilt. The efforts were continued for thirteen years without success. As Ralegh ironically wrote in 1618, Gondomar's readiest way of stopping the Guiana expedition would have been, had he been guilty, 'to discover the great practices I had with his Master against the King in the first year of his Majesty's reign.' In default of direct testimony, apologists for Ralegh's condemnation have even attempted to plead a remark by the French Ambassador, Beaumont, to his Court before the trial that, though there was no sufficient evidence to sustain a conviction, yet the truth was 'Cobham with Ralegh had conducted the practices with the Archduke.' As Hallam observes, Beaumont possessed no more information than the English Government gave out. He arrived at his conclusion against Ralegh on the testimony of Arenberg's intercepted letters, which James had shown him. Of the correctness of the inference from them, Lingard admits, 'we have no opportunity of judging.' That the Frenchman would rejoice to believe a rival diplomatist had traitors for his confederates, and that they had tampered with assassination plots, is obvious. His bias towards such a result must have been so strong as to incapacitate him, even beyond de Thou, for a neutral scrutiny of the facts. Inquirers since have ransacked all sources of information, official and unofficial, English, Spanish, French, and Venetian. No higher criminality has been discovered in him than that he may have been aware of the project of an acquaintance to influence by means of Spanish gold the King's policy. If he were guilty of worse than this, it is a solecism in the history of treasons that in the course of three centuries not a tittle of evidence of it should have been unearthed.

Ralegh, to the last, clung to the chance of rehabilitation through Cobham.

Cobham's Trial. He should have understood the man too well by this time to repose the most slender trust in his truthfulness, generosity, or courage. Privy Councillors examined him after Ralegh's trial, and he repeated his calumnies. On the following Friday he was tried by his peers in the County hall, the great hall of Winchester Castle, known as Arthur's Hall from a picture of the Round Table at the east end. 'Never,' reported Sir Dudley Carleton, afterwards Lord Dorchester, who was present at both trials, 'was there so poor and abject a spirit.' He listened to his indictment with fear and trembling. He confessed he had hammered in his brains imaginations of the matters charged against him, but never had purposed to bring them to effect. He repeated in an incoherent manner his charges against Ralegh. Ralegh, he asserted, had stirred him up to discontent, and thereby overthrown his fortunes. Ralegh had proposed the despatch of a Spanish army to Milford Haven. Ralegh had made himself a pensioner of Spain. As earnest of services for which he expected a salary of 1500 crowns, Ralegh had disclosed to Arenberg State deliberations at Greenwich. Ralegh had nothing to hope from the compiler of this wonderful medley, who was willing to buy his life by calumnies upon his friend. He had nothing to hope from the legal justice of his cause. His only real hope was in a discovery by the Fountain of Mercy that the prosecution of him was a mistake; that he was too precious a weapon in the royal armoury to be thrown away, or be let rust; that though law condemned, the national conscience had acquitted him, and cancelled his sentence. His trust, at all events, in public opinion was justified. In 1603 it was not plain to his contemporaries that not a shadow of evidence had ever existed on which he could justly be sent to trial. They saw no absurdity in the association of his name as a traitor in scurrilous ballads with those of Watson and Brooke. But they had seen him in the dock. He had compelled them to weigh the proofs against him and recognise their hollowness and inconclusiveness. The manliness with which he had stood at bay against Coke's insolence, Cobham's perfidy, and Cecil's damaging apologies for estrangement had brought over to him the sympathy of public opinion. The tide of popular feeling turned, and ceased henceforth to run turbulently against him.

Public Opinion.

The Court had been densely thronged. A multitude of eye-witnesses spread through the kingdom their own 'great admiration.' 'Never man,' writes Sir Toby Matthew, 'spoke better for himself. So worthily, so wisely, so temperately he behaved himself that in half a day the mind of all the company was changed from the extremest hate to the extremest pity.' His demeanour was extolled as perfect; to the Lords humble, yet not prostrate, to the jury affable, not fawning, rather showing love of life than fear of death, to the King's counsel patient, but not insensibly neglecting, not yielding to imputations laid against him in words. Michael Hickes wrote to Lord Shrewsbury that his conduct 'wrought both admiration for his good parts and pity towards his person.' His demeanour and eloquence, Hickes heard, had elicited some tears from Mar and Cecil. It was 'wondered that a man of his heroic spirit could be so valiant in suffering that he was never overtaken in passion.' Carleton's account to Chamberlain was that he answered Coke and the rest 'with that temper, wit, learning, courage, and judgment, that, save it went with the hazard of his life, it was the happiest day that ever he spent. And so well he shifted all advantages that were taken against him, that, were not *fama malum gravius quam res*, and an ill name half hanged, in the opinion of all men he had been acquitted. In one word, never was a man so hated and so popular in so short a time.' James wished to have an independent account of the trial, and had commissioned two gentlemen, Roger Ashton and a Scotchman, to report. They carried the news of the trial to the King at Wilton House. 'Never,' stated Ashton, according to Carleton, 'man spake so well in the time past, nor would in the time to come.' The Scotchman seems to have reported that, 'whereas, when he saw Sir Walter Ralegh first, he was so led with the common hatred that he would have gone a hundred miles to see him hanged, he would, ere they parted, have gone a thousand to save his life.'

Legends.

The shock inflicted upon the national instinct of fairness by the conviction of such a man, on such evidence, and after such a defence, showed itself by legends which clustered round the facts of the trial. 'Some of the jury,' it is related by Francis Osborn in his *Memorials on the Reign of King James*, 'were, after he was cast, so far touched in conscience as to demand of him pardon on their knees.' Coke himself was rumoured to have been astonished at the form of the verdict. He was in a garden resting his brazen lungs and his venomous temper, when his man announced that the jury had brought in Ralegh guilty of treason. 'Surely,' observed Coke, 'thou art mistaken; for I myself accused him but of misprision of treason.' The story, which its narrator, in the anonymous *Observations upon Sanderson's History of Queen Mary and King James*, issued in 1656, 'upon the word of a Christian received from Sir Edward Coke's own mouth,' will appear to any reader of the trial a manifest fable. Not the less does it, like the myth of the fraud by which Cobham's accusing Winchester deposition is alleged to have been procured, testify to the difficulty the public experienced in digesting the judicial outrage upon reason. Similarly must be explained the anecdote, though told by Ralegh himself to the Privy Council after his return from Guiana, on the authority of his physician, Dr. Turner, of Sir Francis Gawdy's death-bed lament that 'Never before had the justice of England been so depraved and injured as in the condemnation of Sir Walter Ralegh.' Gowdy had uttered no word of protest against the shameless misbehaviour of his Chief and the Attorney throughout the hearing. On the contrary, his one remark was against the prisoner. If he really considered the conduct or result of the trial iniquitous, it is a pity he was not more prompt in denouncing it. His judicial sensitiveness needed to be awakened by a fit of apoplexy which carried him off in 1606 to his grave in the next parish, he having turned his own church at Wellington into a dog kennel.

CHAPTER XXI.

REPRIEVE (December 10, 1603).

The nation was doing a great man justice, though tardily. Not even its hero's temporary self-abasement could put it out of conceit with him. One of the many curious surprises in Ralegh's history is the manner in which a sudden change in his demeanour seemed to give the lie to the general admiration. Almost a worse grievance against the Court and its legal tools than their persecution is the effect it had in humiliating and degrading him for a time. Though the proceedings had been a travesty of justice, they had been invested hitherto with a scenic stateliness. Ralegh had borne *Bathos.* himself gallantly. He had kept and left the stage with unfailing dignity. The prosecution had at least evinced the respectable earnestness of stubborn hate. At the moment after the catastrophe the nobility, whether of persecuted greatness or of murderous vengefulness, evaporated. Ralegh's enemies appeared to have lost their motive and plan. They seemed no longer sure why or how they wished to wreak their rage. He, from his condemned cell, demanded justice for wronged innocence in the accents of a detected cut-throat. To the Lords Commissioners he wrote: 'The law is passed against me. The mercy of my Sovereign is all that remaineth for my comfort. If I may not beg a pardon or a life, yet let me beg a time. Let me have one year to give to God in a prison and to serve him. It is my soul that beggeth a time of the King.' He spoke of his fear that the power of law might be greater than the power of truth. He reminded Cecil that he was a Councillor to a merciful and just King, if ever we had any, and that the law ought not to overrule pity, but pity the law.' 'Your Lordship,' he proceeds, 'will find that I have been strangely practised against, and that others have their lives promised to accuse me.' In the same November in *Ralegh's* *Abasement.* which he had told Cecil it would be presumption for him to ask grace directly of the King, he asked it. He assured his most dread Sovereign he was not one of the men who were greatly discontented, and therefore the more likely to be disloyal. He protested he had loved the King 'now twenty years'; that he had never invented treason, consented to treason, or performed treason. He invoked mercy in the name of English law, 'who knowing her own cruelty, and that she is wont to compound treasons out of presumptions and circumstances, does advise the King to be *misericorditer justus.*' In a rather loftier strain he exclaimed, 'If the law destroy me, your Majesty shall put me out of your power, and I shall then have none to fear, none to reverence, but the King of Kings.' But the burden throughout is the pitiful 'Send me my life.'

These prayers by Walter Ralegh to a most dread Sovereign, who happened to be James I, these genuflections of spirit to a Minister who must have been suspected of malevolent jealousy, if not of treason to ancient friendship, present a strange and sad spectacle. Excessive importance should not be attached to the phraseology. Not a little of the apparent abjectness was matter of style: 'What,' Ralegh himself has said, 'is the vowing of service to every man whom men bid but good morrow other than a courteous and Court-like kind of lying?' Much must be allowed for the fashion of the age in dealing with Princes and their Ministers. Grey, no more than Ralegh, could resist the impulse. The Puritan Baron had bidden a magnanimous farewell to his peers at Winchester: 'The House of the Wiltons have spent many lives in their Princes' service; Grey cannot beg his!' Within a few days he was grovelling in gratitude for an insulting reprieve: 'As your mercy draws out my life, I cannot deny it the only object it aspires to, by unfeigned confession and contrition to diminish my offence, and your displeasure.' Not till the Civil War had cleared the atmosphere through which royalty was seen, was the demeanour of subjects to the Sovereign in general conformity with the modern standard of manliness. Ralegh, the Court favourite, the poet, was cast in a more plastic mould than Grey. The suddenness of his ruin may well have thrown him off his balance now, as at the original explosion of the tempest in the summer. The tendency of men endowed with genius like his to indulge in extravagances of dejection when *Its motive.* fortune frowns is notorious. But his long course of importunities to all possessed of the means of helping or hindering in the years after 1603 is not to be explained either by style, or by spasms of despair. Both their impulse and something too of an apology for them are to be found in the basis of his character, which was tough as well as elastic. After the shock of the plunge into the depths he braced himself to the task of rising to the surface, and reaching shore. Life, freedom, wealth, career, were forfeited. He determined to redeem the whole. He availed himself of the instruments at hand, though they were tarnished. He did not scruple to soil his fingers in groping his way out of a sea of mud.

It is necessary continually to remind ourselves, when we are tempted to be incensed at his deportment, of the mode in which he had been treated, of his consuming sense of a mission, and his determination, little short of monomania, to return to its service. He and everybody knew that his conviction was an act of legal violence. There was no prospect of rescue through the machinery of the law from an overwhelming disaster which demonstrated law to be without a conscience or sense of responsibility. As soon as the law with its automatic violence had possession of his case, he felt himself held in a grasp not to be relaxed. He knew he must look outside law for justice as well as mercy. It and its ministers were not intentionally cruel. Simply their craft had assumed a scientific shape from which morality and common sense alike were absent. A defendant had a right to evade the penalties of the most manifest guilt by any loopholes and gaps he could discover in the works. It had the right to pursue him to the death, whether innocent or criminal, so long as the rules of the art were observed. Its point of honour was not to let the accused escape. Ralegh was penetrated with an acute and indignant consciousness of the iniquity of the Court intrigue from which he suffered. He despaired of correcting the wrong by the help of the law which had lent itself to be the agent. His struggle was to salve the malice of law with the remorse of the Prerogative which had been seduced into setting it in motion. The shape his efforts took was by no means admirable. Had he been more uniformly heroic, or less absolutely irrepressible, he would have gone to his prison, and laid himself down magnanimously or passively mute. There, early or late, he would have died. Never would his foes have opened the doors of their own

Doggedness

of Purpose. good will. But his nature was not of that kind. He burnt with a longing to be up and doing. He knew he was caught in toils he could not burst by force. For his career's sake, he condescended to plead with and beseech them through whom alone he could emerge into the daylight. They who have idealized him as a downtrodden martyr will find the Ralegh portrayed by his own pen in scores of letters to princes, statesmen, and nobles, little to their taste. The real Ralegh will not cease to be honoured by all whom the sight of indomitable courage and doggedness in the accomplishment of a purpose moves. Only in his words and style could we wish him to have been less supple and less meek. That we have to wish in vain. He thought too highly both of the objects he meant to attain, and of the strength of those who kept him from them, to be sparing of such slight things as entreaties.

Life was the first article in his programme of ends to be pursued, or losses to be redeemed. He prized life more than most. He had so much to do with a life. Half his work still, as he reckoned, was incomplete. The world was young, and abounded in possibilities. To save himself for life and work was worth playing at servility. He could hardly see the pettiness in a James, in his parasites, in his Ministers, for absorption in their one *Reverence*

essential quality, their ability, as holding headsman and
gaolers in a leash, to keep alive or kill, to bind or let loose. To this age
James is an awkward, ludicrous pedant. The spectacle of Ralegh's
veneration is exasperating. For Ralegh he was a symbol of sovereign
authority, a mysterious keeper of the scales of fate. He represented for
Ralegh a power above courts of law, and entitled to set right their mistakes
or misdeeds. Of his mere will he could free Ralegh from persecution. For
Ralegh he was a redresser of grievances; and he was more. He
impersonated potentiality to do as well as undo. The idea of the
opportunities embodied in an occupant of the throne was too engrossing
for Ralegh to weigh the character of the individual. He imagined himself
not merely pardoned, but trusted by the depositary of boundless national
resources, which he was conscious of an infinite competence to employ.
His admiration of the capabilities of the royal Prerogative, if utilized as he
perceived that they could be utilized, embraced its titular tenant whoever he
might be. He was dominated by an intense sense of all he might accomplish
for the indistinguishable duality of himself and his country, if the King
would. Sincerely he could profess he had loved James ever since he beheld
in him the heir of the national crown.

On November 29, 1603, the priests, Watson and Clarke, underwent the
hideous doom which had been pronounced upon Ralegh. They were
drawn, hanged, and quartered. They still lived when the quartering began.
On December 6 Brooke was beheaded. His last words were: 'There is
somewhat yet hidden, which will one day appear for my justification.'
Nothing ever has appeared. James at Wilton House signed warrants for the
execution of Cobham, Grey, and Markham on Friday, December 10. He
had not the hardihood to sign the warrant for Ralegh's execution; but it is
believed to have been fixed for the Monday after. Queen Anne, it is said,
was interceding for his life. So was the King's host, Lord Pembroke, at his
mother's bidding. Cecil wrote to Winwood, afterwards Secretary of State,
that the King 'pretended to forbear Sir Walter Ralegh for the present, till
the Lord Cobham's death had given some light how far he would make
good his accusation.' James, we will hope, had been staggered in conscience
by the reports of his own messengers from Winchester. He and his
courtiers had won from the criminal law Ralegh's condemnation. They were
still hunting after apologies for the conviction. Watson, Clarke, and Brooke
had supplied none of the missing links. In vain had Commissioners been
examining and re-examining the prisoners. Their forlorn hope was the
agony or recklessness of the two lords and Markham on the scaffold.

Meanwhile, in his prison in the Castle, Ralegh made ready for death. He
had the spiritual assistance of Bishop Bilson of Winchester, whom the King

had deputed to console or confess him. Bishop Bilson, who was said by an admirer to carry prelature in his very aspect, furthered later on the divorce of Lord and Lady Essex. Ralegh found no fault with his behaviour to him, and gratefully characterized him in his History as grave and learned. He satisfied the Bishop of his Christian state; he could not be persuaded

Farewell to his Wife. : to acknowledge the truth of any of the charges against him, unless, very partially, as to the pension. That, he said, was 'once mentioned, but never proceeded in.' The day appointed for his death, he thought, was December 13. He had penned a last farewell to his wife on December 9, 1603. It reads very unlike the All Souls' College paper. He sends his 'love, that, when I am dead, you may keep it, not sorrows, dear Bess; let them go to the grave with me, and be buried in the dust. Bear my destruction gently, and with a heart like yourself.' He gives 'all the thanks my heart can conceive for your many troubles and cares taken for me.' He bids her, for the love she bare him living, not hide herself many days, but by her travail seek to help her miserable fortunes, and the right of her poor child. 'If you can live free from want, care for no more: for the rest is but vanity. Love God, and begin betimes to repose yourself on Him. When you have wearied your thoughts on all sorts of worldly cogitations, you shall sit down by sorrow in the end.' He does not know to what friend to direct her, for all his had left him in the time of trial. 'I plainly perceive,' he continues, 'that my death was determined from the first day.' He asks her, 'for my soul's health, to pay all poor men.' He warns her against suitors for her money; 'for the world thinks that I was very rich.' He prays her, 'Get those letters, if it be possible, which I writ to the Lords, wherein I sued for my life. God knoweth that it was for you and yours that I desired it; but it is true that I disdain myself for begging it. And know it, dear wife, that your son is the child of a true man, and who, in his own respect, despiseth Death, and all his misshapen and ugly forms. Beg my dead body, which living was denied you; and either lay it at Sherborne, if the land continue, or in Exeter church by my father and mother. I can write no more. Time and Death call me away.' Yet he can hardly part with wife or child, and adds still something: 'God teach me to forgive my persecutors and false accusers. My true wife farewell. Bless my poor boy; pray for me. Yours, that was, but now not my own.'

He was more than willing to live. He was not afraid to die. In the apparent

The Pilgrimage. : presence of death his soul, as always, recovered its lofty serenity. With his head, as he thought, on the block, he burst into the grand dirge of the *Pilgrimage*. Such are the variances of taste that a writer of reputation has spoken of this noble composition as 'a strange medley in which faith and confidence in God appear side by side with sarcasms upon the lawyers and the courtiers.' That is a judgment with which few will agree. The poem in the most authoritative manuscript is described as having been composed the night before Ralegh was beheaded. But it can scarcely be doubted that it belongs to the present period, when he was daily expecting the arrival of the warrant for his execution at Winchester. His spirit had 'quenched its thirst at those clear wells where sweetness dwells.' It was bound in quiet palmer's fresh apparel—

> to Heaven's bribeless hall,
> Where no corrupted voices brawl;
> No conscience molten into gold,
> No forged accuser bought or sold,
> No cause deferred, no vain-spent journey;
> For there Christ is the King's Attorney.
> And when the grand twelve-million jury
> Of our sins, with direful fury,
> Against our souls black verdicts give,
> Christ pleads his death, and then we live.

At ten in the morning of December 10 Sir Griffin Markham was conducted to the scaffold, which had been erected in the Castle yard. He had said adieu to his friends, prayed, and was awaiting the axe. Suddenly the spectators in the Castle yard saw the Sheriff, Sir Benjamin Tichborne, stay the *Royal Intervention.* executioner. John Gibb, a Scotch groom of the royal bedchamber, had arrived, almost too late, at the edge of the crowd. He was the bearer of a reprieve. James himself, on December 7, had drawn it, with a preamble: 'The two prestis and George Brooke vaire the principall plotteris and intisairs of all the rest to the embracing of the saiddis treasonabill machinations.' He had kept it back to the last, as well to multiply the chances of eliciting confessions of guilt, as for the sake of the vividness of the stage play. He admired greatly his own ingenuity, and his courtiers applauded enthusiastically. Of the detestable feline cruelty he and they had no shame. Ralegh's window in the Castle overlooked the scaffold. He would be sensible of the interruption of the proceedings. He could not have seen Gibb. He must, says Carleton, 'have had hammers working in his head to beat out the meaning of the stratagem.' Beaumont, the French ambassador, was told by an imaginative reporter that he 'était à la fenêtre, regardant la comédie de ses compagnons avec un visage riant.'

The Sheriff performed his part with a ready gravity which secured the King's approval. He was already a favourite for having proclaimed James on the first news of the death of Elizabeth, before the Council had declared him her successor. For his deserts both now and then the custody of the

Castle soon afterwards was bestowed upon him and his heirs.
He said to Markham, 'You say you are ill-prepared to die; you shall have
two hours' respite.' Then he led him away, and locked him in Arthur's Hall.
Next Grey was brought on the scaffold. He asserted that his fault against
the King was 'far from the greatest, yet he knew his heart to be faulty.' He
too was ready for the axe, when the Sheriff led him away to Arthur's Hall,
saying the order of the execution was changed by the King's command, and
Cobham was to precede Grey. Cobham came, with so bold an air as to
suggest he had heard; but he prayed so lengthily that a bystander ejaculated
he had 'a good mouth in a cry, but was nothing single.' He expressed
repentance for his offence against the King. He corroborated all he had
said against Sir Walter Ralegh as true 'upon the hope of his soul's
resurrection.' The extortion of that confirmation of his calumnies had been
a main object of the whole disgraceful farce. When he had thus bought his
worthless life, the Sheriff brought back upon the scaffold Grey and
Markham to stand beside him. All three were asked if their offences were
not heinous, and if they had not been justly tried and lawfully condemned.
Each answered affirmatively. Then said the Sheriff: 'See the mercy of your
Prince, who of himself hath sent hither a countermand, and hath given you
your lives.' At this the crowd burst into such hues and cries that they went
from the Castle into the town, and there began afresh. Grey said, 'Since the
King has given me my life without my begging, I will deserve life.' Henry
IV was sceptical as to the magnanimity of James. He wrote to Beaumont to
discover if 'Spanish gold' were concerned in the reprieves; if Don Juan de
Taxis and Cecil had used influence for them; 'for it is rumoured that these
persons, backed by money expended by Ralegh, brought the thing about.'
The faith in Ralegh's endless resources and skill prevailed in France as in
England.

CHAPTER XXII.

On December 16, 1603, Ralegh, with his fellow convicts, returned to London. That would have been the close of an ordinary man's career. To him alone it did not seem the end, and he resolved it should not be. He had his life. Liberty and fortune were still to be regained. He looked around him, and endeavoured to retrieve the scattered fragments of his wealth. Like all his peers in arms and politics he had ever believed in the importance of riches. But now he was grasping at the possibility of continuing by money in lieu of his imprisoned self his schemes of a Guiana sovereignty. He was striving to construct out of the wreck of his grandeur a refuge for his wife and his boy from the anguish and dependence of penury. 'Poverty,' he preached to his son, 'is a shame, an imprisonment of the mind. Poverty provokes a man to do infamous and detested deeds.'

Civilly dead.

He was civilly dead. The division of his spoils had commenced before the trial. He had, as has been mentioned, been dismissed in July from his island government. In September Godolphin, High Sheriff of Cornwall, had been directed to take the musters, 'the commission of Lieutenancy granted to Sir Walter Ralegh being become void and determined.' Early in 1604 he formally returned the seal of the Duchy of Cornwall to Cecil. His successor was his connexion, Lord Pembroke. He was stripped of the Rangership of Gillingham Forest, and of the Lieutenancy of Portland, though he would regret the loss of those offices the less that they remained in the hands of their joint tenant, his brother, Sir Carew. His enjoyment of his patent as wine licenser had been suspended, that it might be considered if the post were a monopoly. The Council came to the conclusion that it was not.

Lord   *Nottingham's*

Rapacity. But before Ralegh could collect the arrears from the vintners he was arraigned. Thereupon, not waiting for the result of the trial, the King revoked the patent, and granted it to the Lord Admiral. Nottingham, not content with the profit from new licenses, claimed the arrears. Lady Ralegh remonstrated. She indignantly computed to Cecil in 1604 that the Admiral 'hath £6000, and £3000 a year, by my husband's fall. And since it pleaseth God that his Lordship shall build upon our ruins, which we never suspected, yet the portion is great and, I trust, sufficient, out of one poor gentleman's fortune to take all that remains, and not to look back before his Majesty's grant, and take from us the debts past, which your Lordship knows were stayed from us by a proclamation before my husband was suspected of any offence.' Sherborne was attached. Commissioners for it had been appointed, Serjeant Phillips and Meere. They had pounced upon the domain, and were selling stock, felling timber, and dismantling the castle. Cecil interfered peremptorily by letter, and for a time stayed all proceedings. He is likely to have 'spoken the one word' about the wine licence arrears which Lady Ralegh implored. No more is heard of the Lord Admiral's demand. A more important favour was obtained. In February, 1604, all Ralegh's goods, chattels, and money due to him, though forfeited for treason, were granted by the Crown to trustees for payment of debts owing before his attainder, and for the maintenance of his wife and child. The trustees named were Robert Smith and John Shelbury. Shelbury was Ralegh's steward, 'a man I can better entreat than know how to reward.'

The grant included, beside the wine arrearages, money in the hands of the wine licenser's deputy, William Sanderson. *The Sandersons.* Sanderson was husband to Ralegh's niece, Margaret Snedale. He was father of Sir William Sanderson, writer in 1656 of a *History of Queen Mary and King James*, full of calumnies upon Ralegh. He denied the debt, and claimed £2000 from his principal. Thereupon Ralegh, 'in great anger,' sued him, apparently with success. It is unnecessary to credit the further allegation by the author, supposed to have been Ralegh's son Carew, though more probably somebody inspired by him, of the *Observations*, already cited, upon Sanderson's *History*, that the deputy was for the debt cast into prison, where he died a beggar. On the contrary, slender as is the authority of the historian, as of his critic, it is easier, as well as preferable, to accept Sir William Sanderson's statement, in answer to the *Observations*, that his father and his family continued to be prosperous, and, having resumed amicable relations with Ralegh, remained kind and faithful kinsfolk to the last. It is pleasant to be able to believe that Ralegh disappointed a relative's temporary calculations upon his incapacity of resistance, without acting the part of the insolvent steward of the Parable.

The mercy of the Crown extended for the present to the maintenance even of his rights over the estate of Sherborne itself. A dozen suitors had applied for it, Cecil told a Scotch courtier in October, 1603. But on July 30, 1604, in place of Ralegh's life interest, which was forfeited by the attainder, a sixty years' term of Sherborne and ten other Dorset and Somerset manors, with all other lands escheated, was conveyed by the Crown to trustees for Lady Ralegh and young Walter, should Ralegh so long live. This boon, following the rest, went far towards remedying the overwhelming pecuniary consequences of a judicial crime. The King is entitled to share the credit with Cecil. He was not incapable of caprices of beneficence. Pity, rather than a sense of justice, moved him. He loved to be magnanimous at small cost. He chose to regard Ralegh as a traitor when he was innocent. He reaped from the injustice the additional satisfaction of being exalted by his flatterers into a paragon of generosity for waiving part of the penalties for offences which had not been committed. Ralegh's estate was, however, indebted yet more to Cecil. If he would not, or could not, secure justice for his old ally, Cecil had no desire to see him reduced to beggary. Whatever the cause, Ralegh undoubtedly suffered in purse less than his condemned fellows. Cobham's and Grey's vast patrimonies were wholly confiscated. They subsisted on the charity of the Crown. Markham was sent into exile so bare of means that he had to barter his inlaid sword hilt for *The reck* - *of his Estate.* - a meal. Ralegh was not thus stripped. Only, being guiltless, as they were not, and did not pretend to be, he was not always gratefully content with the morsels tossed back to him. Soon after his removal from Winchester he wrote to Cecil that £3000 a year, from Jersey, the Wine Office, the Stannaries, Gillingham, and Portland, was gone; there remained but £300 from Sherborne, with a debt upon it of £3000. His tenants refused to pay Lady Ralegh her rents. His woods were cut down, his grounds wasted, and his stock sold. Meanwhile he was charged at the Tower, at first, £4, and later, £5, a week for the diet of himself, his wife, child, and two servants. He had to urge the Council to stay the Commissioners at Sherborne, whose rapacious activity had again awoke. He told the Council that the estate, with the park and a stock of £400 in sheep, whatever its valuation by others, brought in but £666 13s. 4d. This has been estimated, perhaps somewhat excessively, as equivalent to an income now of £3333. Out of it he had to pay the Bishop of Salisbury £260. Fees and rates took another £50 a year. His personal property he reckoned at not worth a thousand marks, or £666 13s. 4d. His rich hangings were sold to my Lord Admiral for £500. He had but one rich bed, which he had sold to Lord Cobham before his misfortunes. His plate, which he describes as very fair, was all 'lost, or eaten out with interest at one Chenes', 'or Cheynes', the goldsmith, in Lombard-street.

He thought it hard to be robbed of his revenues. He declared that he could have endured the calamity if penury had been all. Early in 1604 he wrote that, if Sherborne could be assured, he should take his loss for a gain, nothing having been lost that could have bettered his family, 'but the lease of the wines, which was desperate before his troubles.' He did not wish for his wife and son, 'God knows, the least proportion of plenty, having forgotten that happiness which found too much too little.' His one desire was that they should be able to eat their own bread. The interruption of his career was the real and unappeasable wrong. All his virtues made him struggle indomitably against that. He was supported in the contest by the vice itself, if it were a vice, of his abounding egotism. His incapacity for

believing that powers like his could be wasted by the

State, buoyed him up against the direst persecutions. He was unable at heart, whatever his groanings, to regard them as more than passing checks in a game in which he had chanced upon losing cards. He fought for liberty more stubbornly than for his property, that he might resume his work in the world. He complained in January, 1604, that Papists who plotted to surprise the King's person had been liberated, while Cecil's poor, ancient, and true friend was left to perish 'here where health wears away.' Cecil had written kind but cautious lines in another hand, of which Ralegh 'knew the phrase.' They had raised his hopes. Cecil dashed them by declaring to Lady Ralegh early in 1604 that, 'for a pardon, it could not yet be done.' Ralegh did not therefore leave off seeking it. For some time he could not believe that his imprisonment was to be more than transitory. His efforts were directed to the negotiation of terms to which he might consent for the abridgment of the liberty he deemed his right. He did not ask to be 'about London—which God cast my soul into hell if I desire.' He would be content to be confined within the Hundred of Sherborne. If he could not be allowed so much, he was ready to live in Holland. There he thought he might obtain some employment connected with the Indies. Else he petitioned to 'be appointed to any bishop, or other gentleman, or nobleman, or that your Lordship would let me keep but a park of yours— which I would buy from someone that hath it—I will never break the order which you shall please to undertake for me.'

He fretted in mind; and he was ill in body. For several years his health had been impaired. Only periodical visits to Bath for its waters assuaged his ailments. He prayed in vain that he might be suffered to go thither in the autumn after his conviction. His prognostication that, if he 'could not go this fall, he should be dead or disabled for ever,' was not likely to alarm his foes. They affected at all times to be incredulous of the gravity of his infirmities. But there is no reason to question his statement that he was

'daily in danger of death by the palsy; nightly of suffocation by

wasted and obstructed lungs.' His complaints began in the early summer of 1604. After a week's sojourn in the Tower he seems to have been sent to the Fleet, where Keymis was for a short time his fellow prisoner. There bills for his diet show that he was staying between Christmas 1603 and Lady Day, 1604, or rather a few days later. He cannot have gone back to the Tower precisely by Lady Day to stay, for reasons not of State, but of Court. On Monday, March 26, 1604, Easter games were to be performed before the Court at the Tower. Two mastiffs were to be let loose on a lion, and the King wanted to have his fortress-palace cleared, for the occasion, of melancholy captives. A custom prevailed at such festivities of releasing prisoners. There was no intention of liberating the Winchester convicts. So, according to the rumour of the Court, as sent home by the Venetian Embassy, they 'were removed from the Tower and placed in other prisons.' If this statement is to be accepted literally, and to be reconciled with the Fleet bills for food, they must, at some time before Easter, have returned from the Fleet to the Tower, and then, before March 26, been sent back for a brief space to the Fleet. Ralegh had no cause for rejoicing when the time arrived for his permanent establishment in the Tower. After his return it was again, as in 1603, visited by the Plague. He prayed to be taken elsewhere, on the ground that the pestilence was come next door. In the adjacent tenement, with a paper wall between, were, he told Cecil, lying a woman and her child, dying of it. When the Tower was free from the Plague it was still an unsuitable lodging for one of Ralegh's constitution. Moisture oozed constantly into the walls from the wide

muddi ditch. The . *His Ailments.* - cells were bitterly cold, and Ralegh was chilled and benumbed. 'Every second or third night,' he reiterated to Cecil in 1605, 'I am in danger either of sudden death, or of the loss of my limbs and senses, being sometimes two hours without feeling a motion of my hand and whole arm.' In 1606 his physician, Dr. Peter Turner, certified that his whole left side was cold. His fingers on the same side began to be contracted, and his tongue in some sort, insomuch that he spoke weakly, and that it was to be feared he might utterly lose the use of it. Only in consequence of Turner's authoritative representations was Ralegh's chamber changed. In the little garden under the terrace was a lath and plaster lean-to. It had been Bishop Latimer's prison. Since it had been used as a hen-house. Ralegh had already been permitted to employ this out-house as a still room. He was allowed now to build a little room next it, and use it as his habitual dwelling.

Other alleviations of his confinement were granted, particularly in its earlier and again in its concluding years. For an inmate of a gaol, his treatment was commonly not very rigorous. His quarters themselves, though cold, were otherwise convenient. At his committal in July he had been put into the upper chamber of the Bloody tower. Formerly this was called the Garden tower. According to one authority it became known by the more ominous name after Lord Northumberland's death there in June, 1585. Mrs. Lucy

Hutchinson, who was born in the Tower, derives the appellation from a tradition of her childhood, that it was the scene of the murder of the Duke of Clarence. The assassination in it of Edward V and his brother seems to account for it more naturally. On Ralegh's return from Winchester, he was, says Lord de Ros, who was both Lieutenant of the Tower and one of his successors in the Captaincy of the Yeomen, placed in a semi-circular room, lighted by loopholes, in the White tower, and there remained all the years of his imprisonment. That, though a current local tradition, is grossly incorrect, as a Lieutenant of the Tower ought to have known. As, however, Lord de Ros also thought that Ralegh died on Tower Hill, it is the less

- *In the Bloody Tower.* - surprising that he should not have known where in

the Tower he lived. According to another legend equally baseless, he was lodged on the second and third floors of the Beauchamp tower. Really from Winchester he went back to the apartment he had previously inhabited. It had its advantages. A passage in the rear led by a door to the terrace, which has been christened Ralegh's Walk. From it he could look down on one side over a much-frequented wharf to the busy river. On the other it commanded the Lieutenant's garden and green. The suite of rooms accommodated Cottrell, and apparently also John Talbot, Talbot's son, and Peter Dean, who waited on Ralegh. There was space for Lady Ralegh, Walter, and Lady Ralegh's waiting maid. They occupied the room in which Edward V and his brother were murdered. When the Plague invaded their quarters they removed for a time to lodgings on Tower Hill, near the church of Allhallows, Barking. It is uncertain whether there, or in the room of the slaughtered Princes, a second son, Carew, was born to Ralegh and his wife in 1604. On the abatement of the epidemic, Lady Ralegh, with the children, returned.

Ralegh could entertain dependents and acquaintances. His Sherborne steward, John Shelbury, Hariot, his physician Dr. Turner, a surgeon Dr. John, and a clergyman named Hawthorn, were frequently with him. His Ralegh and Gilbert kinsfolk, we may be sure, did not desert him, though there was no especial reason to chronicle their visits. Had fuller details been preserved of his private life, we should doubtless have found mention of his brother Carew, who was living in apparent prosperity at Downton. His employment, as soon as he had the opportunity, of the naval and military services of his nephews, George Ralegh and Gilbert, shows that the family union survived unbroken. Admirers from the West and the Court came to listen to his conversation, and watch his chemical experiments. The Indians he had brought from Guiana had stayed in England. The register of Chelsea Church records the baptism of one of them by the name of Charles, 'a boy of estimation ten or twelve years old, brought by Sir Walter

Rawlie from *Alleviations of Confinement.* Guiana.' After his imprisonment
they were lodged in the Tower, or near. He could amuse himself by
catechising them on the wonders of their land. His freedom of movement
in the early and late stages of his imprisonment, when he had 'the liberty of
the Tower,' roused the envy of fellow prisoners. Grey murmured in 1611:
'Sir Walter Ralegh hath a garden and a gallery to himself.' In his deepest
tribulations he had reverential valets and pages to comb by the hour his
thick curling locks, to trim his bushy beard, and round moustache. Crowds
thronged the wharf below to mark him pacing his terrace in the velvet and
laced cap, the rich gown and trunk hose, noted by Aubrey's cousin
Whitney, and the jewels, of which he retained an ample store.

But he was made in many respects, and at frequent intervals, to feel himself
'a dead man,' possessed of no rights, subject to all sorts of caprices. A kind-
hearted Lieutenant might ameliorate his lot. He had fascinated Sir George
Harvey, who had commenced ill with the suppression of Cobham's letter.
They habitually dined together. Harvey had lent or let to him his garden.
The door of the Bloody tower was suffered to stand habitually open. On
August 16, 1605, Sir William Waad replaced Harvey. He had earned the
post by his keen scent for plots. He came prepared to grudge privileges to
the man who had foiled his inquisitorial cunning. A week after his
appointment to the Lieutenancy he wrote to Cecil, to suggest the
replacement of a lath fence, which ran past the Bloody tower gate, by a
brick wall, as 'more safe and convenient.' His advice was taken, and a brick
wall built. Still he was uneasy. In December, 1608, he complained
indignantly to Cecil that 'Sir Walter Ralegh doth show himself upon the
wall in his garden to the view of the people, who gaze upon him, and he
stareth on them. Which he doeth in his cunning humour, that it might be
thought his being before the Council was rather to clear than to charge
him.' Waad took credit to himself that he had been 'bold in discretion and
conveniency to restrain him again.' For Waad to reprove Ralegh ought to

His Gaoler. have needed boldness. He desired to repress the wife as well
as the husband. Lady Ralegh does not seem to have been sufficiently awed
by the august associations of the Tower. He had to issue an order
forbidding her to drive into the court-yard in her coach. By another solemn
order aimed at Sir Walter, he decreed that, at ringing of the afternoon bell,
all the prisoners, with their servants, were to withdraw into their chambers.
They were not to go forth again for that night.

Until May, 1613, Ralegh had to endure this man's petty spite and
disciplinary pedantry. Then Waad retired, to the great contentment of his
prisoners, though, as it happened, from a cause which did him honour.

Lady Arabella Stuart's chief pleasure during her iniquitous imprisonment was the increase of her stock of jewels. From an order of Council after her death, she would seem to have consulted Ralegh as an expert. Several stones of price had disappeared in 1613. Suspicion was cast upon Waad, or his wife and daughter. Probably they were entirely innocent. The real object was that Carr might introduce a more pliant instrument for foul play against Sir Thomas Overbury. Under pressure of the accusation based on the missing trinkets, Waad accepted £1400 from Sir Gervase Elways, with a promise of £600 more, and vacated his office. Elways became an accomplice in Overbury's murder, and was hanged on his own Tower Hill. But he was less of a martinet than his predecessor. Perhaps his patrons were engaged in too serious crimes to waste their energy in inciting him to petty persecutions of Ralegh. At all events, Ralegh recovered the liberty of the Tower; and the restrictions on the presence of his wife were relaxed.

At no period were his really formidable enemies inside the Tower. Waad himself would not have dared to harass and worry him, if he had not been confident that his tyranny would be approved at Court. His foes there were perpetually on the watch for excuses for tightening and perpetuating his

Fresh Accusations. bonds. He had to defend himself from a suspicion of complicity with the Gunpowder Plot in 1605. Commissioners, of whom Waad was one, were appointed to inquire. Lord Northumberland had been sent to the Tower by the Star Chamber for misprision of treason, on the flimsy pretext of his intimacy with Thomas Percy. He was questioned on his communications at the Tower with Ralegh. Ralegh was questioned on his with the Earl. One day the French ambassador's wife, Madame de Beaumont, came to visit the lions in company with Lady Howard of Effingham. She saw Ralegh in his garden. The Tower contained no lion as wonderful. She asked him for some balsam of Guiana. He forwarded the balsam to the ambassadress by Captain Whitelocke, a retainer of Northumberland's, who happened to have been in her train. Several Lords of the Council were deputed to examine him on his intercourse with Whitelocke, a spy having deposed that he had noticed Whitelocke in the Archduke's company during the summer of 1605. Ralegh had difficulty in persuading the Council that he had seen little either of the Captain, who came only on an ordinary visit, of Northumberland, since the Earl's confinement, or of the French ambassador and his wife. He prayed their Lordships in the name of 'my many sorrows and the causes, my services and love to my country, not to suspect me to be knowing this unexampled and more than devilish invention.' Some of them, with their master, were capable of thinking, or affecting to think, any incredible evil of him, and all belonging to him. It was accounted an alarming circumstance that in the

September of 1605 Lady Ralegh, during a visit to Sherborne, had the old arms in the castle scoured.

In 1607 the Council instituted an inquiry into the manner in which Harvey had played the gaoler. Ralegh was brought before it, and interrogated. So was Edward or William Cottrell, described as 'alias Captain Sampson.' He was found to have been living for some time past at Sherborne, perhaps under his alias, on a pension granted him by Ralegh. In terror, or through an offer of better terms, he now confessed his part in the bygone transmission of messages between Ralegh, Keymis, and Cobham. Again, in 1610 some new and shadowy charges were brought against Ralegh. The Council sat *LadyRalegh's Expulsion.* at the Tower. On Cecil was thrown the task, we will hope, the very ungrateful task, of addressing to him a solemn rebuke. He was subjected to three months of close imprisonment, and his wife was obliged to leave the Tower. An order was served upon her: 'The Lady Raleighe must understand his Majesty's express will and commandment that she resort to her house on Tower Hill or ellswhere with her women and sonnes to remayne there, and not to lodge hereafter within the Tower.' Ralegh prayed earnestly that she might 'again be made a prisoner with me, as she hath been for six years last past, in this unsavoury place—a miserable fate for her, and yet great to me, who in this wretched estate can hope for no other thing than peaceable sorrow.' The offence for which he was censured and immured was never revealed to the public; for the excellent reason, it may be presumed, that to the public it would have appeared frivolous. His true criminality now and throughout is to be gathered from the testimony of Henry Howard in the year following. In July, 1611, fresh rumours of offences committed by him were spread. Howard, now Earl of Northampton and Lord Chamberlain, and another Privy Councillor, were commissioned to inquire. To Howard's taste, his spirit was not at all sufficiently subdued. In a letter to his notable accomplice and pupil, and the future husband of his great niece, Carr, Lord Rochester and Privy Seal, Howard expressed his spite: 'We had a bout with Sir Walter Ralegh, in whom we find no change, but the same boldness, pride, and passion, that heretofore hath wrought more violently, but never expended itself in a stronger passion. Hereof his Majesty shall hear when the Lords come to him. The lawless liberty of the Tower, so long cockered and fostered with hopes exorbitant, hath bred suitable desires and affections. And yet you may assure his Majesty that by this publication he won little ground.' He gained so little that, as he wrote in this year, he was, after eight years of imprisonment, as straitly locked up as he had been the first day.

When his imprisonment was most severe, it was moderate for his guilt if he were guilty. In its times of least oppressiveness it was an enormity, if he were innocent. To himself, who knew that he was guiltless of the treason imputed to him, and was convinced that his gaolers knew it, his imprisonment under any conditions appeared a monstrous iniquity. He could never desist from protesting against the wrong. It was the grievance as much of his enemies that they had him fast in prison, and could neither

Search for Evidence of Guilt. browbeat him into acknowledging the justice

of his doom, nor prove its justice. They had obtained his condemnation rather than his conviction. They were incited by his appeals to redoubled efforts to establish his original guilt. Some, the King for example, may, from rooted prejudice, have believed him guilty. No less than his most malignant and unscrupulous foes they resented furiously their inability to demonstrate it. They regarded it as evidence merely of his abominable craft. The ordinary and extraordinary laxity of his confinement indicated their doubt of his fair liability to any. The intervals of rigour were meant to notify to the sceptical that the Government was at last on the track of evidence which would confirm the equity of everything from the beginning done against him. Constantly he had to stand on his defence against attempts to palliate the effrontery of the Winchester judgment by experimental accusations that he had been tampering with new conspiracies. For ten years the contest proceeded between him and the Court on that basis. He asseverated the right of an innocent man to freedom, and the Court went on searching for proofs of its right to put him into captivity. His adversaries might have been content with the degree of ruin they had wrought if he would have acquiesced in his fall. He insisted on regarding himself as living, though he could not deny that he was civilly dead. He looked forth from his prison on the world as a stage on which he still played a part, and might once more lead. He would keep digging up the buried past. He assumed the offensive against the majesty of the law. He was not patient of injustice because a court of justice was its source. He had the audacity to speak, think, and write, as if he were entitled to canvass affairs of State. From his gaol he became audible in the recesses of the Palace. He troubled the self-complacency of its master by teaching his consort and his heir-apparent to question his infallible wisdom.

*Queen
Anne's Favour.*

Queen Anne perhaps scarcely needed the lesson. She was fond of power, and 'bold and enterprising,' records Sully. Her husband appears to have stood in some awe of her criticisms. She commonly took a line of her own.

Henry Howard, whose policy she had opposed before the death of Elizabeth, insinuated that she was a foolish, garrulous, and intriguing woman. She may not have been very wise, but she had generous emotions and courage. She disliked the Spanish connexion, of which she was at one period esteemed a supporter. She admired Ralegh's great qualities and great deeds. His faithful cousin George Carew, her Vice-Chamberlain, would remind her of them. Lady Ralegh, whom she is said on her first arrival from Scotland to have repulsed, had gained her ear and sympathy. She had, from the time of Ralegh's trial, tried to help him. By a medicine of his invention she believed herself subsequently to have been cured of a violent malady. In gratitude she is reported, or fabled, to have gained the King's consent to a re-examination of Cobham's charge against him. Reference has already been made to the story, as told by Sir Anthony Welldon. Cecil, Lenox, Worcester, Suffolk, Carew, and Julius Cæsar are said to have been deputed to ask Cobham if he had not really accused Ralegh at Winchester. Cobham answered: 'Never, nor could I; but that villain Waad got me by a trick to write my name upon a piece of white paper, which I, thinking nothing, did;

Cobham's Winchester Letter again.   so that, if any charge came under my hand, it was forged by Waad by writing something above my hand.' Then returning to the King the rest chose Cecil for spokesman. He said: 'Sir, my Lord Cobham hath made good all that ever he wrote or said.' Altogether it is a most improbable tale. Waad disliked Ralegh; there is no ground for belief that he would have perpetrated a cold-blooded fraud to gratify his ill-will. He was arrogant and tyrannical, not criminal, as the circumstances of the loss of his Lieutenancy show. The presence of honest and friendly Carew as one of the royal commissioners, renders the account as it stands all but incredible. He certainly would not have been a party to a lying and wicked prevarication. Cecil would not, nor Sir Julius Cæsar. But it is one of the many Ralegh myths, with a possible particle of truth in it, which cannot be sifted out of the mass of fiction.

Ralegh built more hopes on the favour of the Prince of Wales than on that of his mother. Prince Henry was of a high spirit. He would have rejoiced in war at which his father shuddered. Through his mother he made Ralegh's acquaintance in his boyhood, and for him the prisoner was a hero. Everybody has heard his saying: 'Who but my father would keep such a bird in a cage!' Ralegh eagerly responded to the advances of one through whom he might become not only free but powerful. The Prince delighted in the company of Ralegh, who states that he had intended the *History of the World* for him; and he is said to have looked over the manuscript. He consulted Ralegh in 1611 on the proposal by Duke Charles Emmanuel I of Savoy for a double intermarriage. The Elector Palatine was negotiating for the hand of Princess Elizabeth. Spain and the whole Catholic party in

Europe dreaded *Ralegh on a Piedmontese Alliance.* an alliance of the English royal family with German Protestantism. They tried to engage James to affiance Elizabeth to the Duke of Savoy's son, the Prince of Piedmont, and Henry to the Duke's daughter. Ralegh combated the scheme in two Discourses, printed long after his death. The first mainly discussed the plan of Elizabeth's marriage to 'a prince jesuited,' her removal far from her country to a family circle of another faith, a dependent now and ever, as Ralegh not prophetically declared, 'either upon France or upon Spain.' He foreboded how, in default of male heirs in England, 'a Savoyan, of Spanish race, might become King of England.' 'I do prize,' he declared, 'the alliance of the Palatine of the Rhine, and of the House of Nassau, more than I do the alliance of the Duke of Savoy.' In the second Discourse Ralegh argued against the Prince's alliance with Dukes of the blood of Spain, and servants of 'Spain, which to England is irreconcilable.' Such an alliance would increase the jealousy of the Netherlands, a country which was for England a necessary friend. He lamented the present weakness of England, 'through the detested covetousness of some great ones of ours. Whereas, in my time, I have known one of her Majesty's ships command forty Hollanders to strike sail, they will now take us one to one, and not give us a good morrow. They have our own ordnance to break our own bones withal.' Besides, the Prince was only about eighteen. So long as he continued unmarried all the eyes of Christendom were upon him. 'Let him for a while not entangle himself.' When he desired to wed he would find, Ralegh suggested, a French family alliance more honourable and advantageous than a Spanish.

His presumption in meddling with questions of State, and in answering them in a manner opposite to the King's inclination, may have had something to do with the unexplained chastisement inflicted upon him in the summer of 1611. Whatever their cause, rebukes and curtailments of privileges neither silenced him nor lost him the goodwill of his friend. The Prince not long after sought his assistance in the building of a model ship. The vessel was christened 'The Prince,' and it proved an excellent sailer. The prisoner of the Tower wrote about it as if he smelt the sea-breezes. Twenty-nine years earlier he had proved himself a master in the art of ship-building. In his time, as he has recorded, 'the shape of English ships had been greatly bettered.' Much of the credit of the reform is his due. Pett, the best naval architect in the kingdom, in whose family the post of Master Shipwright became almost hereditary, is reported to have been glad to gather hints from him. His communications with the Prince about the ship drew his thoughts back to maritime questions. Beside a letter, admirably terse and critical, to Prince Henry, he composed a treatise minutely practical, called a *Discourse of the Invention of Ships*, and also *Observations concerning the Royal Navy and Sea Service.* Both probably were intended for parts of an elaborate work on *The Art of War by Sea,* which the death of the Prince hindered him from completing. He alludes in the Observations to a *Discourse of a Maritimal Voyage,* as a previous product of his pen, which, unless it be the *Discourse of the Invention of Ships,* has disappeared. Had *The Art of War by Sea* come into systematic being, that might have stood as another of its chapters.

Prince Henry's death was the most cruel blow inflicted on him since his

: *Robert Cecil's Death.* : trial. The disappointment was the severer that it had

been preceded six months earlier by another death on which his friends, and perhaps himself, founded expectations. On May 16, 1612, died Robert Cecil, Earl of Salisbury, and Lord High Treasurer. He was hastening to Court, to countermine his underminers, from Bath, where he had been taking the waters. At the inn at Marlborough he found himself grievously ill. He was removed, it has been variously stated, either to the parsonage, or to the house of a Mr. Daniel, which had formerly been St. Margaret's Priory. There he expired.

A born statesman, Cecil had been condemned by a passion for affairs, and incapacity for dispensing with office, to serve a great sovereign in little ways, and to emphasize or dissemble a feeble sovereign's feebleness. As a friend he could relieve adversity so far as not to cancel it; but he could not pardon in a companion prosperity which threatened rivalry, or risk his share of sunshine by screening a victim of popular and regal odium. By no class was he profoundly lamented. Veteran and well-endowed officials seldom are. Ralegh, it is to be feared, was never among the mourners. He had received benefits from Cecil, and acknowledged them thankfully. He could not forgive an acquaintance, who must have known his innocence of treason, for letting his life be blasted by the charge. He could not understand that the statesman and potent courtier, whose fortunes at no time were visibly clouded, should be unable, or honestly think himself

unable, to lift a persecuted comrade out of the mire. If Cecil did : *Dumb* :

: *Enmity.* : not come effectually to the rescue, he believed, at any rate at

last, that it was because he would not. Cecil read his mind, had no faith in his gratitude, and accounted the duties of a dead friendship discharged by attempts to mitigate rather than to reverse his doom. Harassed by business and the toil of keeping his slippery footing, he would feel chiefly a dull irritation at the captive, whether guiltless or guilty, for the obstinacy of his dispute with accomplished facts. He ought, the Minister, like his avowed enemies, would think, to have acquiesced, and been still. Thus the two went on, mutually scornful and mistrustful, exchanging soft phrases which neither meant. The true condition of their hearts was not hidden from bystanders. They never confessed it one to the other, or frankly to themselves.

Historical scavengers, Aubrey and Osborn, have attributed to Ralegh's pen a coarse and truculent epigram on the dead statesman under the name of Hobbinol. John Shirley, Ralegh's honest but credulous biographer, in 1677, also alleges him to have been the author, 'on very good grounds,' by which probably is signified nothing better than common gossip. Aubrey vouches in support statements made to him by Mr. Justice Malet, who is not known to have had any especial means of procuring information. Mr. Edwards believes it to be genuine. I cannot, though King James's alleged expression of a 'hope that the writer of those lines might die before him,' of which he was so careful to secure the fulfilment, has to be discarded with it. The evidence for Ralegh's authorship is exceedingly weak; and the rude verses are marked by none of his elegance of style. But the attempt to father so wretched a foundling upon him is proof the more of the popular perception of the dissembled estrangement. In a less undignified shape than a scurrilous epitaph on a dishonest shepherd, the bitterness Ralegh felt was sometimes openly exhibited. It is not discernible merely in collective insinuations against men whose ascendency in the royal council had been his 'infelicity.' When he had an opportunity it found a vent in a formal written accusation against the dead Lord Treasurer of having violated his duty to the King and the Exchequer by diverting to his own use the mass of Cobham's forfeited wealth. Gradually, brooding over his wrongs, he had accustomed himself to think Cecil not only the egotist he was, but an unscrupulous plotter, who wished to keep under lock and key a man able to unmask his rapacity. The Minister's death would appear to him to have cleared the board for new and happier combinations in his favour.

Prince Henry.

The Prince of Wales had at eighteen developed a will both resolute and impetuous, to which the death of a veteran statesman like Cecil was sure to have afforded freer scope. He did not disguise either his discontent at the policy of his father's favourite advisers, or his preference for ambitious projects such as Ralegh was known to cherish. Ralegh never had reason to doubt the sincerity of his admiration. There seemed no more ground for uncertainty as to the Prince's immediate influence on his behalf than as to the benefits to be derived from the youth's eventual accession to the throne. Henry was said to have extracted a promise from James of Ralegh's liberation at Christmas, 1612. November came, and the Prince lay dying of a raging fever. The Queen sent to the Tower for the medicine which had cured her. Ralegh despatched it with a letter, asserting that it would certainly heal this or any other case of fever, unless there were poison. A vehement debate followed among the Lords of the Council and the doctors, - *The Prince's Death.* - including the Genevese physician, Dr., afterwards Sir, Theodore Mayerne. Finally, the potion was administered. The patient, who had been speechless, revived sufficiently to speak. But it did not save his life. The populace and the Queen believed that it had been ineffectual because there had been poison. Forty years later, Carew Ralegh referred to the rumour as still credited. At the time it was repeated on the judicial bench. Sir Thomas Monson in 1615 was being tried for complicity in the murder of Sir Thomas Overbury. Coke, become Chief Justice, insinuated with his usual discretion and fairness at the trial that Overbury was poisoned from fear that he might, through hostility to Carr, divulge his guilty knowledge of a similar crime against 'a sweet Prince.'

Prince Henry's death blasted the prospect of Ralegh's ultimate restoration to royal favour, as well as to immediate liberty. It inflicted a less, but very vexatious, disappointment. After a protracted struggle he had been stripped of his Dorsetshire estate. Sherborne, he might have reckoned, was indefeasibly safe. Its enjoyment for his life was covered by the term for sixty years. The settlement of 1602 seemed to have set the inheritance out of danger. But in the course, perhaps, of the legal investigation with a view to the grant of the term for the benefit of Ralegh's wife and children, a flaw was detected in the conveyance of the fee. Little cause as Ralegh had to respect the impartiality of Popham and Coke in criminal procedure, he retained full confidence in their legal learning. To them in 1604, at his own earnest request, the deed of 1602 was submitted by Cecil. Their opinion on it was clear and fatal. They could have given no other. The essential words of a conveyance in trust, that the trustees shall stand thereof seised to the uses specified, had, Popham wrote to Cecil on June 7, 1605, been omitted. Popham believed the omission to have been due to the carelessness of the engrossing clerk. Through it the estate had remained wholly in Ralegh. Consequently, by his attainder it was forfeited. Lady Ralegh sought an audience of James. She prayed him not to take advantage of the forfeiture. With the facility which was compatible equally with generosity and with rapacious injustice, he promised. He directed Cecil to have a grant to her and her children prepared. It never was. At first the preposterous suspicion of Ralegh's sympathy with the Gunpowder Plot may have caused delay. Later the King discovered that he wanted the property for his own purposes. Alarmed at his own propensity for indulging the caprice of the moment, and mindful of the extent to which the Scottish Crown had been pauperized by royal improvidence, he had accepted a self-denying ordinance. By this he bound himself not to grant away the patrimony of the

Crown. For the endowment of favourites he had to rely, therefore, on windfalls from attainders and escheats. Robert Carr now had to be provided for. Sherborne happened to suit his taste, and the Ralegh family had to be ejected.

*Lady Ralegh
and the King.*

Proceedings were commenced in 1607 on the Attorney-General's Information to establish the claim of the Crown. Lady Ralegh again knelt before the King. She implored a waiver of the forfeiture in her and young Walter's favour. James rejected her petition either silently, or, according to Carew Ralegh, with the ejaculation, 'I mun have the land; I mun have it for Carr.' In a petition he addressed to the Long Parliament, Carew related that she fell down upon her knees, with her young sons beside her, and in the bitterness of her spirit invoked the vengeance of Heaven upon those who had so wrongfully exposed her and her poor children to ruin and beggary. James was used to her supplications for justice, and to repulsing them. In the previous autumn she had knelt to him at Hampton Court for her husband's liberty, and been passed without a word. Ralegh himself wasted upon Carr an eloquent prayer that he would not begin his first buildings upon the ruins of the innocent. He entreated him not to 'give me and mine our last fatal blow by obtaining from his Majesty the inheritance of my children and nephews, lost in law for want of words.' He made the attempt after his manner of neglecting no possibility. He can have put little trust in royal justice, and less in a worthless minion's magnanimity. Early in January, 1608, the Court of Exchequer decided against the validity of the conveyance. Chamberlain wrote on January 10, 1608, to *Escheat of Sherborne.* Dudley Carleton: 'Sir Walter Ralegh's estate is fallen into the King's hands by reason of a flaw in the conveyance. He hath bestowed it on Sir Robert Carr. And though the Lady Ralegh hath been an importunate suitor all these holidays in her husband's behalf, yet it is past recall. So that he may say, with Job, Naked came I into the world, &c. But, above all, one thing is to be noticed: the error or oversight is said to be so gross that men do merely ascribe it to God's own hand that blinded him and his counsel.'

Apparently the case was too technically plain against the deed for it to be seriously defended. Ralegh before the formal judgment had assented, under protest, to a proposal for the conveyance of his wife's and son's interest during his life to the Crown for a sum of £5000 to be paid the next year. For the remainder in fee he and she both struggled a while longer. Finally, formal judgment having been given for the Crown on October 27, 1608, they agreed to convey absolutely the entire interest for an annuity of £400, to be paid for the lives of lady Ralegh and young Walter, in lieu of Lady Ralegh's right to jointure out of the estate, and for a capital sum of £8000. In this the £5000 was to merge. The annuity was often in arrear. Part of the £8000 was paid down, and Ralegh lent it on mortgage to the dowager Countess of Bedford. For the rest the Exchequer not very regularly paid interest. The rental of the Sherborne lands was £750. This at sixteen years' purchase was £12,000. Consequently, it has been urged, the Crown did not drive a hard bargain. They who thus argue confess to some perplexity how the property could shortly afterwards have been, as it was, valued against Carr himself at £20,000 or £25,000. They have forgotten that the £750 rental does not allow for the worth of the house Ralegh had built, and for its costly embellishments.

Ralegh, with the certainty of a legal declaration of the forfeiture of the fee, had reluctantly assented to the compromise. He was weary and sick. He would be glad, he wrote, never to hear the place named thenceforth. Not so easily could he divorce himself from it. There was his old bailiff, whose insolent persecution tied him to the estate. In April, 1610, Meere had the effrontery to offer to prove by a letter, probably forged, that Ralegh had

Vicissitudes

of Ownership, promised him £100 a-year to conceal a set of frauds. His own heart cherished a lingering hope of a restoration of the property after all. In 1612 it seemed to be on the point of returning to him. Prince Henry expressed his indignation that a place of so much strength and beauty should have been given away, and had begged it of his father in the summer. James consented, and compensated Carr with £25,000 or £20,000. Ralegh and his friends believed that the Prince meant to bestow it on him with his freedom. On the Prince's death in November it reverted to the Crown, which sold a lease of it to Sir Robert Phillips. The transaction was speedily cancelled, and James gave the place back to Carr for the sum of £20,000, which, if not more, he had received. Three years later Carr's attainder shifted it over once again. Villiers might have had it, and refused. He would not, he said, have his fortune built upon another man's ruins. His contemporaries thought he might have been influenced also by fear of Bishop Osmund's curse upon all who should take Sherborne from the bishopric. Had he accepted it, Felton's dagger would have been considered one of the curse's instruments. At all events, he did not lose by his generous sentiment. Eleven manors were bestowed upon him instead, as was recited in their grant, of the Manor *Sale to Digby.* of Sherborne intended for him. Thereupon the property was sold to Sir John Digby, subsequently Lord Digby of Sherborne and Earl of Bristol, for £10,000, supplemented by gratuitous diplomatic services in Spain. Long afterwards, as we shall see, Carew Ralegh tried to revive the hereditary claim. Ralegh himself ceased to prosecute it after Prince Henry's death.

CHAPTER XXIII.

In prison as in freedom, if Ralegh failed in one effort for the reconstruction whether of his fortune, or of his career, he was always ready for another. He felt all the tedium of the uphill struggle. 'Sorrow rides the ass,' he exclaimed; 'prosperity the eagle.' Never for an instant was he dejected to the extent of faltering in the energy of his protests against the endeavours to suppress him. As Mr. Rossetti has noted in an exquisite sonnet, his mind remained always at liberty. His avocations and *Chemical Researches.* interests were enough to engage a dozen ordinary lives. He had always been interested in chemical experiments. He had studied the qualities of metals. In August, 1602, Carew mentioned to Cecil that he had been sending over to Ralegh from Munster 'many sorts of ore' to prove. Within his Tower garden he equipped an assaying furnace. Cecil occasionally visited it and him to inquire about the results. He is supposed to have written a *Treatise of Mines and the Trial of Minerals.* It has been thought he was associated with Sir Adrian Gilbert in working during Elizabeth's reign the ancient and neglected silver mines at Combe Martin. Long afterwards he agreed to join Boyle in working a Munster copper mine. Beside his furnace he had his laboratory at the foot of Bloody tower. He had always been fond of chemistry. A learned book on it had been dedicated to him as to an expert in the days of his grandeur. Oldys saw in Sir Hans Sloane's library a manuscript collection in Ralegh's own hand of *Chemical and Medicinal Receipts.* Now, in his enforced leisure, he threw himself ardently into the pursuit of experimental philosophy in many directions. He is said to have learnt how to cure common English tobacco in the Tower, so that he made it equal to American. The Royal Agricultural Society a few years since would have been grateful for his discovery. He is known to have discovered in the Tower the art of condensing fresh water from salt. He applied the process during his subsequent voyage to Guiana, though the secret was afterwards lost for two centuries. He was especially eager in the study of drugs. Waad wrote to Cecil in 1605 that he 'doth spend his time all the day in distillations in a little hen-house in the garden, which he hath converted into a still-house.' Sampson, a chemist, served him as operator for twelve years. Materials were brought to him by his old comrades and servants from all parts, and he experimented on their properties. He kept a stock of spices and essences, which sometimes he gave away, and sometimes sold. Great French ladies, we have seen, begged balms of him. A letter is preserved from one Zechelius of Nuremberg, complaining of his neglect to send some sassafras he had promised.

His drugs gained fame for cures, and sometimes for the reverse. He had presented some to Overbury. Ill-natured gossip attributed the death of the

The Great Cordial. - Countess of Rutland on September 1, 1612, to pills of

his composition. The wonder is that in neither case was any sinister motive charged. On the other hand, his Great Cordial or Elixir, which is not to be confounded with his Simple Cordial, was credited with astonishing virtues, and devoutly imbibed. His exact prescription for it is no longer extant. It is not clear whether he ever divulged the quantities as well as the ingredients. As specified by himself it might not have the air of quackery, which, it cannot be denied, surrounds the receipt handed down to posterity. Charles the Second's apothecary, Nicholas le Febre, or le Febure, compounded it for the royal use, and printed an account in 1664. Evelyn relates that he accompanied Charles to see the preparation in 1662. But le Febre, Kenelm Digby, and Alexander Fraser tampered with the original. It is acknowledged that Fraser added the flesh, heart, and liver of vipers, and the mineral unicorn. Other liberties, it may be apprehended, were taken. The receipt as drawn up by le Febre reads like a botanist's catalogue interpolated with oriental pearls, ambergris, and bezoardic stones, to add mystery. The old London Pharmacopœia gave a simpler receipt, in which the ingredients were zedoary and saffron, distilled with crabs' claws, cinnamon, nutmeg, cloves, cardamom seeds, and sugar.

Physical science did not occupy all his leisure. He wrote much. At

Political Disquisitions. - different periods of his imprisonment, which

cannot be precisely fixed, he composed a variety of treatises. He discussed many questions of politics, theoretical and practical. In his *Prerogative of Parliaments* he undertook to prove by an elaborate survey of past relations between the Crown and the Legislature, that the royal power gains and does not lose through regular and amicable relations with the House of Commons. The *Savoy Marriage* is a demonstrative argument against the proposed double family alliance between Savoy and the House of Stuart. Of that, and of his *Discourse of the Invention of Ships*, his *Observations concerning the Royal Navy and Sea Service*, and the *Letter to Prince Henry on the Model of a Ship*, I have already spoken. He composed *A Discourse on War in General*, which is very sententious. From his notebooks he collected, in his *Arts of the Empire* and *The Prince*, better known as *Maxims of State*, a series of wise, almost excessively wise, thoughts which had occurred to him in the course of his eager reading. An essay on the *Seat of Government*, and *Observations concerning the Causes of the Magnificency and Opulency of Cities*, show equal exuberance of learning, chiefly classical, though they cannot be said to be very conclusive. The former reads as if it had been meant for an introduction to a contemplated ampler view of polity. He must have studied not merely general, but economic politics, if the *Observations touching Trade and Commerce with the Hollander and other Nations* be by him. That remains a matter of doubt. Both Oldys and a recent German writer ascribe the work, published under five varying titles, to John Keymer, the Cambridge vintner, who is said to have composed, about 1601, *Observations upon the Dutch Fishery*. Ralegh more commonly has the credit of it. The dissertation, first printed inaccurately, and under a different heading, in 1650, shows minute statistical information, though it propounds, as might be expected, not a few economic fallacies. Its aim is the not very generous one of abstracting the carrying trade from Holland. The author engages, if he should be empowered to inquire officially, to enrich the King's coffers with a couple of millions in two or three years.

Ralegh is alleged to have written on the state, power, and riches of Spain. He has had attributed to him a *Premonition to Princes; A Dialogue, in 1609, between a Jesuit and a Recusant; A Discourse on Spanish Cruelties to Moral and Metaphysical Essays. Englishmen in Havanna*, and others on the relations of France, England, and Spain, and the meaning of the words Law and Right. He expatiated in the field of practical morals in his celebrated *Instructions to his Son and to Posterity*. The treatise makes an unpleasant impression with its hard, selfish, and somewhat sensual dogmatism. In extenuation it must be recollected that it was addressed to a hot and impetuous youth. He cultivated a taste for metaphysics. *The Sceptic* and *A Treatise on the Soul* are exemplifications of it. The former, as it stands, is an apology for 'neither affirming, nor denying, but doubting.' Probably the intention, not carried out, was to have composed an answer in defence of faith. It is affirmed, as matter beyond scepticism, that bees are born of bulls, and wasps of horses. *The Treatise on the Soul* is a performance of more mark. The profusion of its learning is enough to prevent surprise, whatever the quantity of knowledge displayed by the writer elsewhere. It is memorable for a fine burst of indignation at the denial by some men that women possess souls, and for several marvellous subtleties. For instance, the necessity of the theory that man begets soul as well as body, is alleged, since the contrary is said to involve the blasphemous absurdity that God assists adultery by having to bestow souls upon its fruits. In the Oxford edition of Ralegh's works, *A Discourse of Tenures which were before the Conquest* is also included. So versatile was Ralegh that he has thus been assumed to have even amassed the lore of a black-letter lawyer. Its authenticity nevertheless does not seem to have been questioned. That of the *Life and Death of Mahomet* has been, and on very sufficient grounds. The *Dutiful Advice of a Loving Son to his Aged Father* falls within a different category. It is not more likely than Steele's counterfeit letter in the *Englishman* to Prince Henry against the phrase 'God's Vicegerent,' or Bolingbroke's attacks, in Ralegh's name, upon Walpole in the *Craftsman Extraordinary*, to have been put forth with any notion that it would be believed to be his. Some editors have supposed it to be a libel upon him by an enemy. Any reader who peruses it dispassionately will see that it is sufficiently reverent pleading against the postponement of repentance to the hour of death, written by an admirer of Ralegh's style, with no purpose either of ridicule or of imposture.

Posthumous Publications.

Dissertations which were undoubtedly his circulated in manuscript, and were printed posthumously, if ever. *A Report of the Truth of the Fight about the Isles of Azores*, the *Discovery of Guiana*, and the *History of the World*, alone of his many prose writings appeared in his lifetime. The *Prerogative of Parliaments in England* was not published till 1628, and then first at Middleburg. Milton had the *Arts of Empire* printed for the first time in 1658, under the title of *The Cabinet Council, by the ever-renowned Knight Sir Walter Ralegh*. Dr. Brushfield, in his excellent *Ralegh Bibliography*, suggests that Wood may have meant this essay by the *Aphorisms of State*, to which he alludes as having been published in 1661 by Milton, and as identical with *Maxims of State*. Others of his writings have disappeared altogether. David Lloyd, in his *Observations on the Statesmen and Favourites of England*, published in 1665, states that John Hampden, shortly before the Civil Wars, was at the charge of transcribing 3452 sheets of Ralegh's writing. The published essays with his name attached to them do not nearly account for this vast mass. It may be suggested as a possible hypothesis that Hampden's collection comprised the manuscript materials for both parts of the History. Some compositions of his are known to have been lost. That has been the fate of his *Treatise of the West Indies*, mentioned by himself in the dedication of his *Discovery of Guiana*, and also of a *Description of the River of the Amazons*, if it were correctly assigned to him by Wood. Most of all to be regretted, if Jonson or Drummond is to be believed, is the life Jonson, at Hawthornden, alleged 'S.W.', that is, Sir Walter, to have written of Queen Elizabeth, 'of which there are copies extant.' As a writer of prose, no less than as a poet, he had little literary vanity. He wrote for a purpose, and often for one pair of eyes. When the occasion had passed he did not care to register the author's title.

The weightiness of thought, the enormous scope, the stateliness without pedantry or affectation, and the nobility of style, of one literary product

History of the World. of his imprisonment insured it against any such casualty. Of all the enterprises ever achieved in captivity none can match the _History of the World._ The authors of _Pilgrim's Progress_ and _Don Quixote_ showed more literary genius, and as much elasticity of spirit. Their works did not exact the same constancy and inflexibility of effort. Mr. Macvey Napier has well said: 'So vast a project betokens a consciousness of intellectual power which cannot but excite admiration.' Ralegh may himself not have commenced by realising the gigantic comprehensiveness of his undertaking. An accepted theory has been that his primary idea was a history of his own country, not of the world. It has been usual to cite a sentence of the preface in proof. The passage does not confirm the hypothesis. It runs: 'Beginning with the Creation, I have proceeded with the history of our world; and lastly proposed, some few sallies excepted, to confine my discourse within this our renowned island of Great Britain.' Here is no intimation that he had begun by setting before him for his text English history, and that the history of the world was an enlarged introduction. If his own words are to be believed, his survey of universal antiquity was as much part of his scheme as English history. Only, as he proceeded, the mass of details would necessarily thicken, and he would be compelled to narrow his inquiries. Having to choose, he naturally selected the nation which he regarded as the heir of successive empires, a race more valiant than the warriors, whether of Macedon or of Rome. But he distinctly preferred as a historical subject antiquity to recent times. As he says, 'Whosoever in writing a modern history shall follow truth too near the heels, it may haply strike out his teeth.'

It has been conjectured that he had already, before the History received its final shape, experimented on the more contracted or concentrated theme to which he purposed ultimately to devote himself. Archbishop Sancroft

Breviary of the History of England. possessed a short manuscript entitled a _Breviary of the History of England under William the First._ This was printed in 1693 without the Archbishop's consent, under the title _An Introduction to the Breviary of the History of England, with the Reign of King William I, entitled the Conqueror._ Sancroft, a good judge, considered the work in all its parts much like Ralegh's way of writing, and worthy of him. Though the language is more careless than Ralegh's, and the tone is less elevated, there is a resemblance in the diction. But much importance cannot be attached to a general similarity in the style of compositions belonging to the same age. Sancroft had the manuscript from an old Presbyterian in Hertfordshire, 'which sort of men were always the more fond of Sir Walter's books because he was under the displeasure of the Court.' Other manuscript copies also ascribe the authorship to Ralegh. The book, which shows research, but is not very accurate, is almost identical with the corresponding portion of the poet Samuel Daniel's *Collection of the History of England*, printed in 1618, and entered originally in the Register of the Stationers as a *Breviary of the History of England*. Daniel introduces his narrative with the words: 'For the work itself I can challenge nothing therein, but only the serving, and the observation of necessary circumstances with inferences.' Ralegh, though it is not very likely, may have given the fragment to Daniel for use in his history. Clearly he had formed a project of writing a history of England himself. In an undated letter from the Tower he asks Sir Robert Cotton to lend him thirteen authors, 'wherein I can read any of our written antiquities, or any old French history, wherein our nation is mentioned, or any else in what language soever.' It is not impossible that the *Breviary*, if in any way it were his, led him on to his gigantic enterprise, which by its expansion, unfortunately or fortunately, usurped all the leisure he had prospectively appropriated to his native annals. But the composition of an elaborate history by him was no accident, though the choice of the particular subject may have been.

Studies for the History.

Whatever the original design, the History in its final shape demanded encyclopædic research and learning. Necessarily the preparation for it and its composition employed several years. The number is not known. Ralegh is alleged to have begun to collect and arrange his matter in 1607. The date is purely conjectural. Sir John Pope Hennessy imagines that the preliminary investigations may be traced much farther back. Ralegh quotes in his book Peter Comestor's *Scholastica Historia*, an abstract of Scripture history, which has been found, with other remnants of an old monastic library, in a recess behind the wainscot of Ralegh's bedroom, next to his study in the house at Youghal. Mr. Samuel Hayman, the historiographer of Youghal, writing in 1852, states that the discovery was made a few years before, and that the books had probably been 'hidden at the period of the Reformation.' Sir John conjectures that Ralegh may have been taking notes from the collection 'for the *opus magnum* during his frequent Irish exiles.' An objection is that, according to Mr. Hayman, the authority cited by Sir John, Comestor's volume, with its companions, must have been secreted before Ralegh resided at Youghal, and have remained concealed till he had been dead for two centuries. In one sense he had been in training for the enterprise during his whole life; in another the actual work doubtless was accomplished after he felt that he was destined to a long term of imprisonment. He had always been a lover of books. In the midst of his adversities he spared £50 as a contribution towards the establishment of the Bodleian Library. When he was most deeply immersed in affairs he had made time for study. As Aubrey says, probably with complete truth, he was no slug, and was up betimes to read. On every voyage he carried a trunk full of books. During his active life, when business occupied thirteen hours of the twenty-four, he is said by Shirley to have reduced his sleeping hours to five. He was thus able to devote four to study, beside two for conversation. He loved research; and his name is in a list of members of the Society of Antiquaries formed by Archbishop Parker, which, though subsequently dissolved, was the precursor of the present learned body bearing the name. In the Tower he could read without stint. He possessed a fair library. From the company of his books, writes Sir John Harington, he drew more true comfort than ever from his courtly companions in their chiefest bravery.

Care for Accuracy.

Formerly, his reading necessarily had been desultory. For his History it had to be concentrated. He distrusted the exactness of his information, and was willing to accept advice freely. For criticism, Greek, Mosaic, Oriental and remoter antiquities, he consulted the learned Robert Burhill. Hariot had since 1606 been lodging or boarding in the Tower at the charge of the munificent Earl of Northumberland. He, Hues, and Warner were the Earl's 'three magi.' For chronology, mathematics, and geography, Ralegh relied upon him. 'Whenever he scrupled anything in phrase or diction,' he would refer his doubt to that accomplished serjeant-at-law, John Hoskyns or Hoskins. Hoskyns, now remembered, if at all, by some poor little epigrams, belongs to the class of paragons of one age, whose excellence later ages have to take on trust. He is described by an admirer as the most ingenious and admired poet of his time. Wotton loved his company. Ben Jonson considered him his 'father' in literature: "Twas he that polished me.' In the summer of 1614 he became, in consequence of a speech in the House of Commons, Ralegh's fellow prisoner. He is said to have revised the History before it went to press. Ralegh's intense desire to secure accuracy, his avowal of it, and its notoriety, have given occasion for charges against his title to the credit of the total result. Ben Jonson and Algernon Sidney are the only independent authorities for the calumny. But it has been caught up by other writers, especially by Isaac D'Israeli, who seems to have thought charges brought, as Mr. Bolton Corney showed, on the flimsiest evidence, of an impudent assumption of false literary plumage, in no way inconsistent with fervid admiration for the alleged pretender.

Ben Jonson was associated incidentally in the work. He prefaced it with a set of anonymous verses explanatory of an allegorical frontispiece. The manuscript of them was found among his papers. They have always been included in his *Underwoods*. Though the version there differs materially from that prefixed to the History, no reasonable doubt of his authorship of both exists. His omission openly to claim the lines is supposed, not unreasonably, by Mr. Edwards, to have been due to his fear of the prejudice his favour at Court might sustain from an open connexion with a fame so *Borrowed Learning.* odious there as Ralegh's. But a year after Ralegh's death he boasted over his liquor to civil sneering Drummond at Hawthornden, of other 'considerable' contributions. He had written, he said, 'a piece to him of the Punic War, which Sir Walter altered and set in his book.' In general, the best wits of England were, he asserted, engaged in the production. Algernon Sidney, in his posthumous *Discourses concerning Government*, repeated this insinuation of borrowed plumes of learning. Ralegh, he stated, was 'so well assisted in his *History of the World*, that an ordinary man with the same helps might have performed the same thing.' This is all bare assertion, and refuted by the internal evidence of the volume itself, which in its remarkable consistency of style, method and thought, testifies to its emanation from a single mind. Ralegh had himself explained with a manly frankness, which ought to have disarmed suspicion, the extent to which alone he was indebted for assistance. In his preface he admits he was altogether ignorant of Hebrew. When a Hebrew passage did not occur in Arias Montanus, or in the Latin character in Sixtus Senensis, he was at a loss. 'Of the rest,' he says, 'I have borrowed the interpretation of some of my learned friends; yet, had I been beholden to neither, yet were it not to be wondered at; having had an eleven years' leisure to attain to the knowledge of that or any other tongue.' As a whole, the History must be recognised as truly his own, his not only in its multitude of grand thoughts and reflections, but in the narrative and general texture. It cannot be the less his that some of the 660 authors it cites may have been searched for him by assistants.

Period of Publication.

As early as 1611 he must have settled the scheme, and even the title, of the book. On April 15 in that year notice was given in the Registers of the Stationers' Company of '*The History of the World*, written by Sir Walter Rawleighe.' Part may be presumed to have been by that time written, and shown to Prince Henry. Three years passed before actual publication. Camden fixes that on March 29, 1614. Though it is almost impossible to think Camden in error, yet, if the story of the perusal of the manuscript by Serjeant Hoskyns be true, and apply, as has been presumed, to the period of the Serjeant's imprisonment, the publication must have been half a year or more later. The later date would also accord better with a rumour of the suppression of the volume at the beginning of 1615. The publisher was Walter Burre, of the sign of the Crane in St. Paul's Churchyard. Burre published several works for Ben Jonson; and out of that circumstance has been constructed the statement that Jonson superintended the publication of the History for Ralegh. The form was that of a massive folio, at a price vaguely put by Alexander Ross at 'twenty or thirty shillings.' The edition was struck off in two issues, the errata of the first being corrected in the second. None of the extant copies of either issue possess a title-page, or contain any mention of the writer's name. The explanation may be the modesty or the pride which had led him habitually to neglect the personal glory of authorship, apprehension of the odium in which his name was held at Court, or a reason which will be mentioned hereafter. There is an engraved frontispiece by Renold Elstracke, the most elaborate of its kind known in English bibliography. A naval battle in the North Atlantic is depicted, and the course of the river Orinoko, with various symbolical figures. Ben Jonson's lines point its application. All the pages of the volume bear the heading, 'The First Part of the History of the World.'

Defects.

For modern readers a defect of the work is the learning, which was the wonder and admiration of contemporaries. Since Ralegh's time the historical method, and historical criticism, have been entirely changed. The mass of historical evidences has been immensely increased, and their quality is as different as their quantity. Ralegh had studied the researches of his learned contemporaries. He had expended much thought on the reconciliation of apparent inconsistencies. From the point of view of his own time he was successful. Often he satisfied others better than himself. Thus, he acknowledges with vexation his inability to divide exactly the seventy years of the Jewish captivity among the successive kings of Babylon. Had he been not merely a disciple of the great scholars of his age, but himself a pioneer, his dissertations and conclusions would equally have been drowned in the flood of later knowledge. His information is become superannuated. The metaphysical subtleties which he loved to introduce no longer delight or surprise. With all this there is much in the work which can never be obsolete, or cease to interest and charm. He himself is always near at hand, sometimes in front. He does not shun to be discerned in the evening of a tempestuous life, crippled with wounds aching and uncured. He does not repress, he hails, opportunities for sallying outside his subject. He is easily tempted to tell of the tactics by which the Armada was

vanquished, and how the battle *Merits.* might have had another issue had

Howard been misled by malignant fools that found fault. He recollects how he won Fayal. He pauses in his narrative of Alexander's victories to glorify English courage. He does homage to the invincible constancy of Spain, and avows her right to all its rewards, if she would 'but not hinder the like virtue in others.' The story suddenly gleams with flashes of natural eloquence and insight. Nowhere is there stagnation. His characters are very human, and very dramatic. King Artaxerxes is shown wearing a manly look when half a mile off, till the Greeks, for whom the bravery was not meant, espied his golden eagle, and drew rudely near. Queen Jezebel is visible and audible, with her paint, which more offended the dogs' paunches than her scolding tongue troubled the ears of Jehu, struggling in vain with base grooms, who contumeliously did hale and thrust her. There Demetrius revels, discovering at length in luxurious captivity the happiness he had convulsed the world with travail and bloodshed to attain. Pyrrhus is painted to the life, flying from one adventure to another, which was indeed the disease he had, whereof not long after he died in Argos. Characters are drawn with an astonishing breadth, depth, and decision. Nothing in Tacitus surpasses the epitaph on Epaminondas, the worthiest man that ever was bred in that nation of Greece. Everywhere are happy expressions, with wisdom beneath. It is a history for the nurture of virtuous citizens and generous kings, for the confusion of sensuality and selfishness.

The narrative rises and falls with the occasion; it is always bright and apt. Charles James Fox bracketed Bacon, Ralegh, and Hooker, as the three writers of prose who most enriched the English language in the period between 1588 and 1640. The diction of the History establishes Ralegh's title to the praise. It is clear, flowing, elastic, and racy, and laudably free, as Hallam has testified, from the affectation and passion for conceits, the snare of contemporary historians, preachers, and essayists. If Pope, as Spence represents, rejected Ralegh's works as 'too affected' for one of the foundations of an English dictionary, he must have been talking at random. At all events, he contradicted his own judgment deliberately expressed in authentic verse. For style, for wit, mother wit ¦ *The Moral.* ¦ and Court wit, and for a pervading sense that the reader is in the presence of a sovereign spirit, the *History of the World* will, to students now as to students of old, vindicate its rank as a classic. But its true grandeur is in the scope of the conception, which exhibits a masque of the Lords of Earth, 'great conquerors, and other troublers of the world,' rioting in their wantonness and savagery, as if Heaven cared not or dared not interpose, yet made to pay in the end to the last farthing of righteous vengeance. They are paraded paying it often in their own persons, wrecked, ruined, humiliated; and always in those of their descendants. At times it has seemed as if God saw not. In truth 'He is more severe unto cruel tyrants than only to hinder them of their wills.' Israelite judges, Assyrian kings, Alexander, the infuriate and insatiable conqueror, May-game monarchs like Darius, Rehoboam with his 'witless parasites,' so unlike wise, merciful, generous King James and his, Antiochus, 'acting and deliberating at once, in the inexplicable desire of repugnancies, which is a disease of great and overswelling fortunes,' Consul Æmilius, sacking all innocent Epirus to show his vigour, down to Henry the Eighth, 'pattern of a merciless prince,' none of them escaped without penalties in their households; none elude their condemnation and sentences, sometimes, as in the case of Alexander, it may be deemed, a little too austere, before the tribunal of posterity. On moves the world's imperial pageant; now slowly and somewhat heavily, through the domain of Scriptural annals, with theological pitfalls at every step for the reputed freethinker; now, as Greek and Roman confines are reached, with more ease and animation; always under the conduct as if of a Heaven-commissioned teacher with a message to rulers, that no 'cords have ever lasted long but those which have been twisted by love only.' Throughout are found an instinct of the spirit of events and their doers, a sense that they are to be judged as breathing beings, and not as mummies, an affection for nobility of aim and virtuous conduct, a scorn of rapacity, treachery, selfishness, and cruelty, which account better for the rapture of contemporaries, than for the neglect of the *History of the World* in the present century.

Popular Favour.

It was hailed enthusiastically both by a host of illustrious persons and by the general public. The applause rolled thundering on. The work was for Cromwell a library of the classics. He recommended it with enthusiasm in a letter to his son Richard. Hampden was a devoted student of it, as of Ralegh's other writings. It was a text-book of Puritans, in whose number, Ralegh says, if the *Dialogue with a Jesuit* be his, he was reckoned, though unjustly. They had forgotten or forgiven under James his enmity to their old idol Essex. The admiration of Nonconformists did not deter Churchmen and Cavaliers from extolling it. Bishop Hall, in his *Consolations*, writes of 'an eminent person, to whose imprisonment we are obliged, besides many philosophical experiments, for that noble *History of the World*. The Tower reformed the courtier in him.' Montrose fed his boyish fancy upon its pictures of great deeds. Unless for a few prejudiced and narrow minds it, 'the most God-fearing and God-seeing history known of among human writings,' as Mr. Kingsley has described it, swept away the old calumny of its author's scepticism. All ranks welcomed it as a classic. That Princess Elizabeth made it her travelling companion is proved by the history of the British Museum copy of the 1614 edition, which formed part of her luggage captured by the Spaniards at Prague in 1620, and recovered by the Swedes in 1648. With the King alone it found no favour. Contemporaries believed that he was jealous of Ralegh's literary ability and fame. Causes rather less base for his distaste for the book may be assigned. Ralegh had endeavoured to guard in his preface against a suspicion that, in speaking of the Past, he pointed at the Present, and taxed the vices of those that are yet living in their persons that are long since dead. He had interspersed encomiums upon his own sovereign, the 'temperate, revengeless, liberal, wise, and just,' though 'he may err.' His doctrine was, as he has written in his *Cabinet Council*, that 'all kings, the bad as well as the good, must be endured' by their subjects. The murder even of tyrants is deprecated, as 'followed by inconveniences worse than civil war.' But posterity he did not think was debarred from judging worthless rulers; and he tried them in his History. In the eyes of James such freedom of speech, especially in Ralegh, was *lèse majesté*. An explanation by himself of his ill-will to the book, which has been handed down by Osborn, has an air of verisimilitude. In his *Memoirs on King James*, Osborn relates that 'after much scorn cast upon Ralegh's History, the King, being modestly demanded what fault he found, answered, as one surprised, that Ralegh had spoken irreverently of King Henry the Eighth.' He would be more indignant on his own account than on that of King Henry, against whom, says Osborn, 'none ever exclaimed more than usually himself.' James discovered his own features in the outlined face of Ninias, 'esteemed no man of war at all, but altogether feminine, and subjected to ease and delicacy,' the successor of valiant Queen Semiramis, too laborious a princess, as Ralegh held, to have been vicious.

Threatened Suppression.

Commonly it has been believed that the King's sympathy with his caste provoked him to the monstrosity of an attempt to stifle its censor's volume. Chamberlain wrote to Carleton at Venice on January 5, 1615: 'Sir Walter Ralegh's book is called in by the King's commandment, for divers exceptions, but specially for being too saucy in censuring princes. I hear he takes it much to heart, for he thought he had won his spurs, and pleased the King extraordinarily.' The author of the *Observations on Sanderson's History* in 1656 writes to the same effect, but somewhat less definitely: 'It is well known King James forbad the book for some passages in it which offended the Spaniards, and for being too plain with the faults of princes in his preface.' There is no other evidence, and the majority of Ralegh's biographers have simply accepted the fact on the authority of Chamberlain's assertion. Yet it is almost incredible that so extreme an act of prerogative, carried out against so remarkable a work, should have been suffered to pass without popular protests. Ralegh and his wife never complained; and they were not given to suffering in silence. Copies of the first edition are extant in an abundance which, though not absolutely contradictory to the tale, renders it unlikely. Dr. Brushfield, who has made the history of the publication his especial study, conjectures that a compromise with the royal censorship was effected on the terms that a title-page, which he thinks the first, like all subsequent editions, originally contained, should be removed, leaving the volume apparently anonymous. The surmise is ingenious; but it is very hard to believe that such an arrangement, if made, would have excited no discussion. Chamberlain's language, moreover, implies that the book was already in circulation. It would be exceedingly strange if its previous purchasers had the docility to eliminate the title-page from their copies, in deference to an order certainly not very emphatically promulgated. The readiest explanation is that Chamberlain, in his haste to give his correspondent early information, reported to him a rumour, and perhaps a threat, upon which James happily had not the hardihood to act.

Successive Editions.

At all events, the book weathered the storm of royal displeasure, however manifested. A second edition appeared in 1617. Down to the standard Oxford collection of Ralegh's works in 1829, which includes it, eight have been published since. The last folio edition appeared, with a biography by the editor, Oldys, in 1736. Gibbon commends it as the best which had to that time appeared, though it is open to charges of gross carelessness in the printer, and of arbitrary alterations by the editor, to the injury of the sense. The work was popular enough to attract epitomists. Alexander Ross, in 1650, condensed it into his *Marrow of History*, which is rather its dry bones. Philip Ralegh, Sir Walter's grandson, in 1698 printed an abridgment. The *Tubus Historicus*, or *Historical Perspective*, published in 1631, a brief summary of the fortunes of the four great ancient Empires, which bears Ralegh's name on the title page, suggests rather the hand of a book maker. For half a century from the time of the original issue it was an accepted classic. No folio of the period, it has been said, approached it in circulation. Its success tempted Alexander Ross to put forth in 1652 a second part, B.C. 160 to A.D. 1640. The popular favour was enough to have encouraged the author to continue his own design. Two explanations of his interruption of it have been invented. For the first, the eldest authority is W. Winstanley's *English Worthies*, published in 1660. Winstanley, whom Aubrey *Two Fables.* follows, relates that Ralegh, a few days before his execution, asked Burre how that work of his had sold. So slowly, answered Burre, that it had undone him. Thereupon Ralegh, stepping to his desk, took the other unprinted part of his work into his hand with a sigh, saying 'Ah, my friend, hath the first part undone thee? The second volume shall undo no man; this ungrateful world is unworthy of it.' Then immediately, going to the fireside, he threw it in, and set his foot on it till it was consumed. The story is impossible, if only for the circumstance that the publication notoriously was not a failure. At the period to which the fable is assigned a second edition had been printed. So rapid was its sale, furthered, it may be admitted, by the circumstances of the author's death, that a third edition appeared in 1621. As, moreover, has been with prosaic common sense observed, a manuscript of some 1000 printed pages would have taken very long to burn.

The other story is still more complicated, and, if possible, more insolently mythical. John Pinkerton, writing under the name of Robert Heron, Esq., in 1785, in his eccentric *Letters on Literature*, is its source. According to him Ralegh, who had just completed the manuscript of a second volume, looking from his window into a court-yard, saw a man strike an officer near a raised stone. The officer drew his sword, and ran his assailant through. The man, as he fell, knocked the officer down, and died. His corpse and the stunned officer were carried off. Next day Ralegh mentioned the affray to a visitor of known probity and honour. His acquaintance informed him he was entirely in error. The seeming officer, he said, a servant of the Spanish Ambassador, struck the first blow. The other snatched out the servant's sword, and with it slew him. A bystander wrested away the sword, and a foreigner in the crowd struck down the murderer, while other foreigners bore off their comrade's body. The narrator, to Ralegh's assurances that he could not be mistaken, since he had witnessed the whole affair as it happened round the stone, replied that neither could he be, for he was the bystander, and on that very stone he had been standing. He showed Ralegh a scratch on the cheek he had received in pulling away the sword. Ralegh did not persist in his version. As soon as his friend was gone, he cast his manuscript into the fire. If he could not properly estimate an event under his own eyes, he despaired of appreciating human acts done thousands of years before he was born. 'Truth!' he cried, 'I sacrifice to thee.' Pinkerton, whose judgment and veracity were not equal to his learning, led astray both Guizot and Carlyle. Carlyle talks of 'the old story, still a true lesson for us.'

The Fact.

Of the extent to which Ralegh had proceeded in the continuation of his work he had himself informed the public. In his preface he 'forbears to promise a second or third volume, which he intends if the first receives grace and good acceptance; for that which is already done may be thought enough and too much.' At the conclusion he wrote: 'Whereas this book calls itself the first part of the *General History of the World*, implying a second and third volume, which I also intended, and have hewn out; besides many other discouragements persuading my silence, it hath pleased God to take that glorious prince out of the world, to whom they were directed.' His language points evidently to the collection of 'apparatus for the second volume,' as Aubrey says. It may have comprised very possibly not a few such scattered gems of thought and rich experience as are the glory of the printed volume. A Ralegh Society, should it ever be instituted, might have the honour of disinterring and reuniting some of them. No less clearly he indicates that he had not advanced beyond the preliminary processes of inquiry and meditation.

The motive for his abandonment at this point of the thorough realization of his plan was probably a combination of disturbing causes, disappointment, hope, and rival occupations. Prince Henry's favour had brought liberty and restitution very close. With a nature like his the abrupt catastrophe did not benumb; it even stimulated; but it took the flavour out of many of his pursuits. He could no longer indulge in learned ease, and trust for his rehabilitation to spontaneous respect and sympathy. The near breath of freedom had set his nerves throbbing too vehemently for him to be able to settle down, as if for an eternity of literary leisure, to tasks like the *History of the World*, or the *Art of War by Sea*. He began working mines as busily as ever, but in new directions. He sought to make himself recognised as necessary either by the King or by the nation. With the *The Prerogative of Parliaments.* sanguine elasticity which no failures could damp, he tried to storm his way as a politician into the royal confidence a few months after he is said to have experienced as a scholar an effect of the King's invincible prejudice. At some period after May, 1615, he wrote, and dedicated to James, an imaginary dialogue between a Counsellor of State and a Justice of the Peace. Under the title of *The Prerogative of Parliaments in England* it was published first posthumously in 1628, at Middleburg. In his lifetime it circulated in manuscript copies.

A conspicuous instance of the misconceptions of which he was the habitual victim is the view taken of this treatise by Algernon Sidney, and by the judicious and fair-minded Hallam. Its object was to influence the King to call a Parliament. Ralegh's point of view of the royal prerogative was, it must be admitted and remembered, that of a Tudor courtier. It was very different from that which the Long Parliament learnt and taught. But it was liberal for his own day, according to a Tudor standard of liberalism. It was

too liberal for the taste *Hallam's Misconception.* of the Court of James.
Hallam has caught at some phrases couched in the adulatory style, 'so much,' Hallam allows, 'among the vices of the age, that the want of it passed for rudeness.' Ralegh told James in his dedication that 'the bonds of subjects to their kings should always be wrought out of iron, the bonds of kings unto subjects but with cobwebs.' Sidney had already protested against these obsequious phrases; and to Hallam they seem 'terrible things.' He is equally horrified by a statement in the dialogue that Philip II 'attempted to make himself not only an absolute monarch over the Netherlands, like unto the Kings of England and France, but Turk like to tread under his feet all their national and fundamental laws, privileges, and ancient rights.' The tenor of the essay itself only has to be equitably considered to enable its readers to place a more lenient construction than Hallam's even upon the former sentence. Ralegh merely was pursuing his object, with some carelessness, after his manner, as to form. Throughout he endeavoured to sweeten advice he knew to be unpalatable, by assurances that the King need not fear his prerogative would be permanently impaired by deference to the representatives of the people. The language is, for the nineteenth century, indefensible. Taken in connexion with the general argument, it resolves itself into a courtly seventeenth century solace to the monarch for an obligatory return to Parliamentary government.

For the second quotation such an excuse is scarcely requisite. The theories of the royal prerogative in France and in England were not originally dissimilar, profoundly unlike as was the practice. Since, as well as before, the Revolution of 1689, the absolute character of the English sovereignty has been a common theory of lawyers. Blackstone, writing in the reign of George the Third, asserts dogmatically that an English King is absolute in the exercise of his prerogative. Blackstone was able to find room beside an absolute prerogative for the national liberties and Parliamentary privileges. So was Ralegh able. His language seems now unconstitutional, when, in his *Maxims of State*, he distinguishes the English 'Empire' from a 'limited Kingdom'; or when, in this *Prerogative of Parliaments*, he declares that 'the three Estates do but advise, as the Privy Council doth.' To him, however, 'limited' meant more than now, and 'absolute' less. He saw no inconsistency between the theory of royal absolutism and the application of popular checks. Their reconciliation was *Not shared by James.* the purpose of the essay of 1615. That was evident to many excellent patriots of the next reign, who circulated and gloried in a composition which proved the writer their fellow worker. It was too apparent, though not to Hallam, to James, for the dissertation to move him to any kindness. The basis and principle of the discussion affronted all his prejudices. He was not to be beguiled by admissions of his theoretical omnipotence into affection for a wise and constitutional policy, which recognised popular rights. He had no inclination to traverse the golden bridge Ralegh had built for his return within the lines, whether of the Constitution, or of personal justice. In all relations Ralegh was antipathetic to James without consciousness of it. He could declare his implicit belief, in consonance with strict constitutional orthodoxy, that the King loved the liberties of his people, and that none but evil counsellors intercepted the signs of his liberality. He could acknowledge the tender benignity of his sovereign to himself, and throw upon betrayers of the royal trust the shame of his persecution. He could be excessively deferential and grateful in words and demeanour. He could not but act and reason with a mental independence as hateful to James as to Henry Howard, and as condemnatory. Whether he discoursed on Assyrian or on English politics, or on his private wrongs, he sat visibly on the seat of judgment. Nothing but tame silence and spiritual petrifaction could have made his peace at the Stuart Court. It was the one kind of fealty he was incapable of rendering.

CHAPTER XXIV.

THE RELEASE (March, 1616).

No merits of his, and no sense of justice to him, opened, or ever would have opened, his prison doors. But at length it was become inconvenient to keep him under duress. The gaolers who cared to detain him were gone. In their places stood others who had an interest in sending him forth, though with a chain on his ankle. He could never have been brought to trial on a fantastic charge, or been convicted without evidence, unless for the weight of popular odium, which enabled the new Court to trample upon the favourite of the old. Without that he could not have been kept for long

years in *How his Fetters fell off.* prison. Gradually the nation forgot its

habit of dislike, which never had much foundation. Englishmen remembered his mighty deeds. They honoured him as the representative of a glorious and dead past. His fetters were of themselves falling off. Special circumstances helped to shake him free of them. He had protested ineffectually in the name of right. He had pleaded to deaf ears for liberty to serve his country. At length an impression had been produced that the prosecution of his policy might bring money into other coffers beside his own.

He had never ceased to plan the establishment of English colonies in Virginia and Guiana. He regarded both countries as his, and as English by priority of discovery or occupation. From the fragments of his broken fortunes the captive of the Tower had managed to fit out or subsidize expeditions at intervals to both. Every few years the Guiana Indians in particular were reminded by messages from him that their deliverance from the Spaniards was at hand. To Englishmen ores and plants from Guiana recalled the riches of the land, and their title to it. Thus, in December, 1609, we hear that Sir Walter Ralegh had a ship come from Guiana laden with gold ore. His chase after freedom was stimulated by visions of himself once more a leader, and the founder of an empire. The thought grew to be a passion, and almost a monomania.

To gain permission to hazard life, health, and reputation in the western seas, he was ready to subscribe to the most grotesque conditions, which,

Petitions to the Queen. however, do not seem to have impressed

contemporaries as extravagant. He had hoped that the Queen Consort might consent to be lady patroness of his project. In 1611 he solicited her formally. He proffered by letter his service in Virginia. It was his name for

Guiana, in order not to alarm pro-Spanish jealousies. He had been suspected of a design to fly from England under cover of a voyage of discovery. The Queen had faith in him, and he entreated her to give her word for him to mistrustful Cecil. He was willing, if he should not be on his way to America by a day set, to forfeit life and estate. As a security against turning aside to some foreign European Court after his departure from England, he would leave his wife and two sons as his pledges. His wife, whom we can see stooping over him, and dictating the words, 'shall yield herself to death, if I perform not my duty to the King.' If this sufficed not, the masters and mariners might have orders, if he offered to sail elsewhere, to cast him into the sea. Again in 1611 he addressed the Queen. Previously he had propounded to Cecil a scheme for a Guiana expedition, of which he now sent her a copy. He besought her influence on its behalf. She would be acting for the King's sake, that 'all presumption might be taken from his enemies, arising from the want of treasure.' He was scarcely pleading, he said, for himself. 'My extreme shortness of breath doth grow so fast, with the despair of obtaining so much grace to walk with my keeper up the hill within the Tower, as it makes me resolve that God hath otherwise disposed of that business, and of me.'

At this time interest in Guiana and its precious metals had revived. Ralegh had some morsels of merquisite he had himself picked up assayed by a refiner. The man found gold in them. These, or other specimens of Guiana ores, Sir Amias Preston, his old adversary, had seen. Preston had extolled them to Cecil. Ralegh may have discussed their virtues with Cecil in the Tower at one of the interviews in the laboratory, when, he complains, the Minister would listen, inquire, talk of the assay, hold out hopes, and then retreat into an *arrière boutique*, in which he lay unapproachable. A letter to Cecil, with the uncertainty of date which breaks the hearts of Ralegh's biographers, says: 'I have heard that Sir Amias Preston informed | *Golden* | *Bait.* | your Lordship of certain mineral stones brought from Guiana, of which your Lordship had some doubt—for so you had at my first return— secondly, that your Lordship thought it but an invention of mine to procure unto myself my former liberty; suspicions which might rightly form into the cogitations of a wise man.' He assured Cecil that a mountain near the river contained 'an abundance sufficient to please every appetite.' Once he had thought the stones valueless, like other merquisite. He had been convinced of his error by the refiner, who was willing to go and be 'hanged there if he prove not his assay to be good.' To avert suspicion that he meant to become a runagate, Ralegh was ready not to command, but to ship as a private man. He repeated his strange offer to be cast into the sea if

he should persuade a contrary course. The cost would be no more than
£5000. 'Of that, if the Queen's Majesty, to whom I am bound for her
compassion, and your Lordship will bear two parts, I and my friends will
bear a third. Your Lordship may have gold good and cheap, and may join
others of your honourable friends in the matter, if you please. For there is
enough. The journey may go under the colour of Virginia. We will break
no peace; invade none of the Spanish towns. We will see none of that
nation, except they assail us.' His intention was to melt down the mineral
on the spot into ingots, 'for to bring all in ore would be notorious.' In 1610
he had written to a trusted friend of James, John Ramsay, then Viscount
Haddington, and later Earl of Holderness, with similar proposals. He would
follow Ramsay as a private man, or others, and if he recommended a
different course was willing to be drowned. Then, 'if I bring them not to a
mountain, near a navigable river, covered with gold and silver ore, let the
commander have commission to cut off my head there.' Or he would give a
£40,000 bond to boot.

*Overtures to
the Council.*

In 1611, or 1612, he alternated his overtures to the Queen with others to
Lords of the Council, who, it may be gathered from a letter of his, agreed
to become joint-adventurers with him. A plan had been started for sending
Captain Keymis with two ships to Guiana, and enough men to defend him
'from the Spaniards inhabiting upon Orenoche, not that it is meant to begin
any quarrel with them, except themselves shall begin the war.' Captain
Moate, servant of Ralegh's friend, Sir John Watts, had come the last spring
'from St. Thome, where the Spaniards inhabit.' According to him Keymis
might safely go the five miles from the river to his mountain. In this way he
could bring from the mine 'half a ton of that slate gold ore, whereof I gave
a sample to my Lord Knevett.' In default, all the charge of the journey
should be laid upon himself. He was contented to adventure all he had but
his reputation upon Keymis's memory. He warned the Lords, that 'there is
no hope, after this trial made, to fetch any more riches from thence.' But he
submitted to the wisdom of the King and their Lordships. 'Only, if half a
ton be brought home, then I shall have my liberty, and in the meanwhile
my free pardon under the Great Seal, to be left in his Majesty's hands till
the end of the journey.' That precaution later he omitted, and paid the
penalty of dealing in good faith with crowned and coroneted pettifoggers.
At all events, the present proposal gave full notice to members of the
Council of the existence of a Spanish settlement on the Orinoko, which
subsequently Ralegh was accused of having perfidiously concealed from the
King.

His projects, prayers, and expeditions came to nothing at the time. They were not without their effect. They kept the thought of Guiana before the nation. As James in his *Declaration* afterwards asserted, the confident asseveration of that which every man was willing to believe, enchanted the world. To a certain degree it influenced the King and Court. James was not

to Guiana. of a nature to undervalue dignities and opportunities of wealth. While he imprisoned the explorer, he had asserted the title to Guiana acquired through him. He commissioned Captain Charles Leigh in 1604, and, after his death, Captain Robert Harcourt in 1608, to take possession of all from the Amazon to the Dessequebe, with the neighbouring islands. The result was a settlement on the Oyapoco. After three years the colonists abandoned the enterprise, and returned to England. Harcourt experienced the effect of the local renown of Ralegh, and of the success of his efforts to keep alive the recollection of the fealty once offered through him to England. Leonard the Indian, who had resided in England three or four years with Ralegh, obtained for Harcourt supplies he sorely needed. The help was rendered in the belief, says Ralegh, that Harcourt was a follower of his. The natives visited Harcourt's vessel dressed in European clothes, which Ralegh had sent them the year before. They were disappointed at not finding him in command. Leigh's and Harcourt's expeditions confirmed his assertions of the immense possibilities of the country. Harcourt expressly stated his 'satisfaction that there be rich mines in the country.' The actual fruits were so meagre as to demonstrate that supreme capacity was needed to extract its treasures.

Ralegh's adversaries, including James, were as persuaded as his friends of his unbounded ability. They hated him for it. They were covetous of gold and territory. They thought he might justify his boasts, and enrich them as well as himself, if he were let go. Failure, on the other hand, would, they calculated, blast his power to hurt. At all events, in the existing popular mood, it was easier to despatch him at his own expense for their contingent gain to America, than to confine him in the Tower. Their personal relations with Spain supplied rather a motive for his liberation for such a purpose than a fatal objection. James longed for a family league with the Escurial. Spain was reserved and proud, and responded coldly to his advances. He did not care what harm came to Ralegh, upon whom, as Mr. Gardiner says, he knew the Spaniards would fall wherever they found him. Meanwhile he hoped to warm his coy allies by letting loose upon the Spanish Main their and his inveterate aversion. Ralegh was a convenient firebrand to show Spain the harm England, if an enemy, could do. He was a scapegoat to immolate in proof of all England was prepared to sacrifice in return for Spain's love. Suddenly, for many mixed reasons, it was decided to free him. He was to be licensed to discover gold mines and affirm the English title to the Orinoko.

Ralegh's Opportunity.

He himself was at the moment in a strong position for demanding liberty and a commission. The arms and hands which had, according to his expression, abused their Sovereign's borrowed authority to fling stones at him, were now, as with doubtful discretion as well as taste he reminded James in the *Prerogative of Parliaments*, 'most of them already rotten.' Robert Cecil, though nowise to be ranked with Howard as demoniacally malevolent, had evinced no disposition to release him. Certainly he would, if only for Ralegh's own sake, not have abetted his wild quest of Guiana gold. But he too was dead. Robert Carr was worse than dead. The terrible exposure of his and his wife's crimes had made James and his counsellors peculiarly sensitive to public opinion. Hallam thinks it 'more likely than anything else that James had listened to some criminal suggestion from Overbury and Somerset, and that, through apprehension of this being disclosed, he had pusillanimously acquiesced in the scheme of Overbury's murder.' That is Hallam's deliberate view of the King who claimed the right to sit in judgment on Ralegh. The country entertained a similar suspicion. It might have been dangerous to hold a national hero confined under the same prison roof with the principals in the crime. Moreover, a sympathetic politician, Sir Ralph Winwood, was Secretary of State. Personally, Winwood was in high favour with the King, notwithstanding discrepancies in their estimates of the value of a Spanish alliance. Of that he and Archbishop Abbot both were vehement opponents. They thought Ralegh a likely instrument for bringing about a collision with Spain in the most advantageous circumstances. For the moment Winwood's admiration of Ralegh and dislike of Spain, and the King's contrary feelings, together with his general disposition to shift responsibility, worked to the same end. George Villiers was inclined to befriend Ralegh out of opposition to the Howards, who had been Carr's supporters. Henry Howard, Earl of

Northampton, had died in June, 1614. The King Christian. credit of

Thomas Howard, Earl of Suffolk, the Lord Treasurer, was waning. The old Lord High Admiral Nottingham's naval administration had been unsuccessful and wasteful. King Christian, the Queen's brother, when recently in England, had warmly interceded for Ralegh, whom, if Sir Thomas Wilson's reports of subsequent conversations with Ralegh are to be believed, he would gladly have borrowed of James for the Danish navy.

Ralegh believed the King had, on a previous visit, asked for his liberty. That is not certain. Carleton, writing to Chamberlain in August, 1606, stated that Christian had declined the office. In any case he exerted himself on his second visit. The fact must be set off for him against another, that he was a sot, and, as Harington shows, set an evil example of drunken bouts to the imitative English Court. Ralegh wrote to Winwood in January, 1616, on the wealth of Guiana: 'Those that had the greatest trust were resolved not to believe it; not because they doubted the truth, but because they doubted my disposition towards themselves, had I recovered his Majesty's favour and good opinion. Our late worthy Prince of Wales was extreme curious in searching out the nature of my offences; the Queen's Majesty hath informed herself from the beginning; the King of Denmark, at both times his being here, was thoroughly satisfied of my innocency. The wife, the brother, and the son of a King do not use to sue for mere suspect. It is true, sir, that his Majesty hath sometimes answered that his Council knew me better than he did; meaning some two or three of them; and it was indeed my infelicity. For had his Majesty known me, I had not been where I now am; or had I known his Majesty, they had never been so long where they now are. His Majesty's misknowing of them hath been the ruin of a goodly part of his estate; but they are all of them—some living, and some dying—come to his Majesty's knowledge. But to die for the King, and not by the King, is all the ambition I have in the world.'

Gifts of Money.

No further explanation of Ralegh's deliverance might seem to be required. Without the co-operation of these various coincidences which aided his claim to justice, and weakened the resistance to it, he must indeed have remained in prison. But the popular belief was that the immediate agency to which he owed his freedom was neither equity nor policy; it was the prisoner's own money. A half-brother of George Villiers, Sir Edward Villiers, and Sir William St. John, a kinsman of Sir Edward's wife, are alleged in the *Observations on Sanderson's History of King James*, to have procured Sir Walter Ralegh's liberty, and to have had £1500 for their labour. The story has been denied. Unfortunately it is by no means intrinsically improbable. It agrees with Ralegh's confident allusion at his death to the ease with which he could have bought his peace, even after his return from Guiana, if he had been rich enough. There is a miserable consistency in his imprisonment on a false charge of treason, and his release through a bribe to relatives of the King's favourite. He wrote to George Villiers: 'You have by your mediation put me again into the world.' The service cannot be questioned, but its motive.

On March 19, 1616, a royal warrant required the Lieutenant of the Tower to 'permit Sir Walter Ralegh to go abroad to make preparations for his

Ralegh's Fellow Prisoners. voyage.' He then partially or entirely quitted the prison which had been his home for twelve years. Its population had undergone some recent and notable changes and exchanges. Sir George More was Lieutenant. Lord Grey of Wilton had died in July, 1614. To the end he had hoped to be, through the influence of Henry Howard and Carr, set free to serve Protestant Holland against Catholic Spain. More pitiable Arabella Stuart, or Seymour, had entered in 1611. She survived till September, 1615, ever weak, but guilty of no crime except her contingent birthright. Ralegh left in prison Northumberland. This splendid patron of letters, for the dozen years he inhabited the Tower, has been said to have invested it with the atmosphere of an university. He peopled it with students and inquirers, such as Thomas Allen, William Warner, Robert Hues, Torporley, and Hariot. Of an intelligence and capacity which won Sully's admiration, but wayward, scornful, and, for his own interests very little of the wizard he was reputed to be, he had been consigned thither for no guilt, unless, like Ralegh, that he may have consorted with the guilty. An injustice was not wholly fruitless which bestowed on Ralegh the comfort of a companionship of learning. Death, eight years before his release, had freed the last titular chieftain of the Fitzgeralds, whose spoils he had shared; but he left there an older antagonist, Florence McCarthy, the 'infinitely adored' Munster man, who in a neighbouring cell emulated his historical researches. He left Cobham. A rumour current at the commencement of 1616 that Cobham, like him, was to be freed, was not confirmed till 1617, and then only partially. In that year Cobham was allowed to visit Bath for the waters. He was on his way back to the Tower in September, when, at Odiham, he had a paralytic stroke. He was conveyed to London at the

beginning of October, and lingered *Death of Cobham.* between life and

death till January 12, 1619. Probably he expired in the Tower, though Francis Osborn, who had been master of the horse to Lord Pembroke, was told by Pembroke that he died half starved in the hovel of an old laundress in the Minories. The statement of his poverty is in conflict with the fact mentioned by Ralegh in the *Prerogative of Parliaments*, that the Crown allowed him £500 a year till his death for his maintenance. An explanation has been offered that the tale may have been founded on the delay in his burial. His wealthy wife and relatives tried to throw upon the Crown the liability for the cost of an obscure funeral by night at Cobham. But for some unknown reason he appears to have been in pecuniary straits. Camden speaks of his return to the Tower 'omnium rerum egentissimus,' and of his death 'miser et inops.' Certainly he had been, as he deserved to be, more harshly treated in respect of money than Ralegh. On his conviction his estates had been confiscated. Even his valuable library, which, in the Tower, he had retained, was claimed in 1618 for the King's use by the Keeper of State Papers. He had no wife to tend him as had Ralegh. Lady Kildare was more literally faithful than Sir Griffin Markham's wife, who, while he was in exile, wedded her serving man, and had to do penance for bigamy at St. Paul's in a white sheet. But she neglected her husband, whom she had once ardently loved, and allowed him to pine alone. Ralegh's admirers too cannot but despise him, though their feeling is less anger than impatience that so poor a creature should have warped the fate of one so great.

Another and newer prisoner Ralegh left, who was to stay till 1622, as notorious as Cobham, and yet more ignoble. Robert Carr, Viscount Rochester, and Earl of Somerset, had been committed to the Tower on October 18, 1615, on the charge of having procured the murder of Sir Thomas Overbury. The guiltier Countess was joined in the accusation, and committed in April, 1616. Both were convicted in the May after Ralegh's release. They were lodged in Ralegh's old _Carr and his Wife._ quarters, he in the Bloody tower, she in the garden pavilion erected or remodelled for Ralegh's accommodation. It had been hastily prepared for her in response to her passionate entreaties to the Lieutenant not to be put into Overbury's apartment. Carr's imprisonment and Ralegh's liberation are said, in a treatise attributed to Fulke Greville, Lord Brooke, to have given great occasion of speech and rumour. Quips and taunts upon Carr, on the same authority, are imputed to Ralegh. Town gossip was always busy with his name. In the absence of facts it invented. He was capable of sharp epigrams, and may have exulted in the fall of his unworthy supplanter. He would not have condescended to hurl gibes, as has further been alleged, in the face of the miserable being who was succeeding him as tenant of his cell. The story is that, possibly during a visit to the Tower after Carr's trial, he met the convict entering the dark archway from Water Lane, and thereupon remarked aloud: 'The whole History of the World had not the like precedent of a King's prisoner to purchase freedom, and his bosom favourite to have the halter, but in Scripture, in the case of Mordecai and Haman.' As improbably James is reported to have been told, and to have retorted that 'Ralegh might die in that deceit.'

CHAPTER XXV.

Ralegh's freedom was for a period conditional. The King's warrant 'fully and wholly enlarging' him, was not issued till January 30, 1617. From the preceding March 19, or, Camden says, March 29, he was permitted to live at his own house in the city. But he was attended by a keeper, and his movements were restricted. On March 19, the Privy Council had written to him: 'His Majesty being pleased to release you out of your imprisonment in the Tower, to go abroad with a keeper, to make your provisions for your intended voyage, we admonish you that you should not presume to resort either to his Majesty's Court, the Queen's, or Prince's, nor go into any public assemblies wheresoever without especial licence.' Before his *A*

Pilgrimage

Round London. liberation he had been seriously ill. Anxiety, and, it was rumoured, excessive toil in his laboratory at the assaying of his Guiana ores, had brought on a slight apoplectic stroke. A sense of liberty restored his activity. In March or April he handselled his freedom, as Chamberlain wrote to tell Carleton, with a journey round London to see the new buildings erected since his imprisonment. Then forthwith he commenced his preparations for 'the business for which,' as wrote the Council, 'upon your humble request, his Majesty hath been pleased to grant you freedom.' He needed no driving, and he spared no sacrifices.

He collected information from every quarter, and was willing to buy it. He promised, for instance, payment out of the profits of the voyage to an Amsterdam merchant for discovering somewhat of importance to him in Guiana. He arranged on March 27, eight days after his release, for Phineas Pett, the King's shipwright, to build, under his directions, the Destiny, of 450 tons burden. He pledged all his resources. He called in the loan of £3000 to the Countess of Bedford. His wife sold to Mr. Thomas Plumer for £2500 her house and lands at Mitcham. Altogether he spent £10,500. Part he had to borrow on bills. So impoverished was he that, as he related subsequently, he left himself no more in all the world, directly or indirectly, than £100, of which he gave his wife £45. Warm personal friends, of whom he *The Destiny.* always had many, notwithstanding his want of promiscuous popularity, gave encouragement and sympathy. George

Carew, writing to Sir Thomas Roe at the Great Mogul's Court of the building of the Destiny, which was launched on December 16, 1616, 'prayed Heaven she might be no less fortunate with her owner than is wished by me.' Carew, shrewd and prudent, had no doubt of the sincerity of his 'extreme confidence in his gold mine.' Adherents contributed money and equipments. Lady Ralegh's relative, grand-nephew of her old opponent at law, Lord Huntingdon, presented a pair of cannon. The Queen offered good wishes, and was with difficulty dissuaded from visiting the flagship.

Many co-adventurers joined, and contributed nearly £30,000. Unfortunately they were, Ralegh has recorded, mostly dissolute, disorderly, and ungovernable. Their friends were cheaply rid of them at the hazard of thirty, forty, or fifty pounds apiece. Some soon showed themselves unmanageable, and were dismissed before the fleet sailed. Of the discharged a correspondent of Ralegh's pleasantly wrote: 'It will cause the King to be at some charge in buying halters to save them from drowning.' More than enough stayed to furnish Ralegh with mournful grounds later on for recollecting his own Cassandra-like regret that Greek Eumenes should have 'cast away all his virtue, industry, and wit in leading an army without full power to keep it in due obedience.' Of better characters were some forty gentlemen volunteers. Among them were Sir Warham St. Leger, son of Ralegh's Irish comrade, not as Mr. Kingsley surmises, the father, who had been slain in 1600; George Ralegh, Ralegh's nephew, who had served with Prince Maurice; William or Myles Herbert, a cousin of Ralegh, and near kinsman of Lord Pembroke; Charles Parker, misnamed in one list Barker, a brother of Lord Monteagle; Captain North; and Edward Hastings, Lord Huntingdon's brother. Hastings died at Cayenne. He would, wrote Ralegh at the time, have died as certainly at home, for 'both his liver, spleen, and brains were rotten.'

Young Walter.

Young Walter was of the company, and Ralegh and his wife adventured nothing else for them so precious. Walter was fiery and precocious, too much addicted, by his father's testimony, to strange company and violent exercise. He had been of an age to feel the ruin of his parents, and to resent their persecution. In childhood, with the consent of Cobham, and of Cecil as Master of the Court of Wards, he was betrothed to Cobham's ward, Elizabeth, the daughter and heiress of wealthy William Basset, of Blore. On the attainder the contract was broken. The girl was affianced to Henry Howard, who died in September, 1616, a son of Lord Treasurer Suffolk, formerly Lord Thomas Howard. Walter was born in 1593, and in October, 1607, at fourteen, matriculated at Corpus College, Oxford. He was described as, at this time, his father's exact image both in body and mind.

In 1610 he took his bachelor's degree. By 1613 he was living in London. In April, 1615, according to a letter from Carew to Roe, though other accounts variously give the date as 1614 or early in 1616, he fought a duel with Robert Finett or Tyrwhit, a retainer of Suffolk's. It was necessary for him to leave the country. Ralegh sent him to the Netherlands, with letters of introduction to Prince Maurice. Ben Jonson is said to have acted as his governor abroad. That is impossible at the date, 1593, assigned by Aubrey to their association. It is not impossible a year or two after 1613, if not in 1613, when Jonson appears to have been in France. Poet and pupil are said to have parted 'not in cold blood.' It is likely enough, if Drummond's tale be true, as Mr. Dyce seems to believe, that Walter had Jonson carted dead drunk about a foreign town. According to another not very plausible story, retailed by Oldys, the exposure of the tutor's failing was at the Tower, and to Ralegh, to whom Walter consigned Jonson in a clothes-basket carried by two stout porters. Though the particular tales are hardly credible, Jonson's revelries may have laid him open to lectures by the father, and disrespect from the son, which would have something to do with the dramatist's sneer at the memory of Ralegh, as one who 'esteemed more fame than conscience.' At all events, Walter, now just twenty-three, was back from the Continent in time to command his father's finely-built and equipped flagship, the Destiny. He was as full of life as Edward Hastings of disease, and as death-doomed.

Commission
with Omissions.

Ralegh was liberated expressly that he might work out his Guiana plans. He was not pardoned. A royal commission was granted him in August, 1616. He had understood that he was to have a commission under the Great Seal, which would be addressed to him as 'trusty and well-beloved.' Actually, though he and others often seem to have forgotten the difference, it was under the Privy Seal, and he was described as plain 'Sir Walter Ralegh.' The honorary epithets are known to have been inserted originally, and afterwards erased. Similarly, in a warrant for the payment to him in November, 1617, of the statutable bounty of 700 crowns for his construction of the Destiny, an erasure precedes his name. The space it covers would suffice for the expression, 'our well-beloved subject,' usual in such grants. The withholding at any rate of a pardon excited apprehensions. It was matter of common talk. Carew wrote to Roe on March 19, 1616, that Ralegh had left the Tower, and was to go to Guiana, but 'remains unpardoned until his return.' Merchants, it was stated, required security, 'Sir Walter Ralegh being under the peril of the law,' that they should enjoy the benefits of the expedition. His kinsmen and friends, it was said, were willing to serve only 'if they might be commanded by none but himself.' Their scruples had to be pacified by the issue of an express licence to him to carry subjects of the King to the south of America, and elsewhere within America, possessed and inhabited by heathen and savage people, with shipping, weapons and ordnance. He was authorised to keep gold, silver, and other goods which he should bring back, the fifth part of the gold, silver, pearls, and precious stones, with all customs due for any other goods, being truly paid to the Crown. Further, his Majesty, of his most special grace, constituted Ralegh sole commander, 'to punish, pardon, and rule according to such orders as he shall establish in cases capital, criminal, and civil, and to exercise martial law in as ample a manner as our lieutenant-general by sea or land.' The commission did not contain the authority conferred by Ralegh's old Guiana commission to subdue foreign lands. It too is reported to have been originally inserted, and to have been struck out by James.

Unpardoned.

Ralegh must, like his friends and creditors, have been conscious of the risk of sailing without a pardon. Carew Ralegh many years afterwards asserted, that Sir William St. John agreed to procure one for him for £1500 beyond the sum paid for his liberty. According to the *Observations on Sanderson's History*, the benefit was offered by St. John and Edward Villiers jointly, and for as little as £700. A right to abandon the voyage if he pleased was to have been added. Bacon's name is connected with the matter. Incidentally Bacon, who had been appointed Lord Keeper on March 7, 1617, is known to have met Ralegh after his release. He himself relates that he kept the Earl of Exeter waiting long in his upper room as he 'continued upon occasion still walking in Gray's Inn walks with Sir Walter Ralegh a good while.' On the authority of Carew Ralegh, as quoted in a letter to the latter from James Howell in the *Familiar Letters*, he is reported, possibly on this occasion, to have persuaded Ralegh to save his money, and trust to the implication of a pardon to be inferred from the royal commission. 'Money,' said the Lord Keeper, 'is the knee-timber of your voyage. Spare *Advice from, and avowal to, Bacon.* your money in this particular; for, upon my life, you have a sufficient pardon for all that is past already, the King having under his Great Seal made you Admiral, and given you power of martial law. Your commission is as good a pardon for all former offences as the law of England can afford you.' That is the view of so sound a constitutional lawyer as Hallam. His reason for the contention is that a man attainted of treason is incapable of exercising authority. But it can scarcely be argued as a point of law, and it is difficult to believe that a Lord Keeper should have volunteered a dogma of an absolute pardon by implication. Moreover, though, as will hereafter be seen, Sir Julius Cæsar, who was Master of the Rolls, fell into the same mistake in 1618, the misdescription, imputed to Bacon, of the Commission as under the Great Seal, of itself casts doubt upon the anecdote. On the whole, there is no sufficient cause for disputing the statement in the *Declaration* of 1618, that James deliberately, 'the better to contain Sir Walter Ralegh, and to hold him upon his good behaviour, denied, though much sued unto for the same, to grant him pardon for his former treasons.'

In the course of this or another conversation, Bacon, according to Sir Thomas Wilson's note of a statement made to him by Ralegh himself, inquired, 'What will you do, if, after all this expenditure, you miss of the gold mine?' The reply was: 'We will look after the Plate Fleet, to be sure.' 'But then,' remonstrated Bacon, 'You will be pirates!' 'Ah!' Ralegh is alleged to have cried, 'who ever heard of men being pirates for millions!' The Mexican fleet for 1618 is in fact computed to have conveyed treasure to the amount of £2,545,454. It is scarcely credible that Ralegh, though never distinguished for cautious speech, should have been so intemperately rash. Such a confession to Bacon, known to be Winwood's antagonist, who would rejoice to have ground for thwarting the anti-Spanish party at Court, is particularly unlikely. Mr. Spedding himself, while he believes it, regards Ralegh's reply as 'a playful diversion of an inconvenient question.' As a serious statement the saying is not the more authentic that it emanates from Wilson. Naturally it has been accepted by writers for whom Ralegh is a mere buccaneer.

From the first it is evident that Spain and the Spanish faction at the English Court laboured to place upon the expedition the construction which

Count Gondomar. Ralegh's apocryphal outburst to Bacon would warrant.

Don Diego Sarmiento de Acuña, the Ambassador of Spain, better known by the title, not yet his, of Count Gondomar, was the mouthpiece of the view. He offered, as Ralegh in his *Apology* virtually admits, to procure a safe-conduct for Ralegh to and from the mine, with liberty to bring home any gold he should find. The condition he imposed was that the expedition should be limited to one or two ships. The reason Ralegh gave in his paper for declining the arrangement, was that he did not trust sufficiently to the Ambassador's promises to go unarmed. In view of the way Spaniards were in the habit of treating English visitors, he clearly could not with prudence. At all events, for its refusal, if the offer were ever made in a practicable shape, James and his Government are obviously as responsible as he. They might, if they chose, have withdrawn his commission if he rejected those terms. Gondomar was a good Spaniard. He had a patriotic hatred for 'the old pirate bred under the English virago, and by her fleshed in Spanish blood and ruin.' His influence with James was boundless. He could 'pipe James asleep,' it was said, 'with facetious words and gestures.' They were the more diverting from their contrast with his lank, austere aspect. James had supreme faith in his wisdom, to the extravagant extent, according to his own incredible letter in 1622 from Madrid to the King, of having appointed him a member '*non seulement de votre Conseil d'état, mais du Cabinet intérieur.*'

Above all, he held for or against England the key to a family pact with the Escurial. At first he hoped to stop Ralegh's enterprise altogether. So late as the middle of March, 1617, Chamberlain wrote to Carleton that the Spanish Ambassador had 'well nigh overthrown it.' If he could not nip the undertaking in the bud, he had means of stifling it by misinterpreting to James Ralegh's motives, and by informing the Spanish Court how to meet force with force. Ralegh was ordered to explain the details of his scheme, and to lay down his route on a chart. According to Carew Ralegh, whose information may be presumed to have been derived from Lady Ralegh, James *Disclosures to the Spanish Ambassador.* promised upon the word of a King to keep secret these accounts of the programme. At any rate, Gondomar, by his familiar access to the King, was enabled to study the whole, whatever its value. He forwarded all particulars to Madrid. When the fleet had been surveyed by the Admiralty, he had a copy of the official report. He sent it by express to his Government, which despatched it with instructions to America. Cottington, the English Agent at the Spanish Court, was directed to promise that no harm should be done by Ralegh's voyage. The King in his *Declaration* of 1618 said he had taken 'order that he and all those that went in his company should find good security to behave themselves peaceably,' though the intention, the King lamented, was frustrated by 'every one of the principals that were in the voyage putting in security one for another.' There even was a story that the Court had obliged Lords Arundel and Pembroke to engage solemnly for Ralegh's return, that he might be rendered personally liable for any wrong. The foundation for this report may have been that, late in March, as the Destiny was about to sail from the Thames, James, alarmed at Gondomar's prognostications of evil, retailed them to his Council. Ralegh's supporters at the Board reassured him by affirmations of their willingness to give security that no harm should be done to lands of the King of Spain. James, several weeks earlier, at the end of January, had solemnly promised Gondomar, through Winwood, that, though he had determined to allow the voyage, if Ralegh acted in it in contravention of his instructions, he should pay for his disobedience with his head.

Ralegh and his friends knew of the care taken to guard Spanish interests at his cost. He had told Carew, as Carew writes to Roe, that 'the alarm of his journey had flown into Spain, and sea forces were prepared to lie for him.' He was nothing appalled, since, as Carew was informed, he had a good

fleet, *Ralegh's preparations against Violence.* and would be able to land five

or as many as seven hundred men; 'which will be a competent army, the Spaniards, especially about Orinoque, being so poorly planted.' Carew evidently, it will be seen, assumed that Ralegh must expect violence, and might lawfully meet it in kind. James and his Councillors assumed it also, till Ralegh came back empty handed. He openly was arming to be a match in battle for the Spaniards; and his party in the Council with equal earnestness tried to balance the weight there of Spain by another influence. Mr. Secretary Winwood wished in all ways to break with Spain. He urged Ralegh to capture the Mexico fleet. In support of his policy he favoured an intimate alliance with the chief rival Power. He introduced Ralegh to the Comte des Marêts, the French Ambassador. Des Marêts is supposed to have grown apprehensive of a sudden diversion of Ralegh's forces to an attack on St. Valery in the interest of the Huguenots against the Queen Mother. He was glad, therefore, of an opportunity of judging for himself of Ralegh's views. They may already have had communication by letter. French influence had been, it is thought, employed on Ralegh's behalf while he was in the Tower. He had never ceased to maintain relations with the Huguenots, and the French Court appreciated the importance in certain circumstances of his services. The Spanish, Savoyard, and Venetian Envoys had inspected his squadron. On March 15, 1617, the Count too visited the Destiny. He reported the interview to Richelieu a few days later. He soon satisfied himself that St. Valery was not threatened. He told Ralegh that the French Court had sympathised with him in his long and unjust imprisonment, and the confiscation of his property. From another quarter he had heard, he wrote to Richelieu, that Ralegh especially resented the gift of Sherborne to Sir John Digby, who lately had returned from his Spanish mission. He gathered that Ralegh was discontented with James, and with the Court policy. Ralegh expressed his desire for more talk at a less inconvenient time and place. Richelieu had recently described him to Marshal Concini as 'grand marinier et mauvais capitaine'; but he was far from discouraging his overtures. A subsequent interview was held, and described in a despatch several weeks after the meeting. If the Count's memory did not, as Sir Robert Schomburgk thinks, deceive him, Ralegh said: 'Seeing myself so badly and tyrannically treated by my own Sovereign, I have made up my mind, if God send me good success, to leave my

country, and *The Comte des Marêts.* to make to the King your master the first offer of what shall fall under my power.' Doubtless there was just so much truth in the Count's report that a profusion of compliments passed. Des Marêts would express his astonishment at the treatment Ralegh had experienced, and regret that France had not enjoyed the happiness of possessing such a hero, and the opportunity of rewarding him properly. Ralegh would respond in the same key, and assure his French sympathiser that, if an occasion presented itself, he was well inclined to serve the noblest Court in Europe. He is not to be held responsible for the positive summary the Frenchman dressed up of the conversation weeks after it had passed to show Ralegh's effusiveness and his own caution. Des Marêts himself did not at the time treat the talk seriously. He said he replied that Ralegh could betake himself to no quarter in which he would receive more of courtesy or friendship. 'I thought it well,' wrote des Marêts, 'to give him good words, although I do not anticipate that his voyage will have much fruit.'

Before Ralegh left English waters he had further negotiations with France. A Frenchman, Captain Faige, was his companion on the voyage, which commenced March 28, 1617, from the Thames to Plymouth. By this man he sent in May a letter to a M. de Bisseaux, a French Councillor of State. He wrote that he had commissioned Faige to take ships to points in the Indies agreed on between them. The intention was to meet Ralegh at the mine which he *Understanding with France.* counted upon working. Faige, he said, could explain his plan. He asked for a patent, promised, he said, by Admiral de Montmorency, which would empower him to enter a French port, 'avec tous les ports, navires, equipages, et biens, par lui traités ou conquis.' One Belle reported himself to Montmorency as Faige's associate. In that character he obtained Ralegh's letter, and carried it with other papers, and a map of Guiana, to Madrid. There he told the story in the May of the following year. Ralegh's letter to Bisseaux in his handwriting has been seen and copied at Simancas. If he ever received, as is inferred from his admissions to the Royal Commissioners next year, and to Sir Thomas Wilson, the warrant he asked, it was a permit from the French Admiralty. It was not a commission from the French Crown, and, whatever it was, James and his Ministers were parties to its grant.

The whole secret history of the preliminaries to the Guiana expedition forms a tangled skein. The negotiations of Ralegh with France were certainly known to Winwood, and, there can be little doubt, to James also. Ralegh taxed the King by letter in October, 1618, with privity and assent to the arrangement, through Faige, for the co-operation of French ships against the Spaniards at the mouth of the Orinoko. He was not contradicted. Winwood and his section of the Council in good faith preferred a French to a Spanish compact. They did not shudder at the contingency of war. James and the pro-Spanish party concurred for the moment in the playing off of France against Spain, in order to push Spain into the English alliance which they coveted. From the double motive the Government in general encouraged Ralegh to treat with France. That Spain might be frightened he was instigated to an intimacy with French Ministers and plotters. Though he never received a regular French commission, it was allowed to be supposed that one had been issued to him. No French ships were fitted out *Mystifications.* to aid him, or despatched to the coast of Guiana. Nothing, it may confidently be asserted, was ever farther from his thoughts than the surrender of territory he might appropriate to any foreign Crown. All simply was a game of mystification devised for one purpose by Winwood, and, for a different purpose, joined in by James and the rest. The Spanish faction wished to give Spain cause to fancy its foe was being unchained to do his worst against it at his own discretion, and by any agency he chose, unless it should come to terms speedily. A condition of the game, which Ralegh but imperfectly understood, was that it should be played at his especial peril. He was suffered to concert measures with one foreign ally of England against another, at the direct instance of a leading Minister, and with the connivance of the King himself. The King was informed of the intrigue, and knew as much as his indolence permitted of its various steps. He was never obliged to know so much, or to betray such signs of knowing anything, as not to be in a position on an exigency to disavow the whole. This was his idea of statecraft.

The negotiation with the French Government was but one of the threads in the skein. James and his advisers were in a frame of mind in which any foreign adventure had a chance of securing their support. Ralegh, and the popular excitement which had wafted him from a prison to an Admiral's command, were pawns moved by the political speculators of the Court for their own purposes. Wild rumours circulated of objects to which the expedition was about really to be directed. The circumstances of the expedition, the character of its chief, his sudden liberation, and the trust reposed in him, were so extraordinary that all Europe was disturbed. Though Continental thought may, as the greatest of modern historians has said, have visited the memory of Ralegh since with an indifference more bitter than censure or reproach, it was very far from indifferent in 1617. At home cynics disbelieved the sincerity of Ralegh. They ridiculed the notion that, after the iniquitous treatment he had experienced, he would have the folly to come back. Friends apparently were not entirely free from the suspicion that he might be induced, if he failed, to shake the dust of an ungrateful kingdom off his feet. Lord Arundel at parting earnestly dissuaded him from yielding to any temptation to a self banishment, which assuredly he never contemplated. A solicitation of authority to carry Spanish prizes in certain circumstances into French ports is no evidence that he contemplated a change of allegiance. Reports that he had asked the licence may explain why it occurred to Arundel or Pembroke to pledge him against such an use of it.

If acquaintances who felt how ill he had been treated feared he might be beguiled into abjuring his ungrateful country, others deemed the ostensible gold digging aim of the expedition too simple and bounded for his subtle and lofty ambition. Leonello, the Secretary to the Venetian Embassy, writing to the Council of Ten on January 19 and 26, and February 3, 1617,

- *Plot against Genoa.* - described communications between Ralegh, Winwood, and Count Scarnafissi, the Ambassador of Savoy. The Duke of Savoy was waging a war with Spain, which ended in the following September. He would have liked Ralegh to pounce upon Genoa, which was become almost a Spanish port. The project was discussed by Scarnafissi with Winwood and Ralegh, whom Winwood had introduced to him. It is said by Leonello to have been divulged by Winwood to James. James at first was inclined to adopt it. After a few days he recalled his assent. Probably he had given it partly out of pique against the Spanish Court; and now Spain was resuming negotiations for the marriage of the Infanta to Prince Charles. He was, moreover, said Leonello, suspicious that Ralegh might not give him his just share of the anticipated twenty millions of booty. The entire business is not very intelligible. Leonello's three secret despatches disinterred by Mr. Rawdon Brown are the main evidence of the project, and of the degree of Ralegh's participation in it. An examination of the Piedmontese Archives might shed clearer light on the scope and reality of the obscure intrigue. Leonello himself offers no testimony but admissions alleged to have been extorted by him from Scarnafissi. At any rate if credence is to be given to the somewhat suspicious account, the worst guilt for the contemplated piratical perfidy attaches to the crowned accomplice. Sir Thomas Wilson wrote to James on October 4, 1618: 'Sir Walter Ralegh tells me Sir Ralph Winwood brought him acquainted with the Ambassador of Savoy, with whom they consulted for the surprise of Genoa, and that your Majesty was acquainted with the business, and liked it well.' The King never denied the truth of the imputation. From first to last the negotiations, the plots for and against, were, on the side of the English, French, Spanish, and Savoyard Governments, a mere shuffle of diplomatic cards. The one thing in real earnest was the universal propensity to intrigue at Ralegh's expense. Everybody's hands were to be left loose but his.

The preparations for the expedition on the original basis were little affected by the speculative projects for turning it to strange purposes. The Destiny, Jason, Encounter, Thunder, Southampton, and the pinnace Page had sailed from the Thames at the end of March, 1617. Fears of a countermand were said to have hastened their departure. They carried ninety gentlemen, a few soldiers, and 318 seamen, beside captains and masters. There were also servants and assayers. The *Declaration* of 1618 contends, truly or untruly, that no miners were embarked. If it were so, it is strange that the omission should not have been remarked in the West, of all regions. Four ships had been fitted for sea at Plymouth by Sir John Ferne, Laurence Keymis, Wollaston, and Chudleigh. Others arrived later. Want of money caused delay. Captain Pennington of the Star was detained off the Isle of Wight for provisions. He had to ride to London to redeem, with Lady Ralegh's help, his ship's bread. To eke out Captain Whitney's resources, Ralegh sold much of his plate. He raised £300 for Sir John Ferne. No checks, temptations, or expenses daunted him. While he knew, as he wrote to Boyle, 'there was no middle course but perish or prosper,' his idea steeled him against forebodings. He felt inspired to accomplish a national enterprise. 'What fancy,' he exclaimed later, 'could possess him thus to dispose of his whole substance, and undertake such a toilsome and perilous voyage, now that his constitution was impaired by such a long confinement, beside age itself, sickness, and affliction, were not he assured thereby of doing his prince service, bettering his country by commerce, and restoring his family to its estates, all from the mines of Guiana!' The spectacle of his confidence is among the most pathetic tragedies in history.

CHAPTER XXVI.

Orders to the Fleet.

On May 3 he published his orders to the fleet. They were a model of godly, severe, and martial government, as testified a gentleman of his company. Divine service was to be solemnised every morning and evening. The pillage of ships of friendly Powers was rigorously prohibited. Courtesy towards the Indians was strictly injoined. All firearms were to be kept clean. Rules were laid down in the event of an encounter with 'the enemy' at sea. Cards, dice, and swearing were forbidden. The people of the West, and especially Plymouth, had remained faithful in their admiration of Ralegh though an imprisoned convict. They rejoiced at seeing him once more in command of a powerful fleet. On the eve of his departure the Mayor of Plymouth, a Trelawny, 'by a general consent,' at the town's expense entertained the Admiral and his followers. The town also 'paid the drummer for calling Sir Walter Ralegh's company aboard.' On June 12, seven ships of war and three pinnaces sailed from the port. At sea they were joined by loiterers, which brought the total up to thirteen ships, manned by a thousand men. Contrary winds forced them back, first into Plymouth, and next into Falmouth. Again, eight leagues west of Scilly, a gale rose which sank a pinnace, and drove the rest into Kinsale.

At Cork he was cordially welcomed alike by old enemies and old friends. With his inexhaustible vivacity he flew his hawks at Cloyne; he took shares in an Irish copper mining adventure; he provisioned his fleet; he was feasted and admired; he reviewed the past, and anticipated the future. Among those who sought his company were Lords Barry and Roche.

Boyle, now *Boyle's Bargain with Ralegh.* Lord Boyle, came from Lismore, and entertained him. He rode to Lismore and Mogelly. His estate had turned in Boyle's more patient hands into a noble domain with a revenue estimated by Pym in 1616 at £12,000. Boyle gave his own account of his transactions with Ralegh in a letter of 1631 to Carew Ralegh, who wished to have them reviewed. According to this he behaved, and was recognised by Ralegh as having behaved, generously and honourably. Clearly he had no doubt of his own magnanimity. At the time of the attainder the conveyance under the agreement of 1602 was not legally completed. Apparently not all the purchase-money had been paid. Inquisitions were being taken of Ralegh's Irish lands by the Government. Sir John Ramsay, Boyle said, had offered to use his Scotch influence to obtain from the Crown an absolute release of all claims against him, by Ralegh as well as by the Crown, for 500 marks. He preferred to follow the advice of George Carew, who predicted to him after the Winchester conviction that the King would remit Ralegh's forfeiture. He went on dealing with him, though legally incompetent, and had paid him a supplementary sum of £1000 to close the matter. In addition he had to beg or buy a royal confirmation of his title to the lands, when they had been 'found by offices' upon the attainder. Now, in Cork he supplied the expedition with oxen, biscuit, beer, and iron, to the value of 600 marks or more. He gave Ralegh £350 in cash, and a thirty-two gallon cask of whiskey. For three weeks he kept open house for him at Cork. Ralegh, he asserted, reciprocated his hospitalities by a full abandonment of any possible claims he might have made upon the Lismore property. He also contributed evidence towards Boyle's defence against some demands founded by Ralegh's old partner Pyne upon a lease alleged by him to have been granted him by Ralegh many years before, in extension of a shorter term. Ralegh, though on good terms at the time with Pyne, seems to have assured Boyle of his belief that the second demise was a counterfeit fabricated by Meere. His dealings, however, were very complicated, and his remembrance of them necessarily not always clear. In 1618 he became dubious if he had not been too positive against Pyne's title. He requested, on the eve of his death, that he should not be considered a witness either for or against it.

The fleet stayed at Cork from June 25 to August 19. Then it made a fresh start. Off Cape St. Vincent, Captain Bayley, of the ship Southampton, boarded four French vessels, and took from them a fishing net, a pinnace, and some oil. A report of the capture reached Madrid, where it was denounced as piracy. In truth Ralegh had been scrupulous. He insisted on buying the goods of the owners at the price of sixty-one crowns, to the high indignation of Bayley. The captor's argument was that he found the Frenchmen had procured their cargo by piracy in the West Indies, and he, therefore, had lawfully confiscated it. Ralegh did not admit that the charge would, if true, justify him in refusing compensation. Frenchmen and Englishmen alike, he held, could plunder Spaniards 'beyond the line.' Lancerota, one of the Great Canaries, was reached on September 6. The

Fray at Lancerota. islanders happened to be under the influence of a special panic. Barbary corsairs had been ravaging a neighbouring island. Next year they laid Lancerota itself waste. When Ralegh's fleet appeared it was supposed to be the Barbary squadron. Some sailors having landed, three were murdered. Ralegh showed remarkable forbearance. He would suffer no vengeance to be taken. An English merchantman, belonging to one Reeks of Ratcliff, lay in the harbour. Ralegh knew it would have to bear the penalty of retaliation by him. Bayley, however, seized upon the pretext of the broil. He affected to see in that, onesided as it was, evidence of Ralegh's piratical temper. In a fit of virtuous horror at his Admiral who had docked his prize money of sixty-one crowns, he deserted, and sailed home.

At Gomera, one of the Lesser Canaries, the fleet found more hospitality. The Governor permitted the crews to draw water, and buy provisions. Ralegh reciprocated by keeping his men in perfect order. He sent a present of gloves to the Governor's wife, a lady of the Stafford family. She returned fruit, sugar, and rusks. Not to be outdone he rejoined with ambergris, rosewater, a cut-work ruff, and a picture of the Magdalen. He was in the habit of taking pictures with him on his voyages. This interchange of

Sickness in the Fleet. courtesies was the one gleam of human kindness which lighted up for Ralegh his dismal journey. He dwells upon it gratefully in the journal he kept. The manuscript, in twenty large pages, is in the British Museum. It covers the period from August 19 to February 13. Off the Isle of Bravo, sickness attacked the fleet. It was aggravated through the protraction of the voyage by contrary winds from the customary fortnight or three weeks to six. Forty-two men in the flagship died. Among them were Fowler, the principal refiner, Ralegh's cook Francis, his servant Crab, the master surgeon, the provost martial, Captain Piggot, his best land-general, and Mr. John Talbot, 'who,' records Ralegh, 'had lived with me eleven years in the Tower, an excellent general scholar, and a faithful true man as lived.' The ship left Bravo on October 4. On the 12th they were becalmed. At one time a thick and fearful darkness enveloped them. Then the horizon became over-shot with gloomy discolorations. Off Trinidad fifteen rainbows in a day were seen. Ralegh caught a cold, which turned to a burning fever. For twenty-eight days he lay unable to take solid food. He could not have survived but for the Gomera fruit. His ordinary servants were all ill; but he had also pages who attended him. Apparently his illness did not prevent him from keeping a general supervision of the fleet. His journal proves him to have been a thorough and practical seaman.

The fleet arrived off Cape Oyapoco on November 11. Ralegh wrote to his wife on November 17, from the mouth of the Cayenne in Guiana, the Caliana, as he calls it: 'Sweet Heart, We are yet 200 men, and the rest of our fleet are reasonably strong; strong enough, I hope, to perform what we have undertaken, if the diligent care at London to make our strength known to the Spanish King by his ambassador have not taught the Spaniards to fortify all the entrances against us. If we perish, it shall be no gain for his Majesty to lose, among many other, one hundred as valiant gentlemen as : *Indian Affection.* : England hath in it.' But he was not disheartened. Walter was never so well, having had 'no distemper in all the heat under the Line.' He found good faith in Indian hearts, if not at King James's Court. 'To tell you I might here be King of the Indians were a vanity; but my name hath still lived among them. All offer to obey me.' Harry the Indian Chief who had lived two years in the Tower with him presently came. He had previously sent provisions. He brought roasted mullets, which were very good meat, great store of plantains, peccaries, casava bread, pistachio nuts, and pine apples, which tempted Ralegh exceedingly. After a few days on shore he began to mend, and to have an appetite for roast peccary. His crews were still sickly, and rested for three weeks. One of the Adventurers employed his leisure in composing a discourse in praise of Guiana. It contains the orders Ralegh issued to the fleet before he left England; but the information concerning the voyage is meagre. Captain Peter Alley, being ill of a vertigo, was sent home in a Dutch vessel, which traded with Guiana. The narrative went with him. Next year it was printed in London under the title 'Newes of Sir Walter Rauleigh from the River of Caliana,' with a woodcut of Ralegh in band and collar, and a laced velvet doublet.

Ralegh left the Cayenne on December 4, and sailed to the Triangle Islands, now called the Isles of Health. There he organized the expedition to the Mine. It was decided that he should not lead in person. Fever had a second time attacked him. Besides, his officers were unwilling to venture inland, unless he remained behind to guard the river mouth from a Spanish fleet. Sir Wareham St. Leger, the lieutenant-general, also was ill. George Ralegh, who previously had succeeded Piggot as serjeant-major, commanded in St. Leger's place. Apparently Ralegh, who nowhere has specified the exact situation, supposed the Mine was at a short distance from the right bank of the river. Mr. Gardiner, in his *Case against Sir Walter Ralegh*, published in the *Fortnightly Review* in 1867, assumes it was that pointed out to Keymis by Putijma in 1595, though, it must be remembered, Keymis heard of another from the Cacique in 1596. At any rate the precise topographical relation between it and the existing Spanish settlement of San Thome, or St. Thomas, was unknown to Ralegh. : *The new San Thome.* : The town was no longer where it had stood in 1596 when Keymis heard of it. The old site had been deserted at some date which cannot be fixed. The common view has been that the change had been effected before 1611, and that the San Thome which Captain Moate found inhabited by the Spaniards was the new town. That is unlikely, both because Moate would then have identified the actual spot, and on account of Ralegh's description to the King, after his return, of the town as 'new set up within three miles of the Mine.' San Thome at all events in 1618 was twenty to thirty miles lower down than the original town. It was close to the bank, a group of some hundred and forty houses, 'a town of stakes, covered with leaves of trees.' There is no evidence that Ralegh, who must have heard of the transplantation, knew the new town directly blocked the approach to the Mine. Though, however, he was ignorant that in the circumstances a collision was certain, he may well have thought it probable. So must the English Government which had sanctioned his martial preparations. The Spaniards never dissembled their belief that the entrance of foreigners into the American interior was a lawless trespass to be repelled by force. Consequently, he provided against the contingency. Four hundred soldiers and sailors were embarked in five of the ships of least draught, commanded by Captains Whitney, King, Smith, Wollaston, and Hall. The other five, including the flagship, which drew twelve feet of water, were left behind with Ralegh. The land forces were under Walter. The landing and search for the Mine were entrusted to Keymis.

Ralegh's account of his communications to his officers differs from that put forth by the King's Government. According to the official version, he

Ralegh's Instructions to his Captains. at first advised them to commence by the immediate capture of the Spanish town. But, objected one of them, that would be a breach of peace. He is alleged to have answered that he had orders by word of mouth to take the town, if it were any hindrance to the digging of the Mine. The tale rests on the dubious testimony of James's Councillors writing in a desperate panic at an outburst of popular indignation after Ralegh's execution. In itself it is not improbable that Ralegh, with qualifications omitted in the official report, said something at a council of war to this effect. If he suggested a hostile movement at all, he may be presumed to have stated also with right that he spoke by authority. Mr. Secretary Winwood, it is admitted, calculated upon a collision with the Spaniards, and even upon Ralegh's seizure of the plate-fleet. He would not shrink from the capture of a Guiana fort. They alone will treat Ralegh's assertion, if it were his, as 'evidence of his unblushing effrontery,' to whom his accounts are necessarily mendacious, and those of the Court, King James's Court, necessarily honest. In any case the point matters little, as Ralegh is admitted to have himself decided against the plan. His final instructions to Keymis and George Ralegh were that they should endeavour to reach the Mine, as he imagined they might, without a struggle. He bade them encamp between it and the town, which, as he believed, lay beyond. Thus the soldiers would cover the miners as they worked. 'If,' said he, 'you find the Mine royal, and the Spaniards begin to war upon you, you, George Ralegh, are to repel them, and to drive them as far as you can.' To Keymis he said, 'If you find the Mine be not so rich as may persuade the holding of it, and draw on a second supply, then you shall bring but a basket or two, to satisfy his Majesty that my design was not imaginary, but true, though not answerable to his Majesty's expectation.' If there appeared to be many new soldiers, 'so that, without manifest peril of my son and the other captains, you cannot pass towards the Mine, then be well advised how you land. For I know, a few gentlemen excepted, what a scum of men you have. And I would not, for all the world, receive a blow from the Spaniards to the dishonour of our nation. I myself for my weakness cannot be present. Neither will the companies land, except I stay with the ships, the galleons of Spain being daily expected. My nephew is but a young man. It is therefore on your judgment that I rely. You shall find me at Puncto Gallo, dead or alive. And if you find not my ships there, you shall find their ashes. For I will fire, with the galleons, if it come to extremity; run will I never.'

Departure for the Mine.

The expedition started with a month's provisions on December 10. Its progress was slow, and accidents detained Whitney's and Wollaston's vessels. The rest took three weeks to reach the Isle of Yaya, styled by Ralegh Assapana. The isle is opposite to the modern town of St. Raphael of Barrancas. Preparations had been made by the Spaniards to resist further progress. Antonio de Berreo was dead. His son Fernando was Governor-General of New Grenada, with authority over Guiana and Trinidad. But recently Diego Palomeque de Acuña had been appointed to administer those two territories. He was a relative of Gondomar. A copy of the description of the fleet and its intended course, which Ralegh had been obliged to submit to James, had been sent to him from Madrid on March 19, 1617. He had repaired to San Thome. The English were attacked by fire from both banks. Nevertheless, on the evening of December 31, according to Ralegh, they sailed past the town without noticing it. On New Year's Day, 1618, they landed, at eleven in the morning, some little distance higher up. They were ignorant, Ralegh stated subsequently in his *Apology*, of the proximity of the settlement. Their intention simply was to rest by the river, and the next day to set off for the Mine. Pedro Simon, a Spanish historian of the period, differs. He asserts that they landed below the town, and deliberately marched against it. At all events, it cannot be questioned that the Spaniards were fully resolved to stop the advance of the expedition, whether to the Mine or elsewhere. If, as James's commission to Ralegh assumed, Englishmen had a right to make their way to the Mine, they could not be more to blame than the Spaniards for the actual collision. In fact the Spaniards struck the first blow.

They had arranged an ambuscade, and, under Geronimo de Grados, attacked about nine in the evening. Though the Spanish force appears to have comprised but forty-two regular soldiers, the English were thrown into confusion. 'The common sort,' wrote Ralegh, 'as weak sort as ever followed valiant leaders, were so amazed as, had not the captains and some other twenty or thirty valiant gentlemen made a head and encouraged the rest, they had all been broken and cut to pieces.' Ultimately the English drove the assailants back to the town. In front of it Diego Palomeque and the main body of Spaniards were drawn up. The reports of eye-witnesses on the sequel differed. According to one, the pikemen whom Walter led were in advance of the musketeers. According to another, they were behind, when Walter quitted them and rushed in front. In the official *Declaration* it was alleged that Walter, 'who was likest to know his father's secret,' cried to the Englishmen, 'Come on, my hearts; here is the Mine that ye must expect; they that look for any other are fools.' By all accounts he closed with the enemy, and Grados or Erenetta mortally wounded him. His last words were: 'Go on! Lord, have mercy upon me, and prosper your enterprise.' His death excited his men. Diego was slain, and his force routed. The English stormed the monastery of St. Francis, in which some of the fugitives had fortified themselves. San Thome, such as it was, was theirs. They buried Walter, and Captain Cosmor, described in a letter of March 22 to Alley by Parker as leader of the forlorn hope, in one grave, near the high altar in the Church of St. Thomas. On the day of the funeral the belated ships of Whitney and Wollaston arrived.

Notwithstanding the loss of the town, the Spaniards maintained resistance. Garcia de Aguilar and Juan de Lazanna, the alcaldes, with Grados, collected the residue, and constituted a garrison for the women and children in the Isle of la Ceyva. They laid wait for stray Englishmen, and cooped the main body within the town. There discords broke out which George Ralegh had difficulty in pacifying. Not till a week after the occupation did Keymis venture to make for the Mine, though he computed that it was but eight

miles off. At length he equipped a couple of launches. In them he, Sir John Hampden, and others embarked. Near la Ceyva they fell into an ambuscade. Nine out of those in the first launch were killed or wounded. Keymis was discouraged, and turned back, he alleged, for more soldiers. Though not a man afraid of responsibility, he may have shrunk from the prospect, as he intimated, that he might, through Ralegh's sickness, as well as legal disabilities, have to bear it alone. Ralegh's detractors inferred from the inactivity of Keymis that he and Ralegh were as incredulous of the existence of the Mine as, by his own subsequent account, had always been the King. The imputation upon the truthfulness of Keymis is altogether groundless. He had, in his expedition of 1596, ascertained the authenticity of the Mine, at least to his own satisfaction, and brought home specimens of its ore. His fancy wildly exaggerated its riches. There is no reason to suppose that he knavishly invented stories about it. The Spaniards, it is known, had worked gold mines in the vicinity. The excavations were lying idle from the mere want of Indian labourers, whom it had just been declared illegal to press. So lately had the workings been discontinued that, it is said, all the best houses in San Thome belonged to refiners, as the tools in them proved.

George Ralegh for his part refused to give up at once, though his own views were directed rather to colonization than to mining. In boats he ascended the Orinoko to its junction with the Guarico. In his absence the town was repeatedly attacked. English prisoners were barbarously treated. Several, it is asserted, were tortured or butchered. After twenty-five days it was determined to retire, and fire was set to the place. Altogether the English had lost 250 men. They collected some spoil estimated as worth 40,000 reals. Partly it consisted of church ornaments, and a couple of gold ingots reserved for the King of Spain's royalty, but chiefly of tobacco. Three negroes and two Indians were carried off. One of the Indians accompanied the fleet to England, returning afterwards to Guiana.

At Puncto Gallo.

Ralegh meanwhile had stationed himself at Puncto Gallo, now Point Hicacos, on the south-west of Trinidad. He arrived on December 17, 1617, and there he stayed. On account of currents he seems to have thought at one time that he might be obliged to change his moorings. No more conclusive proof can be given of the spirit of the King's *Declaration* of November, 1618, than that it alleges him not to have minded, but rather to have anticipated, the certain starvation of the returning land forces through such a removal from the fixed rendezvous. He wrote to Winwood on March 21, 1618, that with five ships he had daily attended the armada of Spain. But he had been left in comparative tranquillity. Attacks from San Giuseppe he easily repulsed, with no more serious loss than of one sailor and a boy. He amused his leisure by hunting for balsams and other indigenous rarities. Six days after the fight Keymis sent a letter describing Walter's death, and eulogizing his 'extraordinary valour, forwardness, and constant vigour of mind.' An Indian had already brought confused tidings of the occupation of San Thome. Keymis's letter was dated January 8. It arrived, it has been reckoned, on February 14. The day is believed to be fixed by the abrupt closing of Ralegh's journal. After his son's death, 'with whom,' he wrote to Winwood, 'all respect of this world hath taken end in me,' he had no heart to continue it. With the letter Keymis despatched a parcel of scattered papers. A cart-load, he mentioned, remained behind. The consignment is supposed to have included the King of Spain's and his Custom-house Secretary's letters of warning to Diego Palomeque. A copy, some say the original, of Ralegh's own letter to James was in the bundle. Ralegh is reported to have conveyed it home, and to have shown it to the Lords of the Council.

On March 2 the survivors of the expedition rejoined him at Puncto Gallo. Keymis had to confess his crowning failure. Ralegh did not banish him from his board, as the *Declaration* noted with a sneer; but he upbraided him severely for having stopped short of the Mine. He declared that, as Walter was killed, he should not have cared, and he did not believe Keymis cared, if a hundred more had been lost in opening the Mine, so the King had been satisfied, and Ralegh's reputation been saved. There was no kinder or more generous leader than he. His dependents and servants worshipped him. The treatment of Keymis is the one instance in his career of harshness to a

Suicide of Keymis. follower. He would see no force in Keymis's apologies.

He told him that he must answer to the King and the State. Keymis had composed a letter of excuse to Lord Arundel, a chief promoter of the expedition. This he submitted to Ralegh, and asked for his approval. He refused it absolutely: 'Is that,' inquired Keymis, 'your resolution? I know'—or, according to the *Apology*, 'I know not'—'then, Sir, what course to take.' He went away, and very soon a shot was heard. Keymis told a page, whom Ralegh sent to his cabin door, that he had fired the pistol because it had long been charged. Half an hour afterwards his cabin-boy found him stabbed to the heart. The pistol shot had only broken a rib, and he had finished the work with a dagger. Poor Keymis, who was fifty-five at his death, was no 'rough old sailor,' no mere 'sturdy mariner,' as Mr. Gardiner styles the ex-Fellow of Balliol, the writer of Latin verses, the fluent and argumentative chronicler. He was emotional and imaginative. He was fated to be as evil a genius to the leader he adored as selfish, unstable Cobham. He brought much woe upon his friends and himself through blunders committed from the most generous motives, and he was very sternly judged. If the supposed message to Cobham, which formed one of the most damaging charges in 1603 against Ralegh, were a gloss of his own,

concocted from casual talk, he paid for *Harsh Judgments.* his indiscretion

by enduring imprisonment, and braving threats of torture, with a noble fidelity. He suffered yet more cruel penalties for having vaunted the mineral riches of Guiana to enhance the merit of its discovery, until the mirage ended by beguiling his admired chief into irretrievable ruin. Not even death redeemed his memory. His comrades decried him as an impostor and deceiver. 'False to all men, a hateful fellow, a mere Machiavel,' Captain Parker called him, because he did not find his gold mine. Ralegh, for whom he had ventured and borne much, writes of him as an obstinate, self-willed man, and of his doleful end with a coldness which only gnawing despair can explain, not excuse.

The expedition had been vexed by storms and fever on its passage to Guiana. None of its objects on the Orinoko had been attained. To the last it continued disappointing and disappointed; 'continually pursued with misfortunes,' wrote Beecher to Camden, 'as if to prove that God did take pleasure to confound the wisdom of men.' Ralegh already had not been free from danger of discord in his fleet. A page had invented a tale that he kept in his cabin £24,200, which had led some of his crew to conspire to leave him ashore in Trinidad, and sail away. But hitherto he had maintained his personal ascendency. The collapse at San Thome shook the faith of his captains in him. Henceforth they expected him to prefer their wisdom to his own. Whitney and Wollaston planned the plunder of homeward-bound Spanish ships. They would have liked him to abet them. They warned him that he was a lost man if he returned to England. When they could not persuade him, they resolved to go off by themselves. At Grenada they carried their intention into effect. Mr. Jones, chaplain of the Flying Chudleigh, says Ralegh authorised any captain to part if he pleased, as the aim of the voyage could no longer be accomplished. The chaplain may have had the offer narrated to him by a captain who desired his freedom. In itself it is too inconsistent with all we know of Ralegh's views to be credible. He showed the utmost anxiety to keep his forces together. For this purpose he was *Ship Gossip.* willing to let restless spirits hope for indulgence of their thirst both for spoil and for revenge by a combined attempt upon the Mexico fleet. Out of the chaos of ship gossip, the private wishes of officers, and conjectures about their commander's probable intentions, James's apologists wove a theory that he had never meant to seek for a mine, and had always intended to seize the treasure-ships. He was alleged to have confessed on his return that, before the mining project failed, he had proposed the capture of the fleet in the event of its failure. He was said to have admitted in talk with Sir Thomas Wilson in the Tower, that, after the return from San Thome, he formally enunciated to his officers a design to that effect. He was said to have told them that he had a French commission which empowered him to take any Spanish vessel beyond the Canaries. The allegation that, after the collapse of the expedition to San Thome, he had meant to sail for the Carib islands, and leave the land companies to their fate, insinuated that he was projecting some great piracy. His own subsequent contradiction of the issue to him of any commission from the French Crown has been represented by modern writers as a dishonest prevarication. He had, it is asserted, a French commission, though from the French Lord High Admiral, not from the King of France.

Much of this indictment rests upon tainted evidence. When the testimony is respectable, it is for the most part outweighed by Ralegh's own word. At all events, for his alleged intention to have been of avail for the support of a criminal charge it was necessary to prove some act in conformity with it. None could be instanced except the San Thome collision itself, which the Spaniards had brought on. Whether he would have embraced a good opportunity for anything like buccaneering it is difficult to decide. Though the rumours of the fleet, reckless words of his own, other words uttered for some very dissimilar purpose, admissions dishonourably drawn from him and craftily pieced together, and a phrase in a heart-broken letter to his heart-broken wife, need not be accepted as conclusive, it may be conceded that they accord with his and the prevalent English temper. For him England and Spain in America were always at war. 'To break peace where there is no peace,' he wrote, 'it cannot be. The Spaniards give us no peace there.' He stated the literal truth. Spaniards treated unlicensed English voyagers to any part of South America as pirates and felons. He claimed the right of reprisals; and public opinion in England was on his side. English law was not. He might have been amenable to it had he acted upon his idea

- _Ralegh's real Project._ - of Anglo-Spanish reciprocity, and in conformity with the schemes attributed to him by many of his own officers. But he did nothing of the kind. The projects he is known to have entertained indicate that his fancy was travelling in a different direction. His original and desperate thought, after the return of the launches, had still been bounded by Guiana. His wish was to lead a second expedition to San Thome. He meant to leave his body by his son's, or bring out of Keymis's or other mines so much gold ore as should satisfy the King that he had propounded no vain thing. Carew Ralegh's account was that the plan, perhaps on reflection modified from that, was to revictual in Virginia, and return in the spring to Guiana.

Whatever the exact eventual shape of the design, Whitney and Wollaston thwarted its execution by their desertion. At a council of war it was determined to make for home, by way, according to Ralegh's original programme, of Newfoundland. The ships stayed awhile at St. Christopher's. Ralegh took the opportunity to write on March 21 to the friendly Secretary of State. He was not aware that Winwood had died, to his irreparable loss, in the previous October. He had been, like Prince Henry, under the medical care of Dr. Theodore Mayerne, physician to the King and Queen. Mayerne had high repute, and is eminent in English medical history as having introduced the use of calomel. But he is described by a cynical contemporary as generally unfortunate with his patients. The headstrong but generous Secretary was succeeded by Naunton, a ripe Cambridge scholar, whom the favour first of Essex, then of Overbury, and last of Villiers, perverted into a time-serving official, 'close-fisted,' 'zealous and sullen.' For Naunton Ralegh was by no means the hero of the young author of the *Fragmenta Regalia*. By unsympathetic eyes his epistle was to be read. As interpreted by Naunton it was sure to aggravate the ill-will of the King, who would reasonably regard much of it as a censure upon him.

Letter to Winwood.

Ralegh glanced in it at his bodily sufferings and fatigue: 'There is never a base slave in the fleet hath taken the pains and care that I have done; hath slept so little, and travailed so much.' He bewailed his misfortunes, 'the greatest and sharpest that have ever befallen any man.' His brains, he said, were broken with them. So sincere an admirer as Mr. Kingsley takes him literally, and holds that 'his life really ended on the return of Keymis from San Thome.' His contemporaries did not think it. For them he was never even an old man; and it is one of the phenomena in the national feeling towards and about him. To the popular mind he was to the end, though portraits might show him grey and wasted, the brilliant and gallant Knight of Cadiz. Least of all for his enemies was he ever aged and broken. They had too acute a perception of his ability to resist them. They knew that he preserved his powers intact, and was not to be trampled on with impunity. He brought now an all but direct charge of treachery against the King: 'It pleased his Majesty to value us at so little as to command me upon my allegiance to set down under my hand the country, and the very river by which I was to enter it; to set down the number of men, and burden of my ships; with what ordnance every ship carried; which was made known to the Spanish Ambassador, and by him in post sent to the King of Spain.' His future looked to him profoundly black. He glanced, as he well might without treason, at the contingency of foreign service, whether in Denmark, France, or Holland: 'What shall become of me now I know not.' Notwithstanding the royal commission, which, like others, he misdescribed as 'under the Great Seal,' and not the Privy Seal, he was aware that he was

'unpardoned in *Letter to Lady Ralegh.* England.' He went on: 'My poor estate is consumed; and whether any other Prince or State will give me bread I know not.' From St. Christopher's he wrote also to his wife. He had told Winwood he durst not write to her from fear of renewing the sorrow for her son. Yet he could not be silent, though he confessed he knew not how to comfort her: 'God knows, I never knew what sorrow meant till now. Comfort your heart, dearest Bess, I shall sorrow for us both. I shall sorrow the less because I have not long to sorrow, because not long to live.' He expressed a hope, which must be allowed to be ambiguous, that 'God will send us somewhat before we return.' He bids her tell about Keymis to Lord Northumberland, Sir John Leigh, and Silvanus Skory, a London merchant, who had in verse dissuaded him from the Guiana adventure altogether.

From St. Christopher's he sent home his fly-boat, under his cousin Herbert, who afterwards suffered in purse for the association with him. The vessel was laden with 'a rabble of idle rascals, which I know will not spare to wound me; but my friends will not believe them; and for the rest I care not.' This 'scum of men' being gone, he told Winwood he should be able, if he lived, to keep the sea till the end of August, with four reasonably good ships. His object he did not specify. Off Newfoundland the soldiers in his ship, he declared, wanted him to turn pirate with them. They compelled him to swear he would not go home without their leave. Among them were four convicted criminals. These were afraid to set foot in England unless Ralegh obtained their pardons from the Crown. He compromised by landing them at Kinsale, where he touched after a storm had scattered his ships. There is no record that Boyle or other old friends came now to salute him. But Sir Oliver St. John, at the time Lord Deputy, wrote word on May 30 to George

Sympathy. Carew of his arrival, probably on May 24. Three ships, commanded by Sir John Ferne, Captain Pennington, and Captain King, happened also to have taken refuge in Kinsale harbour. St. John expressed his deep sorrow for Ralegh's ill-success, which he attributed to 'the failing and mutinying of those that ought rather to have died with him than left him.' He instructed Lord Thomond to 'secure those captains, mutineers, and their ships.' Captain King was the one loyal man among them. In the *Declaration* of 1618 Ralegh was alleged, as they may believe who will, to have offered the *Destiny* at Kinsale to his officers, and also previously off Newfoundland to some of his chief captains, if they would only set him aboard a French bark, 'as being loath to put his head under the King's girdle.'

CHAPTER XXVII.

He arrived in his flagship the Destiny at Plymouth on June 21. No other ships accompanied him. At the news Lady Ralegh, sorrowing and glad, hastened from London. No painter has tried to portray the meeting, one of the most pathetic scenes in English history. His return had long been provided for by others than his noble wife. Captain Bayley, who stole away

Bayley's Calumnies. from Lancerota early in September, 1617, reached England in October. There he skulked about, spreading his fable that he had deserted because he was persuaded Ralegh intended to turn pirate. He circulated among his friends copies of a journal kept by him while he remained in the fleet, in which that view was enforced. The Lord Admiral, no partial friend of Ralegh's, had his ship and cargo seized, and himself summoned before the Privy Council. But later in October, as has been mentioned, Winwood died. On November 18 the Council wrote to the Lord Admiral to release the vessel and goods. It asked if the Admiral had discovered anything against the Captain, or could clear doubts which had been raised of Ralegh's courses and intentions. Reeks, of Ratcliff, had saved his ship through Ralegh's refusal to gratify the desire of his men for revenge at Lancerota. He arrived in December, 1617, and told how forbearing Ralegh had been, and how treacherous the Governor. Men like Carew had never put faith in assertions by creatures of Bayley's stamp, who 'maliced' him, that Ralegh had turned pirate. 'That for my part I would never believe,' wrote Carew. But the evidence of Reeks convinced for the instant even sceptics. Bayley was committed to Westminster Gate-house. On January 11, 1618, he appeared before the Council. The Council declared he had behaved himself undutifully and contemptuously, not only in flying from his General upon false and frivolous suggestions without any just cause at all, but also in defaming him. Allegations by him of treasonable expressions which he had heard Mr. Hastings report Ralegh to have uttered, were held to deepen his offence. If they were true, it was misprision of treason in him to have concealed the matter for a twelvemonth. An account of the inquiry has been printed by Mr. Gardiner in the *Camden Miscellany* from the Council Register. At its termination he was committed to prison, from which he was not liberated till the end of February. At the Council Carew, Arundel, Compton, Zouch, and Hay had been present. They all were friendly to Ralegh.

By May 13 came the news of the burning of St. Thomas, and Ralegh's well-wishers had no longer strength to defend him. It had reached Madrid earlier. Cottington wrote, on May 3, that the Spanish Ministers had advice of Ralegh's landing and proceedings. He made no comment, unless that the Spaniards were confident Ralegh would discover no gold or silver in those

Piratas! parts. On the arrival of the intelligence in London the story, which it is a pity to have to doubt, is that Gondomar burst into the royal chamber, in spite of assurances that the King was engaged. He said he needed to utter but a single word. It was 'Piratas! Piratas! Piratas!' On June 11 James published a Proclamation. It denounced as 'scandalous and enormous outrages' the hostile invasion of the town of San Thome, as reported by 'a common fame,' and the malicious breaking of the peace 'which hath been so happily established, and so long inviolately continued.' Gondomar had set off on a visit to Madrid. James hoped he would be able to conclude, by his personal representations, the negotiations for the marriage. He was overtaken at Greenwich by a royal messenger with an ill-written letter from Villiers, dated June 26: 'His Majesty will be as severe in punishing them as if they had done the like spoil in any of the cities of England. Howbeit Sir Walter Ralegh had returned with his ship's lading of

A Royal disavowal. gold, being taken from the King of Spain or his subjects, he would have sent unto the King of Spain back again as well his treasures as himself, according to his first and precedent promise, which he made unto your Excellency, the which he is resolute to accomplish precisely against the persons and upon the goods of them the offenders therein, it not being so that he doth understand that the same also shall seem well to the King of Spain, to be most convenient and exemplary that they should suffer here so severe punishments as such like crime doth require.' On his knees George Carew pleaded in vain. James would only promise that Ralegh should be heard. He intimated that he had predetermined the result: 'As good hang him as deliver him to the King of Spain; and one of these two I must, if the case be as Gondomar has represented.' In vain Captain North pictured the miseries which had been endured. He showed no pity for the lost son, the ruined fortune, the shattered hopes. Peiresc wrote from the Continent to Camden to condole on the ill-success of 'miser Raleghus.' James's sole thought was how most profitably to sacrifice him. He held out to the Escurial the prospect of an ignominious death in due course. In the meantime he engaged to indemnify any plundered Spanish subjects out of the offender's property. The offer brought upon him two years afterwards a claimant for tobacco to the value of £40,000. Francis Davila, of San Thome, appears to have succeeded in obtaining £750 of the amount from Ralegh's cousin and comrade, Herbert.

Ralegh on his arrival at Plymouth heard of the King's Proclamation. His follower, Samuel King, who had commanded a fly-boat in the expedition, says in his *Narrative*, written after the execution, that Ralegh had resolved to surrender - *Sir Lewis Stukely*. - voluntarily. The Court did not believe it. The seizure of the Destiny had previously been ordered. On June 12 the Lord Admiral had directed Sir Lewis Stukely to arrest Ralegh himself, and bring him to London. Stukely was Vice-Admiral of Devon, having bought the office for £600. He was nephew to Sir Richard Grenville, of the Revenge. Thus, though subsequently he seemed to deny it, he was related to Ralegh. His father had served in the second Virginia voyage. Ralegh had solicited the favour of Cecil for the family. Stukely could boast of sixteen quarterings, and possessed the remains of a considerable inheritance at Afton or Affeton. But he was a man of broken fortunes and doubtful character. In the second week of July Ralegh, his wife, and Captain King had started for London. Close to Ashburton Stukely met them. Ralegh did not dispute his authority, though Stukely admitted he was without a formal warrant, which, according to his own account, did not reach him till he and his prisoner had arrived at Salisbury. The whole party returned the twenty miles to Plymouth. There for nine or ten days Ralegh, who was sick, and glad of rest, lodged, first at the house of Sir Christopher Harris, and next with Mr. Drake. He saw little or nothing of his keeper, who was selling tobacco and the stores of the Destiny. It has been imagined that Stukely meant to tempt him to fly, and then display his dexterity by intercepting him. The laxity of the supervision and the delay give colour rather to a supposition that the Government wished him actually to escape. That would have relieved it from a heavy embarrassment. Out of affection Lady Ralegh and Captain King had the same desire, and at length they gained his consent. King negotiated with two Rochelle captains, Flory and le Grand, for his conveyance across the Channel. One night King and he rowed off to one of the barks. When a quarter of a mile from the ship Ralegh insisted upon returning. According to one account he seems to have been once more persuaded to start, and again his heart failed him, or perhaps his courage revived. He was still buoyed up with romantic fancies, which he had cherished ever since the disappointment on the Orinoko. Until he saw death or a dungeon yawning in front of him, he kept a fond faith that he should be authorized to lead one more forlorn hope.

Peremptory directions at last came from the Council. Ralegh perceived that he was regarded as a criminal, and he foresaw the end as it was to be. He declared that his trust in the King had undone him, and that he should have to die to please the State. He repented that he had not seized the opportunity to escape, and began to form fresh plans. It has been said that at Plymouth his fortitude deserted him. Mr. Gardiner has suggested the very improbable motive for his aversion from a return to London, that he feared he might be torn in pieces by the mob. It was not courage, but patience, which failed. He could not bear the thought of losing the power to strike another blow for the fulfilment of his darling ambition.

Stukely closed his sales, and set off, we are told, on July 25, though more

Manourie. probably the journey began some days earlier. The company consisted of himself, Ralegh, and Lady Ralegh, with their servants, King, and a Frenchman, Manourie, who is said to have brought Stukely his regular warrant. Manourie, who had been long settled in Devonshire, has been variously described as a physician and as a quack. Two centuries and a half ago the distinction between charlatans and experimentalists was not clearly marked in medical science. Ralegh seems to have suspected that he was a spy, but to have believed in his skill. The man may not have been the medical impostor popular resentment believed him. Undoubtedly he was needy and greedy, and a perfidious rogue. From the first he laid traps. He reported to Stukely, or invented, an ejaculation by Ralegh, on hearing of the orders for London: 'God's wounds! Is it possible that my fortune should thus return upon me again?' He told how Ralegh cried as they rode by Sherborne Park: 'All this was mine, and it was taken from me unjustly.' Nothing could be more true.

They had slept on the night of July 26 at the house of old Mr. Parham, who lived, with his son, Sir Edward Parham, close to Sherborne. Next day, July 27, they journeyed to Salisbury by Wilton. On the hill beyond Wilton, Ralegh, as he walked down it with Manourie, asked him to prepare an emetic: 'It will be good,' Manourie asserted that he said, 'to evacuate bad humours; and by its means I shall gain time to work my friends and order my affairs; perhaps even to pacify his Majesty.' The summer Progress was proceeding. Ralegh knew that, in pursuance of its programme, the King would stay at Salisbury. That night at Salisbury he turned dizzy. Notwithstanding, or because he desired to spare her a discreditable scene,

- *The CounterfeitDisease.* - in the morning Lady Ralegh, with her retinue of servants, continued her journey to London. King went too. He was to hire a boat, which was to lie off Tilbury. According to him, the design was that Ralegh should stop in France till the anger of Spain was lulled. After their departure a servant of Ralegh's rushed to Stukely with the news that his master was out of his wits, in his shirt, and upon all fours, gnawing at the rushes on the boards. Stukely sent Manourie to him. Manourie administered the emetic, and also an ointment compounded of aquafortis. This brought out purple pustules over the breast and arms. Strangers, and after a single visit Stukely too, were afraid to approach. Lancelot Andrewes, then Bishop of Ely, happened to be at Salisbury. He heard, and compassionately sent the best three physicians of the town. None of them could explain the sickness. For four days the cavalcade halted. Ralegh subsisted on a clandestine leg of mutton, and wrote his *Apology for the Voyage to Guiana*, from which I have already drawn for his view of disputed facts. Manourie he employed to copy his manuscript. The wish to compose the narrative is believed by some to have been the sole motive of his artifice. His own subsequent account of it was that he had speculated on an interview with the King. With that view he had compassed a delay. How an apparent attack of leprosy should have helped him to an interview is not very intelligible. Chamberlain wrote to Carleton on August 8 that Ralegh had no audience of James on account of his malady. Probably the ruling motive of the comedy was a passionate desire to win leisure for drawing up his narrative, which he wildly hoped he might find means of bringing before the King during his sojourn at Salisbury. That was the audience he really desired. As soon as the treatise was written he recovered. Not now or afterwards was he at all ashamed of the deception. So given was he to physicking himself, that it occurred to him as a natural thing to use his drugs in order to gain a few quiet literary days. He justified his pretence by the example of David: 'David did make himself a fool, and suffered spittle to fall upon his beard, that he might escape the hands of his enemies.'

The statement which he had stolen a respite to write has been considered by *Consistency of his Position.* Mr. Gardiner, in his *Prince Charles and the Spanish Marriage*, an aggravation of his guilt. The claim it sets up of his right to sweep opposing Spaniards out of his way to the Mine, is treated as an admission that he had founded his enterprise on a lie, and that his sin had found him out. Mr. Gardiner adds he must have known that his case would not bear the light. Apparently this means that he had asserted, or had fraudulently suffered James to infer, that no Spaniards were settled in the vicinity of Keymis's Mine, or were in the least likely to withstand in arms his approach to it; or that he had made a promise, of which the resistance of his men to the Spanish attack was a breach, in no circumstances to fight. These are unproved assumptions. Ralegh, who constitutionally took his instructions from Secretary Winwood, cannot be shown to have given, or been asked for, any positive pledge that in no circumstances would he force his way into the interior of Guiana. The warlike equipment of his fleet, and of the men he led, is evidence that the contingency of a collision with armed Spanish ships and soldiers was contemplated by the Government and prepared for. The nature of the business on which James had despatched him fully authorized the claim in the *Apology*. He was sent to work a mine on the Orinoko, where the whole commercial world knew that Spaniards were settled. James must have known it from many sources. He knew it definitely from Gondomar, whose protests against the expedition were based particularly on it. Any 'guilt' of Ralegh's for letting his followers run the gauntlet of the San Thome garrison, James must share equally for letting him go with an armed squadron to the Orinoko at all.

On the first of August, when the *Apology* was already completed, the King arrived at Salisbury. It is not known whether Ralegh succeeded in having the composition at once laid before him. If the King saw it, we may be

- *Manourie's Story.* - certain that it exerted upon the royal mind the precise

reverse of the conciliatory effect the writer anticipated. Orders immediately were issued that Ralegh should move forward. Thereupon, according to Manourie, Ralegh bribed him with twenty crowns, and an offer of £50 a year, to aid his escape. On the same suspicious testimony, he was furious against the King, and uttered menaces. Ralegh informed Manourie of King's Tilbury project. He said he must fly, for 'a man that fears is never secure.' Further, he asserted his conviction that the courtiers had concluded among them 'a man must die to reassure the traffic which he had broken in Spain.' Manourie pretended Ralegh handed to him jewels and money for the purchase of Stukely's connivance. Ralegh acknowledged he had told Stukely he hoped to procure payment of his debts. Any offers beyond this he denied. At Staines Manourie left. He said to Ralegh, whom he was betraying to prison and death, that he did not expect to see him again while Ralegh was in England. It is a pity his figure cannot be wholly obliterated from Ralegh's biography, on which it is one of several ugly human blurs.

At Brentford a more loyal but as unlucky a Frenchman, David de Novion, came to meet Ralegh at the inn. He brought a message from le Clerc, the French Resident, that he wished to see Ralegh. The Government knew of this, and thought that, by affecting ignorance, it might learn more. On July 30 had arrived a Council warrant for Ralegh's committal to the Tower. It was not at once executed. Before he left Salisbury it had been conceded through the mediation, it is said, of Digby, touched by his apparent infirmities at Salisbury, that he should be conveyed to his own house in Broad-street, for four or five days' rest. He now obtained leave to have that arrangement confirmed or resumed. Naunton told Carleton that he procured the permission on a pretence of sickness, that he might take

medicine at home. Probably it - *Interview with French Agents.* - was granted

that he might be tempted to plan an escape with the Frenchmen, and give the Government an excuse for more rigour. On the night of Friday, August 7, he arrived in Broad-street, where he found Lady Ralegh. On the evening of Sunday, at eight, le Clerc and de Novion came. They showed little caution, speaking freely in the presence of eight or ten persons. They intimated he might count on their help in his flight, and on a good reception in France. The French interest in Ralegh was an anti-Spanish interest. If safe in France he could, it was thought, exercise in some not very apparent way influence in England against the Anglo-Spanish alliance. Queen Anne was understood to prefer vehemently a French to a Spanish bride for Prince Charles. The French dealings with Ralegh, it was believed at the time, had been prompted by the Queen or her confidants. Ralegh seems to have listened to his French visitors with grateful courtesy, but not to have accepted any offer of French assistance. He intended to make his way to France. He would not go in a French vessel.

The plan on which he decided had been concerted with King. A former boatswain of King's, called Hart, had a ketch. Cottrell, apparently Ralegh's old Tower servant, who had once before borne witness against him, had found Hart for King. Before Ralegh reached London, King had arranged with Hart through Cottrell that the ketch should be held ready off Tilbury. Implicit trust was placed in Cottrell's supposed devotion to Ralegh. In reality he and Hart had at once betrayed the whole arrangement to a Mr. William Herbert, not the Herbert of the Guiana Expedition. Herbert told Sir William St. John, who in 1616 had traded in Ralegh's liberation. St. John in company, it would seem from Stukely's subsequent account, with Herbert, had posted off with the news to Salisbury. He had met Stukely and

Preparations

for Flight. his prisoner at Bagshot on the road, and warned the former, who scarcely required the information. Stukely showed such zeal for Ralegh's safety as wholly to delude both him and King. He had obtained a licence from Naunton to enter, without liability, into any contract, and comply with any offer. Though in theory Ralegh was under his charge in Broad-street, he left him full liberty of action. Ralegh's own servants were allowed to wait on him. Stukely borrowed £10 of him. The pretence was a wish to pay for the despatch into the country of his own servants, that they might not interfere with the flight. He promised to accompany Ralegh into France. Ralegh, with all his wit and experience of men, his wife, with her love and her clearness of vision, the shrewd French diplomatists, and honest King, were dupes of a mere cormorant, like Stukely, and of vulgar knaves, like Cottrell and Hart. Without the least suspicion of foul play Ralegh on that Sunday night, after le Clerc and de Novion had left, went down to the river side.

It was a foolish business. Nothing, except success, could have been more woful than all its features and its failure. If the attempt be blamed as rebellion against the law, the correctness of the condemnation cannot be disputed. Ralegh derived no right to fly from the injustice of his treatment. Had he been of the nature of Socrates he would not have thought of flight. His respect for authority was not like that of Socrates. His conscience never particularly troubled him for the immorality of his endeavour to break from custody. It stung him very soon and sharply for the degradation of having run from danger. Flight was unworthy of him, and he acknowledged its shame. But his own account of the temptation to which he yielded may be accepted as truthful. He told Sir Thomas Wilson his intention was to seek an asylum in France from Spanish vengeance, until 'the Queen should have made means for his pardon and recalling.' In England he was doomed, he foresaw, to death or to perpetual confinement; and he believed he had work in life still to do. He feared neither death nor prison for itself. In a paroxysm of despair he clutched the only chance he perceived of reserving his powers for the enterprise he had set them, the overthrow of the colonial monopoly of Spain.

Two wherries were hired at the Tower dock. Ralegh, attended by one of his pages, Stukely, Stukely's son, King, and Hart, set off. Sir William St. John and Herbert followed secretly in another boat. Ralegh wore a false beard and a hat with a green band. Stukely asked King whether thus far he *On the Thames.* had not acted as an honest man. King replied by a hope that he would continue to act thus. Herbert's boat was seen first making as if it would go through the bridge; but finally it returned down the river. Ralegh became alarmed. He asked the watermen if they would row on, though one came to arrest him in the King's name. They answered they could at all events not go beyond Gravesend. Ralegh explained that a brabbling matter with the Spanish Ambassador was taking him to Tilbury to embark for the Low Countries. He offered them ten gold pieces. Thereupon Stukely began cursing himself that he should be so unfortunate as to venture his life and fortune with a man full of doubt. He swore he would kill the watermen if they did not row on. The delays spent the tide, and the men said they could not reach Gravesend before morning. When they were a mile beyond Woolwich, at a reach called the Gallions, near Plumstead, Ralegh felt sure he was betrayed, and ordered the men to row back. Herbert's and St. John's wherry met them. Then Ralegh, wishing to remain in Stukely's custody, declared himself his prisoner. He still supposed the man was faithful. He pulled things out of his pocket and gave them to Stukely, who hugged him with tenderness. *Stukely Unmasked.* They landed at Greenwich, Ralegh intending to go to Stukely's house. But the other crew landed also. Now at last Stukely revealed his true character. He arrested Ralegh and King in his

Majesty's name, and committed them to the charge of two of St. John's men. Ralegh understood, and said: 'Sir Lewis, these actions will not turn out to your credit.' With a generous thoughtfulness for a very different man, he tried to induce King to give himself out for an accomplice in Stukely's plot. King could not be persuaded. Ralegh and he were kept separate till the morning, when Ralegh was conducted to the Tower. As once more he passed within, he must have felt that his tomb had opened for him. King was allowed to attend him to the gate. There he was compelled to part. He left Ralegh, he wrote after the execution, 'to His tuition with whom I do not doubt but his soul resteth.' Ralegh's farewell words to him were: 'Stukely and Cottrell have betrayed me.'

CHAPTER XXVIII.

A MORAL RACK (August 10-October 15).

On the morning of Monday, August 10, Ralegh finally entered the Tower. This time he was made to feel that he was a prisoner indeed. He had meant to ⸨ *Ralegh's Trinkets.* ⸩ transport to France charts of Guiana, the Orinoko, Nuova Regina, and Panama, with five assays of the ore of the Mine. They were on him, and they were taken from him. He was stripped also of his trinkets, except a spleen stone. This and an ounce of ambergris were left with him for his personal use. A gold picture-case set with diamonds was, by his wish, consigned to the Lieutenant of the Tower. There were other ornaments. Among them was a diamond ring, supposed by Naunton to have been a present from Queen Elizabeth, though Ralegh told Sir Thomas Wilson he had never any such of the Queen's giving. There were a Guiana idol of gold and copper, and sixty-three gold buttons with sparks of diamonds. All these were entrusted to Stukely by the Lieutenant of the Tower. It would be strange if some did not stay with their custodian. It may have been with reference to them that Ralegh admitted the traitor to a last interview in the Lieutenant's lodgings on the Wednesday after his committal. We may be sure it was not to affirm, as Stukely declared, that he 'loved him as well as any friend he had in the world.'

More exalted persecutors than Stukely were now let loose upon him. The old game of 1603 was resumed. Lords of the Council and the Law Officers of the Crown worked their hardest to discover that he was a criminal. First on August 17, and twice afterwards, he was examined upon interrogatories by a ⸨ *Examinations by Privy Councillors.* ⸩ committee of the Privy Council, consisting of Lord Chancellor Bacon, Archbishop Abbot, Lord Worcester, Coke, since November, 1616, no longer Chief Justice, Cæsar, and Naunton The examinations were not directed in a way either to do justice to the prisoner, or to elicit the truth, so far as can be discovered from the records of them. Those among the Lords Commissioners who desired something more than merely to extricate their master from a diplomatic difficulty, were incapacitated by an invincible prejudice. All started by taking for granted that the prisoner never intended to search for the Mine, that none existed, and that his single purpose since he prepared for his expedition was to attack piratically the Spanish colonies and commerce. Mr. Gardiner, who is one of his severest critics, acknowledges that they blundered and failed, because they were not content to convict him of having cared simply to find the Mine, and been reckless of the means.

James and his Ministers could convince themselves of the expediency and moral propriety of slaying a man capable, as they believed, of schemes, however qualified, for the capture of the Spanish treasure ships. They saw the difficulty of proving to the country the capital criminality of the avowal of a project never acted upon. They had hoped they might fabricate supplementary treasonable matter out of the communications between Ralegh and the French Agency. After a long competition between a French and a Spanish family compact, the Spanish faction at Court, which was James's own, was absolutely predominant. The Government did not shrink from offending French susceptibilities. In September it arrested and repeatedly examined de Novion, whose diplomatic character was not very definitive. Le Clerc, the resident Agent, was himself summoned before the Council at Hampton Court, and confronted with de Novion. He stood upon his privilege, and refused to answer. The Council solemnly rebuked him for his secret conferences with, and offers of means of escape to, an English subject attainted of high treason, and since 'detected in other heinous crimes.' He was informed he had forfeited, by the law of nations, his immunities, and was required to confine himself to his house. The French Government was wrathful; but it had a weak case. Its conduct, though its original advances to Ralegh had the sanction of the English Ministers, was clearly a breach of diplomatic propriety. The proof against the Frenchmen was of no use towards the end for which the Council laid stress on it. Ralegh, it was seen, could not be accounted liable for overtures he had rejected. The Crown still was thrown back on the chance of confessions by himself for a provision of assignable pretexts for his destruction.

In some way or other reasons had to be discovered. James saw the Infanta's dower of two million crowns and jewels within his grasp. The Spanish Court showed the friendliest disposition. It had expressed its delight at the welcome news of its enemy's capture in the act of flight, and his committal

Pledges to Spain. again to the Tower. Nothing was wanting, James imagined, to crown the negotiations, but an English head which he was very willing to sacrifice. He had given the Spanish Government the option of a public execution either at Madrid or in London. It was impossible that he should disappoint the agreeable expectation. At Court the will to put Ralegh to death was matter of notoriety. The Queen's was the only voice raised loudly against it. They who were ignorant how faded was her influence imagined her protest might still be of avail. On September 23, Sir Edward Harwood wrote to Carleton, that Ralegh was struggling hard for life, and that, as the King was now with the Queen, it was believed he might live. Courtiers in general knew better. On August 29, Tyringham, another of Carleton's purveyors of news, wrote to him: 'It is said that death will conclude Sir Walter Ralegh's troubles. The Queen's intercession will rather defer than prevent his punishment.' Yet ways and means had to be provided, and the difficulty grew rather than diminished, until it was decided to cut the knot. Harwood reported to Carleton on October 3, that 'the King is much inclined to hang Ralegh; but it cannot handsomely be done; and he is likely to live out his days.' As time went on, and the climax was not reached, the gossip of the town, perhaps of the Court itself, spread a rumour that the delay was intentional. Ralegh was said to have been promised his life if he would help towards revelations of the misappropriation of crown jewels or lands at the King's accession, with the connivance of the late Treasurers, Salisbury and Suffolk. The tale may have had some sort of basis in Ralegh's habit of charging Cecil with an abuse of his position to his personal enrichment at the expense of the Crown, from which he was alleged to have taken Hatfield by a profitable exchange, and Cobham's escheated estates. No evidence exists that the question was ever seriously raised, or had any connexion with the delay. Of that the one real cause was the inability of the Court to elicit damning testimony against himself.

To patch up the gaps in the inquiry before the Lords Commissioners, the same system was tried as in the preliminary investigations of 1603. Ralegh

- *Sir Thomas Wilson.* - was placed, from September 11 till October 15, under

a special keeper. The keeper's business, like that of a Juge d'Instruction, was to ransack him, and worry him into supplying a case against himself. For the office Sir Thomas Wilson, Keeper of the State Paper Office, was chosen. As Wilson himself confessed, his arrival produced an impression on the officers of the Tower as well as Ralegh, that 'a messenger of death had been sent.' He had entered the public service as a spy of Cecil's. He was now enjoying a pension for the intelligence he had collected in Spain concerning the Main and Bye Plots. His defect in his new office was an excess of zeal in suspiciousness. He began by regarding Ralegh as an arch hypocrite, and a lying impudent impostor, from whom the truth could be extracted only by 'a rack, or a halter.' Though otherwise a man of some learning, and a diligent guardian of the public records, he seems to have been very ignorant of physics. He thought Ralegh was an empty boaster for his statement that he could distil salt-water into fresh by means of copper furnaces. He treated his ailments, which Ralegh's somewhat hypochondriacal temperament may have a little exaggerated, as wholly feigned, 'that he might not be thought in his health to enterprise any such matter as perhaps he designeth.' Their symptoms, the swollen left side and liver, the painful sores over his body, the ague-fits, his lameness from the Cadiz wound, he conjectured were caused by the patient's own applications. With his wife to share his watch, he was given absolute control. No person was to have speech with Ralegh, unless in his hearing. The Council was to be told all he observed. He was cunning, though he was fond of enlarging on his simple honesty. He had a high sense of his own importance, and magnified his very extensive powers. He was furious with the door-keeper of the Council for delaying one day to carry in a message from him while the Council was deliberating. He quarrelled with Sir Allen Apsley, now Lieutenant of the Tower, for withholding the keys of Ralegh's apartment at night.

Apsley, a near connexion by his third wife of Villiers, through whom he had *The Apsleys.* been enabled to buy his office, must have been an acquaintance of Ralegh's. He had served in the commissariat department in the Cadiz expedition, and in Ireland. His second wife was niece, and almost adopted daughter, of George Carew. On Ralegh's return to the Tower, his old lodgings in the Bloody tower being tenanted by Lord and Lady Somerset, he was quartered in the Lieutenant's own house. There he was sure of hospitable treatment, both on account of the past, and as one of the persons eminent in learning and in arms, for whom, we are told, Sir Allen had a singular kindness. He had the especial happiness of association there with the third Lady Apsley, the mother of Lucy, afterwards the noble wife of Colonel Hutchinson. Lady Apsley was interested in physical science. Mrs. Hutchinson has recorded how her mother, as well from curiosity as from her abounding benignity, which made her desire that the illustrious prisoner should be comforted and diverted, persuaded the less scientifically enlightened Sir Allen to tolerate his chemical investigations. Sir Allen allowed her an income for herself of £300 a year. Among other good works on which this 'mother' of the Tower spent her pin-money, was the payment of the cost of Ralegh's experiments. According to Mrs. Hutchinson, herself a capable surgeon, Ralegh taught Lady Apsley in return many valuable chemical prescriptions. After a time he was removed to good quarters in the Wardrobe tower, looking over the Queen's garden. With that arrangement Wilson professed himself much dissatisfied. He affected to apprehend communications between Ralegh and confederates outside. Finally he had his way. Against the wishes of Apsley, as much as his own, Ralegh was transported to a little upper room in the Brick tower. 'Though it seemeth nearer Heaven, yet,' wrote Wilson to Naunton, 'there is there no means to escape but into Hell.' It had been *'Chemical Stuffs.'* occupied by his servants when he was confined in that building for his offence of 1592.

He was not allowed now to have the attendance of his own valet. He was threatened with separation from the 'chemical stuffs,' with which he loved constantly to drench himself from phials containing all spirits, sneered ignorant Wilson, but the spirit of God. The Tower physician could not tell what they were. He, and apparently Sir Allen Apsley too, at first apprehended another attempt at suicide. They need not. Ralegh, landless, ruined, had no longer aught to gain by self-destruction for his family. Apart from a sense of religious duty, he had every motive for reserving his head for the block, for wishing to 'die in the light.' Wilson's employers might not have been sorry had his view been different. Though sometimes the conversation turned on the topic of noble Roman suicides, Ralegh showed no inclination to take his own life. Wilson said with a taunt he did not abstain out of principle, but simply because he, who knew not what fear was, 'had no such Roman courage.'

It would be unfair to Wilson and to his confederate Naunton, who had hoped that the other would 'not long be troubled with that cripple,' to infer that they were disappointed at Ralegh's reluctance to disembarrass the Court by self-murder of the trouble of him. There can be no doubt of the dishonesty of the devices Wilson adopted to secure him for the block. He tempted him with mendaciously ambiguous declarations that, if he disclosed all he knew, the King would forgive him, and do him all kindness. Wilson, James, and Naunton were engaged in a common conspiracy, that the first, without directly pledging the royal word to a grant of grace, should

coax *Promises in the King's Name.* from Ralegh a confession by allowing him to fancy such a pledge had been given. Naunton's rebukes, as well as Wilson's own avowals to him, indicate that Wilson all but positively bound the King. He need scarcely have resorted to falsehoods, which did not impose upon his prisoner. Ralegh's experience of the King's justice and clemency had been too long and intimate for him to be deluded by a Sir Thomas Wilson. Though he had a right to tax the King with promises given in the King's name, he did not hope, he told Wilson, thus to save his life. 'He knew that the more he confessed, the sooner he should be hanged.' But he was not unwilling to talk and write. He wished, absurd as seemed to Wilson his pretension to such a possession, 'to discharge his conscience in all things to his Majesty.' He rejoiced besides in an opportunity for clearing up obscurities in his career. Ultimately he grew reserved with Wilson, as may easily be understood. At first, before he had thoroughly gauged his companion, he conversed freely. He discoursed almost too freely and fully for Wilson's ability to condense the whole into a narrative which would be plausible enough to give the King a sense that they were on the verge of real discoveries. Wilson complained to Naunton that he often tried to gain information by talking on matters which might lead to it.

From the Tower, though one biographer believes it was from Devonshire, he wrote to the King, asking why it should be lawful for Spaniards to murder thirty-six Englishmen, tying them back to back, and then cutting their throats, yet be unlawful for Englishmen—'O miserable English! O miserable Ralegh!—to repel force by force.' The Spanish atrocities are not disputed. The strange thing is that historians who condemn Ralegh's alleged violence to Spaniards never seem to suppose he was really resentful of them. They treat his indignation as factitious. Another letter he appears, at Wilson's instigation, to have written to the King on September 17 or 18, which has been lost or suppressed. In it, from an indorsement, dated September 19, on Wilson's covering letter, it seems that he asked for an examination of one Christofero, the Governor of Guiana's mulatto valet, whom Keymis had brought from San Thome. He would be able to speak, it was mentioned, of 'seven or eight several mines of gold that are there.' It was not *Apology for Flight.* convenient to order any such examination.

Ralegh wrote other letters from the Tower. He wrote to Villiers, to explain, not so much to him or his master, as to his own wounded self-respect, the one act of which he was really ashamed. It was his ineffectual flight, that 'late and too late lamented resolution.' He recounted to deaf ears the dreams on which he had brooded of permission to lead yet another expedition in search of his El Dorado; his despair, when the peremptory summons by the Council to London demonstrated to him that his vision of treasures and glory was to be extinguished for ever by actual or virtual death. In a much bolder letter to George Carew, intended for the King's perusal, which sounds more like a manifesto to the English nation, he frankly avowed the things he had left undone as well as the things he had done, and his reasons. He admitted he had not, in his description of his project, reminded the King that the Spaniards had already a footing in Guiana. Though the King's advisers were as well aware as himself of the foundation of the original San Thome, he was willing to facilitate the King's efforts to purge himself individually of complicity with the attack on a Spanish settlement. He admitted further that his patent did not formally authorize him to remove the Spaniards when they blocked the path to the Mine. His defence was that he required no distinct authority. The natural lords of Guiana had acknowledged Elizabeth their sovereign, and the Spaniards had no title to forbid the entry of Englishmen. He did not deny his responsibility for the capture of San Thome as part of the operations for the discovery of the Mine, and he justified it. His right to march about Guiana without let or hindrance was, he contended, implied in the Royal commission. Unless the King's title to Guiana were clear, his entrance for any purpose could not have been sanctioned. If Guiana were Spanish soil, he would have been as manifestly a thief for taking gold anywhere out of it, and the Crown as manifestly an accessary to theft, as the Spaniards now asserted him to be a peace breaker.

As may easily be imagined, these were not confessions of the sort James desired. 'Farrago istius veteratoris' was the description applied to them by Wilson in his classical moments. 'Mountebank's stuff' he called them when writing for less classical eyes than the King's. Naunton affected to despise them as 'roaring tedious epistles.' They were as little satisfied with the undressed disclosures which they ungenerously endeavoured to obtain through Lady Carew and Lady Ralegh. Lady Carew was made to question him on his communications with the French Agent, and also to question the Agent. She reported the Agent's answer to her interrogation what

Ralegh was *Detention of Lady Ralegh.* to have done or to do in France if he had succeeded, or should succeed, in escaping thither. It was: 'Il mangera, il boyera, il fera bien.' Nothing more material was extracted from Lady Ralegh. She had been committed on August 20 to the custody, in her own house in Broad-street, of a London merchant, Wollaston. He was relieved of the disagreeable duty on September 10, 'for his many great occasions and affairs.' Another merchant, Richard Champion, succeeded him. He was forbidden to allow any to have access to her, save only such as he should think fit. Eventually she was subjected to the supervision of Wilson. No crime was imputed to her. The object of the lawless outrage was the interception of admissions in the letters husband and wife were encouraged to write. All were submitted to the King's prying though lazy eyes. Naunton remarked on one occasion to Wilson: 'I forbear to send your long letter to the King, who would not read over the Lady's, being glutted and cloyed with business.' The correspondence told little any of the conspirators cared to learn. The letters breathed a trust and affection James never inspired. None of the State secrets he expected to detect were revealed in such a note as from Ralegh in September: 'I am sick and weak. My swollen side keeps me in perpetual pain and unrest;' or in her reply: 'I am sorry to hear amongst many discomforts that your health is so ill. 'Tis merely sorrow and grief. I hope your health and comforts will mend, and mend us for God.'

Mr. Gardiner's Case against Ralegh.

By this time the Government recognised that it had done all in its power for the completion of its case against Ralegh. Students of the proceedings will think the same. They have cause to be grateful to Mr. Gardiner for marshalling the medley in his essay under that title in the *Fortnightly Review.* With the fullest desire to be impartial, he sums up strongly against the defendant; and his skill and patience in the collection of evidence are such as to ensure that he has neglected nothing available for a decisive condemnation. According to him, Ralegh was guilty of a flagrant breach of the conditions on which his expedition was authorized. He had pledged his own faith and that of his friends and companions that he could reach and work his Mine in Guiana without attacking resident Spaniards, or trespassing on lands in Spanish occupation. James, it is said, was not inconsistent with his own principles in sanctioning an enterprise thus qualified. The King's doctrine, frankly stated by Mr. Gardiner, was that nothing less than occupancy carried the right to territorial dominion; and it had been declared to him that the locality of the Mine was not occupied by Spaniards. He was sceptical of the existence of the Mine, and he was mistrustful of Ralegh's disposition to comply with the compact. The national eagerness, however, for the adventure, and the confidence of Ralegh's well-wishers, overpowered his reluctance. He was moved also by the venial hope of a vast influx of innocent profit into his empty Treasury. From the first it was understood plainly that the admiral accepted the entire responsibility for the maintenance of a peaceable attitude towards Spanish possessions. The postponement of a pardon was a sign. Ralegh's conduct in despatching his men to a spot where a collision was inevitable, indicated a deliberate disregard of his covenants. James could not have known that the situation of the new San Thome necessitated a conflict, if the Mine were to be approached, since Ralegh himself had in England not been aware of the resettlement. As soon · *The King's good Faith.* · as he heard, his duty was either to retire, or to choose a fresh route. He did neither, and thus fairly laid himself open to the punishment he had invoked before he started. Mr. Gardiner does not allow that James is chargeable with double dealing which should have tied his hands as against Ralegh, on account of the disclosure of Ralegh's memorial and plans to Gondomar. The memorial, which, Mr. Gardiner is sure, included no specification of the place of the Mine, would tell the Ambassador little of novelty or practical importance. Besides, Mr. Gardiner believes Ralegh was aware that it was to be shown. Finally, Ralegh's designs against the plate fleet, and his intrigues with Savoy and France, in Mr. Gardiner's opinion, sufficiently demonstrate his want of scrupulousness. The evidence of them would naturally disincline the King for passing indulgently over proved violations of agreement. On the whole, he concludes, 'no one who now constructs a narrative of Ralegh's voyage on the basis of a belief in his veracity will be likely to obtain a hearing.'

It is a large indictment resting upon a very slender basis. The question of the alleged schemes of freebooting, none of which issued in action, has been considered already. For the present its relevancy depends on the answer to the main charge of an unlicensed and deliberate rupture by

Ralegh of the peace between his own Sovereign and the King of Spain. For a determination of the point it must be remembered how much Mr. Gardiner concedes in Ralegh's favour, as well as how much he decides adversely. If . *Weakness of the Case.* . San Thome had remained in 1618 where it was in 1596, and Spanish troops, having taken up a temporary post a score or so of miles lower down, had from that barred the quiet passage of young Walter and Keymis, Mr. Gardiner apparently must have exonerated Ralegh. He would have been safe within his commission, which appointed him leader of an armed force for the obvious purpose of resisting impediments to his progress about Guiana, unless where Spaniards were in immediate possession. Warfare with Spaniards in Guiana is not in itself represented as criminal. His sole offence was in combating them voluntarily on ground they positively occupied. The same defence which he might have conclusively urged if soldiers, descending from the original San Thome, had blocked his transit, is justly pleadable for his men's voyage on the Orinoko past the new town. Guiana in general being free to Englishmen, it is manifest that a settlement on the bank could not appropriate the channel. The whole question of the guilt or innocence of Ralegh on James's reading of international law, is narrowed to the minute issue whether the Spaniards or the Englishmen on the particular scene of the fight were the aggressors. Whatever the decision upon that, it is difficult to see how it could properly affect Ralegh. His right and his duty were to find and take possession of the Mine, if it were not in Spanish hands, as nobody alleges it was. He was entitled to break through obstacles in his way, so long as he did not violate actual Spanish soil. Lawfully he sent his comrades along the Orinoko. If on their road the Spaniards compelled a contest, neither Ralegh nor his subordinates were in fault. If his captains compelled it, he cannot have been liable, unless he be proved, as he has not been, to have so instructed them. In any event, when all Spanish officers in America notoriously deemed an Englishman a pirate who entered the Orinoko without their leave, and King James claimed authority to send his subjects wherever in Guiana Spaniards were not permanently planted, it is unreasonable to throw the liability for an armed brawl between Spaniards and Englishmen in Guiana upon the English chief. His Sovereign, who with eyes open despatched him with an armament to work a mine of prodigious value, cannot be permitted to shift on him the odium of a bloody struggle because the goal turned out to be some eight miles off, instead of the twenty more or less at which both master and subject had judged it to be.

The design of the Government had been to discover proof of fresh crimes since Ralegh's liberation in 1616, and to try him for them. It had failed. Much of the testimony it had painfully collected was dubious, vague, biassed, interested, or plainly corrupt. Such as it was the Council either would not, or could not, rely upon it for a conviction. Ralegh's transactions with the Frenchmen were unwarrantable, if its view of them were correct. But they had resulted in nothing, and they were a continuation of relations which it had itself promoted. At San Thome, if he *Difficulties of the Government.* were liable for his men, as partially he did not deny, though he might have denied it, he had broken the King's peace by an invasion of Spanish territory, if Guiana were Spanish. He maintained that it was as much English as it was Spanish, if not more; and they neither dared, in the existing state of national opinion, nor perhaps cared, to gainsay the doctrine. His alleged schemes for the maritime spoliation of Spaniards may well have been to his mind lawful. All English seamen, and the nation at large, believed that the articles of peace between the two kingdoms did not extend beyond the Equator. In the latest treaty with Spain, that of 1604, the Indies and their trade were intentionally not mentioned, on account of the insoluble difficulties arising out of the Spanish determination to shut the region to free European trade. For Ralegh and a multitude of Englishmen, and Spaniards also, England and Spain were in America always at war. Neither national nor international law countenanced the doctrine. Any Englishman who had devastated Spanish commerce in the West Indies, would, during a large part of Elizabeth's reign, have been amenable to criminal justice, if the State had prosecuted. But the State then was not inclined to prosecute for such acts. During the next reign some statesmen continued to hold, like the people, that there was no peace beyond the Line. If there were peace, the State could not have proceeded against Ralegh for the thought of breaking it. The single criminal act proved was his attempt at escape. For it he might have been tried and punished. But the most triumphant prosecution on such a charge would not have given the Government the pound of flesh it owed to Spain. Nothing less was of use.

The administration floundered about in futile efforts. Perpetually it was deluded by a sensation of solid ground which immediately slipped from under its feet. It was the more enraged with Ralegh that he seemed to be ever offering clues, which only led astray. It imputed its embarrassment to his cunning. He had no intention to deceive, or even to abstain from promoting a revelation of the truth, which he did not fear. Simply he and it were radically at cross purposes. They were mutually unintelligible. The sincerity of his ardour for the attainment of a footing in Guiana is unquestionable. He was honestly eager for it in the Tower, in Trinidad *Ralegh's real Motive.* after the return from San Thome, at Plymouth, when he was grovelling in counterfeit madness at Salisbury, and when he was a fugitive on the Thames. But Guiana was not his real end. Guiana was the means he had finally and deliberately chosen to inflame the English people and Crown with an inextinguishable ambition for the creation of an American empire. He did not much mind how the national imagination was kindled, provided that it caught fire. His motive was patriotic and vast, and his judges and accusers, conscientious men like Cæsar and Abbot, as well as others, had not the faintest understanding of it. All except the motive was talk, much of it reprehensible talk, but much not truly reported; and his censors let their prejudices seduce them into treating the entire mass as evidence of facts and acts. If he ever instructed his officers to commence the *The Rest Talk.* expedition to the Mine by taking the initiative in an attack on San Thome, the direction was confined to talk. If, whether before or after the San Thome incident, he spoke of the capture of the plate fleet, that was nothing but talk. Captain Parker's report of the project of Ralegh and St. Leger for lying in wait for homeward bound ships referred, if not wholly untrue, to talk, like his own and Whitney's similar plans. When Ralegh told his wife he hoped for something ere his return, that was talk. If he ever said he should not come back, that was talk. If he boasted of a French commission, and affirmed his preference for France, that was talk. The entire pile of charges against him, proved, unproved, or disproved, was talk. All began and ended in talk, unless that Bayley captured French boats, and Ralegh redeemed them; that the Lancerota islanders murdered English sailors, and he did not retaliate; that the San Giuseppe Spaniards were aggressors, and he bore it; and that the garrison of San Thome laid an ambush for his men, to hinder their access to a district which his Sovereign had commissioned him to enter, and were soundly beaten for their hostility.

The Government was in a dilemma. It meant to put Ralegh to death, and the process was as behindhand as at Ralegh's return to Plymouth, or more so. Spain had the promise of his blood, as soon as it should decide whether itself or England were to provide the scaffold. On October 15 the Spanish Legation in London received the answer of the Escurial. Philip III had no mind to accept the odium before Europe of murdering a redoubtable foe. He expressed his preference for an execution in England, and at once. Only in one way could the object be effected. Ralegh must be put to death, not ostensibly for San Thome, but for the Main Plot. Both for Ralegh and his heroic wife the immediate results were solacing. There was no need for tormenting either further for the concoction of a fresh indictment, if the original indictment retained strength to do the work. A warrant was addressed to Wilson for Lady Ralegh's release from his supervision. By another he was discharged from attendance upon her husband. Ten days earlier he had pretended to pray the King's leave to give up his trust at the

Tower. He said he was anxious to resume the arrangement of the State papers of the previous six or seven years. For Ralegh at all events it was a happy respite to be restored, for the last dozen days of his Tower life, to the honest keeping of Sir Allen, and the charitable offices of Lady Apsley.

CHAPTER XXIX.

Bacon, his fellow Commissioners, and the Law Officers were consulted by the Crown on the fitting procedure for the setting up of the old conviction. Coke seems to have been deputed by the other Commissioners to embody in legal form their unanimous opinion, which Bacon, as Lord Chancellor, delivered to James on October 18. The only copy in existence is in Coke's

Two Courses. handwriting. It was to the purport that Ralegh, being attainted already of high treason, could not be drawn in question judicially for any crime since committed. The Commissioners recommended one of two courses. The first was for the King to issue his warrant for execution upon the conviction of 1603. At the same time, as Ralegh's 'late crimes and offences were not yet publicly known,' a printed narrative of them might be published. The Commissioners agreed that such a course could legally be pursued. Some among them would see as clearly, though they might not feel as indignantly, as the modern Whig historian, that 'no technical reasoning could overcome the moral sense which revolted at carrying the original sentence into execution.' Consequently, an alternative method, to which the Commissioners 'rather inclined,' was suggested in Coke's paper; one 'nearest to a legal procedure.' There was a precedent in certain proceedings against Lady Shrewsbury. According to it, Ralegh might be called before the whole body of the Council of State, with the addition of the principal Judges, some noblemen and gentlemen of quality being invited to act as audience. He should be told he was brought before the Council rather than a Court of Justice, because he was already civilly dead. Then he should be charged in regular form by counsel with his acts of hostility, depredation and abuse. He should be heard in his defence; and adverse witnesses should be confronted with him, as Cobham had not been. With that which concerned the Frenchmen the Commissioners thought he should not be charged. Therein he had been passive rather than active; and without it the case appeared to the Commissioners to be complete. Moreover, they doubtless suspected Ralegh could show that in the French negotiations he had not acted alone. Finally, said the memorial, the Council and the Judges assisting would advise whether his Majesty might not with justice and honour give warrant for Ralegh's execution upon his attainder, in respect of his subsequent offences.

Objections to an
open Inquiry.

James dictated a reply to the Commissioners, which is extant in the writing of the secretary of Villiers. He objected to the second proposal in its original form for two main reasons. The procedure, though proper against a Countess, would be too great honour against one of Ralegh's state. It would not be 'fit, because it would make him too popular, as was found by experiment at the arraignment at Winchester, where by his wit he turned the hatred of men into compassion.' Consequently, the King modified the arrangement by an omission of the Judges, and of the element of partial publicity through the presence of a selected audience. The members of the Council who had conducted the previous examinations were directed to sit as a quasi-criminal Court. But they sat with closed doors, and their sitting was kept strictly private. From a letter at Simancas, written on November 6 by a Spanish Agent in London, Julian Sanchez de Ulloa, to his Government from hearsay, it may be gathered that the inquiry was held on October 22, and lasted for four hours. No complete account has been discovered of the course it took, in consequence, Mr. Spedding, in his *Life of Bacon*, supposes, of the destruction of a mass of Council Chamber papers in the fire of January 12, 1619, at the Banqueting House. That is possible. As the Commission sat as a Court, not as a Council, the explanation is not incompatible with the circumstance that the Council Register for 1618, which, as it happens, did not suffer from the conflagration, contains no allusion to a meeting of the Council on October 22. Nevertheless it is more likely that the want of official record is due to the extreme anxiety of the King's advisers for secrecy. They were afraid of popular feeling. The fact of the imitation trial might have been itself doubtful, but for a fragmentary sketch in a volume of Sir Julius Cæsar's notes, preserved among the Lansdowne Manuscripts in the British Museum. The report, which breaks off in the middle of a sentence, is on Council paper, and may have been drawn up for official use, if not with a view to ultimate insertion in the Privy Council Register. In Mr. Spedding's opinion only the first sheet has been kept, and the condition of the paper seems to me clearly to favour the hypothesis. He believes that the full note contained additional evidence against Ralegh, for instance, on the question of the expedition's provision of mining tools, with his replies to it, and the decision of the Commissioners upon the whole. The report, in its existing form, needs to be ⸱ *Sir Julius Cæsar.* ⸱ eked out with the suggestions, necessarily not very sympathetic, in the subsequent Royal *Declaration* of Ralegh's line of defence against the charges. Such as it is, it must be read with caution and uncertainty. Cæsar, who was Master of the Rolls, was generous, and, for a Jacobean placeman, just. The only grave imputation on his memory is his connivance, as a Commissioner, at the collusive divorce of Lady Essex. It is not impugning the good faith of any reporters of proceedings, like the present, against Ralegh, to look sceptically at their narrative. Law reporters in general had lax notions in those days of the distinction between actual statements and inferences by themselves as to the construction they bore. Coke's Reports show it abundantly. Cæsar in particular would feel in no way bound to mechanical accuracy. His endeavour would be to give the prevailing force and significance of the charges, of the defence, and of the evidence; the impression they made upon him with a view to his judicial conclusion. We know the judgment formed in advance by him and his colleagues on the mendacity of Ralegh's account of the motive of his enterprise. That could not but warp a compendium by him of an investigation instituted in order to find a legal justification for a capital sentence on a presumed impostor and pirate.

Sir Henry Yelverton, the Attorney-General, leading for the Crown, took for his theme the conduct of the expedition. He was obliged to try to excuse the King for his authorization of an adventure alleged by himself to be an imposture. His Majesty had been induced, by the hope of 'his country's good,' to grant a commission, which, it should be noted, Cæsar describes as 'under the Great Seal.' The King, Yelverton was not ashamed to suggest, had ⹂ *Charges and Defence.* ⹂ been the dupe of Ralegh, who invented the Mine to regain his liberty. He could not, it was argued, have meant to mine, since he carried no miners or instruments. He had a French commission to assail Spaniards. In reliance on that he had ventured to direct an attack on San Thome. On its failure he was in a mood to depart, and leave his poor company behind him helpless. He had anticipated lucrative booty from the town. Disappointment at its meagreness helped to incite him to schemes for the capture of the Mexico fleet. Much indignation was spent by Sir Thomas Coventry, the Solicitor-General, in his turn, on 'vile and dishonourable speeches, full of contumely to the King,' which, on the word of Stukely and Manourie, he supposed Ralegh to have uttered. Coventry stigmatized them as marking especial and flagitious ingratitude. 'Never was subject so obliged to his Sovereign as he.'

Ralegh, in his reply, repudiated with his wonted courtesy the assertion that he had received extraordinary marks of royal lenity. His release from the Tower he claimed as a tardy reparation for a protracted wrong. 'I do verily believe,' he exclaimed, 'that his Majesty doth in his own conscience clear me of all guiltiness in regard to my conviction in the year 1603. Indeed, I know that his Majesty hath been heard to say, in speaking of these proceedings, that he would not wish to be tried by a Middlesex jury.' He added Dr. Turner's report to him of Mr. Justice Gawdy's death-bed censure of his condemnation. But he denied that he had in fact uttered the abuse imputed to him by Stukely and Manourie. His only ill speech of his Majesty had been: 'My confidence in the King is deceived.' It was deceived. The charge that he had never meant to work a mine he met by references to refiners, and tools and assaying apparatus, costing him £2000, that he had conveyed with him. To the accusation that he had broken the King's peace with Spain, he retorted that the aggression proceeded from the Spaniards. He had not directed any attack upon them. His only object in despatching an armed force had been that the soldiers might take up a position between the town and the Mine while the rest were at work. The mere attempt to reach the Mine was no offence, unless Spaniards had an absolute territorial title to the soil of the region in which it lay.

The Commission could not affirm an absolute claim on behalf of Spain. It was reduced to rely upon accusations that he had from the beginning harboured piratical intentions, and counted upon the assistance of France for their accomplishment. Sir John Ferne, who had left him, reported to the Commission talk by him as if he had meant to turn buccaneer, and also to enter the French service. Apparently that was the belief of some of his

Designs against the Plate Fleet. officers, though several may have alleged it simply to excuse their desertion, and to guard against counter charges by him. In any case the theory seems to have been founded upon the most superficial proofs. Of any piratical acts of his, or practical service rendered to France, he could confidently challenge the Law Officers to produce the smallest proof. But on the solitary charge of a design to seize the plate fleet the Commission was in possession of a morsel of corroborative evidence. It confronted him with another of his runaway captains, Pennington, and also with Wareham St. Leger. They testified to admissions of his intention to lie in wait for the plate fleet. According to Cæsar's note, after their testimony he could no longer adhere to his denial, and 'confessed that he proposed the taking of the Mexico fleet if the mine failed.' How far he positively admitted it, and how far Cæsar inferred to his own satisfaction from Ralegh's mode of receiving the evidence that he could not really contradict it, cannot be ascertained. As has been remarked, all depends on how the thing was said. If Cæsar's summary of the proceedings had been

handed down in a more *The Explanation.* complete form, it might itself have impressed posterity otherwise than the evidence impressed him. By the allusions in the Royal *Declaration* it may be seen that Ralegh was far from being overwhelmed by St. Leger's and Pennington's testimony. In the first place he appears to have asserted that the words concerning the plate fleet were spoken after, and not before, the search for the Mine had been defeated, and that the plan was propounded by him merely to keep the fleet together through the tempting vision. If he had ever before said anything to the same effect, 'it was but discourse at large.' Without regard to the strength or weakness, the sufficiency or insufficiency, of his defence, as to which Mr. Spedding concedes that the remains of Cæsar's note afford scanty materials for a conclusion, there can be no question that the Commissioners paid little respect to his arguments. If they ever embodied their opinion, as Mr. Spedding thinks probable, in words, he certainly is correct in his conjecture that it was wholly condemnatory.

According to Ulloa's account, Bacon wound up the proceedings by addressing a solemn rebuke to Ralegh for the injury he had done to Spanish territories, and by telling him that he must die. Perhaps, however, the Spaniard's informant antedated the Lord Chancellor's announcement, which may be identical with that, hereafter to be mentioned, of October 24. At all events, a privy seal seems to have been sent to the Judges, 'forthwith to order execution.' Jacobean Judges could commit monstrous injustices. They liked to be unjust according to precedent. They demurred, and a conference of them was called. At this, on October 23, it was decided that a privy seal was not enough. It was determined that Ralegh should be brought to bar on a writ of Habeas Corpus addressed to the Lieutenant of the Tower. He was to be asked if he could urge any objection to an award of execution; 'for he might have a pardon; or he might say that he was not the same person.' As a preliminary he was called next day before the Council at Whitehall. He was informed that he was to be executed on his old sentence. His reply is not recorded. If he argued on behalf of his life, it was to no purpose. He was more fortunate with his petition that he might be beheaded, and not hanged. For that amount of benevolence the Council intimated its willingness to hold itself responsible.

A second privy seal came to the Justices of the King's Bench. Their Chief, Coke's successor, much more polished and discreet than he, was Sir Henry Montagu, afterwards Lord Treasurer, Lord President, and Earl of Manchester. His Court was simply commanded to proceed according to

law, as it was : *Before the King's Bench.* : called. Ralegh had been suffering

from an attack of ague. On October 28, at eight, he was awakened with the fit still upon him. He was served with a summons to appear forthwith at Westminster. As he passed along the corridor an old servant, Peter, met him. While he was under Wilson's custody his own domestics had been withdrawn. They had since been allowed to attend him. One of Peter's duties had been to comb the hair, no longer flowing and thick, of his head, and his beard, for an hour a day. Ralegh had left off the practice for a time. As he told Wilson, 'he would know first who should have his head; he would not bestow so much cost of it for the hangman.' Peter had doubtless at his return brought his master back to the old usage. He now reminded

Ralegh that he was going forth with his head undressed. Ralegh replied with a good-humoured question, 'Dost thou know, Peter, of any plaster that will set a man's head on again, when it is off?'

He was at Westminster soon after nine. After the Winchester conviction had been read, Yelverton, as Attorney-General, briefly demanded execution. He was more courteous than Coke had been in his place, and more dignified. 'Sir Walter Ralegh,' he said, 'hath been a statesman, and a man who, in regard to his parts and quality, is to be pitied. He hath been as a star at which the world hath gazed; but stars may fall, nay, they must fall when they trouble the sphere wherein they abide. It is therefore his Majesty's pleasure now to call for execution of the former judgment, and I require order for the same.' Ralegh held up his hand. He told the Court that 'his voice was grown weak by his late sickness, and an ague he had at that instant upon him; therefore, he desired the relief of a pen and ink.' Montagu told him he spoke audibly enough. So he proceeded with his defence. He argued, as Bacon is rumoured to have argued at Gray's Inn, that the King's commission for the late voyage, with the power of life and death, amounted to a pardon. Montagu interrupted him. Nothing about his voyage was, he said, to the purport. Treason was never pardoned by implication. On this Ralegh put himself on the King's mercy. He urged that in that judgment which was so long past, both his Majesty was of opinion, and there were some present who could witness, that he had hard usage. If his Majesty had not been anew exasperated against him, he was sure he might, if he could by nature, have lived a thousand and a thousand years before advantage would *Execution granted.* have been taken of the judgment. Montagu answered that for all the past fifteen years he had been as a man dead in the law; but the King in mercy spared him. He might think it heavy if it were done in cold blood. But new offences had stirred up his Majesty's justice to revive what the law had formerly cast upon him. The Chief Justice continued in a solemn strain, not without eloquence: 'I know that you have been valiant and wise; and I doubt not but you retain both these virtues, for now you shall have occasion to use them. Your faith hath heretofore been questioned; but I am resolved you are a good Christian; for your book, which is an admirable work, doth testify as much. I would give you counsel; but I know you can apply it unto yourself far better than I am able to give it you. Fear not death too much, nor fear death too little; not too much lest you fail in your hope, nor too little lest you die presumptuously.' He ended: 'Execution is granted.'

Ralegh said he had no desire 'to gain one minute of life; for now being old, sickly, in disgrace, and certain to go to it, life was wearisome to him.' But he prayed for a reasonable delay; he had something to do in discharge of his conscience, something for the satisfaction of his Majesty, and something for that of the world. Above all, he besought their Lordships that, when he came to die, he might have leave to speak freely at his farewell. He called God, before whom he was shortly to appear, to witness that he was never disloyal, as he should justify where he need not fear the face of any King on earth. So, with an entreaty to them to pray for him, he was led away to the Gate-house.

James and his confidants were not allowed to carry out their iniquity without remonstrances. Already the Queen had exerted once more her waning influence for Ralegh. He had appealed to her in solemn verse from his prison in the name of his innocence and friendlessness. She was now on her death-bed, dropsical, gloomy, and neglected. It was whispered that she was *The Queen'sIntercession through Villiers.* disturbed in her reason. She preserved at least sufficient intelligence to be horrified at the wrong which was being prepared, and the stain threatened to the memory of her husband's reign. She responded to Ralegh's petition by an earnest letter to George Villiers. She had, at Archbishop Abbot's solicitation, recommended Villiers to the favour of James. He exhibited the most obsequious deference to her as well as to the King. Her letter, of which the precise date is unknown, is addressed to 'My kind Dogge.' That was the name by which Villiers affected to like both of them to call him. She wrote: 'If I have any power or credit with you, I pray you let me have a trial of it, at this time, in dealing sincerely and earnestly with the King, that Sir Walter Ralegh's life may not be called in question.' Her intercession with her truant Consort through his favourite was not more successful than her pleadings with himself had been. As vainly young Carew Ralegh prayed, without date or superscription, for the life of 'my poor father, sometime honoured with many great places of command by the most worthy Queen Elizabeth, the possessor whereof she left him at her death, as a token of her goodwill to his loyalty.' The lad, now about *Other Petitioners.* thirteen, or rather they who dictated his memorial, must have been very simple to suppose that Elizabeth's favour was a passport to James's compassion. On his death-bed James Montague, who died in July, 1618, Bishop of Winchester, and is transformed by Wilson in his journal into the Earl of Winchester, had previously begged of James one thing, the life of Ralegh; 'a great offender,' Montague called him, 'who yet was dearly respected of the late noble Queen.' In his choice of reasons the prelate seems to have been as injudicious as the boy. As fruitlessly were solicitations addressed to the King by Lady Ralegh, and by persons described generally as in great favour and esteem with him. All were repulsed. James, says Francis Osborn in his

Traditional Memoirs, 'did so far participate of the humour of a pusillanimous prince as to pardon any sooner than those injured by himself.' He was unconscious of any such malignity. It is pathetic to observe his utter freedom from suspicion that posterity could help characterizing him as resolute, wise, and just for his persecution of Ralegh, and not as a wretched trickster.

Ralegh's own main anxiety was to settle his affairs in the first place, and to secure that none suffered pecuniary detriment, much or little, through his fault or negligence. When that was assured, he next longed to clear his fame, in death, of every slur and taint. In November, for discharge of his conscience, he gave to Wilson a testamentary note, that he had never let to Captain Caulfeild land near Sherborne Castle, which John Meere claimed by a counterfeit grant of his to Caulfeild. He mentioned further that, before his departure from Cork to Guiana, he had written in prejudice of H. Pyne's lease of Mogile Castle, and in favour of Lord Boyle's claim. Since that time, better bethinking himself, he desired the opinion he gave at Cork might be no evidence in law, and that it should be left to other proofs on both sides. He requested Lady Ralegh, 'if she should enjoy her goods,' to be kind to Hamon's wife, and in any case to the wife of John Talbot, his servant in the Tower, who had died in Guiana: 'I fear me, her son being dead, she will otherwise perish.' He added that an account ought to be exacted from Stukely of the tobacco he had sold at Plymouth, and also of the parcel he had sent down the river, 'the Sunday that we took boat.'

When he prayed a 'respite,' it was not that he was scared at the approach of death. His mind was never brighter and happier. To this moment may well be attributed, as it has been by popular tradition, his composition of the couplet:

> Cowards may fear to die, but courage stout,
> Rather than live in snuff, will be put out.

Assuredly he was not one of the cowards. But his career had been confused and tumultuous. He would have been glad of a little leisure and quiet for unravelling some of the knots. He understood his enemies and events too

Warrant

for Execution. well to be surprised that his shrift was to be short. Before his appearance at the King's Bench, Bacon had drawn the warrant for execution, and James had signed it. Naunton wrote to Carleton, the general depositary of confidential gossip, on October 28, that the warrant for execution had been drawn up, and sent to the King for signature; only, 'it had better not be talked about, as it is de futuro contingente.' James, meanwhile, was restlessly hunting to and fro between Oatlands, Theobalds, and Hampton Court. He was composing meditations on the Lord's Prayer, and dedicating them to Villiers. The warrant, though he was then in Hertfordshire, was dated the day of the scene in the King's Bench. It was directed to the Chancellor. It dispensed with 'the manner of execution according to his former judgment, and released Sir Walter Ralegh of the same to be drawn, hanged, and quartered.' The royal pleasure instead thereof was to have the head only of the said Sir Walter Ralegh cut off at or within the Palace of Westminster.

CHAPTER XXX.

Ralegh was confined in the Gate-house of the old monastery of St. Peter. It was a small two-storied building of the age of Edward III, standing at the western entrance to Tothill-street. The structure embraced two adjoining

The Gate-house. gates, with rooms which had been turned into prison cells. By the side of the gate leading northwards from the College-court, was the Bishop of London's prison for convicted clerks and Romish recusants. With the other gate westwards was connected the gaol of the Liberty of Westminster, to which Ralegh had been committed. The Abbey was visible through its barred windows. Ben Jonson had been confined in it. Eliot, Hampden, and Selden were to be. Lovelace sang there to stone walls. Esmond's name may be added to the list of its glories. Ralegh had been afraid the King might prevent him from speaking, or from being heard. He feared that the space for his friends would be narrow. As he crossed Palace Yard to the Gate-house he had asked Sir Hugh Beeston, of Cheshire, to be there. 'But,' he said, 'I do not know what you may do for a place. For my part, I am sure of one.' Many came to the prison to bid farewell. Among them, according to Sir William Sanderson, was his father, the ex-deputy Licenser. Ralegh was lively and cheerful. To those who grieved he said: 'The world itself is but a larger prison, out of which some are daily selected for execution.' There is no reason for doubting the sincerity of his content. He had striven manfully for a life which for him meant the exercise of fruitful energy. He rejoiced in death, when, from no remissness of his, it closed his labours. His kinsman, Francis Thynne, advised him: 'Do not carry it with too much bravery. Your enemies will take exception, if you do.' His friends were afraid of the 'pride' which had provoked Henry Howard. 'It is my last mirth in this world,' replied he; 'do not grudge it to me. When I come to the sad parting, you will see me grave enough.'

Fearless of Death.

By desire of the Lords of the Council, Dr. Robert Tounson, Dean of Westminster, and afterwards Bishop of Salisbury, attended him. Tounson wrote on November 9 to Sir John Isham: 'He was the most fearless of death that ever was known; and the most resolute and confident, yet with reverence and conscience. When I began to encourage him against the fear of death, he seemed to make so light of it that I wondered at him. He gave

God thanks, he never feared death; and the manner of death, though to others it might seem grievous, yet he had rather die so than of a burning fever. I wished him not to flatter himself, for this extraordinary boldness, I was afraid, came from some false ground. If it were out of a humour of vain glory, or carelessness of death, or senselessness of his own state, he were much to be lamented. He answered that he was persuaded that no man that knew God and feared Him could die with cheerfulness and courage, except he were assured of the love and favour of God unto him; that other men might make shows outwardly, but they felt no joy within; with much more to that effect, very Christianly; so that he satisfied me then, as I think he did all his spectators at his death.' A reputation for free thinking once established is tenacious. Though Ralegh satisfied a Chief Justice, a Dean of Westminster, and men like Pym, Eliot, Hampden, of his orthodoxy, he did not satisfy all. Archbishop Abbot three or four months later wrote to Sir Thomas Roe that his execution was a judgment on him for his scepticism.

He did not allude, wrote Tounson, to 'his former treason.' As to more recent imputations, he could not conceive how it was possible to break peace with Spain, which 'within these four years took divers of his men, and bound them back to back and drowned them.'

Later arrived his wife. She had spent the earlier hours in trying to induce the Council to mediate with the King. Before she came she had learnt from a friend that it refused to beg the life, but authorized her to dispose of the corpse. At the Gate-house first she heard he was to be beheaded on Friday morning, October 29. That was Lord Mayor's Day, the morrow of St. Simon and St. Jude. It appears to have been selected, that the City pageant might draw away the crowd from hearing him, and seeing him die. As he and *A last Farewell to his Wife.* she were consulting how she was to vindicate his fame, if he should be hindered from speech on the scaffold, the Abbey clock struck twelve. She rose to go, that he might rest. Then, with a burst of anguish, she told him she had leave to bury his body. 'It is well, dear Bess,' said he with a smile, 'that thou mayst dispose of that dead, which thou hadst not always the disposing of when alive.' On her return home, between night and morning, she wrote to 'my best brother,' Sir Nicholas Carew, of Beddington: 'I desire, good brother, that you will be pleased to let me bury the worthy body of my noble husband, Sir Walter Ralegh, in your church at Beddington, where I desire to be buried. The Lords have given me his dead body, though they denied me his life. This night he shall be brought you with two or three of my men. Let me hear presently. God hold me and my wits.'

Ralegh, when his wife left him, wrote his last testamentary note. It was a rehearsal of the topics on which he meant to speak on the scaffold. If his mouth were closed it was intended to be a substitute. He repeated in it his constant affirmation of his loyalty: 'If,' he said, 'I had not loved and honoured the King truly, and trusted in his goodness somewhat too much, I had not suffered death.' Then the poet awoke in him. He wrote in the Bible which he gave to Dean Tounson the famous lines:

> Even such is time, that takes in trust
> Our youth, our joys, our all we have,
> And pays us but with earth and dust;
> Who, in the dark and silent grave,
> When we have wandered all our ways,
> Shuts up the story of our days;
> But from this earth, this grave, this dust,
> My God shall raise me up, I trust.

Early in the morning came Tounson again, and administered the Sacrament. Tounson wrote in the letter to Sir John Isham, from which I have already quoted, that Ralegh hoped to persuade the world he died an innocent man. *'Innocent in the Fact.'* The Dean objected that his assertions of innocence obliquely denied the justice of the Realm upon him. In reply he confessed justice had been done; that was to say, that by course of law he must die; but he claimed leave, he said, to stand upon his innocency in the fact; and he thought both the King, and all who heard his answers, believed verily he was innocent for that matter. Tounson then pressed him to call to mind what he had done formerly. Though perhaps in that particular for which he was condemned he was clear, yet for some other matter, it might be, he was guilty, and therefore he should acknowledge the justice of God in it, though at the hands of men he had but hard measure. Here Tounson says he put him in mind of the death of my Lord of Essex; how it was generally reported that he was a great instrument of Essex's death. If his heart charged him with that, he should heartily repent, and ask God forgiveness. To this he made answer; and he said moreover that my Lord of Essex was fetched off by a trick, of which he privately told Tounson. He was, testifies Tounson, very cheerful, ate his breakfast heartily, and took tobacco, and made no more of his death than if it had been to take a journey.

Before he quitted the Gate-house a cup of sack was brought. After he had drunk it the bearer asked if it were to his liking. 'I will answer you,' said Ralegh, 'as did the fellow who drank of St. Giles's bowl as he went to Tyburn: "It is good drink if a man might but tarry by it".' Now arrived the

Sheriffs. They conducted him to Old Palace Yard, where a large scaffold had been erected in front of the Parliament-house. Though the space had been narrowed by barriers, a great multitude had collected. It included, according to John Eliot, who was present, enemies as well as friends. Ralegh was dressed in a black-wrought velvet nightgown over a hair-coloured satin doublet, a ruff band, and a black-wrought waistcoat, black cut taffeta breeches, and ash-coloured silk stockings. On account of his ague he wore under his hat a wrought nightcap. Seeing in the crowd an old man with a very bald head, he inquired why he had ventured forth on such

a *His Good-humour.* morning; whether he would have aught of him. 'Nothing,' was the answer, 'but to see him, and pray God for him.' Ralegh thanked him, and grieved that he had no better return to make for his good will than 'this,' said he, as he threw him his lace cap, 'which you need, my friend, now more than I.' Being pressed on by the crowd, he was breathless and faint when he mounted the scaffold; but he saluted with a cheerful countenance those of his acquaintance whom he saw. Lords Arundel, Doncaster, Northampton, formerly Compton, and Oxford—son of Sir Walter's enemy—stood in Sir Randolph Carew's, or Crues's, balcony. Other Lords, Sheffield and Percy, sat on horseback near. Sir Edward Sackville, Colonel Cecil, Sir Henry Rich, were among the spectators. The assemblage is said to have included ladies of rank. The morning was raw, and a fire had been lighted beside the scaffold for the Sheriffs, while they waited before going to the Gate-house. They invited him to descend and warm himself. He declined; his ague would soon be upon him; it might be deemed, he said, if he delayed, and the fit began before he had played his part, that he quaked with fear.

Proclamation having been made by the Sheriffs, he addressed his audience. Tounson's, and another account prepared, it would appear from a statement of the Dean's, for the Government by one Crawford, do not materially differ. They seem both to be honest, if not fluent. He commenced by explaining, not complaining, that he had the day before been taken from his bed in a strong fit of fever, which might recur that morning. Therefore, he hoped they would ascribe any disability of voice or dejection of look to that, and not to dismay of mind. Hereupon he paused and sat down. Beginning again to speak he fancied they in the balcony did not hear. So he said he would raise his voice. Arundel replied that the

company would rather come *Rejoices to'die in the Light.'* down to the scaffold. Northampton, Doncaster, and himself descended, mounted the scaffold, and shook hands with Ralegh. Then he resumed: 'I thank God that He has sent me to die in the light, and not in darkness, before such an assembly of honourable witnesses, and not obscurely in the Tower, where, for the space of thirteen years together, I have been oppressed with many miseries. I thank Him, too, that my fever hath not taken me at this time.' He proceeded to excuse his counterfeit sickness at Salisbury: 'It was only to prolong the time till his Majesty came, in hopes of some commiseration from him.' He dwelt more seriously on two or three main points of suspicion conceived by the King against him. They, he believed, had specially hastened his doom. One was connected with his supposed intrigues with France. He gave an indignant denial to this charge of practices with foreigners, at any rate without the qualification expressed in the testamentary note he had composed during the night, 'unknowing to the King.' The mistrust had, he was aware, been strengthened by his projects of flight from Plymouth and London. Those luckless schemes had, he asserted, no affinity to thoughts of permanent expatriation and foreign service. Simply he had reckoned that he could more easily make his peace at home while he was safe at a distance. Another cause of odium had been Manourie's tale of his habit of reviling the King. That he declared mere lying: 'It is,' he said, 'no time for me to flatter, or to fear, princes, I who am subject only unto death; yet, if ever I spake disloyally or dishonestly of the King, the Lord blot me out of the book of life.'

Even at this supreme moment he respected the Throne, as much from real reverence for Royalty, as from fear of harm after him to wife and child. He did not repeat his protest against the mock conviction of 1603. He uttered no scorn of the King's betrayal to the Court of Spain of the plan of his

Denial of Stukely's Calumnies. expedition. In general he was content to defend himself; he was sparing of attacks. Only his 'keeper and kinsman,' Stukely, he could not pass over in silence. Having received the Sacrament he forgave the man; but he held himself bound to caution the world against him, out of charity to others. He repudiated warmly a calumny against Carew and Doncaster, that they had advised him to fly. He ridiculed the transparent mendacity of Stukely's story of a promise of £10,000; for 'if I had £1000, I could have made my peace better with it than by giving it to Stukely.' He disclaimed indignantly the statement Stukely had attributed to him, that he had been poisoned at Parham's house. Sir Edward Parham, he said, had been a follower of his; Parham's wife was his cousin-german; and Parham's cook once was his. As untrue was the story that he had been conveyed into England against his will. On the contrary, 150 soldiers held him a close prisoner in his cabin. They extorted an oath that he would not go to England without their consent; 'otherwise, they would have cast me into the sea.' Unless he had won over the master-gunner, and ten or twelve others, to return home, and had drawn the ship to the south of Ireland, he had never got from them. It had even been alleged that he never meant to go to Guiana, and that he knew of no gold mine; that his intention only was to recover his liberty, which he had not the wit to keep. But his friends had believed in his honesty when he started. He reminded Arundel of the Earl's request in the gallery of the Destiny that, whether the voyage were good or bad, he would return to England. Thereupon he had given his word that he would. 'So you did,' cried Arundel; 'it is true, and they were the last words I said to you.' Next, he alluded to the slander, circulated 'through the jealousy of the people,' that at the execution of Essex he had stood in a window over against him and puffed out tobacco in defiance of him. He contradicted it utterly. Essex could not have seen him, since he had retired to the Armoury. He had bewailed him with tears. 'True I was of a contrary faction, but I bare him no ill-affection, and always believed it had been better for me that his life had been preserved; for after his fall I got the hatred of those who wished me well before; and those who set me against him set themselves afterwards against me, and were my greatest enemies.'

'And now,' he concluded an address of which the eloquence is not to be judged from the halting reports, 'I entreat that you will all join with me in prayer to that great God of Heaven whom I have grievously offended, being a man full of all vanity, who has lived a sinful life in such callings as have been most inducing to it; for I have been a soldier, a sailor, and a courtier, which are courses of wickedness and vice. So, I take my leave of you all, making my peace with God.' 'I have,' he said, 'a long journey to take, and must bid the company farewell.'

Preparing for the Block.

With that the Sheriffs ordered that all should depart from the scaffold, where he was left with them, the Dean, and the executioner. Having given his hat and money to some attendants, he prepared himself for the block, permitting no help. Throughout, wrote on November 3 Mr. Thomas Lorkin to Sir Thomas Puckering, 'he seemed as free from all manner of apprehension as if he had been come thither rather to be a spectator than a sufferer; nay, the beholders seemed much more sensible than he.' Having put off gown and doublet, he called for the axe. There being a delay, he chid the headsman, 'I prithee, let me see it!' Fingering the edge, he remarked to the Sheriffs with a smile: 'This is a sharp medicine; but it is a sure cure for all diseases.' Then, going to and fro upon the scaffold upon every side, he entreated the spectators to pray to God to bestow on him strength. Arundel he asked, as if he expected the wish to be granted by James, to 'desire the King that no scandalous writings to defame him might be published after his death.' To a question from Tounson he replied that he died in the faith professed by the Church of England, and hoped to have his sins washed away by the precious blood of our Saviour Christ.

Finally, the executioner spread his own cloak for him to kneel on, and, falling down, besought his forgiveness. Ralegh laid his hand on the man's shoulder, and granted it. To the inquiry whether he would not lay himself eastwards on the block, he replied: 'So the heart be right, it is no matter which way the head lies.' But he placed himself towards the east, as his friends wished it. He refused the executioner's offer to blindfold him: 'Think you I fear the shadow of the axe, when I fear not itself?' He told the man to strike when he should stretch forth his hands. With a parting salutation to the whole goodly company, he ejaculated: 'give me heartily your prayers.' After a brief pause he signed that he was ready. The executioner stirred not. 'What dost thou fear? Strike man, strike!' commanded Ralegh. The executioner plucked up courage, struck, and at two blows, the first mortal, the head was severed. As it tumbled the lips moved, still in prayer; the trunk never shrank. An effusion of blood followed, so copious as to indicate that the kingdom had been robbed of many vigorous years of a great life.

CHAPTER XXXI.

SPOILS AND PENALTIES.

The Remains.

A shudder is said to have run through the crowd of spectators as the axe fell. The trunk was carried from the scaffold to St. Margaret's Church, and buried in front of the Communion table. A single line in the burial register, 'Sir Walter Rawleigh Kt.,' records the interment. James Harrington, author of _Oceana_, occupies the next grave. Why Ralegh's body was not taken to Beddington is unknown. Long afterwards a wooden tablet was fixed by a churchwarden on the wall of the south aisle of the chancel. A metal plate framed, and painted blue with gilt letters, was substituted. In 1845 that was replaced by one of brass, at the expense of several admirers of Ralegh's genius. It bears the uninspired words: 'Within the chancel of this church was interred the body of the great Sir Walter Ralegh, on the day he was beheaded in Old Palace Yard, Westminster, October 29, 1618. Reader, should you reflect on his errors, remember his many virtues, and that he was a Mortal.' Four verses from the pen of Mr. Lowell, inscribed on a painted window, erected a few years since in the church, more worthily commemorate the piety of American citizens to the planter of Virginia.

The head was shown by the executioner on each side of the scaffold, as the head of a traitor. Afterwards it was inclosed in a red velvet bag. With the velvet gown enveloping the whole, it was conveyed to Lady Ralegh's house in a mourning coach which she had sent. It was embalmed; and she kept it ever by her for the twenty-nine years of her widowhood. Bishop Goodman of Gloucester, who, though King James's poor-spirited apologist, admired Ralegh, relates that he had seen and kissed it. On Lady Ralegh's death the charge of it descended to Carew Ralegh. It has been stated, and has been denied, that it was buried with him at West Horsley, and was seen when the grave happened to be opened. For another story, that finally it was deposited with the body at Westminster, there is no authority.

Lady Ralegh lived to educate her son. For his sake she strove for Ralegh's books. They were, she said, 'all the land and living which he left his poor

Carew Ralegh.

child, hoping that he would inherit him in those only, and that he would apply himself by learning to be fit for them, which request I hope I shall fulfil as far as in me lieth.' Carew was thirteen at his father's death. In the spring of 1621, at the age of sixteen, he entered Wadham

College as a gentleman commoner. When he quitted Oxford his relative, Lord Pembroke, who more than twenty years before had interceded at Wilton for his father's life, introduced him at Court. James frowned; he said he was like his father's ghost. He travelled, and, returning next year on the accession of Charles, petitioned for restoration in blood. His prayer was granted only on the obligatory terms of his surrender of any title to Sherborne. In compensation he received a reversion of the £400 a year, Lady Ralegh's Treasury allowance in place of jointure or dower from Sherborne. By the same statute which relieved him from the legal disabilities of the attainder Sherborne was confirmed to the Digby family. He married the wealthy young widow of Sir Anthony Ashley, his father's comrade at Cadiz, and had by her two sons, Walter and Philip, and three daughters. He wrote poems, one of which was set to music by Henry Lawes, and was a Gentleman of the Privy Chamber. In that capacity he attended Charles I when a prisoner at Hampton Court. He may have thought of Charles rather as the brother of Prince Henry than as the son of King James.

He seems to have dreamt of recovering both his father's Irish and English estates. Strafford, on behalf of the Church, had questioned the soundness of Boyle's title to Lismore. The doubt of the validity of Boyle's tenure, though it equally affected Sir Walter's right, may have suggested to Carew somewhat later an attack on him in his own interest, probably on the score of the inadequacy of the price paid to Ralegh. Lady Ralegh had already, in 1619, set up a claim to dower, on the ground that her consent to the sale in 1602 had not been obtained. Boyle intimated that he should meet Lady Ralegh's demand by the legal objection that the wife of an attainted man is not dowerable. But, on the merits, he insisted in answer, as well to her as, afterwards, to Carew Ralegh, that he had in fact, between 1602 and 1617, given ample pecuniary consideration. Neither she nor her son went beyond a protest.

Carew was more pertinacious in his efforts to recover Sherborne. That was supposed to have been forfeited by the flight of Digby, now Lord Bristol, to France on the establishment of the Commonwealth. Carew petitioned the House of Commons for its restitution to himself. His petition, which in

Claim to Sherborne. details was not everywhere as accurate, expressed

righteous indignation at an attainder obtained on charges 'without any proofs, and in themselves as ridiculous as impossible.' He declared in the document his intention to 'range himself under the banner of the Commons of England.' The memorial was referred to the committee for the sale of the estates of delinquents. That reported him 'a fit object of the mercy of the House.' But he advanced no further, in consequence, as is believed, of the influence Lord Bristol was still able to exert. Monk conferred on him the Government of Jersey, and Charles II offered him knighthood, which he waived. Sir Henry Wotton, as quoted by Anthony Wood, commended him as of 'dexterous abilities.' Wood, while he does not dissent, adds that he was 'far, God wot, from his father's parts, either as to the sword or pen.' At least he understood his father's greatness, and clung proudly to his memory.

From Walter Ralegh, at all events, if not from his family, his enemies and persecutors, with their parasites, might think they at last were freed. Their perseverance had been unwearied. For fifteen years they were pursuing him, and they had hunted him down. They had shown versatility as well as virulence. As his son Carew has said, they had obtained his condemnation as a friend to Spain, and his execution, under the same sentence, for being its enemy. Now all, old bloodhounds and young, proceeded to enjoy their hard-won victory. To commence at the bottom, Manourie, 'a French physician, lately sent for from Plymouth,' as early as November received his wages, £20. Sir Lewis Stukely's expectations and deserts were larger. While he lingered at Plymouth he had disposed of part of the stores from Ralegh's ship. Sir Ferdinando Gorges and others completed the work for the Crown as soon as Ralegh had been executed. Some of the tobacco had been brought to London, and sold by Stukely. Ralegh accused him of appropriation of the *Blood Money.* proceeds. He had accepted gifts of jewels from his prisoner on the journey. To his custody were entrusted the trinkets carried by Ralegh about him on the flight to Gravesend. On December 29 the Exchequer was ordered to pay to him 'for performance of his service and expenses in bringing up hither out of Devonshire the person of Sir Walter Ralegh, £965 6s. 3d.'

One more of the hirelings expected to be paid, the Keeper of State Papers. Wilson had failed to spy out treason in Ralegh's talk in the seclusion of the Tower, or in the correspondence with Lady Ralegh. He did not the less crave a fee for his good intentions of treachery. James recognized his claims, to the inexpensive extent of an order to the Fellows of Caius College, Cambridge, in January, 1619, to elect him to their vacant Mastership. The King's letter described him as a man of learning and sufficiency, who had performed faithful service. The letter, as an indorsement by Wilson notes, was never sent. Perhaps the Fellows were found to be prepared to put to the test the King's assertion that he would 'take no denial.' Balked of academical alms, Sir Thomas was driven to importunities three quarters of a year later for payment of his wages for the six weeks' attendance upon Ralegh.

He was more promptly successful in rapacity for the public, it must be admitted, than for himself. Ralegh had stripped himself, or been stripped, before his death, of any possessions ordinarily recognized as available for spoil. His cargo and stores had been seized and converted into money by Stukely, or by other Devonshire officials. His ship had been brought into the Thames as Crown property. The Government accounted itself generous for granting to the widow, in lieu of it and its contents, £2250, the bare equivalent of the purchase money of her Mitcham estate which she had

Ralegh's Library, and Instruments. · expended upon its equipment. Nothing

remained of his but his papers, his instruments, and his books. Covetous eyes were fixed upon them. Wilson wanted them, though, it is fair to say, not for himself. As Keeper of the Records he had a sincere taste for curious books. He urged the King to appropriate Ralegh's library of three hundred volumes on history, divinity, and mathematics, together with Cobham's collection of a thousand. By royal warrant in November he was authorised to seize the whole. The globes and mathematical instruments were to be delivered to the King or the Lord Admiral. The books were to be 'left where they were'; that is, it is to be presumed, they were to remain in the Tower. As if in shame the warrant assigned a reason for the confiscation of Ralegh's library. It could, it alleged, be of 'small use to Sir Walter's surviving wife.' Lady Ralegh judged differently. She implored Lady Carew, who was acquainted with Wilson, to mediate with him that she might be 'no more troubled, having had so many unspeakable losses, as none of worth will seek to molest me.' Before the end of 1618 Wilson had fetched away all the mathematical instruments, one of which had cost £100. Lady Ralegh had, she affirmed, been promised their return, but had not recovered one. He was now requiring the books. She would not grudge them, she asseverated, for his Majesty, if they were rare, and not to be had elsewhere; but Boyle, the bookbinder or stationer, had, she was informed, the very same. The ultimate result of the aggression and her resistance is not known. It might be of public interest if it could be ascertained. In addition to printed volumes Wilson had asked for the sequestration of Ralegh's manuscript treatise on the Art of War, and of a full account by him of all the world's seaports, and for their deposit in the State Paper Office. He could value thoughtful work, though he persecuted its author. Diligently as the State Papers have of recent years been explored, it is not impossible that the two compositions may yet be discovered, carefully buried in a mass of worthless muniments by their spy-keeper.

James had his share too of the immediate profits from the tragedy of Palace Yard, over and above a few more or less scarce books. Apart from his incurable private aversion for one of the three greatest Englishmen of his reign, he had, in butchering Ralegh, been the direct agent of the Spanish

Court. From Spain he sought his real reward. He enhanced his demand by the immensity of the loss he had inflicted upon England. Cottington, the instant the news of the execution reached the Legation, told the Spanish King. Philip III showed, he reported, much contentment with the hearing.

Spanish Debt of Gratitude to James. Rushworth, in his *Historical Collections*, has preserved a letter described as from a great Minister of State to Cottington. In it the English Agent in Spain was urgently instructed to enforce upon the Spaniards their debt of gratitude to James, who had 'caused Sir Walter Ralegh to be put to death, chiefly for the giving them satisfaction.' He was to let them see 'how in many actions of late his Majesty had strained upon the affections of his people, and especially in this last concerning Sir Walter Ralegh, who died with a great deal of courage and constancy. To give them content, he had not spared a man able to have done his Majesty much service, when, by preserving him, he might have given great satisfaction to his subjects, and have had at command upon all occasions as useful a man as served any prince in Christendom.' A fitting response was made. Cottington was able to report 'so much satisfaction and contentment as I am not able to express it.' The Spanish Council of State admitted the obligation to James for the sacrifice of the brightest jewel of his Crown. It advised Philip to thank the King of England by an autograph letter. That was James's payment.

Ralegh's various persecutors were in the right to enjoy their victory betimes. They had not the opportunity for long. The country awoke at a bound to the injury which had been done it. On the miserable tools it first poured out its indignation. Long before the final catastrophe its anger had been gathering against Stukely. On August 20 Chamberlain wrote to Carleton that Sir Lewis Stukely was generally decried. After the execution no measure in execrations was observed. He was christened Sir Judas. Stories, probably fictitious, of the contempt with which he was visited, were greedily devoured. 'Every man in Court,' it was reported, 'declines Stukely's company as treacherous.' The High Admiral, who himself had *Odium of Stukely.* battened on plunder from Ralegh, was rumoured to have threatened to cudgel the betrayer from his door. Stukely had been visiting Nottingham House on some duty connected with his office of Vice-Admiral of Devon. He complained to the King, who befriended him, of the affronts he received. The answer was said to have been: 'Were I disposed to hang every one that speaks ill of thee, there would not be trees enough in all my kingdom to hang them on.' According to another tale, reported by J. Pory to Carleton, the King replied to his protestation of the truth of his accusations: 'I have done amiss; Sir Walter's blood be upon thy head.' In vain he endeavoured to defend himself through the press. On August 10 he had printed a short *Apology* for his conduct as Ralegh's keeper. In it he took up the only practicable ground, that he had simply obeyed the orders of the Crown. After Ralegh's execution he was stung by the obloquy he had incurred into the publication of a formal indictment of the memory of the dead. On November 26 appeared a rhetorical document, which he had retained the Rev. Dr. Sharpe to help him in drawing up. It was entitled the 'Humble Petition and Information of Sir Lewis Stukely, touching his own behaviour in the charge committed to him for the bringing up of Sir Walter Ralegh, and the scandalous aspersions cast upon him for the same.' Fact and fiction are audaciously mingled in the narrative. As a specimen of its temper may be mentioned the statement that Ralegh in the Gate-house asked its keeper, Weekes, if any Romish priests were under his charge. The insinuation was that the Protestant hero would have liked an opportunity of reconciliation to the Church of Rome before his death.

Such calumnies increased the popular wrath. The whole nation exulted in the tidings within a few months that their author was about to be indicted for the capital offence of clipping coin. Manourie was arrested at Plymouth on the same charge. He accused his friend, whose old confederate in clipping and sweating coin he had been. By way, it is to be feared, of embellishment of a tale of righteous retaliation, it was reported that Sir Lewis had been caught on Twelfth Night within the precincts of the Palace of Whitehall in the act of clipping the very gold pieces, the wages of his perfidy, paid to him on the previous New Year's eve. He was confined first in the Gate-house, and then in the Tower, in Ralegh's old cell, and in due course *A Convicted Criminal.* was tried. Fruitlessly he endeavoured to shift the crime on his son, who had absconded. A servant confessed his master had followed the practice for the past seven years. The evidence was overwhelming, and he was convicted. It was a 'just judgment of God,' men said, 'for Sir Walter Ralegh's blood.' James, Mr. Gardiner says, 'thought he owed something to his tool, and flung him a pardon.' According to the popular rumour it was a gift for a tangible consideration. He had to beggar himself to buy it. His office of Vice-Admiral of Devon was forfeited, and it was filled by Eliot. He slunk away first to his home at Afton, where all, gentle and poor, banned him, and thence to Lundy Isle. There, amid the ruins of Morisco's Castle, he died mad on August 29, 1620. His treason has conferred on his obscure name an infamous immortality. He was equally an enemy to himself and to King James, whom his accommodating perfidy tempted to perpetrate the final injustice. But it must be remembered that but for him Ralegh would have lingered for a few years more of weary life on foreign soil, and dropped into an unhonoured grave. To him English history is indebted for a heroic scene, and Ralegh for a glorious close to his splendid but checkered career. The mind shudders at the thought of the bathos into which a little remorse in that contemptible villain would have plunged his victim.

Public vengeance was not satisfied with the self-wrought retribution on Stukely. It ranged lower, and it ranged higher. It condescended to spurn *Manourie's Defence.* the tool of a tool. Manourie, too, had to publish his apology. He called God to witness that Stukely had bribed him to lay traps for Ralegh, and to put into his mouth malcontent speeches. All the evil he told of his ally was believed. His professions that his own admitted baseness had been provoked by resentment of Ralegh's spontaneous abuse of the King were received with incredulity or unconcern. On the fact, Captain King's word in his *Narrative* in answer to Manourie was accepted in preference to the Frenchman's. The *Narrative* was not printed, but circulated extensively in manuscript. Though it is no longer discoverable, Oldys seems to have read it, and he has quoted passages in his life of Ralegh. 'Never,' in it asseverated King, 'in all the years I followed Sir Walter, heard I him name his Majesty but with reverence. I am sorry the assertion of that man should prevail so much against the dead.' He need not have feared that it had prevailed, or would prevail, with the nation. That scarcely spared a thought to Manourie, unless to curse him as a mercenary liar. But in the emotion stirred by Ralegh's death it was soon evident that the people had grown indifferent to the degree of its hero's personal loyalty, or the reverse. The flood of enthusiasm for him swept away the interest in his guilt or innocence in respect of particular charges. Public opinion hallowed him as saint and martyr, and put the Court and Government on their defence.

The vehemence and volume of national emotion at the abandonment of Ralegh to the spite of a faction were a surprise to the King and his advisers. They seemed unable to comprehend its character and direction. They believed, or pretended to believe, that a demand was being raised for a new trial of his offences. They could not, or would not, see that the only question was of the distribution of punishment among his persecutors. Something, however, manifestly had to be done, and at once. One purpose of Stukely's *Petition* had been to pave the way for a 'declaration from the State,' for which the Petitioner formally asked. The Committee of the Council had recommended in Coke's paper of October 18, and the King had approved, the issue of such a manifesto simultaneously with the despatch of Ralegh to the scaffold. Its preparation had been immediately taken in hand. *The Royal Declaration.* The reason for the delay in publication is unknown. Probably the royal editor was extremely fastidious. Whatever the cause of the procrastination, at last, on November 27, the day after Stukely's *Petition*, an apology appeared with the authority of the Crown. James himself supplied part of the contents, 'additions,' wrote Bacon to Villiers, 'which were very material, and fit to proceed from his Majesty.' Naunton and Yelverton also assisted in the composition. The arrangement of arguments and, though marred by royal and other interpolations, the diction have been traced to the serviceable hand of the Lord Chancellor. Ralegh and Bacon had long been intimate with one another. They had never been enemies, or even rivals. In his History Ralegh had cited with applause Bacon's *Advancement of Learning*, and other works. He had testified that no man had taught the laws of history better, and with greater brevity, than that excellent learned gentleman.

Bacon fully reciprocated the admiration. He snatched at opportunities for placing on record his delight in Sir Walter's pretty wit, and adventurous spirit. If it be an excuse for his share in the persecution of the man and his memory, he was animated by no personal antipathy. But his skill had been retained for those who were hounding Ralegh to death, as it had been retained for the destruction of his old patron Essex. He did not now let his conscience afflict itself at the thought that he was about to gloss an act, which a historian, not very friendly to the sufferer, has said 'can hardly be dignified with the title of a judicial murder.' Neither passion, *Bacon's part in it,* pique, nor fear, inspired his pen. His function in official life, as he interpreted it, was to be the advocate of authority; his feeling for any but scientific truth was never acute; and he had positive pleasure in the employment of his intellectual dexterity, whatever the object. Acting on that system he did the best he could with the case put before him on the present occasion. His and its misfortune was that it was irretrievably bad. His instructions were that Ralegh had gained his pardon by a lie; that there was no Mine, and that he never supposed there was any; that he went to harry and plunder Spaniards, and for nothing else; when he found spoil was not to be had as easily as he had anticipated, he had determined to desert his men, and fly to the East Indies, or stay behind in Newfoundland. The King was supposed to have, with his wonted and infallible sagacity, made the discovery of Ralegh's knavery long since. That royal hypothesis of stark imposture, and no enthusiasm, was the clue which the Lords Commissioners, with Bacon at their head, had obsequiously borrowed to hale Ralegh to the scaffold. It was the strange sophism out of which Bacon again was set to compose a sedative for the popular emotion.

He had to begin by apologizing for the King, both to the indignant nation and to the King's own injured sense of consistency. He had to try to extricate his master from the cruel dilemma, either of having been an accomplice in a scheme now denounced by himself as a pirate's conspiracy, or of having betrayed, out of cowardice and cupidity, a faithful servant to foreign vengeance. That is the meaning of the exordium of this pamphlet published in November by the King's Printers, Bonham Norton and John Bill: 'Although Kings be not bound to give account of their actions to any but God alone; yet such are his Majesty's proceedings, as he hath always been willing to bring them before sun and moon, and carefully to satisfy all his good people with his intentions and courses, giving as well to future times as to the present true and undisguised declarations of them; as judging, that for actions not well founded it is advantage to let them pass in uncertain reports, but for actions that are built upon sure and solid grounds, such as his Majesty's are, it belongeth to them to be published by open manifestos. Especially, his Majesty is willing to declare and manifest to the world his proceedings in a case of such a nature as this which followeth is; since it not only concerns his own people, but also a foreign prince and state abroad. Accordingly, therefore, for that which concerneth Sir Walter, late executed for treason—leaving the thoughts of his heart, and the protestations that he made at his death, to God that is the Searcher of all hearts, and the Judge of all truth—his Majesty hath thought fit to manifest unto the world how things appeared unto himself, and upon what proofs and evident matter, and the examination of the · *His Majesty's* · *Honour and Justice.* commanders that were employed with him in the voyage—and namely of those which Sir Walter Ralegh himself, by his own letter to Secretary Winwood, had commended for persons of worth and credit, and as most fit for greater employments—his Majesty's proceedings have been grounded; whereby it will evidently appear how agreeable they have been in all points to honour and justice. Sir Walter Ralegh having been condemned of high treason at his Majesty's entrance into this kingdom; and for the space of fourteen years, by his Majesty's princely clemency and mercy, not only spared from his execution, but permitted to live as in *liberâ custodiâ* in the Tower, and to enjoy his lands and living, till all was by law evicted from him upon another ground, and not by forfeiture—which notwithstanding his Majesty out of his abundant grace gave him a competent satisfaction for the same—at length he fell upon an enterprise of a golden mine in Guiana. This proposition of his was presented and recommended to his Majesty by Sir · *His Princely Judgment.* · Ralph Winwood, then Secretary of State, as a matter not in the air or speculative, but real and of certainty; for that Sir Walter Ralegh had seen of the ore of the mine with his eyes, and tried the richness of it. It is true that his Majesty, in his own princely judgment, gave no belief unto it; as well for that his Majesty was verily persuaded that in nature there are no such mines of gold entire, as they described this to be; and if any such had been, it was not probable that the Spaniards, who were so industrious in the chase of treasure, would have neglected it so long; as also for that it proceeded from the person of Sir Walter Ralegh, invested with such circumstances both of his disposition and fortune. But nevertheless Sir Walter Ralegh had so enchanted the world with his confident asseveration of that which every man was willing to believe, as his Majesty's honour was in a manner engaged not to deny unto his people the adventure and hope of so great riches, to be sought and achieved at the charge of volunteers; especially, for that it stood with his Majesty's politic and magnanimous courses, in these his flourishing times of peace, to nourish and encourage noble and generous enterprises for plantations, discoveries, and opening of new trades.'

The main and misleading principle in the minds of the authors could not but dislocate and discolour facts. Those were carefully culled which made for a given conclusion. Incompatible evidence was omitted altogether. The 'Declaration of the Demeanour and Carriage of Sir Walter Ralegh, as well in his Voyage as in and since his Return, and of the true motives and inducements which occasioned his Majesty to proceed in doing justice upon him, as hath been done,' is a shuffling excuse for a baseness. The mass of it is an accumulation of hearsay evidence. Its chief object was to depict Ralegh as a man whom nobody need regret; to sneer away his lustre and *An Apology for an Apology.* dignity. With this sordid view the trivial episode of the malingering scene at Salisbury is described with sickening minuteness. Few writers of authority have ventured to applaud the treatise. An exception is Mr. Spedding, who could not well let judgment pass against his idol without a word of defence for one of the worst blemishes in a pitiful official career. He shows here as elsewhere his admirable diligence in the collection of evidence; but he cannot be said to have shed any new light either on Ralegh's character, or on the part Bacon played in his slaughter, and in the endeavour to blacken his memory. For him both the King and the keeper of the King's conscience had no option but to put Ralegh to death. According to him the King's sanction of warlike preparations implied no understanding that it might be necessary to use them. According to him the commission to conduct an armed squadron and soldiery to a mine on the banks of the Orinoko conveyed no right to break a hostile Spanish blockade of the river. According to him, though in defiance of contemporary testimony, Ralegh alone employed violence; the San Thome garrison 'offered no provocation whatever, except an attitude of self-defence.' On these principles, while he laments the tardiness of its appearance, he necessarily considers the *Declaration* straightforward, honest, and convincing. National opinion judged differently. It treated the whole as a piece of special pleading. In fairness it must be granted that, had it been much more cogent, it would have had as little effect. Chamberlain had prophetically written to Carleton on November 21, while it was known to be in process of composition, that it 'will not be believed, unless it be well proved.'

CHAPTER XXXII.

More judicious or less prejudiced observers than James and his confidants would have suspected earlier the rise of the popular tide of sympathy and indignation. Strangers had remarked the tendency before the execution. A

Popular Indignation. Spanish Dominican friar in England on a secret political mission had, Chamberlain told Carleton in October, been labouring for Ralegh's life from dread of the ill-will towards Spain which his death would cause. Many Englishmen were much nimbler than official and officious courtiers in perceiving the blunder. A great lord in the Tower, who may be presumed to have been Northumberland, another correspondent of Carleton's told him, had observed that, if the Spanish match went on, Spain had better have given £100,000 than have had him killed; and if not, that England had better have given £100,000 than have killed him. Pory assured Carleton, writing on October 31, that Ralegh's death would do more harm to the faction that procured it than ever he did in his life. As soon as his head was off, the authorities had to be hard at work suppressing ballads which were being sung in the streets against his adversaries. The jeer of the London goldsmith, Wiemark, 'the constant Paul's-walker,' that he wished such a head as had just been severed from Ralegh's body had been on Master Secretary's shoulders, was but a sample of a storm of sarcasms upon the Government which ran through the town. The anger displayed by Naunton and Villiers a couple of years later at the appearance of so poor a satire as Captain Gainsford's *Vox Spiritus, or Sir Walter Ralegh's Ghost*, which was being circulated in manuscript, and their zeal in suppressing it, testify to the durability of the alarm excited in the Court. It was no momentary and evanescent impulse. Dean Tounson had written on November 9, of Ralegh's execution, that 'it left a great impression on the minds of those that beheld him; inasmuch that Sir Lewis Stukely and the Frenchman grow very odious. This was the news a week since; but now it is blown over, *Its Durability.* and he almost forgotten.'

The good Dean underrated the solidity and reasonableness of English feeling. The nation might not care to linger over creatures like Stukely and Manourie, even to execrate them. Its grief for Ralegh was a lasting sentiment. A spectator of his death declared that his Christian and truthful manner on the scaffold made all believe that he was not guilty of treason nor of malpractices. So sudden a conversion of the kingdom to faith in his innocence and heroism would have been almost as irrational as the original acquiescence without proof in his criminality, had it been as abrupt as it seemed. It would have been as short-lived as Dean Tounson anticipated, if its growth had been as gourd-like. In fact the nation only at the instant ascertained the state of its mind. The mood itself had been in course of formation for years.

Ralegh, as we have seen, had been cordially detested in his day of ascendency. All a reign's odium naturally condenses itself upon a royal favourite. His elaborate courtesy did not produce the effect of affability. His lavishness was thought ostentation. His good nature, for he was good natured, had too much an air of condescension. The scorn of rivals or his superiors in rank he met with scorn. His exploits by land and sea, as impartial critics noted, heightened instead of pacifying malignity. Later exposure to settled Court dislike blunted the edge of popular enmity; it hardly turned it into kindness. The national attitude towards Ralegh, downtrodden and harassed, long showed curiosity more than affection. The kingdom wondered what he was doing, or would do. Formerly it had believed, with repugnance, in his ability to extricate himself from all difficulties, whether of war or of intrigue. It retained the same faith in the indomitable resources of the prisoner of the Tower, without much active sympathy, though without antipathy. He died; and the wonder, the observant admiration flamed into a fury of passionate regret. For six and thirty years Ralegh had been before its eyes, and in its thoughts, for good or

Popular Forgetfulness. - evil. It could not imagine him not at its service; and he was irreparably gone. A reserve of force, upon which the nation unconsciously had depended in the event of any emergency, had been thrown away. A light in England had been extinguished. The people forgot how it had misconstrued and reviled him. It forgot how passively it had borne to see him worried by malicious rivals and upstart strangers. On the instant he became for it the representative of an era of national glory sacrificed to sordid machinations. The executioner's axe in Palace Yard scattered a film which had dimmed the sight of Englishmen for an entire generation. Death vindicated on Ralegh's own behalf its title to his panegyric: 'O eloquent, just, and mighty Death!'

The nation persisted in grieving for him. The instruments of his destruction, courtiers and Ministers, it pursued with a storm of immediate hatred. Loyalty or awe of the Prerogative secured the Sovereign's person for the time from open reproaches. The country was willing to suppose that the King had been misled by evil counsellors, and had quickly repented of the iniquity. Spain, two years later, assisted Austria to dethrone the Elector Palatine and his Stuart wife. A story was invented that James, in anger at the news, exclaimed he would demand the Spanish general's head.

A courtier, it was fabled, dared to question whether Philip would be as facile and obliging as James had been. 'Then I wish,' groaned James, 'that Ralegh's head were again on his shoulders.' Posterity has been less ready to make any excuse for James, even the excuse of a selfish contrition. His memory has paid with interest for his escape at first from his rightful share in the obloquy. His injustice as an individual weakened the national faith in royalty. The wrongs suffered from the State caused Ralegh to be regarded as a martyr to freedom, which he was

An Idol of the Constitutional Party.

not. The growing party of champions of constitutional liberties watched over and exalted his fame. Pym, in his note-book of *Memorable Accidents*, has entered under the year 1618: 'Sir Walter Ralegh had the favour to be beheaded at Westminster, where he died with great applause of the beholders, most constantly, most Christianly, most religiously.' Hampden could not bear that any fragments of his writing should be lost. Cromwell pored over his History. Milton printed his essays. Eliot at the date of the execution was twenty-eight. He had long been a friend, and still followed the fortunes, of Villiers. He did not belong yet to the popular party. So far was he from forgetting the spectacle in a week that, many years after, he recalled the whole in a glow of enthusiasm both for the King's victim and the Devon hero. He wrote in the *Monarchy of Man*, which he did not complete till 1631, that all history scarcely contained a parallel to the fortitude of 'our Ralegh'; that the placid courage of 'that great soul,' while it turned to sorrow the joy of the enemies who had come to witness his sufferings, filled all men else with emotion; 'leaving with them only this doubt, whether death were more acceptable to him, or he more welcome unto death.'

Something both of political and religious partisanship mixed with and exalted the zeal of Pym, Hampden, Eliot, Cromwell, and Milton for the foe of Jesuits and Bishops, the scapegoat of a Stuart's infatuation for Spain, the survivor of a Court which had believed in the present grandeur of England, and a future more splendid still. The feeling was wonderfully tenacious. Ralegh remained for the generation which witnessed his death, and for the next also, the patriot scourge of a still detested Spain. Gradually that especial ground of kindness for him subsided, along with the aversion on which it rested. English hatred of Spain has long been so obsolete a sentiment as to be virtually inconceivable. Not many care to thread the mazes of the plots he was alleged to have countenanced, or of those contrived against him. His acts have been relegated to a side channel of history. Yet for Englishmen his figure keeps its prominence and radiance. It is the more conspicuous for the poverty of the period in which a large and calamitous part of his career was spent. As the student plods along one of the dreariest wastes of the national annals, his name gleams across the tedious page. When from time to time he flits over the stage, the quagmire of Court intrigues and jobbing favouritism is illuminated with a sparkle of romance.

He is among the most dazzling personalities in English history, and the most enigmatical. Not an action ascribed to him, not a plan he is reputed to have conceived, not a date in his multifarious career, but is matter of controversy. In view of the state of the national records in the last

Perplexities. century, it is scarcely strange that Gibbon himself should, after selecting him for a theme, have recoiled from the task of marshalling the chaos of his 'obscure' deeds, a 'fame confined to the narrow limits of our language and our island,' and 'a fund of materials not yet properly manufactured.' Posterity and his contemporaries have equally been unable to agree on his virtues and his vices, the nature of his motives, the spelling of his name, and the amount of his genius. No man was ever less reticent about himself; and his confessions and apologies deepen the confusion. He had a poet's inspiration; and his title to most of the verses ascribed to him is contested. He was one of the creators of modern English prose; and his disquisitions have for two centuries ceased to be read. He and Bacon are coupled by Dugald Stewart as eminent beyond their age for their emancipation from the fetters of the Schoolmen, their originality, and the enlargement of their scientific conceptions; and a single phrase, 'the fundamental laws of human knowledge,' is the only philosophical idea connected with him. His name is entered, rightly, in the first rank of discoverers, navigators, and planters, on account of two countries which he neither found nor permanently colonized. He was a great admiral, who commanded in chief on one expedition alone, and that miserably failed. He had in him the making of a great soldier, though his exploits are lost in the dreary darkness of intestine French and Irish savageries. He was a master of policy, and his loftiest office was that of Captain of the Guard. None could

be kinder, or *Failures and Inconsistencies.* more chivalrously generous, and he practised with complacency in Munster treachery and cruelty which he abhorred in a Spaniard of Trinidad. He had the subtlest brain, and became the yokefellow of a Cobham. He thirsted after Court favour, and wealth, and died attainted and landless. He longed to scour the world for adventures, and spent a fourth part of his manhood in a gaol. He laid the foundation of a married life characterized by an unbroken tenor of romantic trust and devotion, by doing his wife the worst injury a woman can undergo. The star of his hopes was the future of his elder son, and the boy squandered his life on an idle skirmish. He courted admiration, and, till he was buried in prison or the grave, was the best hated man in the kingdom.

Had he been less vivacious and many-sided, he might have succeeded better, suffered less, and accomplished more. With qualities less shining he would have escaped the trammels of Court favouritism, and its stains. With powers less various he would have been content to be illustrious in one line. As a poet he might have rivalled instead of patronizing Spenser. In prose he might have surpassed the thoughtful majesty of Hooker. As an observer of nature he might have disputed the palm with Bacon. He must have been recognized as endowed with the specific gifts of a statesman or a general, if he had possessed none others as remarkable. But if less various he would have been less attractive. If he had shone without a cloud in any one direction, he would not have pervaded a period with the splendour of his nature, and become its type. More smoothness in his fortunes would have shorn them of their tragic picturesqueness. Failure itself was needed to colour all with the tints which surprise and captivate. He was not a martyr to forgive his persecutors. He was not a hero to endure in silence, and without an effort at escape. His character had many earthy streaks. His self-love was enormous. He could be shifty, wheedling, whining. His extraordinary and indomitable perseverance in the pursuit of ends was crossed with a strange restlessness and recklessness in the choice of means. His projects often ended in reverses and disappointments. Yet, with all the shortcomings, no figure, no life gathers up in itself more completely the whole spirit of an epoch; none more firmly enchains admiration for invincible individuality, or ends by winning a more personal tenderness and affection.